Preface

Although this book addresses issues directly related to the requirements of the City and Guilds 7307 Further and Adult Education Certificate and Certificate in Education (FE), it should also prove to be of value to all who teach in the post-school sector of education and training.

As so many vocational courses are starting to use a competence approach, it was thought important that competences were used in this book. At the start of each chapter a list of competences and associated performance criteria are outlined and, within the text, suggestions are made for the collection of evidence which might be used to show competence. The collection of such evidence could be useful as the basis of a portfolio to be used either on a course of teacher training or for the accreditation of prior learning and experience.

The text stresses the need for careful and thorough preparation and planning. A range of teaching strategies is explored with the emphasis placed upon the effective use of student centred activities and the need to maximise the quality of communication within the learning environment. A chapter is devoted to " student learning" which outlines some of the educational theory which is so important in the underpinning of practice. The practical aspect of making visual aids is explored with an equal emphasis regarding how adults learn. Assessment of student learning is covered with a separate chapter dealing with course and self evaluation. Finally the role of the teacher and the importance of continual professional development is discussed. Throughout the book the teacher has the opportunity to check understanding and reflect upon the associated competences.

Both authors are with the Department of Education and Administration at New College, Durham.

Acknowledgements

We would like to thank members of the Further Education Teacher Training team at New College Durham for their contribution to debates and discussions over many years and, in particular Phyll Bryning and Alan Lilley. We would also like to pay tribute to our teacher students from whom we have learned a great deal especially during practical teaching visits. Of these, special thanks must go to Carl Gill, Janice Flint, Janet Ford, Andrew Lindley and Carolyn Piggford whose original ideas have greatly enhanced this book.

Our thanks go to all at Business Education Publishers, particularly Gerard Callaghan for his clear and concise graphics, Moira Page and Caroline White, whose help was invaluable in producing this publication, and Paul Callaghan, general editor, whose positive attitude and professionalism have been a constant source of motivation in writing this book.

Finally thanks to Margery, Susan, Timothy, Martin and Ruth for their tolerance, patience and understanding as this book was being written.

All errors and omissions remain the responsibility of the authors.

Durham

July 1992

IHR

SW

Table of Contents

Chapter 2
Student Learning 55

Chapter 4

Learning Aids

Chapter 5
Planning and Design for Teaching and Learning

Chapter 6

Communication and the Teacher

Chapter 7
Assessment of Student Learning

315

Chapter 8

Evaluation of Self and Teaching

Table of Figures

Chapter 4

Chapter 5

Chapter 6

Chapter 7

Chapter 10

Chapter 1
An Introduction to Teaching

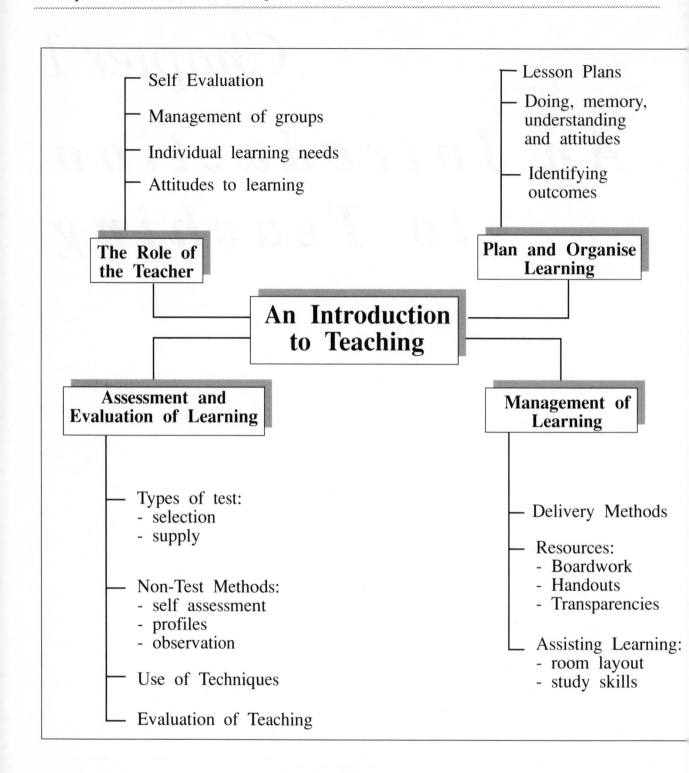

- Self Evaluation
- Management of groups
- Individual learning needs
- Attitudes to learning

The Role of the Teacher

- Lesson Plans
- Doing, memory, understanding and attitudes
- Identifying outcomes

Plan and Organise Learning

An Introduction to Teaching

Assessment and Evaluation of Learning

- Types of test:
  - selection
  - supply
- Non-Test Methods:
  - self assessment
  - profiles
  - observation
- Use of Techniques
- Evaluation of Teaching

Management of Learning

- Delivery Methods
- Resources:
  - Boardwork
  - Handouts
  - Transparencies
- Assisting Learning:
  - room layout
  - study skills

Overview of Chapter 1

This chapter is a free standing basic teacher training course for teaching adults. It equates to the requirements of a Regional Stage 1 and Part 1 of the City and Guilds 7307 courses. It discusses the role of the teacher together with the basic techniques of planning, management and assessment of learning. Thus, it covers the *basic* competences required by the teacher to teach adult students.

Competences Related to this Chapter

The teacher competences and associated performance criteria related to this chapter are:

Overall Competence – *Establish an Effective Approach to Teaching and Learning*

Competence	Performance Criteria
1. Adopt a Teaching Role	(a) Comment upon individual learning needs within a group. (b) Create positive attitudes to learning. (c) Discuss methods of group management. (d) Initiate self evaluation of teaching.
2. Plan and Organise Learning	(a) Identify learning outcomes. (b) Relate topics to outcomes. (c) Produce plans for learning sessions. (d) Identify ways in which learning is recognised. (e) Use learning resources. (f) Relate content, structure and sequence to student needs.
3. Manage Learning	(a) Use methods of delivery that are appropriate to the group. (b) Organise the environment in a way that assists learning. (c) Use appropriate language. (d) Use appropriate resources. (e) Use appropriate methods to assess learning. (f) Encourage feed back from learners.
4. Assess Learning and Evaluate Teaching	(a) Assess prior learning of the group. (b) Analyse strengths and weaknesses of the learners. (c) Identify and confirm strengths and weaknesses of learners. (d) Give constructive feedback on progress to learners. (e) Carry out evaluation of teaching and learning.

Competences

1. The Role of the Teacher

1.1 Creating Positive Attitudes to Learning

Traditionally the role of the teacher has been as a purveyor of information: the teacher was the fount of all knowledge. This suggests a picture of students sitting in rows in front of the teacher who is talking and passing information to students with the aid of a blackboard with the students either passively listening or, if the teacher is lucky, taking their own notes.

This, of course, is not true any more. The modern teacher is a facilitator: a person who assists students to learn for themselves. Instead of having students sitting in rows, they are likely to be all doing something different; some doing practical tasks, some writing, some not even in the room but in another part of the building using specialist equipment or looking up something in the library. All of the students might well be at different stages in their learning and in consequence, the learning is individualised to suit individual requirements and abilities.

This change from the traditional model is the result of a number of factors. First, it is recognised that adults, unlike small children, have a wealth of experience and are able to plan their learning quite efficiently. Second, not all individuals learn in the same manner so that if a teacher talks to students some might benefit, but others might not. Third, everyone learns at their own pace and not, of necessity, at the pace set by the teacher. Hence, the individualising of learning has definite advantages.

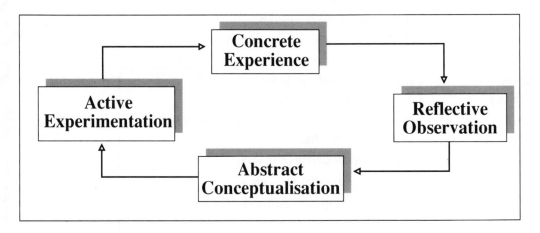

Figure 1.1 Kolb's Four Stage Model of Learning

Research into the ways that people learn has not provided teachers with any specific answers. If it had, all teachers would be using the same techniques. However, researchers have identified that learning is more effective if it is based on experiences: either direct experiences or those that are read about. Of the two the former is likely to be more effective than the latter. Thus, concepts that are able to be practised or seen, are likely to be learned better. D. A. Kolb (1984) suggests a cyclical approach to the learning process and we show this in the learning model in Figure 1.1. The model is a representation (in this case, in words) of how learning takes place.

Kolb suggests that learning from experience is not sufficient but that students must be made to apply what they have learned, to new situations.

This is, in effect, a three stage process involving (a) experience, (b) reflection, and finally (c) learning. Thus, in order for learning to take place, students have to be given experiences (activities) and *also* made to reflect upon those experiences and to think about them. Kolb has made specific references as to how the experiences and the periods of reflection are to take place. The 'concrete experience' is followed by an activity asking learners to reflect on the experience (reflective observation) and this leads to the next stage which involves placing what has been experienced into the body of knowledge that has previously been learned (that is adding more aspects to the concept that the learner already possesses). This he calls 'abstract conceptualisation'. This, again leads to an activity which asks the students to apply the experience in some way (active experimentation) and test it with what has previously been learned.

Our task as teachers is to make this process work in some way and the Basic Teaching Model gives us some help with this. The Model suggests that we start with what we want out students to learn (the objective or 'terminal behaviour' of the students) go through 'entry behaviour' (what the students already know about the topic), 'instructional techniques' (this involves Kolb's experiences and reflections) until finally assessing what has been learned. Thus, the model involves the aspects in Figure 1.2.

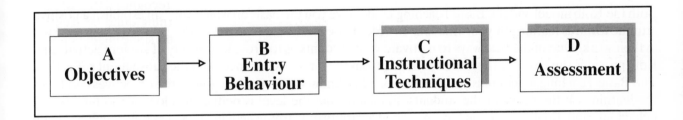

Figure 1.2 Aspects of the Basic Teaching Model

The model sub-divides the teaching process into four components and, in so doing, provides us with an uncomplicated yet fairly adequate concept of the teaching process so allowing us to plan and implement an effective learning sequence.

Objectives involve the determination of what our students should be able to do when they have completed a segment of instruction. Objectives vary in scope and character and we will discuss them in some detail in Chapter 5. They can consist of very general statements of aims or much more specific objective statements or competences. Determining our objectives is first in the sequence because knowing where we are taking the students, means there is more likelihood of us getting them there.

Entry behaviour describes the student's level of understanding of the topic *before* instruction begins. It refers to what the students have previously learned about the objective, their intellectual abilities and development, their motivational state and their learning abilities.

Instructional techniques describes the teaching process, expanded in Kolb's model, which results in those changes in student behaviour that we call 'learning'.

Finally assessment consists of tests and observations that we use to determine how well the student has achieved the objectives. If this assessment tells us that all the students, or even some of them, have fallen short of their objectives, then one or more of the previous components of the model may need adjustment. The feedback loops shown in Figure 1.3 provide the complete diagram.

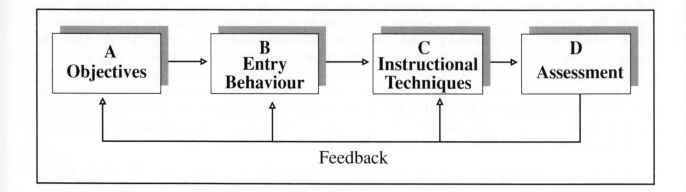

Figure 1.3 Complete Basic Teaching Model

Both the Kolb model and the Basic Teaching model give you the basis on which you can establish a positive attitude towards learning by your students. In order to be motivated to learn, students have to be interested in their work. One of the best ways to motivate your students, is to provide a variety of student activity and Kolb provides the basis for this: variety coming from the direct experiences and the subsequent reflection. The Basic Teaching model tells you that you need to know where you are going (the objectives), to focus the learning on the needs of the students, to ensure that the level is neither too low or too high (entry behaviour) and, finally, after you have provided a variety of learning activity, to assess how much has been learned.

Your role as a teacher is to provide a positive learning environment and it will help you to do this if you take all of these aspects into consideration. Without a positive environment, your students will not reach their full potential. They will find their learning boring, will not devote the required time to it and, even during periods of learning, will find their minds wandering.

1.2 Individual Learning Needs – Adult Expectations

All students are individuals and no two students learn in the same way. One student may prefer to read information and to learn individually. Another student may have problems with reading and only learn through direct experiences by actually doing things. A third may learn through a mixture of experience and being made to think about that experience and learn best as a member of a group where competition is an important element in the learning process. Thus, although you may have a number of students in a class, they are all individuals and need to be treated as individuals.

The question for you is "How do you treat a class of students as individuals"? Adult students (and, in this context, post-16 year olds are classed as adults) all have their own individual expectations and it is important that you meet these. Your students have all, either successfully or unsuccessfully, completed at least eleven years of primary and secondary education and some will have also completed a number of years of tertiary education. During this time they have built up a series of expectations which have been based on their previous experiences. Your task is to find what are their preferences, to concentrate upon those that have been successful and play down those that have been unsuccessful. There are four main general expectations that are common in adult learners and we describe each of these below.

First, adults *expect to be taught*. Adults become involved in post-16 education and training for a variety of reasons but in the main they come of their own volition. This, often for the first time in their life, is education because they choose it. Previously at school, their attendance had been mandatory. Because the students choose to give up their own (or their employer's) time, they have expectations that they *will* learn as a result of their attendance and their hard work. In consequence they expect you to teach them.

This, of course, does not mean that you have to talk or lecture to them the whole time. Kolb has already shown us the importance of variety in instructional techniques. It does, however, mean that you need to find out the techniques that are most appropriate to individuals and to teach each individual according to their needs and preferences.

Second, adult students *expect to have to work hard*. Adults have already come to the realisation that education does not come easily and that success only comes from hard work on an individual basis. They know that not only will they have to concentrate in the learning environment, but that they will also have to devote some time to private study. Your task is to make sure that they do work hard both in the learning environment and outside it at home.

The third main adult expectation is that the *work is related to the vocation*. All too often, especially in secondary education, students are not too sure why they have to learn the subjects they are asked to study and may be too immature to recognise that learning for its own sake is a useful exercise, and be useful in later life. In post-16 education, it is important to make these links clear and to make sure that all of our students know why they are being encouraged to work hard. Generally, classes of students are grouped into specific vocations like secretaries, caterers, or electricians. Even so, a secretary who is employed by one firm has slightly different needs than one who is employed by a different firm. In consequence, you not only have to relate the work to that required by secretaries in general but to an individual secretary employed by a specific firm. This means that you must set exercises that can be adapted to individual requirements, making sure that some of the exercises are work based.

The fourth and final adult expectation is that your learners *expect to be treated as adults*. In children's education it is necessary to establish a degree of discipline and much of the role of the teacher is related to this. Adults do not need this and, although we may become exasperated on occasions, we must not show it. We must accept the students' comments and questions with all of the seriousness with which they are presented. We must not be rude to our students as they are liable to remember that rather than the subject matter. Adults tend to be much more intense about their learning and this is what makes teaching adults so satisfying and, in consequence, we must not treat them in an offhand manner. In short, we must treat our students as adults with all that entails.

Each of these four expectations, although stated in general terms, need to be interpreted as an individual need. Your students may vary in age from sixteen to over sixty. They are different sexes, different marital states, have different backgrounds, different requirements and all have been through different experiences. If you are to treat them as individuals, the more you can find out about them (both in class and outside of it) the greater the likelihood of you being able to treat them as individuals, relate their learning to their needs and, in consequence, improve their learning potential. Kindness, empathy and sincerity will always reap dividends with the adult learner.

1.3 The Management of Groups

All experienced teachers are able to remember their first teaching session; the first time that they stood in front of a class of students. They generally remember the room, the group of students, the subject content and, more importantly, how nervous they were. It should be said that the main reason for this remaining in the memory is due to the nervousness, the impact that it made on the teacher. The first time that you teach a group of students is a nerve racking experience. This is due to the fact that we are not used to coming into contact with a group of students who all have their own expectations and who are all different. We are not used to managing a group of people.

Much of the art of the management of groups of students lies in preparation. You must always be prepared and be ready for any eventualities. This means that you must be ready to change your prepared teaching plan and strategy both for the group and for individuals.

Generally, all sessions, whether they are classroom, laboratory or workshop based, should have an introduction, a development and a conclusion and as such, all of these lesson phases present you with opportunities for both group and individual activities.

Follow the basic teaching model that we discussed earlier and relate this to the three phases of a lesson. In the introduction (which includes an assessment of the immediate needs of individuals – their entry behaviour) the group activities can include question and answer or a discussion of the objectives of the session to find out what your students already know about the topic. The development phase may involve you in some formal input of the material to be covered but, following the Kolb model, students should then reflect and conceptualise the material. This can be achieved by completing some sort of group exercises (discussion groups, role play, group problem solving, gaming) to assist the learning process. The final conclusion phase is to find out how much the students know and this might be achieved through a group assignment. The activities related to each of the lesson phases are summarised in Figure 1.4.

Lesson Plan	Basic Teaching Model Aspect	Group Activity	Individual Activity
Introduction	Objectives	Question and answer or discussion	Notes on session objectives
	Entry Behaviour		Entry behaviour test
Development	Instructional Techniques	Group work to apply learning	Notes on lecture
			Completing examples to apply learning
Conclusion	Assessment	Group assignment	Test

Figure 1.4 Activities Related to Lesson Phases

With this type of group activity, the question is asked "How do we manage the groups?" In effect, the role of the teacher in group work is very different to that when students are working individually or when you are controlling the learning through lecture or other forms of formal teaching method. With group work the students control both the pace and the direction of the learning; they need to pool their knowledge and learning styles so that they learn from each other. Your role is to provide information *only* when it is asked, to point your students in the right direction (for example, where they might find the information that they require) but *not* to supply the answers. If groups are straying from the point or from the right direction, you can ask questions to bring their minds back but do not tell them the direction. Your role is that of guide and counsellor and not as the purveyor of information. This is summarised in Figure 1.5 giving the possible teacher and student roles for the different learning situations.

Learning Situation	Teacher Role	Student Role
Lecture-type situation	Control of time and pace of learning. Giving information and help.	Listening and taking notes.
Individual work	Assisting learners to know and apply their learning.	Asking questions. Working at own pace.
Group work	Guiding groups of students but *not* telling them.	Learning from each other by pooling knowledge. Learning and displaying group skills (leading and following). Working at pace of the group.

Figure 1.5 Teacher and Student Roles in Learning Situations

1.4 Self Evaluation of Teaching

The only person that you can change is yourself. You might think that you change other people, and we often attempt to change them, but unless they want to change, they will not do so.

At the end of a teaching period a teacher usually reflects on how well or how badly the session has been; what were the 'highlights' and what were the 'lowlights'. This, however, is often only a thought process, a 'gut' reaction of what has occurred. Evaluation needs to be systematic if you are to get a realistic picture of what you are good at and what aspects need more thought and practice.

The only true evaluation is self-evaluation. Only when we learn to assess our own performance and make judgments on our own can we really change ourselves. We get all sorts of assistance in evaluating ourselves but, unless we make our own judgments, we will find all sorts of excuses why someone else's evaluation is invalid or unreliable. If, however, we involve ourselves in self evaluation and then make excuses, the only person that we are fooling is ourselves.

Checklists, rating scales and questionnaires all help us to evaluate what we do with our students. Probably one of the most helpful methods is to keep a diary of what has gone on in our learning sessions. The type of headings that you might consider in such a diary are given in Figure 1.6 with associated questions. These questions can be used as a checklist, or alternatively you can rate yourself on a, say, four point scale (one for poor and four for excellent) for each of the aspects, or you might make comments alongside each of the aspects.

Alternately, you might like to design a pro-forma that can be used to make a diary for each of a series of lessons. You can use the proforma to write a sentence or two about each of the aspects of your teaching. The summation of the completed pro-formas can then form a diary for the series of lessons. Such a pro-forma is shown in Figure 1.7 with some suggested headings.

Aspect	Question
Preparation	Have you: * analysed the topic/subject area? * indicated expected student learning? * identified the needs of your students? * selected appropriate teaching strategies? * written systematic lesson plans? * selected and prepared learning resources?
Presentation	* implemented selected teaching/strategies * responded flexibly to classroom situations? * used learning resources effectively? * conformed to safety requirements?
Classroom Relationships	* secured student participation in your lesson? * provided leadership to your students? * promoted a classroom climate which facilitates learning?
Communications	* used appropriate language registers? * developed students' communication skills? * effectively employed skills of non-verbal communication?
Assessment	* used an assessment method to consider if the objectives have been achieved?
Subject Matter	* demonstrated mastery of your subject matter?

Figure 1.6 Headings and Questions for a Self-Evaluation Diary

Preparation:	How successful was the preparation?
Entry Behaviour:	Was the entry behaviour as expected?
Aims/Obejctives:	Were the aims/objectives achieved?
Teaching Strategies:	What teaching methods were most successful?
Aids:	Were the aids successfully designed and used?
Classroom Relationships:	Why was the class climate either successful or unsuccessful?
Assessment:	What assessment techniques were most successful and why?
Subject Matter	What was most successful in achieving the required learning?

Figure 1.7 Pro-forma for Self-Evaluation of a Lesson

The questions in the above example not only ask *what* but they also ask *why* and that second part is important in your self evaluation. Whatever system you devise for yourself, it should be quick and easy to complete; if it is long and complex you will tend not to do it. However, the type of form above when completed for, say, eight to ten consecutive classes, will form a comprehensive 'diary' of your activities, indicating what went well and what went not so well, for that group of students.

> *Possible Evidence to Show you have Achieved the*
> *Competence*
> *'Adopt a Teaching Role'.*

The type of evidence that you might collect to show that you have achieved the competence involves:

(a) Take one of your classes and find out what the students expect from attending the course. You might ask questions like:

    (i) Why did you join the course?

    (ii) What do you expect to do on the course?

    (iii) What will you do at the end of the course?

(b) For one of your classes, show how you have applied either Kolb's four stage model of learning, or the basic teaching model, or a combination of each of these.

(c) Take, say, three individual students (a good student, an average student and one who is not so good) and, by talking to them, find out what are their expectations in terms of:

    (i) What they expect from you?

    (ii) What work they expect to do in the teaching environment and at home?

    (iii) How the work on the course is related to what they do at work?

    (iv) How the course is different/the same as their work at school?

Using these expectations, indicate how you will treat these learners as individuals.

(d) Design a series of 'diary' headings for one of your classes or for individuals and complete these for successive sessions for a period of time. On completion, state what you have found out in general terms, what you have learned and what you might do differently and why if you were starting the teaching again.

> *If you want to check your understanding of your Role as a Teacher, try the following progress check*

Progress Check 1.1

1. Complete the diagram of the Basic Teaching Model by naming each of the four components of the teaching process.

A	B	C	D

2. Identify the three phases that are used in the majority of lessons. Suggest at least two activities that could be used for each of these phases.

3. The following stages are identified by a teacher teaching 'Safety in the Workshop'.

    A. Visiting a factory where machines are in operation.

    B. Discussing own experiences in the College workshop.

    C. Taking notes in a lecture about the importance of machine guards.

    D. Operating a machine safely in the College workshop.

Classify each of the stages as 'concrete experience', 'reflective observation', 'abstract conceptualisation', or 'active experimentation' by completing the table below with a letter (A – D) of the appropriate stage. Hence, give the sequence that would satisfy Kolb's learning cycle.

Letter of Teaching Stage (A-D)	Kolb's Classification
	Abstract Conceptualisation
	Active Experimentation
	Concrete Experience
	Reflective Observation

2. Plan and Organise Learning

2.1 Identify Learning Outcomes

It is important for you to know where you want your students to finish and what you want them to learn. In this way you know when they have got there. In educational language, this involves you indentifying the learning outcomes. These *learning outcomes* can be stated as aims and objectives. They are dealt with in greater detail in Chapter 5 but, at this stage, it is only necessary to state that they are what the students will be able to do by the end of their learning.

Aims are *goals* that are set, either by you as teacher or by the curriculum designers in the curriculum documents (syllabus), to state what the learning will achieve. They are 'ultimate' goals to indicate what the students will be able to do at the end of the course, or subject; they give direction for both the teaching and the learning. Aims can be written at different levels. Course aims are fairly general and are designed to describe the overall purpose of the course. At a subject level they are more specific and are even more specific at lesson level. Examples at the different levels are:

Course Aim:	To provide an introduction to the vocation of catering;
Subject Aim:	To develop the skills required in kitchen work;
Lesson Aim:	To give a working knowledge of the standard methods of cooking by roasting.

These statements are of most use when they are stated in terms of student behaviour; what the learners will be able to do at the end of the course, subject or lesson. Learning outcomes at lesson level are often stated in terms of objectives as opposed to aims. However, at this stage, it is sufficient to identify these as student terminal behaviour. Chapter 5 gives details of writing objectives.

2.2 Doing, Memorising, Understanding and Attitudes

The way in which we learn depends to a certain extent on the type of learning that is involved. There are three main types (or domains) of learning and each type has different 'rules' associated with it for the teaching. The three domains are:

Psychomotor:	relates to the measurement of the student's manual skill performances and, therefore, the performance required will involve the manipulation of objects, tools, supplies or equipment. Performances which are primarily psychomotor include:

typing a letter;
constructing a wall;
driving a car;
drawing a picture.

Cognitive:	includes those learning behaviours which require 'thought processes' for specific information such as 'define the terms', 'select a suitable

material' and 'summarise the topic'. All of these involve thought processes (i.e. thinking).

Affective: the behaviour required in this domain involves the demonstration of feelings, emotions or attitudes towards other people, ideas or things. For example the student might be asked to:

- demonstrate an increased awareness of environmental pollution;

- show concern for safety in the workshop;

- display an appropriate attitude towards a frightened patient.

The learning required of the student related to each of the domains is quite different and, indeed, the learning in the cognitive domain at the level of knowledge is different from that required for understanding (as these are two different levels within that domain).

Teaching Students to Learn to DO Something (Psychomotor Domain)

Learning to *do* something (learning a psychomotor skill) usually involves three distinct aspects:

(i)   *Purpose*   In order to learn a skill the student needs some understanding of what it is that is to be achieved – that is the aim or objective.

(ii)   *Procedures*   Skills need some procedures or rules that are necessary in order to complete them efficiently.

(iii)   *Practice*   All skills need practice so that they are completed correctly, quickly and, like riding a bicycle, automatically. This part is very important so that the movements are *right* from the start, unlearning of wrong movements can be difficult to rectify.

Thus, as the word 'psychomotor' suggests, learning in this domain involves a 'psycho' aspect – a cognitive aspect which must be remembered or understood, and a 'motor' aspect – the movement and co-ordination between brain and limbs (usually, but not always, the hands).

Psychomotor skills are usually learned either from a demonstration or from written instructions or, preferably, from a mixture of the two.

When demonstrating a skill to students you should:

(i)   give emphasis to the required body movements; which hand and foot is being used, when sight, sound, smell and touch are required;

(ii)   encourage students to *ask questions* until they understand what is being done;

(iii)   emphasise the key points so that the sequence is learned and any difficult aspects can be concentrated upon. These points could be highlighted on a chalkboard or in a handout or noted by the students themselves.

(iv)   ensure that all safety aspects are covered.

Demonstrations should be short as, in the main, students will be inactive, watching what is being done. Anything that you do that can give students an activity will help them to concentration upon the important points, for instance get them to complete a handout, noting the key points, sketching some aspects, or, even assisting. If the demonstration is too long consider dividing it into two parts.

Demonstrations are designed to assist with the cognitive aspects of learning. Give the students some practice as soon as possible; too long a gap between the demonstration and the subsequent practice will mean that they may have forgotten many of the points.

Teaching Students to Memorise (Cognitive Domain)

Some students have good memories while others are not so good (and the same might be said of teachers!). Memory relates to the factual information which is the basis of all subjects. It is not concerned with understanding but only with the *recall* of the factual information.

You can help your students to memorise information by:

(i) verbal or visual association; that is grouping things together verbally (like knife, fork and spoon) or keeping the location of things always the same (like the layout of the kitchen and the drawers so that equipment can always be visualised in the same place and, hence, remembered).

(ii) repetition; we remember our telephone number by dialling it time and time again. We can do the same with facts. By writing them out a number of times, repeating them aloud as in poetry, listening to a tape several times or reading a number of times.

(iii) testing; this is a form of repetition which asks learners to recall and repeat the information either verbally or in writing.

(iv) special aids like rhyme rules (30 days has September, etc.) or mnemonics (ROYGBIV) which can either be designed by you for your learners or by the learners themselves.

A number of conditions help good recall. These include: (a) trying to avoid errors; (b) the more testing the more the learning takes place; (c) the more the students concentrate, the more they will be able to recall; (d) the greater the importance of the learning, the more effective it will be, and (e) the more students can relate the material to other things that have been learned previously, the greater the likelihood of recall.

Type of Learning	Helpful Activities	Unhelpful Activities
Doing	Identifying key points from a demonstration followed by practice.	Errors must be prevented
Memorising	Practice in the form of repetition and testing.	Errors must be prevented
Understanding	Errors can be helpful . Learners should ask questions, make comparisons and solve problems.	Repetition is unhelpful

Figure 1.8 Helpful and Unhelpful Activities for Different Learning

Teaching Students to Understand (Cognitive Domain)

Learning to *understand* something involves giving answers to the questions of "Why" and "How". Students need to give explanations or summaries to show that they understand something.

To summarise these points learning to *do* something involves learning a procedure and then practising it; avoiding errors if possible.

Memorising involves using various methods to enable students to recall facts; practice, in the form of repetition or testing is helpful and, as with learning to do something, errors must be prevented if possible. Learning to *understand* something is different in a number of crucial aspects. Repetition is *not* helpful whereas errors *can be*. Another difference lies in the fact that memorising and doing, once accomplished, are always practised or repeated in the same way. By contrast, understanding is an active mental process involving thoughts which link or group ideas together in a *new* way in our minds.

Helping students to understand involves making sure that they ask questions so that the topic makes sense to them. They must be made to work at making comparisons and trying to solve problems. Thus, there are three techniques that you might use to help students understand; questioning, making comparisons and solving problems.

Getting students to ask questions can be achieved by them asking you as teacher or by them asking other students. Thus, a discussion on the topic can assist understanding. Questions such as 'Why' usually identify the reasons for what goes on and are more likely to be helpful. 'Who', 'What', 'Where' and 'When' only gain information and are not helpful for understanding.

After finding out by questioning as much as they can about the new facts or ideas, you can ask students 'How is the information the same or different from ideas that you have already'? Questioning is being used here for the specific purpose of comparing what is known with what has been recently learned.

Working out a problem expands students' understanding by making them adapt and transfer the body of knowledge that they have to a variety of different circumstances.

Teaching Students to Learn Attitudes (Affective Domain)

The learning of attitudes is equally, if not more, important than the learning of cognitive and psychomotor elements. It could be argued that, unless your students have the 'correct' attitude (whatever that might be), then other learning is superfluous.

Attitudes like 'showing concern for safety', 'working effectively as a group member' and 'checking work after completion' are all important aspects for your students. But, how do you teach them? You can tell students again and again about an incorrect attitude but, unless they really see the necessity for it and internalise it as part of their character, then they are not likely to display it.

The most effective technique for the teaching of attitudes is to set up a discussion (that is a discussion itself, or case study, role play and so on, all of which involve students discussing with each other) where students can learn from each other. Adult students are more likely to listen to their peers about the importance of attitudes than they are from you.

2.3 Production of Plans for Learning Sessions

It is evident from the previous section that:

(a) the type of plan for a learning session depends upon the learning that is required for that session. The requirements are different for a psychomotor skill session compared with a knowledge session;

(b) it is important to classify the requirements of a session into the domain that it predominantly falls and, if it involves cognitive learning, the level in that domain.

We have already said from the Basic Teaching Model (Section 1.2) that the formulation of objectives (or aims) for a session provides the starting point. Within these objectives (or aims) lie the clues to the required domain through the verbs that are used. These are summarised in Figure 1.9.

Domain	Possible Verbs (student behaviours)
Psychomotor	Show skill in, assemble, build, cook, design, fillet, mend, paper, sing, weigh
Cognitive (Knowledge)	Know, define, label, list, name, outline, state
Cognitive (Understanding)	Understand, interpret, translate, explain, give new examples, summarise
Affective	Appreciate, ask, choose, answer, comply, study, check

Figure 1.9 Student Behaviours Related to Domains of Learning

Thus, the wording of the required student behaviour can indicate the domain into which the learning predominantly falls. Of course, as we have already said, the requirement of a psychomotor skill also relies upon cognitive knowledge and attitudes and vice-versa. What we have discussed in the previous section now has to be put into practice with the design and production of a plan for a learning session (lesson plan).

Lesson Planning

A lesson plan has two functions:

1 a strategy or plan for 'teaching'.

2. a series of *cues* to be used during the lesson.

It is not to be confused with *lesson notes* which are details of the actual subject matter content of the session. The lesson plan is intended to help you to proceed logically without being bound to your notes, but, even with detailed planning, every eventuality cannot be catered for, so the lesson plan is essentially tentative and flexible. A lesson plan should not limit you in your approach and it should contain sufficient flexibility to cater for circumstances as they arise in the session.

You can usefully divide your lesson plans into two:

(a)   Initial information; and

(b)   Body of the plan.

The initial information should contain:

1.   The title of the lesson.

2.   Details of the class (name, size, etc.).

3.   The time of the lesson.

4.   The expected entry behaviour of the class (expressed in terms of what the students should know or be able to do).

5.   The aims/objectives of the lesson (expressed in the same sort of terms as the entry behaviour)

An example of initial information is shown in Figure 1.10.

Title:	Calculating Area
Class:	First Year Business Studies – 18 Students
Time:	9.00 - 10.00
Entry Behaviour:	Multiplication of numbers, shapes of plane figures
Objectives:	1. Explain how to calculate the area of plane shapes 2. Solves problems relating to area

Figure 1.10 Sample Initial Information in a Lesson Plan

Once the essential preliminaries have been completed you need to plan the strategy. Planning should relate to the principles stated at the start of this chapter (that is following the Kolb and Basic Teaching Models). You will need to plan an introduction, a development and a conclusion within the time available, give students an experience, make them reflect on the experience and provide variety for them so that they are motivated throughout the session.

Planning a Cognitive Lesson

The expansion of the three phases of a lesson (introduction, development and conclusion) depends upon the type of learning and the subject matter.

Planning a cognitive lesson depends whether the aim or objective relates to knowledge (memorising) or understanding. For a lesson based on knowledge there needs to be an emphasis on verbal or visual association, repetition and testing, whereas, for a lesson based on understanding questioning, comparing with what is already known and problem solving is appropriate.

You may find the following steps helpful when you are planning a lesson where information is to be remembered:

1. Tell the student *what* is expected to be learned and *why* it is important that it is learned.

2. Provide a meaningful context to the information to be learned. Logically organise the information.

3. Relate new information with previous experience or learning.

4. Provide for adequate practice and reinforcement of correct responses.

5. Assess students' performances.

If, on the other hand, the objectives of the lesson require that the students understand the subject matter and are required to solve problems to show their understanding, you will find the following steps useful.

1. Tell the students the lesson objectives

2. Assess the students' entry behaviour for the concepts and principles they will need in order to solve the problem.

3. Have students recall the necessary concepts and principles.

4. Provide verbal direction to the students' thinking (an algorithm or paradigm) short of giving them the solution to the problem.

5. Verify students' learning by requiring them to give a full demonstration of the problem solution.

The headings that can usefully be employed for the expansion of the three phases are:

1. *Time*	It is helpful to give an indication of the time that is likely to be needed for each of the phases and each of the sub-topics within a phase.
2. *Content*	This should be restricted to brief cues or key words and they should be made to stand out clearly.
3. *Teacher Activity*	This should specify the straegies which are intended to be used during the lesson. If a question or questioning technique is to be used then *key* questions should be stated.
4. *Student Activity*	The parts played by students should be clearly stated so that variety can be planned. Students should have a change of activity at least every 15 minutes.
5. *Aids*	All audio-visual materials should be specified.

An example of the body of the plan using the introductory information from Figure 1.10, might be as shown in Figure 1.11.

Time	Content	Teacher Activity	Student Activity	Aids
9.00	**Introduction** Assess entry behaviour	Questions about multiplication	Answering	
9.10	Objectives	Tell students objectives and the importance of them	Listening	OHP
9.05	**Development** Area of Square	Exposition	Listening	Handout A1
		Individual Tutorials	Examples	
9.20	Area of triangle	Individual Tutorials followed by chalkboard	Groups to predict the formula	Handout A2
		Individual Tutorials	Examples	
9.35	Area of parallelogram	Individual Tutorials	Individuals to predict formula	Handout A3
9.45	**Conclusion** Review of formulae	Questions with C/B overview	Answers	
	Test		Individual work	
10.00	**End**			

Figure 1.11 Sample Body of a Plan for a Cognitive Lesson

Planning a Psychomotor Skills Lesson

We have all learned psychomotor skills. These include walking, tying our shoe laces and riding a bicycle. These, however, were learned automatically. They might have taken quite a long time to learn and might have been learned by trial and error. You are required to teach psychomotor skills so that they are learned in the most effective way and this generally means them being learned quickly and with a minimum of error.

Five steps can be identified in the teaching and learning of a skill. These are:

1. Analyse the skill.

2. Assess the entry behaviour of the student.

3. Arrange for training in the component parts.

4. Describe and demonstrate the skill.

5. Arrange for the three basic learning conditions of contiguity, practice and feedback.

Each of these steps will be examined in detail.

1. Analyse the Skill

The first step involves a detailed analysis of the skill so that it is broken down into its constituent parts, the sequence of operation is identified, and the key abilities are noted. For example, if you assume that you are teaching 'sharpening a Pencil with a Knife' the skills analysis will involve for a right handed person:

To cut wood:

1. Hold pencil in left hand about 2.5 cm from the end.

2. Hold knife in right hand and rest blade with blunt edge uppermost at an angle of about 30 degrees to the centre line of the pencil.

3. Cut off wood with slow, sure cuts removing pressure at the end of the stroke.

4. Rotate pencil in left hand to take equal cuts around the pencil.

5. Cut until about 5 mm of lead is exposed from the wood, equally around the circumference.

To put point on lead:

6. Position knife so that it makes an angle of approximately 90 degrees with the centre line of the pencil.

7. Sharpen lead with swift sure strokes rotating pencil in left hand.

From this analysis the key abilities can be identified as:

(a) Ability to keep the angle of the knife around the pencil constant.

(b) Ability to judge angle of knife for correct depth of wood.

(c) Ability to remove pressure towards the end of the stroke of the knife.

(d)   Ability to sharpen exposed lead to a point without breaking the lead.

2. Assess the Entry Behaviour

The skills analysis results in a chain of activities in the form of a sequence of component skills. You must make sure that the students have learned all of the pre-requisite skills. For example, in the sharpening of a pencil you must make sure that the student can cut with a knife, hold the knife at 30 and 90 degrees and so on.

3. Arrange for Training of Component Skills

This provides opportunity for the student to:

(a)   learn any missing links in the chain and to develop the required abilities; and

(b)   learn the skill components (or some of them) so well that they can focus attention on new aspects of the more complex task that is being learned.

4. Describe and Demonstrate the Skill to the Student

Describing and demonstrating is a very important and skilled part of your job. It is necessary to show students the chain involved in the skill and the links in the chain. This part of the learning of the skill is, for the students, the cognitive part; they must learn to verbalise the skill so that they *know* what is required and, secondly, the demonstration provides a clear visual picture of what is required in completing the skill, what the task will look like after each stage. The demonstration method is described in Chapter 3 and will not be discussed here. Sufficient to say that it is an important part of your job.

5. Arrange for the Three Basic Learning Conditions

The first condition for efficient and effective learning is *contiguity*, that is the almost simultaneous occurrence of the links in the chain so that each part of the chain is linked. Once the links are contiguously formed, they occur almost simultaneously. Thus, you must teach students the correct sequence, co-ordination and timing. To achieve this you can teach students (a) the whole method involving all of the links being learned at one time, or (b) the part method involving sub-dividing the skill into sections and learning a section at a time. For a complex skill, the part method has the advantage that the simple skills can be mastered before the more complex ones. It does, however, have the disadvantage that the sections have then to be joined.

The other conditions are *practice* and *feedback*. Practice should be given directly after the demonstration so that students do not have chance to forget what is required . Feedback is the information to the students about their performance. Feedback can be intrinsic (which comes from within the student by, for example, noting the finish produced or by the kinaesthetic or sensory feel of doing the job right) or extrinsic (which is provided by someone else like you as the teacher). The best type of feedback is intrinsic because you will not always be available to provide information to the student. In consequence, any form of extrinsic information should always lead to the provision of intrinsic feedback. For this reason feedback should be immediate or given as soon as possible after the event.

Using the pencil example, intrinsic feedback could be given through telling students the criteria of acceptable performance and them ensuring that the lead does not break during the sharpening process.

Extrinsic feedback could be given by you commenting upon the angles of the knife during the practice periods and through assessment of both process and product.

The Skills Lesson Plan

As with a the cognitive lesson, the main components of a skills lesson involve introduction, development (demonstration, explanation, practice and assessment) and conclusion.

Introduction

It is vital to arouse interest in the first few minutes of a skill lesson. For a new topic, a short clear statement of what the students are going to be doing (the aim/objective) and why it is important for them to be doing this. The importance can often be the link with what they are doing at work. In a continuation lesson testing the work already completed will focus attention on the subject and provide the necessary link with the previous lesson.

Development

A demonstration of the skill to be learned can follow the introduction. This should be followed by an explanation of the key points which can usefully be reinforced with questions and answers. As soon as possible each student should be given the opportunity to practice the skill so that the sub-tasks are integrated. The necessary extrinsic feedback can be given on a one-to-one basis during the practice period to complement the intrinsic feedback that should be encouraged.

When students have practised the skill sufficiently to become competent, they can be tested. This assessment may need to be followed by a further period of practice if sufficient competence has not been achieved.

Conclusion

You should plan the ending of the lesson with just as much care as the introduction and development. Sufficient time must be allowed for the cleaning of the practical area, returning tools and equipment and washing (if this is required). You should plan a short period in which you summarise what has been learned and prepare students for the next session. A useful summary is to place all of the student work on the bench and to formally, but anonymously, assess each piece of work. In this way the students see what their peers have achieved as well as having the main points emphasised.

The example plan given in Figure 1.12 on the next page shows the design of a lesson to teach the sharpening of a pencil with a knife.

Title:	Pencil Sharpening
Class:	First Year – 18 Students
Time:	2.00 - 3.00
Entry Behaviour:	Use of knives – Know 30 and 90 degrees
Objectives:	1. Show skill in sharpening a wood pencil with a knife so that 5 mm of lead is exposed concentrically

Time	Content	Teacher Activity	Student Activity	Aids
2.00	**Introduction** Assess entry behaviour	How do you use a knife?	Answering	
2.05	Objectives	Tell students objectives and importance of sharp point in drawing	Listening	OHP
2.15	**Development** Removal of wood	Demonstration	Watching	
		Tutorials	Practice	Pencils & Knives
2.30	Sharpen to a point	Demonstration	Watching	
		Tutorials	Practice	
		Assessment	2nd Practice	Template
2.45	**Conclusion**	Display on front desk of all pencils for critique Identification of criteria	Listening Identification and notes	
2.55			Clearing away and returning equipment	
3.00	**End**			

Figure 1.12   Sample Psychomotor Skills Lesson Plan

> *Possible Evidence to Show you Have Achieved the*
> *Competence*
> *'Plan and Organise Learning'*

The type of evidence that you might collect to show that you have achieved the competence involves:

(a) Stating the aims/objectives of either a course, subject or lesson in which you are involved and stating how they will be achieved and why.

(b) Classifying each of the aims/objectives into the domain which they predominantly fall and, for those in the cognitive domain, stating whether they are at the knowledge or understanding level.

(c) Choosing an aim/objective in each of the domains and stating, with reasons, how you would achieve the necessary learning.

(d) For a session that you are to teach in the near future, writing a lesson plan and giving a rationale for activities that you have included in each of the phases of (a) introduction; (b) development; and (c) conclusion.

(e) For the planned lesson asking your tutor, or a colleague, or your line manager to sit in on the session and to provide for you a critical analysis of your performance using the headings and questions in section 1.4 of this chapter as the basis.

> *If you want to check your understanding of your role in Planning and Organising Learning, try the following progress check*

Progress Check 1.2

1. What are the three phases of a lesson plan?

2. Describe a lesson plan in your own words.

3. The two sections of a lesson plans are:

    (a) introductory information; and

    (b) a breakdown of the topic.

    Indicate what might be included in each of these sections.

4. What is the difference between 'memory' and 'understanding'?

5. What are the helpful activities that can be given to students for:

    (a) learning to 'do';

    (b) learning to 'memorise'; and

    (c) learning to 'understand'?

3. The Management of Learning

3.1 Methods of Delivery

A teaching strategy is defined as "a combination of student activities supported by the use of appropriate resources to provide a particular learning experience (process) and/or to bring about the desired learning (product)". Notice, in the definition, the emphasis is placed firmly on the needs of the student and not on the teacher. A teaching strategy is what you do for the benefit of student learning. There is a vast range of teaching strategies, some of which are detailed in Chapter 5. Here it is sufficient that you familiarise yourself with that range and know what each of them entails. Some of the more popular strategies are outlined below.

Lecture	One way communication by the teacher with no feedback from students. May last from 5 minutes to more than two hours.
Question and Answer	Teacher-centred interaction with the students.
Group Discussion	A network of interaction between students with the teacher setting the discussion but subsequently playing only a minor role.
Practicals	Real or simulated situations with students learning from experience.
Tutorial	Interaction between the teacher and one or a small group of students providing opportunity for guidance and support.
Individual Learning	Situations where students work alone with books, equipment and other resources.
Demonstration	Teacher shows the basic steps and sequence of a skill or the main attributes of a concept with students watching.
Seminar	Students either individually or in small groups are set a task to research and from which they report their findings to the whole group and lead a subsequent discussion.
Case Study	The examination of a real or simulated situation so that learning can take place through the discussion of each of its facets.
Role Play	Students are invited to enact, in the training situation, the role they will be called upon to play in their job of work.
Project	The particular task is laid down by the teacher but the lines to be followed to achieve the objectives are left for the student to decide. Projects have an end product and tend to be integrated activities.
Assignment	Similar to a project but usually of shorter duration and not as open-ended.
Problem Solving	Teacher sets a problem which students solve either individually or in groups.

It has already been suggested that the use of one strategy may be more appropriate in a given situation than another. To teach the making of a specific meal through a series of practical sessions is likely to be more effective than through a lecture. Research into the advantages and limitations of the various methods, however, is not always clear cut. It is possible to make some crude choices, based on the way that you analyse your objectives. Figure 1.13 makes suggestions for the crude choices of matching strategies to objectives.

When your objective is to teach a motor skill	When your objective is to impart knowledge and understanding	When your objective is to change attitudes
Assignment Demonstration Individual Practice Tutorial Project	Case Study Project Seminar Individual Learning Problem Solving Lecture Question and Answer Assignment	Case Study Discussion Role Play

Figure 1.13 Matching Strategies to Objectives

You will see from the table that if the objective involves psychomotor skills the strategies are the practical ones, if the objective involves learning attitudes then the strategies associated with discussion are available and, if the objective is cognitive then the more formal teacher-centred strategies are applicable with others added for variety and individual work. Making the choice, of course, does not mean that a lecture (for instance) cannot change attitudes, or that role play will not impart knowledge.

3.2 Resources to Supplement Strategies

You will remember from the previous section that the definition of a teaching strategy was given as a combination of student activities supported by appropriate resources. The main resources (or visual aids) with which you should have familiarity and be able to use fairly effectively are:

Chalk and whiteboard or flipchart — can be used as a planned visual aid but also to give a resumé of student work like responses to questions.

Handout — information given to students on paper which can either be given complete to supplement a lecture or incomplete to provide a student activity. Worksheets fall into this latter category.

OHP transparency — pictures or words projected onto a screen which are used to provide students with the information needed to reach the lesson objectives. Used like a chalkboard but with the advantage that the transparencies can be prepared prior to the lesson to save time in writing.

Chapter 4 goes into some detail about the design and use of resources. In this Chapter you should be able to use the three main ones suggested above with a degree of skill, know when to use them in the lesson plans that you design and, in consequence, prepare them skilfully.

You must remember that resources are an extremely useful aspect of your teaching repertoire. They can:

(a)   provide concrete experience (Kolb Model);

(b)   motivate and arouse learner interest;

(c)   increase retention (we remember more what we see than we do of what we hear);

(d)   provide variety in learning,

(e)   provide experience not otherwise easily obtained;

(f)   make better use of class contact time;

(g)   improve your communicative skills.

With all of these advantages, you must ensure that you are skilful in the design and use of resources.

A great variety of information can be presented on handouts and transparencies. The type of presentation method you choose will depend upon the sort of information that you are dealing with and the facilities that you have available. The best method will be the one which will most *clearly* and *simply* illustrate the idea that you are seeking to teach.

Boardwork

Figure 1.14 suggests some guidelines that you can use for your boardwork including chalk, white or flipchart.

Boardwork	
Preparation:	Keypoints and diagrams should be planned on lesson plan.

Lettering:	Minimum size should be 5cm upper case and 3cm lower case.
	Lower case is easier to read than upper case.
	Emphasis can be given by:
	    * UPPER CASE
	    * colour
	    * underlining
	    * s p a c i n g
	Avoid symbols, abbreviations, vertical or angled words

Diagrams:	Avoid clutter. Use colour but not too much to be confusing. Label directly, avoid a key. Use templates for accuracy and recurring need.
Location:	Ensure it is visible to all learners and is suitably lit.
Testing:	Check visibility from rear of room. Avoid Obscuring students' vision.

Figure 1.14 Guidelines for Boardwork

Handouts

Handouts are useful in the presentation of information and as worksheets. They may be loosely categorised as:

Information handouts

These aim to provide learners with the information needed to achieve the lesson objectives. They may be further divided into:

(a)   Notes that relate directly to the content of the lesson, for example an overview of the main points of a lecture, a summary or outline of an experiment, a full transcript of a seminar.

(b)   Supporting handouts which may be used to introduce a session, give formal statements such as definitions or formulae, present data to support arguments, e.g. graphs or maps.

Worksheets (Incomplete handouts)

The student is expected to write on the handout either during the lesson or afterwards. Workcards are similar to worksheets but the crucial difference is that they are reusable because the students do the associated work on a separate page.

You should give various considerations in using handouts. The following questions need answering before you decide to design and duplicate the handout.

(a)   Why use a handout? Is it to save time and make the learning easier for the students?

(b)   At what stage in the lesson do you intend using the handout? Remember that, if they are Information Handouts, it is better to give them at the start of your lecture/exposition as they can then be read at the same time as listening to you.

(c)   Are the students clear as to how they can use the handout? Do they use it as background to be read later? Do they make their own notes on it? There is nothing worse than spending time, effort and money on their design and duplication and find that they are subsequently left on the desks or, even worse, in the wastebasket at the end of the lesson!

(d)   What type of handout do you intend to use? In general, an incomplete handout is preferable to the information type. The former can be personalised and you can ensure that they are read and used.

(e)   Do you intend to assess the students' use of the handout? This is a useful way to ensure that the material that they contain is learned. One way which this can be achieved is to plan the questions that you are to ask in order to draw out the information from the class, which students then write in the appropriate spaces provided.

Preparing Handouts

The layout and presentation of an handout will depend on the sort of information with which you are dealing. Choose the best format to clearly and simply illustrate the idea you are seeking to teach. Remember your aim is to provide motivation and to ensure achievement. The handout should be clear, logical, straightforward, concise, error free and legible. The use of computer word processing and desktop publishing facilities have greatly enhanced legibility and presentation although there is a school of thought which says that handwritten sheets are more popular as they show the care and concern that has been taken with their preparation.

You must write at a vocabulary level which will be understood by the student. Simple, short sentences rather than complex, compound ones are more likely to be understood. Illustrations are invaluable; a picture can be worth much more than words and a table is more likely to be looked at than a paragraph.

You should avoid large blocks of type. Presenting students with three of four pages of closely typed text can visibly bring wrinkled brows and audible sighs from a class. 'White space' makes a handout easier to read. If possible colour should be used where it is necessary to differentiate between different aspects but remember that black and one colour is the norm. For differentiation purposes, different phases, topics or subjects can be duplicated on different coloured paper.

OHP Transparencies

The Overhead Projector, where you project an image from an acetate sheet on to a screen, has several advantages including:

(a) it can be used in daylight conditions;

(b) you face the class whilst using the projector and can therefore more easily control the group;

(c) it can be used in conjunction with other aids like the chalkboard and charts;

(e) material can be prepared before a lesson or can be developed as the lesson proceeds;

(f) material can be stored and used again.

You should, ideally, site the OHP 'off centre', as shown in Figure 1.15 on the following page, and then turned so that the projected image is directed diagonally towards the screen which should be placed in the darkest corner at the front of the room.

You may find it necessary to adjust the screen to avoid a 'keystoning' effect where the image at the bottom of the screen is wider than at the top with the result that it is distorted. To prevent this, tilt the top edge of the screen towards the projector.

Operating the OHP

You should follow the following principles when using the OHP:

(a) face the students at all times;

(b) stand or sit to one side of the projector and not behind it; you will obscure the image if you do stand behind. All writing on the transparencies should be done from the side;

(c) place the prepared transparencies on the projector with the light *off*. Switch off between each transparency;

(d) if it is necessary to *point* at the transparency this should be done by pointing at the projector and *not* at the screen;

(e) do not move the projector while it is hot as this may reduce the bulb life.

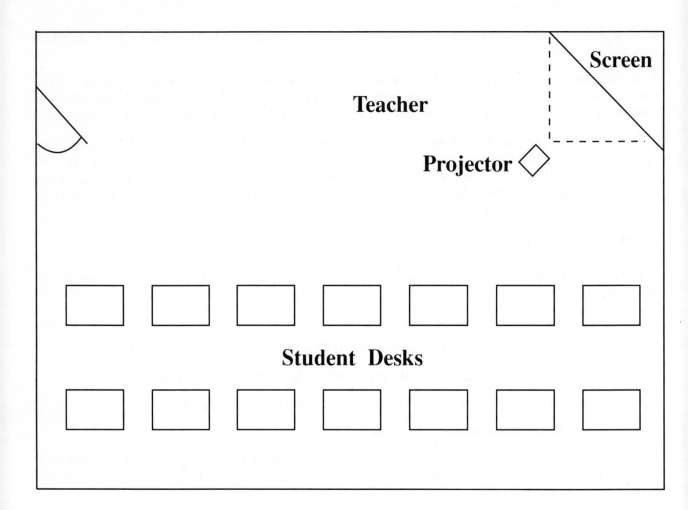

Figure 1.15 Position of an Overhead Projector and Screen

Preparing Transparencies

(i) Materials

The transparency material is made from acetate sheet and different thicknesses are available. The thicker material is easier to use and handle than the very thin.

Two types of ink pen are available: spirit based (usually having a black body) and water based. If a permanent transparency is to be produced, then use a spirit based ink pen. Both are available in the major colours but you should beware of yellow as it does not project at all well. If you have to erase the ink from a spirit-based pen, as you may need to do when drawing diagrams, special erasing spirits are available, but Gin or Whiskey is just as good! Also, special erasers are available on the market.

Adhesive lettering such as '*Letraset*' can be applied directly to the acetate film. However, if colour is required, ensure that OHP quality is used otherwise the light will not shine through the colour and the image will appear black.

Care should be taken when using photocopies from books, magazines or other published material. Apart from the laws relating to copyright, the printing can be too small for classroom purposes. If you do resort to this, ensure that you enlarge the print prior to copying onto acetate film.

Once a transparency has been completed it can be worthwhile fixing the sheet of acetate onto a card mount. This will prevent thin acetate from curling when it is displayed on the projector and the transparency is easier to handle. However, if you prefer to file transparencies with your notes in a prong file, this may not be advisable. Thicker acetate with holes punched along the edge may be the answer in this case.

(ii) Considerations of use

Although commercial transparency material is available, this tends to be quite expensive and many teachers prefer to prepare their own. If you do this you must give careful thought to how you are going to use the aid and how you will integrate them with other learning activities. That is:

(a) What do you expect the students to do while the transparency is being projected?

(b) Are they to make notes or copy in full the material on display? If the latter is to be the case, should an associated handout be prepared and used?

(c) What questions are to be asked to draw out information from the students?

(iii) Key Design Principles

Often, transparencies have far too much material on them. They are cluttered and it is difficult to differentiate between the aspects of the topic. The overall principle relates to simplicity: plenty of 'white space' is an important characteristic to remember. So you should:

(a) keep the transparency simple. Preferably, a transparency should deal with only one main point. Too much information or detail is distracting and confusing;

(b) use large lettering (a minimum of 6 mm in height) and, as with boardwork, lower case is easier to read than upper case;

(c) have only 6–7 words per line and only 10 lines or less to a single transparency;

(d) do not overuse colour but some colour is useful for highlighting purposes;

(e) water based pens can easily be erased (even with moisture on hands when using the transparency) so use spirit based permanent ones when you intend to store the transparency for future use;

(f) desktop publishing facilities give a professional look to your transparencies which can be duplicated on plain paper copier acetate which is available in the libraries of many institutions.

3.3 Assisting Student Learning

It is evident that a very important task for you is to make learning as easy and as enjoyable as possible for your students. We have already laid down some principles like:

- all students learn differently, at their own pace and in their own way;

- students' experiences should be interspersed with periods of reflection;

- different strategies are applicable for different domains of objectives;

- a variety of teaching strategies are most likely to be useful to a class of students to maintain motivation;

- well designed and correctly used visual aids assist the learning process.

All of these, and more, are means which you can use to assist your students in their learning. You must think about the environment of your classrooms and workshops and make them as amenable to the learning process as possible.

We have already discussed some aspects in the section dealing with the use of visual aids, like the sighting of the overhead projector, the design of handouts and the use of the chalkboard. There are, however, others that you must consider.

Room Layout

The traditional image of post-16 teaching is fast disappearing and you should assist it to disappear. This old image is one which involves a lecturer, chalk and talk, teacher centred methods that are syllabus bound and examination oriented, dictated notes, pitching the teaching at the average ability level, rows of desks and despotic teacher control.

For courses which involve a practical bias, to the above list can be added practical sessions where the teacher's demonstration is more or less faithfully reproduced (often a week later) by the students and theory sessions isolated from their associated practicals.

You should assist the disappearance of this mode of teaching and learning. You should see yourself as a facilitator with much of your work being done out of the classroom in preparation for individualised learning: you should value resource-based learning where student participation and activity is high, curriculum negotiation is common and the teaching of transferable skills takes place at all stages.

In order to accommodate this change, your classroom has to become more of a resource centre and less of a lecture room. You need to have books, magazines and articles readily available for your students. The walls need to be covered with charts, drawings, photocopied articles and the like, about the subject. They also require constant changing so that they keep up with the changes in the curriculum area being followed. The desks need to have a flexible format so that they can easily be moved from the more formal situations, to groups of them being put together for discussions and then apart for individual work.

Study Skills

If you are to follow this more modern image, you are likely to encounter difficulties. Difficulties from your more traditionalist colleagues and also difficulties from your students. Even students expect the traditional approach and will only complain when this old style is not performed satisfactorily. More and more courses of post-16 education and training are beginning to require the new approach to be adopted, but change is always slow. So, why should you try to introduce new approaches, given the likely resistance? There are a number of possible reasons which were given by Anne Robinson (FEU, 1987) and adapted here:

- The exam results might be better.

- You should not rely on always teaching traditional courses and should be developing some of the skills that the newer FE courses require.

- Even if it does not improve the end product (the exam results), development of more interactive teaching may improve the quality of experience of the course and the process of learning.

- You should value some degree of student independence in learning for its own sake which should make students more adaptable and able to learn for themselves.

If students are to be asked to learn for themselves then you should assist them in this process and teach them the study skills that are necessary for this to take place. In its many forms, teaching study skills basically means teaching people to learn effectively from whatever 'delivery mode' is being used either presently, or in a more general sense, as a life skill. The common study skills are described in detail in Chapter 6 but, in general terms those often required by adults are:

- planning a project or an assignment

- reading (SQ3R – Survey, Question, Read, Recall, Review)

- taking notes
  (a) from a lecture
  (b) from a book

- essay writing

- planning study time

You need to consider including the teaching of these skills, particularly in the beginning part of your courses, in order to assist your students in their learning. They are going to have enough difficulty with the subject matter without having the added problem of not knowing how to study effectively.

Possible Evidence to Show you have
Achieved the Competence
'Manage Learning'

The type of evidence that you might collect to show that you have achieved the competence involves:

(a)   for a lesson plan that you have designed, stating why the teaching strategies that you have chosen are appropriate for that session;

(b)   for a session that you have taught, describing how you have organised the environment in a way that assists learning. In this you should include, not only the room and the groupings that you might have used, but the resources that you have chosen together with the reasons for their choice;

(c)   giving a description of the techniques that you have used with both individuals and groups of students to assist them with learning. This can include organising the environment as well as the teaching of study skills.

*If you want to check your understanding
of your role in Managing Learning,
try the following progress check*

Progress Check 1.3

1. For each of the teaching strategies below, write a short description to indicate what is involved in each.

   (a) Demonstration

   (b) Lecture

   (c) Discussion

   (d) Project

   (e) Question and answer

   (f) Tutorial

2. State at least five advantages of using visual aids.

3. For one of your classes, decide a study skill that is lacking in some of the students and decide how you would introduce it to them and improve their proficiency with it.

4. Assessment of Learning and Evaluation of Teaching

You must make many decisions in your teaching job. Some of these are:

- which students are successful;

- what teaching strategies to use;

- where to start instruction depending on the ability of the students;

- what additional instruction is to be given to less successful students;

- when students have achieved the objectives.

The basis upon which you make these decisions is generally related to information that you collect. This information is often based on tests that you give to your students. A test is:.

> *a systematic procedure for measuring a sample of a student's behaviour in order to evaluate that behaviour .*

Thus a distinction is drawn between assessment and evaluation. Assessment is the provision of information (generally through testing) whereas evaluation involves the making of judgements based on the information that has been collected.

So, assessment is the process of *obtaining information* about how much the student knows and evaluation involves using that information to form *judgements* which, in turn, are to be used in *decision making*.

The three concepts that are outlined are:

Information: facts about students, materials, resources, processes, and so on that you need to collect.

Judgments: interpreting the facts or information to help determine present conditions or predict future performance.

Decisions: deciding upon a course of action from among several alternatives.

The Basic Teaching Model on shown earlier in this Chapter in Figure 1.3 shows that assessment is required at two major stages of the process. You will need to assess the entry behaviour of your students and you will need to make an assessment to see how well they have achieved the objectives after the learning has taken place. Thus, assessment of the student is necessary for the following types of instructional decisions. The list is not exhaustive and you could think of many more decisions that follow assessment tests. It does, however, illustrate the various points.

- identifying where to start instruction

- planning remedial action for students

- identifying student learning difficulties

- finding student readiness for learning new topics

- improving teaching methods or aids

- planning activity-wide groupings of students
- grading students.

4.1 Types of Assessment Test

Achievement testing usually involves the use of certain instruments. These include:

- a written test;
- an oral test, or;
- a practical test.

There are, however, many objectives in education for which tests are not appropriate. For these objectives, non-test methods need to be employed. Some of the techniques used for this purpose are:

- self-report techniques;
- observational techniques;
- profiles.

As all courses require a variety of objectives for their successful completion, it is necessary that you use a variety of test and non-test instruments to decide if all your objectives are being met by your students.

It is not our intention in this chapter to make you expert in the design of the various types of test, only to make you familiar with the different types together with where they might be most appropriately used. In this way you can include them in your lesson plans in order to take the decisions described above. Greater detail will be found in Chapter 7.

A written test is made up of a variety of questions. One way of classifying these is from the point of view of how the students are expected to respond. They can either:

- select the right response from a set of given responses (called selection-type questions) or
- supply the answer to a given question (called supply-type questions).

Selection Type Questions

Items of the selection type include alternate choice, multiple choice and matching block types. The time needed to answer this type of question is only a matter of seconds.

Alternative Choice Type

Items of this type, also known as true-false items, contain statements for which there are only two possible responses. The type of responses can be:

- true or false
- yes or no
- agree or disagree.

Students are required to choose the correct response.

Example

Circle T if the statement is true or F if it is false.
Litmus paper turns red in an acid solution.   T   F

Multiple-Choice Questions

Multiple-choice questions consist of two parts: a stem and a number of options. The *stem* consists of the question or statement which must be answered by choosing one of the options. The *options* are plausible answers or concluding statements from which one option must be selected.

Example

Circle the option which best answers the question.
Which of the following substances is the hardest?   —   Stem

A. Quartz
B. Diamond   ⌐ Options
C. Carborundum
D. Glass

Matching Block Questions

The matching block type consists of a series of premises in one column, and the response options are listed in another column. The student is asked to select the response options that match each of the stems.

Example

Here are two columns. Match the decimals in the in the left-hand list with the appropriate prefix in the right-hand list by completing the table.

Decimal	Prefix
(i) 0.000 001 (ii) 0.000 000 001 (iii) 0.001 (iv) 0.01	a. centi b. milli c. pico d. micro e. nano f. deca

Table

Decimal			
0.000 001	0.000 000 001	0.001	0.01
Letter of Appropriate Prefix			

Supply Type Questions

Questions of this type include short answer, structured response essay, extended response essay and practical questions. The time needed to answer this type of question is much longer than for the selection type.

Short Answer Questions

There are two types of short answer questions:

(a) Where a question is posed and the student supplies the answer by using a word or phrase.

e.g. In what year did the first person land on the moon?

(b) Where an incomplete sentence is given and students must complete it by inserting the appropriate word or phrase.

e.g. In the year .... the first person landed on the moon.

Structured Essay Questions

This is an essay-type question taking 15–25 minutes to answer, but the response is structured for the student. This type can include calculation questions.

Example

Using the following headings, state briefly how to grow a lettuce crop in the open:

(a) soil preparation

(b) sowing

(c) thinning

(d) harvesting

Essay Type

In this type no restrictions or limits are placed on the student responses. Again, they are usually allocated 15–25 minutes to answer.

Example   Give a brief account of growing an outdoor lettuce crop.

Practical Test

The term practical 'test' refers to a test in which students perform a practical exercise according to instructions prepared in advance and assessed according to a marking scheme.

The practical test involves the completion of psychomotor skills. This type of test might also be called an assignment or project when it involves the completion of written work to accompany the psychomotor skills.

Example

The following example shows how such a test can be operated and consists of specific instructions for the students and a marking scheme which will also be given to them.

Task   Apply undercoat and gloss paint to wall surfaces by brush.

Preparation   You will require a wall area (plaster, plaster board or building board) of between 7 and 8 sq. metres with a height of at least 1.5 metres and a cutting edge of at least 4 metres. The surface should be prepared, made good and ready to receive undercoat.

The test is to be organised over two days to allow sufficient drying time. Colours must be selected with care to ensure that no opacity weaknesses reduce your chance of meeting the standards.

Instructions

1.   Protect the surrouding area.

2.   De-nib surfaces.

3.   Apply one coat of undercoat by brush.

4.   Wet or dry flatten to a smooth even surface.

5.   Apply one coat of alkali type gloss finish by brush.

6.   Check and clean tools and equipment and return to store after each process.

7.   Clean surroundings after each process.

8.   Check assessment schedule for standards to be achieved.

Assessment

Standard of Finish	Tolerances	Yes	No	Comments
Are bits and nibs visible but not excessive?				
Are brush marks laid off correctly and not pronounced?				
Is work free from grinning				
Does work have full even gloss?				
Free from runs and tears?	1 run 5mm max.			
Free from curtains?	1 allowed 50mm max.			
Free from misses?	Invisible from 1m			
Etc.				

4.2 Non-Test Methods

We suggested at the start of this section that there were some objectives where it is inapplicable to use tests and that non-test methods had been developed for this type of objective. The objectives that are applicable to these methods include:

- Communicating effectively with a range of people and in a variety of situations.

- Showing a capacity for organisation and leadership.

- Working safely with a range of equipment and materials to an agreed standard.

- Identifying own strengths and weaknesses.

- Recognising the need for a personal career plan.

These objectives are all affective domain objectives which deal with attitudes and personal competences.

Self Assessment Techniques

You can argue, especially in the case of adults, that the only true assessment of the type of objective or competence identified above, is self assessment. No one else really can know how well a person is able to 'communicate with a range of people' or 'recognise the need for a personal career plan'. The only true assessment is that made by the individual. Hence, self-assessment is becoming widely recognised as an important assessment technique especially when used with adults.

When you adopt this technique, you will need to identify the objectives or, even better, competences that are to be achieved together with explicit criteria for assessment for each of the competences, so that students have a clear idea upon which to base their self-assessment.

Profiles

A profile is a way of reporting student achievements; it is not an assessment technique in itself. Profiles can be used during the course of study with students to provide a basis for action by both students and teachers *and*, at the end of the course, to provide a basis for action by employers and teachers. They also provide a system of reporting progress on areas (that is the affective domain areas) that are difficult to assess when using the traditional techniques of assessment. Thus, profiles attempt to pass on information to students, employers and other teachers about student progress and achievements in all areas of study.

You will see that several types of profile are discussed in Chapter 7. One type, the 'Free Response' type is given as an example in Figure 1.16. Others have much greater structure than this and are more firmly linked to lists of objectives or competences.

The intention is that this will be completed by you as the teacher but that you will discuss it with your student and, more importantly, get the student to sign it. This is of particular importance where goals are to be set for the student in the space for areas where improvements need to be made. It has already been stated that profiling is a *process*; it takes place in a on-going (formative) framework. There are four basic principles that you should follow when profiling. It:

1. requires one-to-one teacher-student reviews on a regular basis;

2. involves negotiation with individual students;

3. is a strategy which allows students to:

    • reflect on their success and failure;
    • take responsibility for their own learning, development and assessment;

4. should record positive statements of achievement with respect to:

    • abilities and skills demonstrated;
    • personal qualities exhibited;
    • tasks and activities experienced.

Please comment on the following:

Communication Skills:

Practical and Numerical Skills:

Attitude to Training:

Planning and Problem Solving:

Manual Dexterity:

Computer Literacy:

Aptitude and Areas for Improvement:
(give here areas in which the student shows a particular aptitude and areas in which improvements need to be made)

Signed: **Teacher:**   **Student:**   **Date:**

Figure 1.16 Sample Free Response-Type Profile Sheet

Observation Techniques

It has become realised over the past few years that the traditional techniques of assessment (like examinations involving paper and pencil tests) are very unreliable and are not really valid for what they are intended. They only assess the end product and, generally, completely neglect the process that is involved in achieving that product. In consequence, the instruments that have been used for some time in the assessment of practical work have become more widely accepted for other tasks and are based on *direct observation*.

This observation is necessary to increase the validity and reliability of the assessment procedures. The observation may take place over a relatively long period of time or may be related to the assessment of a specific task. It is evident that this technique can assess the process elements of a task as well as the finished product.

There are four common methods of direct observation but the first of these, although included here for the sake of completeness, is unreliable and not really suggested for common use. The four methods are:

(i) *Global impression:* which is essentially a 'look and see' technique. The method is very unreliable but is a useful first step when starting to develop an assessment procedure.

(ii) *Semi-structured:* consists of a number of open questions which have been determined in advance and are relevant to the different aspects of the task. The observer writes answers and/or comments during and after the observation. The example for gloss painting a wall (above) is of this type.

(iii) *Rating schedules:* are where the rater gives a score on a scale of the impression of each component of the task on a scale from poor to good.

(iv) *Checklists*: are where the rater marks, usually with a tick or a cross, whether the student did or did not carry out the specific features of a task.

Examples of each of these methods is detailed in Chapter 7.

4.3 When to Use the Different Techniques

Each of the type of assessment techniques can be used in a variety of situations. One of your roles is to decide which type to use in a particular situation. Some suggestions for this are made in Figure 1.17.

Assessment Type	Possible Uses
Multiple Choice	Measurement of a variety of learning outcomes such as vocabulary, facts, explanations and applications. Providing diagnostic assessment of entry behaviour or to assess objectives quickly at the end of a session.
Alternate-Choice	These are not particularly helpful as they are very susceptible to guessing.
Matching Block	Testing of lower level knowledge (matching dates with events and symbols with units). When associations between things are to be identified.
Short Answer/completion	The learning outcome is to recall rather than to recognise information. Simple computational problems. When a selection type is too obvious.
Structured and Extended Essay	When the objectives specify writing or recall rather than recognition of information. When the sorting and presentation of an argument is required.
Practical	When the assessment of psychomotor skills is necessary.
Self Assessment	Especially useful for adults where affective and high level cognitive assessment required.
Profile	For on-going assessment during a course to give and negotiate specific feedback to students.
Observation	Particularly for psychomotor and affective domain objectives.

Figure 1.17 Situations where Different Assessment Techniques may be Used

4.4 Evaluation of Teaching

The Basic Teaching Model which was first given on page 6 of this chapter, and is reproduced again on the next page, gives you the basis for the evaluation of your teaching performance. Here if the feedback loop from the assessment tells you that the objectives have not been achieved by the students, you must consider: (a) if the objectives were correct, or (b) if the entry behaviour of the students was lacking, or (c) whether the teaching strategies that you adopted were inappropriate.

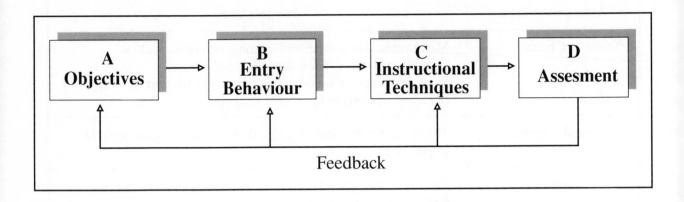

We have already suggested that you evaluate your own teaching. As part of this process you should also involve your students in your evaluation. Students, especially adults, can provide invaluable information about your performance that cannot be collected from any other source.

Information needs to be collected from students about the aspects of the Basic Teaching Model. Such information can be collected by questionnaire or through interviewing students (or a mixture of both). You need to design your own questionnaire or schedule but it is not the intention to go into questionnaire design in this chapter. However, an example questionnaire is presented in Figure 1.18.

It will be seen that this questionnaire has both open response aspects where students are invited to write their own comments, and closed response ones where students rate their choice on a 5-point scale.

In deciding the design of your questionnaire you should first consider what you want to find out. This can reflect the things that you think that you do well and things that you think could be improved. The answers that students give to the questions can either confirm or otherwise challenge these thoughts.

In relation to your course, indicate your views on the following issues by circling the appropriate numbers or ticking the appropriate methods:

1. Are the subject aims being fulfilled?

   Fully   5   4   3   2   1   Not at All

2. Do you think that the classroom assists you with the learning process?

   Helpful 5   4   3   2   1   Unhelpful

3. Do you feel that there are adequate resources?

   Adequate 5   4   3   2   1   Totally Inadequate

4. Are the resources used effectively?

   Effective 5   4   3   2   1   Under-used

5. Which of the teaching methods have you experienced?

   Tick as appropriate and which you would like to experience.

Experienced	Method	Wish to Experience
	Lecture Group Discussion Seminar Role Play Practical Demonstration Use of Handouts One-to-one talks Other (state)	

6. Have you found the content of the subject:

   Simple   5   4   3   2   1   Difficult

7. Do you feel that your progress has been monitored:

   Adequately 5   4   3   2   1   Not at all

8. Do you feel that your progress is:

   Satisfactory 5   4   3   2   1   Unsatisfactory

9. Any other comments:

Figure 1.18 Sample Questionnaire for Students on the Effectiveness of their Course

> ### Possible Evidence to Show you have Achieved the Competence
> ### 'Assess Learning and Evaluate Teaching'

The type of evidence that you might collect to show that you have achieved the competence involves:

(a)   For a lesson plan that you have designed, plan a test to assess:

    (i)   the entry behaviour of the students, and

    (ii)   the achievement of the objectives.

State why you have chosen a particular type of test question.

(b)   Using the results of the tests in (a,ii) above, evaluate how the students, individually, and as a group, have achieved the objectives of the session.

(c)   Design and distribute a questionnaire to students about the effectiveness of either a lesson or a subject. Analyse the results given by students and judge the effectiveness of the teaching. If you were to repeat the session(s), what changes would you make?

If you want to check your understanding of your role in Assessing Learning and Evaluating Teaching, try the following progress check

Progress Check 1.4

1. State three different types of assessment technique and, for each type, state the possible uses.

2. Describe the main differences between assessment and evaluation.

3. Under what headings would you evaluate one of your lessons?

Further Reading and References

Further Reading relating to the topics in this chapter can be found in the following:

Bligh, D   *What's the Use of Lectures?*, Penguin, 1971 – Gives a good comparison (from research) of different teaching and learning methods.

Buzan, T   *Use Your Head*, BBC, 2nd Edition, 1989 – A book written from a series of BBC TV programmes which gives suggestions for thinking and studying (e.g. mind maps).

City & Guilds   *Constructing Practical Tests*, City & Guilds, 1979 – A short practical guide to the construction of practical tests which is useful for teachers of practical subjects.

De Cecco, J P   *The Psychology of Learning and Instruction,* Prentice Hall, 1968 – A very useful tome dealing with the theory of instruction of cognitive, affective and psychomotor learning. Not easy first reading but is a useful volume for 'dipping' into.

Gronlund, N L   *Stating Behavioural Objectives for Classroom Instruction*, Macmillan, 1970 – A product of the '60s approach to instruction but very helpful in the design of aims and objectives.

Kolb, D A   *Experiential Learning – Experience as a Source of Learning and Development,* Prentice Hall, 1984.

Law, D   *Uses and Abuses of Profiling*, Harper, 1984 – A practical guide to both the design and use of profile documents.

Lovell, R B   *Adult Learning*, Croom Helm, 1980 – The mechanisms and processes of adult learning covering individual characteristics to the social context in which learning takes place are included in this easy to read book.

Minton, D   *Teaching Skills in Further and Adult Education*, Macmillan, 1991 – All aspects of study skills, lesson preparation and communication skills to visual aids, assessment and testing are covered. There is also a section giving an overview of the major theories of learning.

Nierenderg, G   *The Complete Negotiator*, Souvenir Press, (London), 1982 – Guidelines to the negotiating process.

Perrott, E   *Effective Teaching: A Practical Guide to Improving Your Teaching,* Longman, 1982 – A very practical book giving guides to lesson planning, questioning and communication in the classroom.

Robinson, A   *Study Skills,* FEU, 1987

Rowntree, D   *Assessing Students: How Shall We Know Them?*, Harper and Row, 1977 – A practical guide to student assessment.

Walkin, L   *Teaching and Learning in Further Education*, Stanley Thornes Ltd., 1990 – A practical book covering all of the topics in this introductory chapter.

Chapter 2

Student Learning

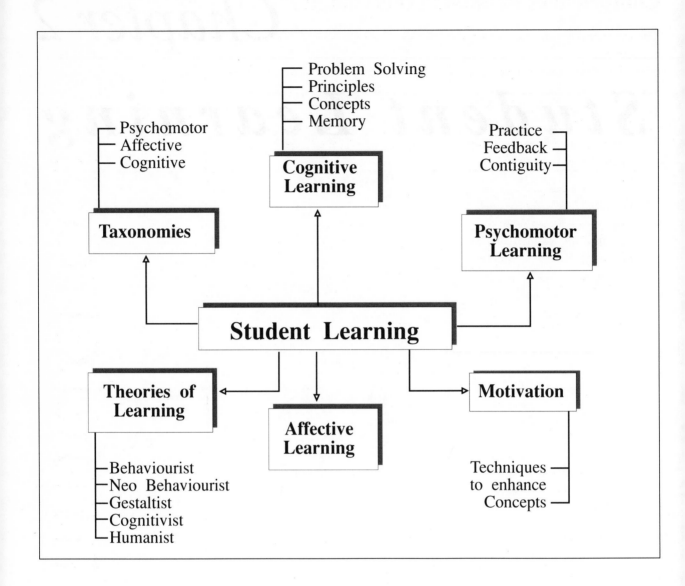

Overview of Chapter 2

Competences Related to this Chapter

The teacher competences and associated performance criteria related to this chapter are:

Overall Competence – *Use positive aspects of theory in the design of lessons*

Competence	Performance Criteria
1. **Identify the characteristics of the three taxonomies.**	(a) The levels in the taxonomy of at least two of the domains are used.
2. **Demonstrate effective design of learning sessions through the identification of variables which effect learning.**	(a) Uses psychological factors when teaching concepts, principles and problem solving. (b) The factors which enhance student memory are used effectively. (c) In the teaching of motor skills, uses contiguity, feedback and practice effectively. (d) Plan to have an influence on student attitudes.
3. **Use the components of a range of theories of learning.**	(a) Consider the main components of learning theory from: – behaviourist; – cognitivist; and – humanistic models (b) Evaluate the effectiveness of the models for your own teaching
4. **Identify variables which influence student motivation.**	(a) Consider student motivational techniques.

1. Introduction

As teachers we tend to think that teaching is all about teachers and our role; in fact the most important aspects of the educational process are the students and what they learn. This leads us to consider what we mean by 'learning'.

As you read the educational literature and, more specifically, educational psychology, you find many differences in theories and definitions. You need to decide which you understand and which make sense to you.

Learning is about change: developing a new skill, understanding a scientific law, changing an attitude. The change is not merely incidental or natural in the way that our appearance changes as we get older. Learning is a relatively permanent change, usually brought about intentionally. When we attend a course, search through a book, or read a discussion paper, we set out to learn!

Other learning can take place without planning, for example experience. If you wallpaper a room and then paint the ceiling you could learn that you should paint the ceiling first. Some of our learning can be more dangerous, for example we might discover that a knife is very sharp. Generally with all learning there is an element within us of wishing to remember and understand why something happens and to do it better next time.

This chapter is about the theoretical underpinning that is provided for us by educational psychology. It is important that we are able to relate what we do in the classroom to some theory. If we do not do this, then the way that we teach is likely to be ad-hoc; we try something out of a whim as opposed to considering it logically and relate it to research. Unfortunately, for every aspect of research that tells us to do something a particular way, there is another piece that suggests, not necessarily the opposite, but a different way.

For the multitude of teachers that staff the nation's classrooms and workshops, theory is all right for the theorists but in the meantime they have to get on with the job. One cannot help but sympathise with this attitude in view of the contribution that theorists have made to education practice. Not that the theorists themselves are particularly at fault since the financial support to make theorising possible has often been very difficult to gain. In consequence, theorists are somewhat thin on the ground especially in UK and much of this work has been carried out in America (with much of the literature, especially prior to 1960's, coming from there).

Without theories in education, the practice in classrooms and workshops would not change. Without theory there would be a tendency for us to teach in the same manner that we were taught, and for teacher training to consist of 'sitting with Nellie'. 'Nellie' is the factory worker who has been doing the job for years to whom new recruits are attached while they learn the job. 'Sitting with Nellie' has been recognised by industry as an extremely inefficient method of job training and few teachers would consider the totality of the role if they were taught in this manner. And yet, at the time of writing, there is a movement to increase the time that trainee teachers spend in schools watching others and then trying their own hands as a major part of their initial training.

Educational theory has, as its base, psychology and the study of behaviour. As teachers, it is argued, we need to know how people behave under certain circumstances so that we can optimise their learning through the provision of conditions that make it as easy a process as possible. For instance, how do we help our students to memorise the material in our subject, how do we help them understand the concepts and principles, does their attitude to both learning and the subject have a bearing on how they learn, and so on?

2. The Three Domains

Writers tend to separate learning into three main groups or domains. These are the psychomotor, cognitive and affective domains. Each will be considered in turn.

Those skills which are concerned with physical dexterity, for example changing a wheel and giving an injection, fall into the *psychomotor* domain. Both of the tasks do need knowledge but, predominantly, they are physical skills which need practice.

Knowledge and knowing the 'how' and the 'why', the thinking skills, fall into the *cognitive* domain. Examples include 'stating the names of the major bones in the body', 'explaining why we have tides'. Both of these require thought processes to be accomplished.

The third domain and one we often neglect is the *affective* domain. This is concerned with attitudes. Examples in this domain include 'the need to eat a healthy, balanced diet', 'the need for equality of opportunity for all', and 'politeness'. These deal with feelings and emotions and are different from the examples in the other domains.

Already, in Chapter 1, we have introduced these three domains but here we need to look at them in more detail in order to consider the conditions that are likely to make learning easier.

Learning in these three domains often needs different teaching and learning approaches. They are often considered in isolation but in practice learning may occur simultaneously in all three.

3. Learning Taxonomies

As teachers we tend to concentrate upon teaching our subject matter and the best or most logical order in which to teach the topics. As we see in this chapter, we teach a variety of topics at different levels and the educational literature leads us to believe we need to teach each issue in the most appropriate way. This prompts us to consider the importance of domains and levels, or degrees of difficulty, within each domain. This classification of levels is known as a 'taxonomy'. Each of the three domains needs to be considered in turn.

The levels in the cognitive domain were identified by Bloom (1960) and the levels in the affective domain by Krathwohl et al, (1964). Modified versions of these are shown in Figure 2.1 and Figure 2.2 respectively. When learning is taking place at one of the higher levels, it is important that the student has the requisite lower levels of learning upon which to base the subsequent learning. This, again, shows the importance of entry behaviour.

Levels in the cognitive domain range from the lowest level of knowledge (remembering or recall) to the more complicated thinking processes required for evaluation. As you will see from Figure 2.1, to accomplish objectives at any level, objectives at the lower level need to be achieved first. For example, in order to achieve the application level the student must first possess knowledge and comprehension.

The affective domain also includes levels, but instead of the development from the simple to the complex

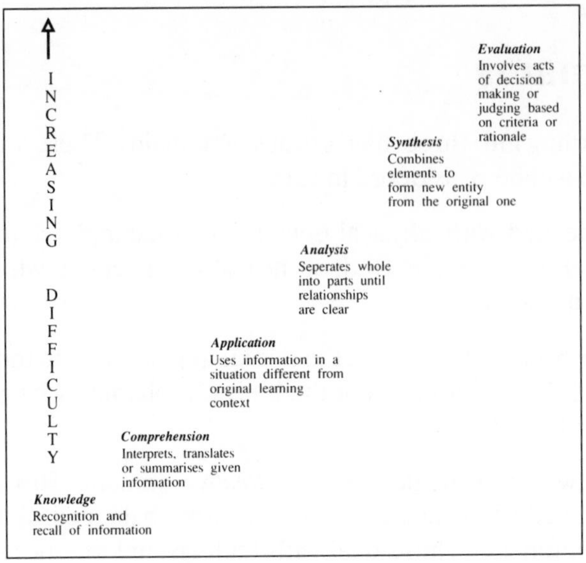

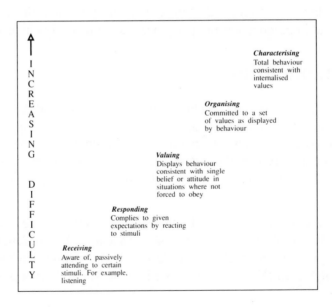

Figure 2.1 Major Categories in the Cognitive Domain

Figure 2.2 Major Categories in the Affective Domain

found in the cognitive domain, each succeeding level involves more internalising of the feeling or attitude. That is, the behaviour becomes a part of our total way of responding. In the lower levels of the domain the student is simply provided with the necessary information with which to know what an appropriate response is: the student is only required to *passively* attend to and be aware of the information. The highest level is only achieved when the student has *internalised* the information. At this level the feelings or attitudes have become a way of life. Thus, if this is related to, say, safety in the workshop, at the lower level the student is told about the safety rules and, in order to achieve the objective, listens attentively to them. At the highest level these rules will be automatically applied without thinking about them no matter what the situation or place as they have become internalised, automatic, and a way of life. Dave (1975) has produced a taxonomy for the psychomotor domain and this is shown in Figure 2.3. This taxonomy is similar to that in the cognitive domain in that it progresses from the simple to the complex of, in this case, skill development. A psychomotor skill consists of tasks that are integrated into a co-ordinated whole. It is developed in stages from the imitation of a model to the point at which performance becomes automatic or habitual. As can

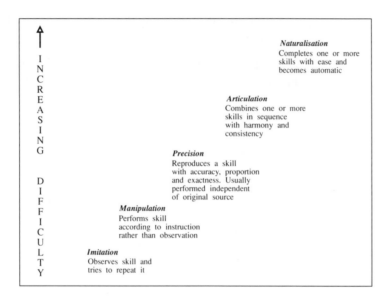

Figure 2.3 Major Categories in the Psychomotor Domain

be seen from Figure 2.3 each successive level within the domain requires more complicated forms of psychomotor skills and/or a combination of several skills into a co-ordinated sequence. The usefulness of each of these taxonomies lies in their operation in the classroom as they are applied to learning. There are three aspects of importance: (i) entry behaviour; (ii) writing and identifying levels of objectives; and (iii) assessing the learning of the objectives.

In terms of entry behaviour its assessment relates to a level lower than that required by the objectives. The writing of objectives need to be at an appropriate level within the domain and the choice of methods are more applicable for some levels than they are for others. Also, the classification of objectives into levels allows you to sequence your teaching from the simple to the complex. Finally, the assessment needs to be at the level at which the objectives have been stated. Thus, the construction of test questions needs to be at the appropriate level of the objectives.

Possible Evidence to Show You Have Achieved
the Competence
'Identify the characteristics of the three taxonomies'

The type of evidence that you might collect to show that you have achieved the competence involves:

1.   Classification of the aims of your subject into:

   (a) the domain into which each predominantly falls;

   (b) identification of the highest level within that domain that is intended by each.

2.   Writing a series of objectives at different levels in each of the domains.

If you want to check your understanding of the three taxonomies try the following progress check.

Progress Check 2.1

1. Define the:

    - six levels in the cognitive domain;

    - five levels in the affective domain; and

    - five levels in the psychomotor domain.

2. State the three main aspects of importance of the use of the taxonomies in the classroom as they are applied to learning.

4. Why use Models?

There is a good deal written about, 'how to teach', and 'how students learn'. This comes from the experience of many people over many years. When we have just started in teaching, we are often pleased to survive but as confidence grows, we can learn a good deal from the plethora of books which are available. These books often contain theories and models which the writers feel 'work' and are useful. You need to be careful to consider the context of that model – how old were the students, what was their previous experience, what resources were available, how long did it take? You can try some of these models. If they help your teaching, then that is something that you can use in future. However, some models do not work well at the first attempt. You can reflect upon this and try to find out why and give the model another chance.

4.1 Pedagogy vs. Andragogy Models

A pedagogical approach may be described as a teacher dominated learning situation. Often the teacher does all or most of the talking, dictates the pace of learning (or rather the pace of teaching!) and the students are rather passive.

An andragogical approach places more emphasis on what the learner is doing. Andragogy is all about how adults learn. Knowles (1970) stated that adults prefer to learn in a different way from that of children. Much of educational theory is based upon assumptions. Knowles identified assumptions such as, adults prefer to be self directing rather than being totally dependent on a teacher and adults have a fund of experience which helps them to learn. Mezirow (1981) considered andragogy to be an organised and sustained effort to assist adults to learn in a way which enhances their capability to function as self directed learners. Aspects which help the andragogical process include:

    (i)   helping learners to understand how to use learning resources;

    (ii) helping learners to assume responsibility for their own learning, (some validating bodies such as BTEC expect this);

    (iii) help the learners make decisions about how they learn best;

    (iv) help the learners to think about the learning process and reflect upon what they have learned;

    (v) make the learning as active and participative as possible.

At first glance this appears to make the teacher redundant! This is far from true. What it does mean that the teacher role is different and many feel much more enjoyable.

5. Learning and the Cognitive Domain

The cognitive domain, like the other domains as we have seen has various levels of learning. The easiest is remembering facts, relationships, laws etc,. More difficult is understanding why relationships occur and predicting requires concept attainment and ability to link concepts to form principles. A further step is the ability to use all these skills in order to solve problems. Perhaps the most logical approach is to consider how memory works and then move up the taxonomic hierarchy to problem solving.

5.1 Memory

As teachers we often present our students with facts and knowledge and leave it to them to select and find a means of remembering these key issues. We should plan the learning to enhance memorability and a study of how we think memory works is helpful.

The model shown in Figure 2.4 is a simplified vision of how we think the memory system functions. Although it is simple it appears to be helpful.

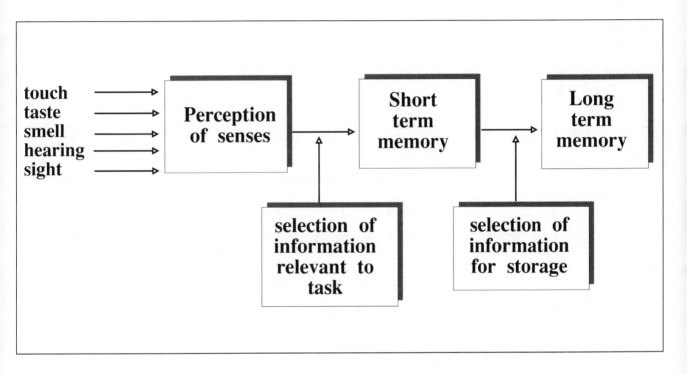

Figure 2.4 Simple Model of Memory

The ability to retain and recall information is called memory. Experience and experiments suggest there are three stages to the memorising process: sensory stage; short-term memory; and long-term memory. Each may be considered in turn.

The first stage is perception. The senses gather a vast amount of information and it appears that much of this is ignored. However some signals are given particular attention and active use of these signals is known as perception. Gathering of the same signals by different people leads to differences in perception because of their different experiences and abilities.

In your teaching you can help the perception process by using a variety of signals, appealing to the senses, perhaps by the use of audio visual aids. You may have to supply information, i.e. set the scene, before the appearance of the stimuli.

The short-term memory appears to retain the immediate interpretation of events. Information goes into the short term memory quickly and is available for rapid recall. The short term memory is a very busy area which perhaps accounts for the fact that its capacity is limited.

The long term memory appears to have a huge capacity. If you can get information into the long term memory – and the purpose of the first two stages is to filter material that is appropriate to long term storage – then it may be stored almost indefinitely.

You may know remember incidents from your childhood, going back many years, depending upon how old you are!

Our task then is to help students to remember. Here are some common ways to do this:

1. *Verbal Association* Group or pair things together e.g. bat and ball; knife, fork and spoon.

Make unlikely associations e.g. chalk and cheese, oil and water.

Make up a story linking things together.

2. *Visual Association* Group things together and visualise them in their relative positions.

Write a list and visualise that list.

3. *Repetition* Write out a number of times, repeat aloud a number of times.

Listen to a tape several times.

Read over and over again.

4. *Self test* Used with repetition.

5. *Part test* If there is a great deal to be learned then break the material into manageable lots and remember these smaller parts.

6. *Rhyme rule* 30 days has September etc.

7. *First letter* Colours of the Rainbow –
Red, Orange, Yellow, Green, Blue Indigo, Violet.
*R*ichard *O*f *Y*ork *G*ave *B*attle *I*n *V*ain

8. *Spelling Association* Stationery – E for envelopes.

The following conditions appear to help recall:

- *Errors*   Try to avoid making errors.

- *Recency*   You tend to remember things which have happened recently.

- *Frequency*   The more you make recall active, via testing, the more likely you are to remember.

- *Intensity*   The better the concentration – the better the recall.

- *Importance*   You remember the most important things to you (at the time).

- *Feelings*   Your state of mind affects the quality of learning. If you are upset about a domestic issue then your ability to enhance recall will be reduced.

- *Association*   The more you can associate and relate new material to existing knowledge, the better the recall.

5.2 The Learning of Concepts

When learning a new topic or subject, the key to understanding is when we grasp the basic concept(s). This makes teaching concepts a key skill. We probably teach many concepts without analysing how we teach them. There are several concept attainment models described in the literature and there is also a reasonable amount of agreement on the key features of teaching concepts.

Before we can teach concepts we need to understand what a concept is. It is considered to be 'a class of stimuli which have common characteristics'. These can be objects, events or persons. For example a *book* is an object - there are many different varieties of books but we can differentiate between what is a book and what is a newspaper, or magazine. A *party* is an example of the 'event concept' while *teachers*, *bakers* and *doctors* are examples of 'people concepts'. Note that 'War and Peace', 'Ruth's 18th Birthday Party', and 'Mr Chips' are not concepts, they are particular examples of each concept.

Concepts have attributes and an attribute is a distinctive feature of a concept. For example a red triangle has two attributes; colour and shape. The more complex the concept then, generally speaking, the greater the number of attributes. Some attributes are more important than others and these are known as dominant attributes.

Perhaps you are wondering why we have concepts and need to teach concepts. Concepts reduce the complexity of learning because we can categorise objects according to their concept rather than having to remember each individual set of stimuli. Concepts also reduce the need for constant learning. We can classify new sets of stimuli ourselves rather than having to be told what it is. Concepts help in communicating with each other and hence with the learning.

There are two main types of concept: concrete and abstract. Concrete concepts are often those we can see, for example, a car, a house, a book. Abstract concepts are a little more difficult and are often defined in many ways for example democracy, poverty. Clearly concepts are important in learning and it is useful to consider how we can help our students attain them. De Cecco and Crawford (1974) provide a step by step approach and this is shown in Figure 2.5.

Step 1	Describe the performance expected of the students after they have learned the concept. *This is what we often call the objective, the competence or the learning outcome.*
Step 2	Reduce the number of attributes to be learned in complex concepts and make the important attributes dominant.
Step 3	Provide the students with useful verbal mediators. *Here we help the students by giving the names of attributes and features and ensure that they know these before we attempt to teach the concept itself.*
Step 4	Provide positive and negative examples of the concept. *This is seen as a very important step. This helps the students to discriminate among the attributes: those which form part of the concept and those which do not.*
Step 5	'Present examples in close succession or simultaneously' This process helps with contiguity and reduces unwanted learning.
Step 6	'Provide occasions for students responses and the reinforcement of these responses. *This really takes place with Steps 4 and 5 and gives feedback to the students.*
Step 7	Assess the learning of the concept. *This final step may not be considered to be part of the concept attainment process but is obviously helpful feedback.*

Figure 2.5 De Cecco's Model of Concept Teaching

If we take an application of the De Cecco's model to the teaching of the concept of a bridge we can see the way in which the learning is structured.

Step 1	The student will be able to identify bridges given a range of structures.
Step 2	Show a picture of a simple bridge and discuss the main features (attributes).
Step 3	Use names for the attributes e.g. span, support, structure, communications.
Step 4	Preesnt pictures of several structures, some of which are bridges, some of which are similar e.g. pylon, crane or road.
Step 5	Display pictures on wall or in quick succession using slide projector, OHP, or charts.

Step 6	With Steps 4 & 5.
Step 7	Test, perhaps in the local area.

Other writers have similar models. Stones (1983) stresses the importance of planning how to teach concepts. His model is based upon 12 stages which are in three phases as shown in Figure 2.6.

A   PRE-ACTIVE

1.   Make a task analysis of the teaching objectives to identify the key concepts involved, the subordinate concepts, specific examples, methods of presentation, students' activities and modes of evaluation.

2.   Ascertain students' prior knowledge. If this is not possible plan for diagnosis at the interactive stage.

B   INTERACTIVE

3.   Give a preliminary idea of the nature of the new learning.

4.   Explain terms to be used in labelling the new concepts and their attributes and call to mind existing concepts relevant to the new learning.

5.   Provide initially a series of simplified exemplars with few attributes to facilitate identification of the criterial attributes.

6.   Increase the salience of the criterial attributes to enable students to discriminate between criterial and non criterial attributes.

7.   Provide a series of exemplars sequenced to provide a complete range of criterial attributes as economically as possible.

8.   Provide non-exemplars in counterposition to exemplars to enhance discrimination between criterial and non-criterial attributes.

9.   Provide new exemplars and non-exemplars and ask the students to identify the exemplars. Provide feedback for each discrimination.

10.   Encourage the students to use their own language in explaining the nature of the concepts.

11.   Provide suitable cueing throughout to ensure that students gradually become independent in their ability to identify novel exemplars of the concepts.

C   EVALUATIVE
(This process is naturally much the same procedure as would be applied in diagnosing prior level of ability.)

12.   Present novel exemplars of the concepts for the students to identify and/or discriminate from non-exemplars

---

Figure 2.6 Stones' Model of Concept Teaching

Rowntree (1982) has a similar model but considers that there is no need to apply each step every time you teach a concept. He thinks this is too time consuming and that the model should be reserved for the more difficult concepts. This model is shown in Figure 2.7.

Isolate the concepts	–	from the facts, principles, examples, etc of our subject matter.
Define each concept	–	dictionary-type definitions to begin with, perhaps.
Examine model examples	–	to sharpen the definition by deciding which features of the examples are essential to the concept and which are incidental.
Examine counter examples	–	to further establish the essential character of the concept by identifying features that would negate it.
Examine border	–	line examples to clarify our understanding of the crucial features of the concepts by considering cases where it 'almost' applies or applies only 'in a way'.
Consider invented examples	–	testing the concept by inventing imaginary cases that might really stretch the features we have identified for the concept.
Compare personal contexts	–	in recognition that the concept will have different connotations for different individuals (which may or may not hinder communication).
Examine related concepts	–	studying one concept leads us into seeing how it fits into the surrounding network of concepts.
Elucidate the principles	–	concepts are related to other concepts in principles (rules, theorems, axioms, generalizations, statements) which constitute the message(s) of the subject matter, and the key principles need to be identified and classified (e.g. as empirical, evaluative, or semantic statements).

Figure 2.7 Rowntree Model of Concept Teaching

Joyce and Weil (1990) have a three phase model (Figure 2.8) which has ten stages. Although each model has differences, they contain many similarities. It may be useful to think about a concept which you will be teaching in the near future and use one of the models to structure your teaching.

PHASE ONE **Presentation of Data and Identification of Concept**	PHASE TWO **Testing Attainment of the Concept**
Teachers present labelled examples Students compare attributes in positive and negative examples. Students generate and test hypotheses. Students state a definition according to the essential attributes.	Students identify additional unlabelled examples as yes/no. Teacher confirms hypotheses, names concept, and restates definitions according to essential attributes. Students generate examples.
PHASE THREE **Analysis of thinking strategies**	
Students describe thoughts Students discuss role of hypotheses and attributes. Students discuss type and number of hypotheses.	

Figure 2.8 Joyce and Weil Syntax of the Concept Attainment Model

5.3 *The Learning of Principles*

In the literature, concept and principle teaching are closely related because a principle is a statement of the relationship between two or more concepts. Principles are sometimes called rules or generalisations.

Some examples of principles are:

(i)   four plus ten equals fourteen;

(ii)   all men are created equal;

(iii)   three dimensional objects have six sides.

The following are statements and phrases but are *not* principles:

(i)   evergreen trees;

(ii)   the Conservative party won the last election;

(iii)   John made the strongest structure.

The first set of statements qualify as principles because they state relationships among concepts. The first, for example, states the relationship among five concepts: four; plus; ten; equals; and fourteen. The second relates four concepts: all; men; created; and equal. The second set of statements are not principles: evergreen trees is a concept, in the second statement the Conservative party is the only concept and so no relationship is stated.

It is sometimes useful to think of principles as 'if-then' statements. For example, *if* you add four to ten, *then* you obtain fourteen; *if* an object has six sides, *then* it is three dimensional. The advantage of phrasing a principle as an if-then statement is that the statement then indicates the proper ordering of the component concepts. Only the proper ordering of the concepts results in satisfactory learning of the principle.

De Cecco (1974) op cit has a model (Figure 2.9) which is similar to the concept attainment model.

---

1.   Describe the performance expected of the students after they have learned the principle.

2.   Decide and indicate which concept or principles the students must recall in learning the new principle.

3.   Assist the students to recall component concepts.

4.   Help the students to combine the concepts in the proper order.

5.   Require the students to demonstrate the principle fully.

6.   Require the students to give a full statement of the principle.

7.   Verify the students' learning of the principle.

8.   Provide for practise of the principle and reinforcement of the students' responses.

Figure 2.9 De Cecco's Steps in the Teaching of a Principle

When teaching principles in the near future you may wish to use this model as a framework for your teaching.

5.4 The Learning of Problem Solving

Moving further up the taxonomy of the Cognitive domain brings us to Problem Solving. Problem Solving may be regarded a high level activity since it usually involves using two or more principles. This separates it from lower order puzzle solving.

A similar model to those used in the teaching of concepts and principles may be used for problem solving. The steps are:

Step 1	State the learning intentions
Step 2	Ensure students know the relevant concepts and principles and ask the students to recall them
Step 3	Give indications or guidelines to the solution without providing the solution.
Step 4	Assess the learning outcomes.

Practice with problem solving, in a structured manner, often helps students.

The following, reported in Gage and Berliner (1975) of Mager's work, are considered important principles in the solving of problems:

- habitual ways of doing things do not solve difficult problems;

- problems would not be difficult if they could be solved through habitual ways of solving problems;

- a person should not stay in a rut but should keep an open mind for new meanings;

- if someone fails to solve a problem, they should put it out of their mind and seek a new problem;

- solutions to problems appear suddenly and cannot be forced.

Experiments have been completed which suggest that problem solving can be enhanced through careful structuring of the teaching. The suggested sequence is:

(i) ensure students understand the problem completely and then get them to state it in general terms;

(ii) find the major solution strategies;

(iii) list alternatives within the solution strategies;

(iv) evaluate the alternatives and choose the best.

Figure 2.10 is an example of the use of this sequence as suggested by Gage and Berliner (op cit).

State the problem in general terms.	Find major solution strategies	List alternatives within the solution strategies	Evaluate and choose the best
Increase the attention of students in class.	Vary the methods of presentation of the subject matter.	Shout at them	Will work if used occasionally; could frighten some students.
		Move about; create novelty and surprise; stop talking, etc	Must gather evidence of attitude change.
	Vary materials to be learned.	Switch texts.	Must gain approval of course team. Expensive. More exercises in new text will help.
		Add films/videos. Use programmed learning.	As above.
	Change rewards being offered.	Give consumable rewards for test performance.	Expensive to provide sweets May foster competition.
		Release class early; Punish when inattentive.	

Figure 2.10 Application of Problem Solving Model

This is only one of the models of problem solving that is suggested by educational psychologists and it is usually attributable to technological problems. However, not all problems are of a technological nature, and different techniques are suggested for (a) science and (b) business studies. These other models are described in Chapter 6 where they are considered as a study skill which, when taught, will assist students in their study habits.

> *Possible Evidence to Show You Have Achieved the Competence 'Demonstrate effective design of Cognitive lessons through the identification of variables which effect learning'*

The type of evidence that you might collect to show that you have achieved the competence involves:

1. From a lesson plan that you have designed, identify the conditions that you have applied to assist the students to memorise the relevant information.

2. For one or more of the following, using a lesson plan, identify the steps that you have used to assist the learning of:

    – a concept

    – a principle

    – a problem solving situation.

Possible Evidence

If you want to check your understanding of your ability to demonstrate effective design of learning sessions through the identification of variables which effect learning in the cognitive domain, try the following progress check

Progress Check 2.2

1. State at least four of the common ways to assist students to memorise information.

2. State at least four conditions that are necessary to aid the memory process.

3. Define a concept.

4. What sequence of steps might be used in the teaching of a concept?

5. Define a principle.

6. What sequence of steps might be used in the teaching of a principle?

7. What sequence of steps might be used to assist the learning of a technique of problem solving?

6. Learning and the Psychomotor Domain

We have all seen skilled tradesmen performing their trade, skilled demonstrations on the television such as 'throwing' pottery, hanging a door, and so on. We often pause and watch with much admiration. It can be motivating and we want to emulate their performance. We usually fail to achieve their high standards even when it looks so easy. Even when we match their standards, with say home decorating, the skilled person is so much quicker. This brings us to the realisation that there are two types of performance;

- Unskilled performance which tends to lack consistency and smoothness

- Skilled performance which is consistent, smooth, co-ordinated – in fact 'second nature'.

Although we tend to concentrate upon the physical part when we teach psychomotor skills, there usually is, of course, a cognitive element and an affective aspect.

A person skilled in a range of their professional tasks of, say, a nurse, a graphic designer, a carpenter, or hairdresser usually exhibit the following characteristics:

- adaptable/flexible;

- clear sense of purpose;

- quick;

- accurate;

- professional/stylish;

- consistently good results;

- good condition;

- smooth and rhythmic;

- cool and calm.

All of the above need training, thought, effort and practice. Fitts (1967) suggests that there are three phases to achieving a skilled performance. These are

(i)   the cognitive phase

(ii) the fixative phase

(iii) the autonomous phase.

It can be argued that, in post-16 education, only the very basic skills are learned to the third of these phases. Many of the skills that we teach are only learned to the second, fixative, phase where they are correctly completed but still require thought and, in consequence, do not have the speed associated with them that are exhibited by the craftsman who can complete them without thought (that is, automatically, with all of the attributes suggested above).

The *cognitive phase* involves considering and talking about the background information. It consists of 'knowing' how to complete the skill, what the steps involved are, and how they might be combined.

This would include:

- procedures;

- essential knowledge;

- precautions;

- standards;

- things to look for;

- things to avoid.

This should be quite a short phase and is usually completed through a teacher demonstration. Thus, the main teaching skill in this phase involves assisting the students to memorise the information and the conditions for this are the same as those described earlier for the cognitive domain.

The *fixative phase* involves acquiring the correct patterns of behaviour and the elimination of errors through initial practice. Thus we need to:

- give the students an opportunity to inquire about the skill;

- practice the skill;

- give feedback on performance.

The *autonomous phase* is the final stage. Speed and accuracy are enhanced as the skill becomes more automatic. Speed, rhythm and concentration should increase at this stage. It may be difficult to notice when the student changes from one phase to another since the process is gradual.

Clearly, a key feature of skill acquisition is practice. Practice can be massed or distributed. Massed practice involves large blocks of time where the students practise without breaks. Distributed practice involves short practice periods, say ten minutes with breaks between each period. It is considered that distributed practice is the most effective of the two because, in massed practice, fatigue soon sets in when initially practicising. There needs to be high concentration in the initial stages of practice and students find such a high level difficult to sustain. Thus, short bursts of practice are more effective.

Feedback is an important part of learning a skill. Intrinsic feedback comes from the task itself, i.e. through the senses, and is immediate. Extrinsic feedback comes from outside the task. Feedback of this nature often comes from ourselves, the teachers. Feedback on knowledge and skills is needed until mastery is achieved. Feedback at the mastery stage is still needed so that the learners can feel confident that they have achieved the standard.

A good deal of the literature used in the UK related to educational psychology is indigenous or from the USA. An interesting writer is the Russian, Galperin. (Galperin and Simon (1957)) He experimented with two main approaches.

The first, and traditional approach, was to explain how to perform the task, and allow the student to perform the task under teacher supervision.

The second method was the teacher carrying out the task: the student watches and helps by directing and prompting. The second method was found to produce better results, perhaps because the students concentrate upon the task elements and organisation of their own learning

De Cecco discusses some useful conditions which enhance the learning of skills. He suggests that contiguity, the almost simultaneous occurrence of the stimulus and the response, is important. We may call this timing or co-ordination. This means that the proper order of sub skills is important.

Feedback, De Cecco suggests, is also of prime importance for the successful learning of a skill during student practice. Students should complete the skill correctly from the start of their practice as unlearning of incorrect movements is difficult. Hence, teacher feedback can assist in stopping these incorrect movements.

Part training is where the students receive instruction on the first subtask, then the second sub task whilst still practicing the first subtask and so on. This may be compared with the whole training method where the students receive instruction and practice on the entire sequence. There is evidence to show that the whole training is more effective.

Gilbert (1962) perhaps confuses the situation by reporting that Mathetics produces superior results. Mathetics is reverse contiguity i.e. first teach the student the final task, then the penultimate task whilst practicing the final task and so on.

As you can see the effectiveness of teaching psychomotor skills would benefit from more research. What are the implications for teaching? De Cecco would advocate an approach similar to the following:

Step 1	*Analyse the skill* At the planning stage, you need to consider body position, movements, sequence of movements, turning etc.
Step 2	*Assess the entry behaviour* This is where to determine what the students can do already. It is important to look for bad practice and eliminate it at this stage.
Step 3	*Describe and Demonstrate the skill*
Step 4	*Provide opportunity for the three basic learning conditions viz, Contiguity, practice and feedback*

Perhaps your best approach is to select and try a range of methods, consider the outcomes and develop an approach which you find suits you and your learners. What may happen is that one approach suits a particular skill or task, where a second approach is more appropriate to a different skill.

Possible Evidence to Show You Have Achieved the Competence 'Demonstrate effective design of Psychomotor lessons through the identification of variables which effect learning'

The type of evidence that you might collect to show that you have achieved the competence involves:

1.　　From a lesson plan that you have designed, identify the conditions that you have applied to assist the students to complete the skill effectively.

2.　　For one or more of the following, using a lesson plan, identify the steps that you have used to assist the learning of:

　　　– memorising the skill; and

　　　– practicing the skill.

If you want to check your understanding of your ability to demonstrate effective design of learning sessions through the identification of variables which effect learning in the psychomotor domain, try the following progress check

Progress Check 2.3

1. State the components of a 'second nature' skilled performance.

2. What are the three stages, according to Fitts, of a skilled performance?

3. What is meant by distributed practice and why is it considered preferable when learning a psychomotor skill?

4. Identify the suggested four steps in the teaching of a psychomotor skill.

7. Learning and the Affective Domain

The affective domain is perhaps the most difficult domain in which to teach and there tends to be relatively less literature concerning attitudes. We could set out to change attitudes and in fact we are often required to change attitudes with regard to health and safety, or we may change attitudes without knowing so. The latter category is where attitudes are caught not taught! For example if we are perpetually late starting our classes then we often find students late in attending; if our boardwork is untidy then students' notes often reflect this. In these cases, the students are using us as a role model and we need to be aware of this. Attitudes are learned and may have roots in the emotions but may also have a major element of knowledge.

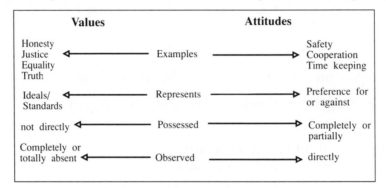

Figure 2.11 Comparison between Values and Attitudes

We all tend to have a value framework i.e. a set of standards or ideals and these are linked to attitudes. Figure 2.11 compares values and attitudes. Attitudes have three components each of which may vary in intensity. These are:

Knowledge	– What the student knows
Emotion	– What the student likes or dislikes about the subject
Action	– What the student does to express feelings of like or dislike

Davies (1981) believes that you cannot change attitudes before the change of behaviour but it is better to change behaviour before there is an attitudinal change, A great many intelligent people smoke or eat an unhealthy diet and know they do so but are unable to change. However, if the behaviour is changed first then attitudinal change is more likely to take place. So, how can we plan to change students' attitudes? The following guidelines appear to be helpful.

1. State intended learning outcomes (e.g. objective)
2. Small group discussions
3. Student centred rather than teacher centred learning
4. High levels of participation by each individual. Peers can have a major influence on attitudes. (Think of fashion!)
5. Role play and simultaneous discussion.

Attitudinal change often takes a long time. You can force change by using rewards or punishments and gain what appear to be rapid results but it is usually only a short term change. However, if you encourage participation, then this slower process tends to be long term and to all intents and purposes – permanent.

Possible Evidence to Show You Have Achieved the Competence 'Demonstrate effective design of Affective lessons through the identification of variables which effect learning'

The type of evidence that you might collect to show that you have achieved the competence involves:

1. From a lesson plan that you have designed, identify the conditions that you have applied to assist the students to learn an attitude.

2. Comment upon the conditions that have been helpful in changing attitudes.

3. Why do you think some students are reluctant to change their attitudes?

If you want to check your understanding of your ability to demonstrate effective design of learning sessions through the identification of variables which effect learning in the affective domain, try the following progress check

Progress Check 2.4

1.   What are the main differences between 'values' and 'attitudes'?

2.   What are the three components of an attitude?

3.   Why is discussion generally thought to be helpful in the learning of attitudes?

8. Motivation

8.1 Concepts related to Motivation

Motivation is a key factor in successful learning. A less able student who is highly motivated can achieve greater success than the more intelligent student who is not well motivated. Students may come to us highly motivated and all we have to do is maintain this motivation. However most groups of students tend to have some highly motivated students, across the range to one or two who appear to have no motivation. Our task, then, is to maximise motivation. To do this we need to consider the concepts related to motivation.

Interest – Students with an interest in a subject tend to pay more attention to it and study it to a level greater than we demand. Their attention and workrate is high with a correspondingly higher quality of learning. Our task is to develop and maximise this interest.

Need – There are several possible needs but the most common student needs are:

- need for achievement e.g. success in reaching a goal;
- need for affiliation e.g. friendly relationship with other persons including you, the teacher;
- need for dominance and this is attained by obtaining leadership, power or control over others e.g. getting the best results in the class.

Attitude – Emotions, and feelings are important. So if students get pleasure out of calculations then they will enjoy working with activities involving calculation, or if they get satisfaction from working with their hands, they will learn psychomotor skills well.

Aspirations – A student may have a particular aim in mind. If they pass your course then they can enter another course which will then qualify them to practise a chosen profession. Motivation can be classified into intrinsic motivation and extrinsic motivation. Intrinsic motivation may be defined as motivation without apparent reward ie studying for its own sake. Many writers say this is the best form of motivation. Extrinsic motivation depends upon external stimuli, which we, as teachers, may have to provide

8.2 Teaching Techniques to Provide Extrinsic Motivation

The following guidelines in the provision of extrinsic motivation are the result the experience of many teachers. Most of the techniques appear to be effective with most groups most of the time. They are relatively easy to use.

Verbal Praise – Feedback to the students such as 'good answer' or 'that's an interesting observation' give the students social approval and such praise appears to be a powerful motivational technique. Care needs to be taken not to over praise so that the most appalling work is praised. Some students, mostly extroverts, appear to respond to blame rather than praise. Your comments to your learners are important. Think of when you have a teaching practice visit. You would expect your tutor to identify your good practice and reinforce that and be positive towards desirable behaviour.

Test results/marks – Results of periodic tests and feedback on assignments are important to your students so that they can see that they are making progress. Poor results should be used to diagnose and remedy learning difficulties – not just left and ignored.

Arousal – Humans, even your students, are naturally curious and like suspense and to explore. We need to use this natural curiosity to enhance motivation. Most subject have features which perplex and baffle students with their apparent contradictions. 'Why should that happen when I expected this to happen?'. This is a powerful stimulant provided the puzzlement does not last too long and lead to frustration.

Unexpected – As teachers, we tend to have our favourite ways of teaching which allows the students to predict the style of learning. This may allow the learner to relax and feel comfortable but it is motivating to have an unexpected event so that the interest of the students is aroused. For example, if the problem-solving has been theoretical - introduce a very practical problem. Change the arrangement of the furniture in the room. Instead of setting the test yourself – ask the students to design the test. Again, this approach could be over used and lose its effect.

Use material familiar to the students – When students are learning, they often have problems with new material and research shows that using examples that are familiar to the students eases the learning. This may involve you in learning a little yourself like the current fashions and that 'Welded Apricot' is the name of the latest pop group so that these can be used in your teaching.

Unusual Contexts – Once you feel concepts or principles are learned you can ask your students to apply them in unusual situations. For example, the law of supply and demand applied to say 'classic cars'. Note that students learn better when attaining concepts with familiar examples but applying them in an unfamiliar situation.

Games and Simulations – Games and simulations motivate students to participate in the learning. Take care to ensure that the learning is reinforced and by the end of the topic the students know why they played the game.

Minimize adverse effects – There are a great many issues which reduce motivation and your job is to try to *minimize* these influences. You can add to this list no doubt:

- listening to a dull, boring teacher;
- listening to an uninteresting teacher;
- test which are too hard or too easy;
- no feedback on progress;
- pace too fast/too slow;
- sitting for too long;
- poor lighting/heating/acoustics;
- being told they are unlikely to understand something;
- waiting for help from the teacher;
- being told that the topic is difficult.

> *Possible Evidence to Show You Have Achieved*
> *the Competence 'Identify variables which*
> *influence student motivation'.*

The type of evidence that you might collect to show that you have achieved the competence involves:

Carry out some of the motivational techniques below and evaluate their effectiveness:

- verbal praise;
- good test marks;
- puzzlement;
- an unexpected event;
- unusual contexts;
- games.

> *If you want to check your understanding of tour ability to identify variables which influence motivation, try the following progress check*

Progress Check 2.5

1.   Explain three concepts related to motivation.

2.   Identify five teaching techniques which you might use to enhance the motivation of your students.

3.   Why is intrinsic preferable to extrinsic motivation?

9. The Main Theories

There is a great deal written about how we learn and there is a great range of theories. The purpose of the final part of this chapter is merely to introduce you to some theories so that you can read those areas which appear to be most useful to you at the moment.

The five main areas are Behaviourism, Neo-behaviourism, Gestalt (Insight), Cognitive Development, and Humanists.

9.1 Behaviourism

The origins of behaviourism are in the early 20th Century. At that time it was thought that human activity or learning could be predicted and explained by studying the behaviour of animals. The essentials of the work involved animals responding to stimuli, that is stimulus-response (S – R). The learning model became more refined with the study of the effect of conditioning.

Pavlov, one of the early workers in the field, proposed the hypothesis of conditioned learning and used experiments with dogs to provide evidence to support the hypothesis. Basically, he linked a specific sound with the provision of food which, of course, caused salivation. After some time the mere sound caused the dogs to salivate.

Watson, another of the early workers in the field, thought that sensations, feelings and instinct were not a necessary part of the study of learning. The only area of interest is what the 'subject' is doing in response to the stimulus. He rejected the concept of memory. Instead, he said that responses were due to learning and we respond when we meet those stimuli again. Learning, he said, was a question of strengthening stimulus-response bonds. Conditioning, therefore, became important and habit forming was considered to be significant.

Both Pavlov and Watson have been criticised as they were considered to only think in mechanistic terms and extrapolated the results of their work with animals to predict human behaviour. Stimulus-Response, however, is quite a powerful action as we all know when we smell our favourite food cooking. The effect of conditioning is also important. We can all probably remember an unpleasant episode at school which put us off a subject for the rest of our lives.

Another early worker, Thorndike, showed in experiments that pleasurable experiences tended to reinforce stimulus-response bonds and 'discomfort' reduced these bonds. There are clear links to rote learning when Thorndike said that there was a need to maximise the strength of a bond. To do this, he suggested that the number of times and duration of the link should be maximised. Also associated with this work was the fact that external reward was seen as being effective, whereas punishment was less important.

9.2 The Neo-behaviourists

Tolman, Skinner and Gagné are, perhaps, the best known neo-behaviourists. They provided a more human perspective in that they considered the human mind to be selective in its actions and does not simply respond to stimuli.

Tolman's work showed that he felt that humans use their beliefs and feelings when responding to stimuli and that there is a need to consider the whole rather than isolated stimulus-response incidents. In other words, humans seek a purpose and that people have a 'cognitive map'. This is a set of relationships appropriate to different stimuli. So the learner has to fit new learning into a pattern, that is 'what leads to what'. Motivation comes into learning theory according to Tolman. The importance of a logical learning sequence was shown and the students need to *apply* their new learning in order to test its validity.

Skinner placed great importance on 'operant conditioning' where an operant is a series of actions which a learner completes. Through reinforcement of the learning, the learning quality becomes greater. Skinner's approach was highly structured. He stated that teachers need to identify what learning they wish to take place and then select 'reinforcers' which will help to maintain the desired behaviours. Such a reinforcer may only be a nod of the head in agreement. Skinner's work showed that it is important to reward the learner frequently in the early stages of learning, then at random or at a fixed interval subsequently. In the early stages of learning, each successive step in the learning process should be as small as possible so that rewards can be given as reinforcement.

Gagné recognised that the design of the teaching had to match the type of learning that was taking place. He listed eight learner characteristics which would influence the way in which the 'instruction' would take place. His eight types of learning are:

1. *Signal Learning*: learner associates exact response to stimuli.

2. *Stimulus-Response Learning*: learner associates exact responses to stimuli.

3. *Chaining*: learner acquires a number of S-R bondings as, for example, in changing a car wheel.

4. *Verbal Association*: verbal chains are acquired.

5. *Multiple Discriminations*: learner discriminates between apparently similar stimuli and makes the correct response.

6. *Concept Learning*: concepts are classes of stimuli and the learner can recognise these classes.

7. *Rule Learning*: chains of two or more concepts often called 'principles' or 'laws'.

8. *Problem Solving*: the discovering of relationships where rule learning is applied.

Gagné suggests that these eight types of learning are in a hierarchy with the lower types being needed as pre-requisites for the higher ones. He also suggests that it is valuable to have a sequence to instruction and such a sequence can usefully be based on the learning types. This, he suggests, might be:

- inform the students what they are expected to do, that is, tell them the objectives;

- question the students to find out what they know already, that is, determine their entry behaviour;

- use cues to form the chains of concepts or rules;

- question students so that they can demonstrate their learning;

- ask students to make a verbal statement of the rule.

This list can be compared with De Cecco's model for concept attainment.

As may be seen, the teacher designs the learning programme to ensure that students have the lower orders of learning before they progress to the higher levels. Planning for feedback is the key feature of the approach advocated by Gagné and is a characteristic of neo-behaviourism.

9.3 The Gestaltists

'Gestalt' comes from the German for pattern or structure. This indicates that the Gestaltists are interested in the overall perspective as opposed to the behaviourists who are concerned with a series of incremental actions. In other words, the whole is greater than the sum of the individual parts: it is the pattern which is important. Understanding, according to Gestaltists, is based upon *insight*. Insight has a particular meaning to those of the Gestalt school. It is when the student suddenly becomes aware of the relevance of the behaviour or learning. We have all experienced a sudden flash of inspiration - and this is a form of insight. The characteristics of insight are that the solution to a problem comes suddenly, the solution can be applied to similar problems in different contexts and the solution can be retained over a period of time.

Gestalt psychology has some basic laws which are of interest. They may well be evident from your own teaching.

1. *Figure-ground relationships*

   Perceptions are organised into figures or features which stand out from their background. As you look at this page, the print is, as you think, the key part, but the spaces are just as important.

2. *Contiguity*

   Proximity in time and space influences how we group things. The closer they are, the more likely they are to be grouped and linked together.

3. *Similarity*

   Items which are similar tend to be grouped or classed together.

4. *Law of Praganz*

   Figures will be perceived in their best possible pattern of form.

5. *Closure*

   Figures, or items, which are incomplete, may be perceived as complete because we tend to complete the figure or 'fill in the gaps'.

6. *Transposition*

   Patterns and figures may be distorted or changed to some degree but they can still be recognised.

As with all the schools of psychology, Gestaltists have their critics. The above laws have never been 'proved' and there appears to be a lack of factual or empirical evidence. Insight is also difficult to observe and measure (although this does not mean that it does not happen). Many subjects, or parts of subjects, do not need insight. For example, learning the times tables does not require a 'flash of inspiration', rote learning is probably the most efficient way.

9.4 The Cognitivists

Behaviourists place their focus on the task and the Stimulus-Response model. The Cognitivists, on the other hand, place their focus on the students and how they gain and organise their knowledge (that is, cognize). Students do not merely receive information, but actively create a pattern of what it means to them. The implications of this are that, if you have a class of sixteen students, they probably have sixteen slightly different understandings. The students 'fit' their new learning onto their own existing mental structure.

Dewey defined learning as 'learning to think' and the process of learning is not just doing something, such as a task, but *reflecting* and learning from this.

The teacher is the key to Dewey's work because, he says, the teacher must plan for reflective thinking to take place. Education being firmly linked to social growth was one of Dewey's main claims.

Bruner was insistent that students must be taught *how* to analyse problems and *how* to think for themselves in order to become independent learners. The implications of this include that teaching a lot of factual information is unproductive since the learner forgets most of it in a relatively short time and will use very little of it. However, teaching generalities is efficient as generalities can be applied in a number of situations over a period of time.

Bruner considers the learning process as the learning of acquiring new information, transforming that learning with regard to existing knowledge and then checking it against the new situation. So, knowledge is a process rather than a product. Models are constructed by the learner which explain the existing but can also predict what might be.

Bruner sees the teacher's role as one of facilitating the student's own discovery – known as 'inquiry training'.

Ausubel sees the key to effective learning as the learners relating their new learning to existing cognitive structures. He advocates the use of 'advance organisers' (that is, bridges between what the students know and what they need to know). Such an organiser is a short description of the new material *before* the lesson so that the students are prepared to accept the new materials.

9.5 Humanists

Since about 1960, beginning with the publication of A S Neill's 'Summerhill', a new movement aimed at criticising and improving education in fundamental ways has gathered momentum. The movement has been particularly attractive with post-16 education whose students have been unhappy with their own schooling. It seemed to respond to their own resentment with the regimentation, pressure, competition, and so on. The movement has had several names: 'new romanticism', 'open schooling' and 'alternative education', but is now generally termed 'humanistic education'.

Summerhill, in southern England, is an 'open', private school where the education of the whole person is considered more important than subject matter. No pupil is forced to attend classes but go only when they want to. The school 'rules' are made through a school committee on which every pupil and staff member have one vote.

Neill recounts the story of how he tried to get football stopped in the corridor outside his office through the committee. Initially he was outvoted and it was not until he had brought it up on several occasions that he managed to get it accepted.

Neill argues that the apparent freedom allowed pupils to gain an education that the conventional kind of schooling was not capable of providing. Although the academic successes of the school were low, and HMI tried unsuccessfully to close the school on several occasions, Neill argued that if one of the ex-pupils of Summerhill gained an interview, they were more likely to get the job than someone from a conventional educational background.

The Humanist school of psychology, then, was developed as a reaction against behaviourism because its proponents saw behaviourism as reducing the concept of the human being. The person was seen as being worthy of dignity and teachers needed to develop qualities of worth and self esteem. These involved helping each person to make the most of themselves that they could.

Maslow is best remembered for his work on motivation. His hierarchy of human needs is well known and is a feature of many management books. Essentially, Maslow states that needs must be satisfied before effective learning can take place. If a student is tired, cold and hungry, then the quality of learning will be reduced. The student who feels threatened in the learning situation is unlikely to learn effectively. Our task as teachers is to create an environment where students feel part of a group and that their contribution has worth.

Rogers' thinking is similar to Maslow's. He felt the need to place the student at the centre of the learning process through active self discovery rather than having to respond to stimuli. He stated that humans are essentially 'good' and that they have a desire to develop and grow. The job of the teacher, in his view, is to generate the conditions and environment for students to develop their own self concept.

The key to effective, long term learning is based upon experiential learning which has the following features: personal involvement, stimulation of feelings and thinking, self initiation and self evaluation. The behaviourists see the need to structure and control the learning whereas the humanists see it as essential to trust the learners to follow their own learning programme at their own pace and direction. Active learning by doing is seen as the key but some form of reflection through evaluation is essential. More recently Kolb, as described in Chapter 1, has completed work in the humanist vein.

The humanist approach is quite different to what was (and, perhaps, is) the perceived way in which adults learn. Schools have always stated that they want to educate the whole person rather than train them for an occupation. Colleges tended to keep to subject matter and link their courses to specific occupational areas – in fact the recent legislation ensures that employers have considerable influence over colleges via their governing body.

9.6 Teaching and Learning Approaches

Inductive and deductive approaches

The differences and similarities of inductive and deductive approaches are, perhaps, best seen through simple examples.

Suppose we wished our students to gain an understanding of magnetic forces. We could give the students a magnet and a number of items made from a range of different materials. The students are then allowed to explore the use of the magnet and the various items made from the different materials. The students may then list items attracted to magnets and those not attracted. You may have to prompt this stage. The list may be as follows:

ATTRACTED BY MAGNET	NOT ATTRACTED BY MAGNET
pen	plastic pen
chair leg	paper
watch	cup
paper clip	wood
hair clip	clothes
spoon	
zip	

You can then ask the students to make a statement which summarizes their observations.. It may be that they say metals are attracted by the magnet. A more sophisticated test would indicate only some metals are attracted by the magnet. The students can then be given more objects and asked to predict which items would be attracted.

A second, alternative approach could be to give out magnets, telling the students that magnets attract (some) metals but not objects made from other materials. Question and answer could then be used to ask the students to predict, then test, whether the magnets will attract various materials.

The two methods have some commonality. Essentially the content and equipment are the same. Both methods depend upon the generalization that magnets attract (some) metals.

However there are significant differences. In the first case the students make observations about specific examples and then make and test a general statement. This process of moving from specific examples to generalized statement – or law is called an *inductive* approach and would be advocated by humanists. In the second case the generalization was stated and then tested using specific examples. This process of working from a general statement and using specific examples is known as a *deductive* approach and would be advocated by behaviourists.

Both approaches have their benefits, and choice of approach may depend upon the topic under consideration. Also some students in your class will prefer an inductive approach whilst the other students may learn better with the deductive one. It could well be that the best approach is to use a mix of the two throughout the course.

A Constructivist's approach to Learning

As teachers we tend to make assumptions about the 'entry behaviour' of our students. We tend to think that the students know nothing about the topic or they know a good deal. The truth is likely to be somewhere between the two extremes and will differ from learner to learner. As we saw with concept attainment, it is important that the learners do not have misconceptions before they even start to learn the concept.

The constructivists' view is that we identify the learners' current ideas which they may well have to modify or abandon before they can construct new meaning.

The key assumptions of this constructivist perspective (as described by Driver and Bell (1985)) include:

1.   What the learner currently believes, whether it is correct or incorrect, is important.

2. Despite having the same learning experience, each individual will construct on individual meaning which only they hold.

3. Understanding or constructing a meaning is an active and continuous process.

4. Learning may well involve some conceptual changes.

5. When a learner constructs a new meaning, they may not believe it but may give it provisional acceptance or even rejection.

6. Learning is not a passive process, but active, and depends upon the learners taking responsibility to learn.

A simplified model of the Constructivist approach is shown in Figure 2.12 below.

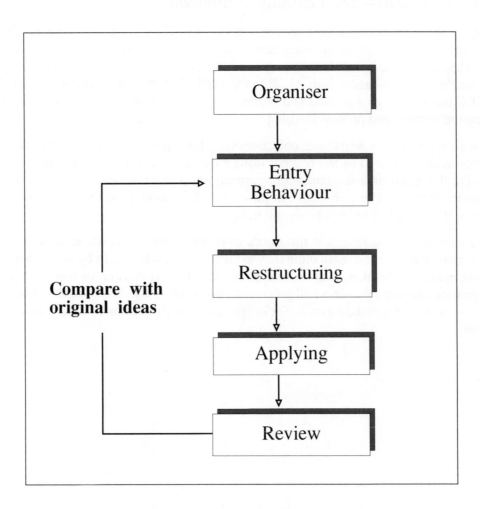

Figure 2.12 Model of the Constructivist Approach

The process starts with an outline of what is going to be learned. This allows the learner to prepare the way for new ideas. The teacher should then try to ascertain the entry behaviour of the students (i.e. what they think now) by, say, question and answer. This may reveal quite a high level of learning or some strange ideas which will inhibit the correct learning which is hoped will take place. Correction of these misconceptions may then be addressed.

The restructuring phase follows – and although this restructuring process is the responsibility of the learner, the teacher needs to lead and facilitate this approach. The teacher may achieve this by designing appropriate practical activities and/or discussions or explorations. The students can try their ideas in new, different situations. The review stage is when the students reflect upon their ideas and how they have changed since the start of the learning.

9.7 Overview of Models – The Learning Continuum

Figure 2.13 gives an overview of the main models together with their prominent aspects. The implications for us as teachers is to decide which approach best suits our students and subject and to organise ourselves accordingly. That is not to suggest that we only use one approach; at different times and with different students we may use a combination. Indeed, often the curriculum materials lead us to a combination. For example BTEC use a mixture of process and product approaches where both the subject matter and the core skills require product and process learning.

The *behaviourist* approach has, as its base, objectives stated in terms of specific, observable outcomes. The teaching needs to be structured by the teacher using a deductive approach with extrinsic motivation. At the other end of the spectrum is the *humanist* approach where the individual student sets the goals to be achieved from the learning. The individual is at the centre of the model due to intrinsic motivation and the innate desire of the individual to be curious and to learn.

The teaching approach to complement this needs to be inductive to allow the students to discover for themselves. If goals are set in the curriculum they would be process based. In between these two extremes is the *cognitive* model which takes its aims from both ends of the spectrum. Its base is that of the subject itself which provides its own structures and procedures for learning and the student would be subjected to guided discovery with provision being made for insight to occur. Both inductive and deductive approaches would be used.

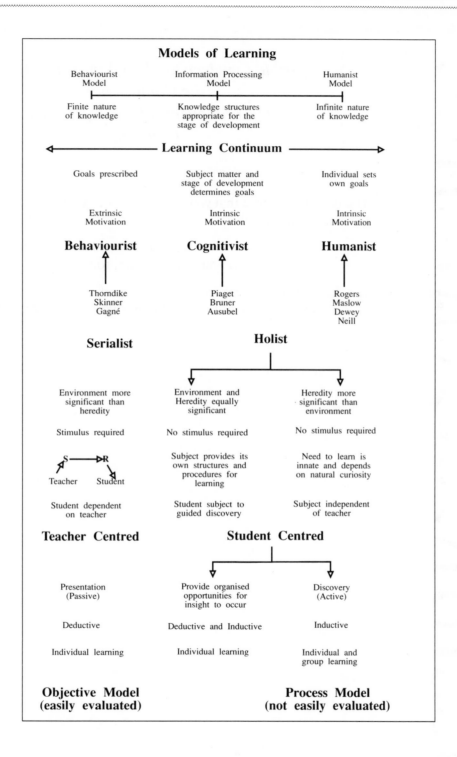

Figure 2.13 Overview of Models of Learning

---

*Possible Evidence to Show You Have Achieved
the Competence
'Use the Components of a Range of Theories of
Learning'.*

The type of evidence that you might collect to show that you have achieved the competence involves:

1.   Showing how you use a particular model of learning and state the reasons why you consider it appropriate.

2.   Evaluating the effectiveness of a particular model through some determination of how it is better than other models.

If you want to check your ability to use a range of learning theories try the following progress check

Progress Check 2.6

1. Define each of the following through giving their main characteristics:

   - behaviourism;

   - gestaltism;

   - cognitivism;

   - humanism;

   - constructivism.

2. Choose a topic that you have taught recently using a deductive approach and state how you would teach it inductively.

3. Classify the following theorists into behaviourists, cognitivists and humanists:

   - Rogers – Maslow

   - Piaget – Skinner

   - Thorndike – Ausubel

   - Bruner – Gagné

   - Neill – Dewey

Further Reading and References

Further Reading and References relating to the topics in this chapter can be found in the following:

Bloom B. S.	*Taxonomy of Educational Objectives, Handbook 1: Cognitive Domain.* David McKay. 1956.
De Cecco, J.P. and Crawford, W.R.	*The Psychology of Learning and Instruction,* Prentice Hall, 1974.
Dave, R.H.	in Armstrong, R.J. et al. *Developing and Writing Behavioural Objectives,* Educational Innovators Press, 1975.
Davies, I.K.	*Instructional Technique,* McGraw Hill, 1981.
Driver, R. and Bell, B	Students' Thinking and the Learning of Science, *School Science Review*, March 1986 pp 443-456.
Fitts, P.M. and Posner, M.I.	*Human Performance*, Brooks Cole, 1967.
Gage, N.L. and Berliner, D.C.	*Educational Psychology*, Houghton Mifflin, 1983.
Gagné, R.M	*The Conditions of Learning*, Holt Rienhart and Winston (NY), 1973.
Galperin, D.	in Simon, B, *Psychology in the Soviet Union*, Routledge and Kegan Paul, 1957.
Gilbert, T.F.	Mathetics: The Technology of Education, *Journal of Mathetics*, 1st July 1973.
Joyce, B. and Weil, M.	*Models of Teaching*, Prentice Hall, 1990.
Krathwohl, D.R. et al	*Taxonomy of Educational Objectives, Handbook 2: Affective Domain,* David McKay, 1964.
Knowles, M	Andragogy: an emerging technology for Adult Learning (1770), in Tight, M, *Adult Learning and Education*, Croom Helm, 1983.
Meziorow, J	A Critical Theory of Adult Learning (1981) in Tight (op cit).
Rowntree, D.	*Educational Technology in Curriculum Development,* Harper, 1982.
Stones, E.	*Psychology of Education: a pedagogical approach*, Methuen, 1983.

Chapter 3

Teaching Strategies and Learning Styles

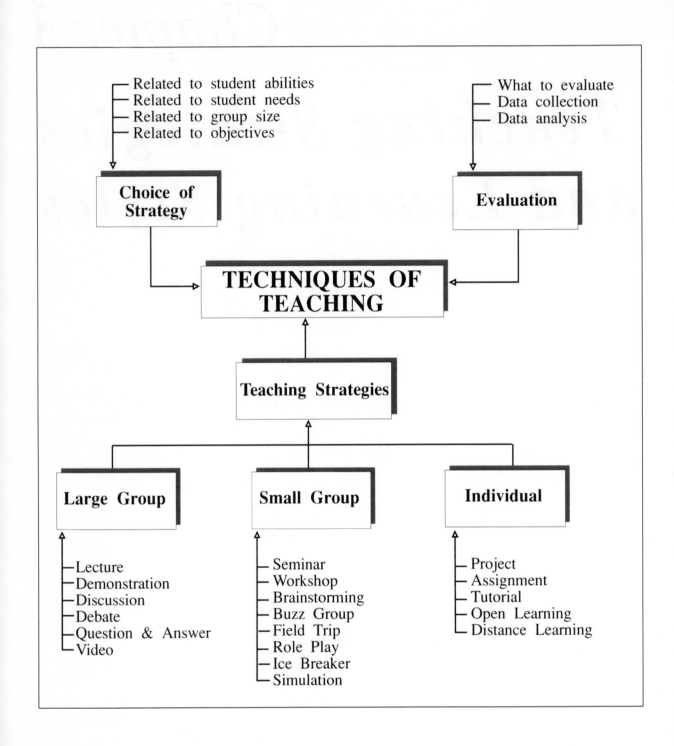

Overview of Chapter 3

Competences Related to this Chapter

The teacher competences and associated performance criteria related to this chapter are:

Overall Competence – *Use a range of teaching techniques appropriately.*

COMPETENCE	PERFORMANCE CRITERIA
1. Deliver a programme of learning sessions.	(a) Deliver teaching sessions to meet specified and/or negotiated group needs. (b) Ensure strategies are relevant to specific objectives and characteristics of students. (c) Encourage a positive attitude to learning.
2. Manage learning activities.	(a) Adapt the learning environment to optimise learning. (b) Encourage a positive attitude to learning. (c) Use a variety of teaching strategies. (d) Manage both your own and your students' time. (e) Ensure appropriate group management/leadership

Teaching Strategies

1. Introduction

When you reflect upon how you were taught at school, college or university you probably remember the teacher talking a great deal and being in control in a relatively quiet classroom. Your role as a student was probably passive, perhaps answering questions and writing notes.

During your first few months in teaching, you tend to adopt an approach with which you are comfortable and able to feel in control of things. Often you model your teaching upon those who taught you. This may mean you give out information by talking and working on the chalkboard. Perhaps there are some question and answer sessions and even a test. This is the usual way to gain confidence in teaching a group of students. However, if we were all to continue in this manner, there would be little change in education and certainly no innovation.

Once you feel confident in the teaching role, you are then able to experiment with how students learn and with ways in which to improve the effectiveness of their learning. In the previous chapter we outlined the substantial body of theory available to those who wish to influence the quality of student learning. On first reading, some strategies may appear to be a recipe for anarchy. When you try a new strategy it may not work at first. Sometimes you need to keep trying variations before it becomes effective. One aspect of experimenting with a range of teaching strategies is that it is challenging, demanding and rewarding, despite the failures. It keeps your interest in teaching – which may waver after the first few years.

You may reflect upon how you were taught and consider the 'modern' or current techniques. You will recognise that there are fashions in education. There is pressure from Government, HMIs, Examining Bodies, Management and others for different ways of teaching. You should start to consider the range of teaching strategies available, explore them and build up your experience, expertise and confidence over a wide range of approaches.

One of the fascinations of teaching is that what works really well with one group of students on one occasion, does not work at all well with a very similar group in a similar situation. Even more interestingly you will find that some strategies which usually work well with a group, are not effective with every topic. This means that you have to read the signals you receive from your students, such as body language, and respond, perhaps with a different approach.

2. Application of Teaching Strategies

There are many teaching strategies described in the literature and we will examine the most common or popular in this chapter. You will find considerable overlap between them and so we have grouped the strategies into those which are suitable for large groups, small groups and for individuals. Of course, you can use most of these strategies in all three situations. You can use some strategies within other strategies, for instance using buzz groups within a lecture. As usual in education, there are few answers which are totally right or totally wrong. Some strategies appear to be more effective with certain students in certain situations. Figure 3.1 on the following page shows the possible applications of various teaching strategies and relates each of them to the three domains, indicating the degree of student participation. Such a general

TEACHING STRATEGY	DOMAIN		
	COGNITIVE LOW — HIGH	AFFECTIVE LOW — HIGH	PSYCHOMOTOR LOW — HIGH
Lecture	X X X		
Demonstration	X X		X X
Team Teaching	X X		X
Discussion	X X	X X	
Debate	X X	X X	
Question & Answer	X X X		
Video	X X	X X	X X
Seminar	X X	X X	
Laboratory/Workshop	X X	X	X X X
Gaming/Quiz	X X	X X	
Brainstorming	X X		
Buzz Group	X X	X	
Field Trip	X	X	X
Role Play	X	X X X	
Ice Breaker		X X	
Simulation	X	X	X X
In Tray	X	X	X X
Case Study	X X		
Project/Assignment	X X	X X	X X
Tutorial	X X	X X	
Open/Distance Learning	X X		

Figure 3.1 Application of Teaching Strategies in the Three Domains

relationship can only be a guide and in this chapter we will describe a range of strategies. Students appreciate variation and would tire of the same, few strategies. Your task is to become adept at using as many strategies as you can and to choose the most appropriate ones for each group you teach.

2.1 Choice of Teaching Strategy

Your choice of teaching strategy is often related to your own individual style. An overriding factor for you may be the need to adopt those strategies that most suit your personality. However, there are some overall 'rules' that you might like to consider. These relate to two aspects. The first is the type of objective that you want your students to achieve. The second is the number of students you have to teach. Although we describe each separately, you should consider them together in making your final choice of which teaching strategy to use.

2.2 Choice of Teaching Strategy related to Objectives to be Achieved

The basic teaching model that we described in Chapter 1 showed us that objectives are at the heart of teaching and that all other aspects flow from them. Thus, when you come to choose your teaching strategy it is logical that you make the domain and level of objective you are seeking to achieve the basis for the choice. In Chapter 1, Figure 1.13, we also linked objectives to teaching strategies. For example, we suggest that the most appropriate way to learn a motor skill is through demonstration and individual practice; to gain knowledge and understanding, a lecture and question and answer are appropriate; and to develop students' attitudes towards issues then you might use discussion to best achieve the objective. In Figure 3.1 we take this a stage further. The figure splits the domains into the different levels that we examined in Chapter 2 and then suggests that different strategies are more appropriate for the lower level objectives in a domain than for the higher levels. Thus a lecture might achieve low level objectives (such as knowledge and comprehension), while to achieve the higher levels (for instance, synthesis and evaluation) then you might find a debate or seminar more appropriate.

2.3 Choice Of Teaching Strategies based On Group Size

Let us look at another means of categorising teaching strategies – a simple category and one close to common usage – namely one based on group size. At one extreme a 'group' may consist of only one student, an individual working alone. In such circumstances you could use methods such as projects or assignments, tutoring and individually prescribed instruction such as open learning.

Next in order of group size we have small groups of, say, between 5 and 20 students. With such a group you may find that a discussion method is suitable. The conventional classroom size for post-16 education and training is a group of between 10 and 20 students. With such groups the approach often adopted is what is traditionally called 'classroom teaching' which consists of a mixture of methods. Because this form of teaching is most frequently used you might consider it a strategy in its own right. The nature of such classroom teaching will vary considerably from one teacher to another. It will often have a short (say, 5 minute) lecture, followed by question and answer, perhaps some small group discussion and some individual work.

The final group size we shall consider is when the group is greater than, say, 20 students. Such large groups can lead to difficulties in dealing with individuals and so you may have to resort to strategies such as lecture and demonstration.

We have already said that little definite advice has emerged from research about teaching strategies. However, Gage and Berliner (1975) describe research completed by Olsen. 18,500 classrooms were observed by trained observers. They looked for 'indicators of quality' in student behaviour that fostered

(a) individualisation, (b) interpersonal regard, (c) group activity and (d) creativity in classes of different sizes. A higher test score indicated a greater occurrence of the types of desirable activity.

Olsen found, as shown in Figure 3.2, that higher 'quality' scores were associated with the styles of classroom activity that entailed smaller groups (laboratory work and discussion), and, as shown in Figure 3.3, that mean 'quality' scores decreased regularly as class size increased. However, he concluded that class size should not be considered in isolation when choosing teaching strategy.

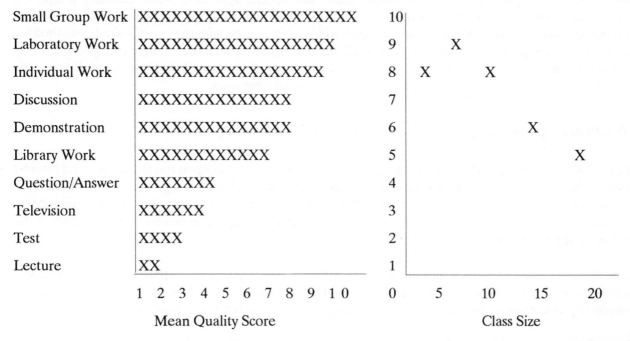

Figure 3.2 'Quality'– Teaching Strategy   **Figure 3.3 'Quality'– Class Size**

2.4 Choice of Teaching Strategy related to Needs and Characteristics of Students

We can think of choice of teaching strategy in terms of classroom management. How you choose your teaching strategy has a direct influence on how you manage your classroom. It has been said repeatedly in this book that students learn in different ways: an approach that is appropriate to one student may well be inappropriate for another. Some people learn better in a group through the interaction with both the teacher and other students. Others find interaction difficult and use the group sessions for gathering of information and only learn when they are on their own. Some learn by reading and listening, others learn through the application of the knowledge gained.

When we accept this premise we realise the importance of providing a variety of learning activities for our students. We might start off by *telling* them, next provide a group activity and finally provide an individual application activity. In this way, the coverage of the content is through a number of different strategies in the hope that one of them will appeal to all of the students and ensure that students learn in a manner appropriate to themselves.

One method that you might use when considering your choice of teaching strategy to meet students' needs is to negotiate with them. You might ask, from a range of options, the type of strategy they prefer and use this along with other aspects before you make your final choice.

2.5 Choice of Strategies related to Ability of Students

Your classroom management needs to be related to the ability of your student group and your choice of teaching strategy, you needs to be related to your students' ability. It is no good lecturing to students and expecting them to take their own notes if they are either not able to do this or not used to it.

The ability of students relates to their temperament and special aptitudes. When choosing a teaching strategy you need to consider the attention span of the student and the ability they have to be able to cope with the adopted approach. More mature students will be able to cope with the use of a similar method for a more protracted period while the less mature will need to benefit from more changes in approach. It may be that the less mature, or less able, will have an attention span of not more than ten minutes. If this is the case, changes in approach will have to be considered for each time span.

2.6 Choice of Teaching Strategies related to Motivation of Students

There is no doubt that the choice of teaching strategy can have an effect upon the motivation and interest of the student. The manner in which the teacher approaches the teaching strategy will have an effect upon motivation: an enthusiastic approach is more likely to motivate than a dull approach. In consequence, to encourage a positive attitude to learning, you should not yourself appear to be disinterested either in the content or the approach.

Some students enjoy working with others. If this is the case, group teaching approaches might give you better results than individual approaches. This could be particularly important in the achieving affective domain objectives where the use of discussion groups, role play or seminars might be effective.

Figure 3.4 gives an overview of some of the aspects that you might consider in making your choice of teaching strategy. Added to this, of course, is your own personal preference and your ability to cope with specific methods.

Aspect Related to Choice	Points to Note
Objective to be achieved	Both the domain and the level in the domain need to be considered.
The size of the group	Different methods are more appropriate to different sizes of class.
The needs and characteristics of students	Student needs and the characteristics of student need to be considered. This might involve negotiation.
The ability of the student	Ability and 'intelligence' need to be considered.
The motivation of the student.	Appropriate strategies can motivate an individual to learn.

Figure 3.4 Aspects to be Considered when Choosing Strategies

> *Possible evidence to show that you have achieved the competence 'Deliver a Programme of Learning Sessions'*

1. For a series of lessons (say, three contiguous) state the teaching strategies that you have used or are to use. Justify your choice in terms of:

   – intended learning outcomes;

   – group size;

   – the needs of the students;

   – the ability of the students;

   – the motivation of the students.

> *If you want to check your understanding of delivering a programme of learning sessions, try the following progress check*

Progress Check 3.1

1. List the teaching strategies you currently use and, for each of them, state:

    (a) whether they are teacher or student-centred;

    (b) the dominant domain with which you use them;

    (c) whether they are used with large, small or individual groups.

    Are your statements in line with the suggestions in the readings above?

2. Identify any domain(s) which is (are) not addressed. Are the strategies appropriate to the intended learning outcomes and objectives?

3. State two teaching strategies which are appropriate for each of the following;

    – cognitive domain objectives;

    – affective domain objectives;

    – psychomotor domain objectives;

    – large groups of students;

    – small groups of students;

    – individual work.

3. Teaching Strategies

In order to make the choice of teaching strategy it is important that you are familiar with each and where it might best be used. The following pages give you a description of each of the stategies, where they might be used, guidelines relating to preparation and presentation and, finally, the merits of each. For ease of reference the methods are divided into the three group sizes to which they are most applicable: large groups, small groups and individual. The sub-division is shown in Figure 3.5.

Group Size	Appropriate Strategy	
3.1 **Large Group** **(N = > 20)**	3.1.1 3.1.2 3.1.3 3.1.4 3.1.5 3.1.6	Lecture Demonstration Discussion Debate Question and Answer Video
3.2 **Small Group** **(N = 5 - 20)**	3.2.1 3.2.2 3.2.3 3.2.4 3.2.5 3.2.6 3.2.7 3.2.8 3.2.9 3.2.10	Seminar Laboratory/Workshop Gaming/Quiz Brainstorming Buzz Groups Field Trip Role Play Ice Breaker Simulation Case Study
3.3 **Individual** **(N = < 5)**	3.3.1 3.3.2 3.3.3	Project/Assignment Tutorial Open/Distance Learning

Figure 3.5 Teaching Strategies Related to Group Size

3.1 Strategies Appropriate to Large Groups

The strategies that are appropriate to large groups (and this, you will remember, has been defined as groups of greater than 20 students) are lecture, demonstration, discussion/debate, question and answer and video. Large group teaching is often an administrative convenience: that is, it is beneficial for all students to come together for a fixed time to cover specific subject topics. It is a continuation of what pre-16 year old students are used to and it is a traditionally accepted method of learning.

However, in recent years, large group teaching has fallen into a certain amount of disrepute. The lecture method is accepted in universities and polytechnics as 'part' of the learning experience where large groups are conveniently brought together in the initial stages of a subject to motivate their subsequent learning by other means (for example seminar, tutorial and individual learning). Research into the lecture method has shown that the amount of information that is remembered is not nearly as much as might have been expected. In consequence, alternative strategies have increased in popularity while large group approaches are not used as much as they have previously been.

Large group teaching strategies, then, are suitable when:

(a)   the basic purpose is to disseminate information;

(b)   the material is not available elsewhere;

(c)   the material must be presented and organised in a particular way for a specific group;

(d)   it is necessary to arouse interest in the subject;

(e)   the material need only be remembered for a short time;

(f)   it is necessary to provide an introduction to an area or directions for learning tasks to be pursued through some other teaching strategy.

3.1.1 Lecture

What it is ?	– a lecture involves the teacher talking to the students about the subject. There is little, if any, chance of any two-way communication. An interesting description of a lecture is: "You tell them what you are going to tell them, you tell them, and you tell them what you have told them." In other words, the lecture has an introduction to the content, the detail is then presented, and finally there is a summary of the lecture.
When is it used ?	– either in the classroom or workshop to pass information to the class in a cost-effective manner (i.e. to a group of students in a short time by one person). Thus, it is used to pass knowledge only: if understanding is required a subsequent different strategy will be used.
Example:	– explaining a concept to a group of learners.

Guidelines:

(a) Preparation	– extract key points from the topic;
	– prepare visual aids (OHP transparencies, handouts, chalkboard) to supplement the verbal material;
	– consider how to introduce and conclude.
(b) Presentation:	– avoid monotone voice and be loud enough for the room;

	– emphasise (by repetition, visual aids etc.) key points;
	– assist learners in their note taking;
	– avoid words that learners will not understand and be sure to define technical words;
	– include an introduction and a summary.
Relative Merits:	– a teacher can reach a large number of students
	– conveys a large amount of material in short time;
	– teacher has complete control (unless listeners rebel!);
	– little opportunity to question teacher (often one way communication);
	– little or even no feed back regarding the effectiveness of the learning;
	– need for a large, comfortable perhaps purpose built room;
	– need to be a communication expert
	– large group could be off putting to teacher;
	– students are often passive;
	– little use of teaching skills
Summary:	– lecturing skills are an essential part of your teaching repertoire. It is often completed without the preparation needed to ensure success. It must have a beginning, middle and end. (Introduction, development and conclusion) and must be supported by other strategies in order to both consolidate and assess the learning which has taken place

The period of concentration of students is not very long. Some authors tell us that ten minutes is the maximum amount of time that an individual can concentrate. To assist this, the development of a lecture should be carefully structured. For instance, if your topic is 'fishing' you might structure it as shown in Figure 3.6. Such an organisational breakdown into sub-topics allows breaks to be made so that the topic is divided into manageable 'chunks' of information which will cope with different concentration spans. The sub-topics need to be sequenced in such a way that students can follow the flow of information.

Attention can also be maintained if you constantly change the communication channel. You need to vary the stimuli between the auditory and visual channels constantly during the lecture.. The importance of visual stimuli (chalkboard, overhead projector, chart) cannot be over-stressed and it is useful to use a variety of different visual aids.

Making a case for active learning is especially relevant for lecturing. None of us in our academic careers has escaped sleep during at least one lecture even when we are moderately interested in the topic. The case for associating an incomplete handout, encouraging students to make their own notes, or asking questions even when the group is large, is easily made.

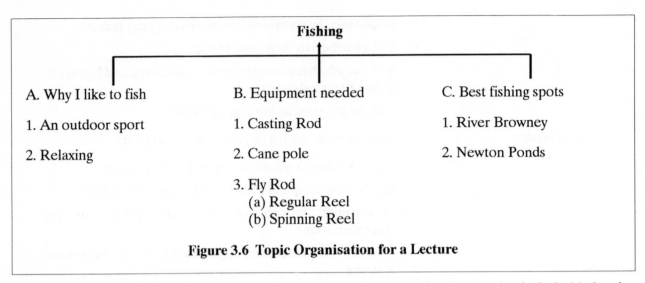

Figure 3.6 Topic Organisation for a Lecture

Other techniques that can be associated with the lecture so that you maintain attention include (a) showing enthusiasm for the topic; (b) ensuring vocal inflection, gesturing and maintaining eye contact; and (c) adding a touch of humour (but not too much).

3.1.2 Demonstration

What it is ?	– the technique is usually associated with demonstrating a practical skill. It often introduces the skill; its point and importance. The skill is demonstrated after which the students practice the skill.
When is it used ?	– in the practical situation to introduce a new skill to a group of students to rectify faults with individuals.
Example:	– giving an injection; changing a car wheel; wallpapering.
Guidelines:	
(a) *Preparation*:	– identify key points;
	– relate theoretical underpinning to key points;
	– rehearse to ensure all equipment is working and that you can use it;
	– ensure all students can see even small equipment and processes;
	– time your demonstration. If it is more than, say 10 minutes, consider sub-dividing into a series of demonstrations;
	– consider how to make the students active (e.g. helping, completing a handout, answering questions, predicting the next step, noting results);

	–	consider how to emphasise safe working practices.
(b) Presentation:	–	clear introduction (why important, where used);
	–	name of tools/equipment;
	–	check entry behaviour;
	–	do not show how not to complete the skill;
	–	stress key points and show links between them;
	–	monitor safety aspects;
	–	check learner understanding.
Relative merits;	–	when performed well, the demonstration can be highly motivating – better than a verbal description;
	–	theory and practice can be linked;
	–	pace of demonstration can be varied i.e. slowly, at normal speed, and in stages;
	–	learners usually enjoy actively doing things;
	–	expert demonstrations may be available via the video.
Summary:	–	the first stage in learners acquiring a skill. It must be well prepared, key points identified, learners involved and must be followed by individual learner practice and feedback.

A skilled demonstration is characterised by its speed and dexterity. You need to try to remember the problems you had when you were learning. These are likely to be the 'key abilities' similar to those that were discussed in Chapter 1 when we were talking about the skill of sharpening a pencil with a knife. Some skills are difficult for you to slow down because when you do, you loose the 'flow' (the links in the chain of stimulus-response relationships). A golf swing, slicing an onion, and plastering a wall are all difficult to slow down.

In order to overcome this problem of speed a useful sequence to follow is:

(i) complete the demonstration at normal speed without commentary;

(ii) repeat the demonstration with commentary stressing the key points, asking students questions (what comes next? can you hold this? will you fill that?);

(iii) ask a student to repeat the demonstration with all of the students watching;

(iv) ask another student to repeat the demonstration with a third one giving a commentary.

You do not need to complete all of these stages of course but they are possibilities. Remember that you are helping the students to *verbalise* (to remember in their own minds) the stages or steps involved in the skill. And, as you will remember, repetition is helpful in helping students to remember.

Points (iii) and (iv) above are useful because, when you are not directly involved in demonstrating the skill, you can concentrate more upon the teaching aspects: you can more easily identify the key points and tell students to expect them, to watch out for them, or ask them what they are, without having to stop the student who is completing the demonstration.

Also getting students to demonstrate is useful for highlighting the problems that exist in the completion of the skill. You should *not*, in your demonstration, show students the wrong way of doing things. They may remember only the wrong way and think that it is the correct one. However, when a student is completing the demonstration with the others watching, they are likely to do things incorrectly so that these points can be forcibly made by you.

A demonstration is a very visual teaching technique and students generally enjoy the use of this method. However, you should remember that it is not an opportunity to 'show off' your aptitude which has been gained over, perhaps, years of practice, but it is a an ideal opportunity for teaching.

The above strategy has linked the method to the initial stages of skill learning but it can also be used for the teaching of concepts. If you are able to visually demonstrate the concept, then all of the above benefits of the strategy can be maintained. For example if you are teaching Pythagoras Theorem (in a right angled triangle the square on the hypotenuse is equal to the sum of the squares on the other two sides. We are sure that you all remember that!) then this can be demonstrated by using a model as shown in Figure 3.7.

A model can be made (either out of card or coloured acetate to go onto the overhead projector) of the triangle abc and of the squares on side 'a' and 'b'. The squares on these two sides can then be replaced onto side 'c' showing that the square on the hypotenuse (side 'c') is equal in area to the square on the other two sides. Students are more likely to remember this visual demonstration of the concept than they are a formula written on the chalkboard.

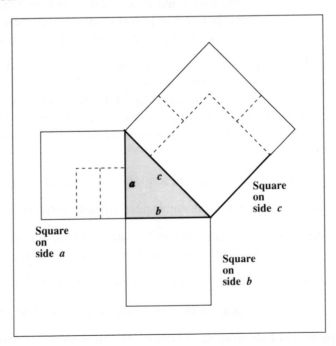

Figure 3.7 Demonstration of a Concept: Pythagoras Theorem

3.1.3 Discussion

What it is ? — the students are actively involved in talking to each other about an issue of mutual concern. Your job is to manage the situation so that learning takes place.

When is it used ? — discussion is often used to help solve problems, or to explore issues and take decisions. It is a useful way of exploring attitudes and to help change unhelpful or antisocial attitudes.

Examples — Treatment of Young Offenders; preventative medicine.

Guidelines: — discussion must be carefully pre-planned. A clear intention or objective is needed and ground rules need to be established. Timing is a crucial issue as is the need to reduce your own involvement whilst trying to ensure all can participate. The topic should be easily understood by all students. Ensure that the room layout is conducive to a discussion.

(a) Preparation: — must be relevant to an objective;

— do learners need to research the topic?

— consider size of group and room layout so that all participate (i.e. small groups and intimate areas);

— consider if a semi-structured handout will assist coverage of topic.

(b) Presentation: — tell students how long they have for discussion;

— tell the students how the results are to be fed back;

— your role is (a) to provide information and not answers; (b) to monitor the discussion: and (c) to try to ensure all participate;

— assist learners to summarise the main points as a conclusion, and finally you must summarise the main issues.

Relative merits : — can be used following a video or lecture in order to reinforce the learning;

— very useful for changing attitudes;

— involves the students – and quiet members of the group can emerge as leaders;

- can be very creative;

- needs a summary;

- can encourage students to become more articulate;

- students and teachers need to develop discussion skills;

- can be risky;

- may take a relatively long time.

Summary:
- high learner participation but you need to develop the necessary management skills;

- remember to arrange the furniture in the room so the communication in the discussion is enhanced.

The seating plan is very important for discussion and, as we said above, the room must be suitable (or made suitable) if you are to use this strategy successfully. Figure 3.8 shows an ideal situation where desks have been removed and students are seated so they can both see and hear each other. The 'network' has been decentralised so that there is no focal point - the students are seated in a circle.

If there is a focal point (for example, someone sitting in the middle) some students are likely to look to this person for a lead and will not participate as an 'equal partner'. If it is not possible to remove the desks, then they should be arranged in a square or circle so that all of the students can see and hear each other and, again, there should be no focal point. However, desks can provide a barrier behind which the more introvert students might hide.

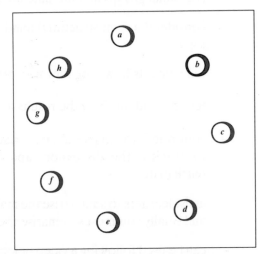

Figure 3.8 Decentralised Student Seating for a Discussion

Often the results of the discussion will need to be fed back to either the whole group or to you as teacher. This needs to be made clear at the start and it is useful to let students decide who is to do this. However, it is useful that they make this decision at the start of the discussion period so that individual can make the necessary notes and preparation (or ensure that another student does it for them).

3.1.4 Debate

What is it ?	– a debate is very similar to a discussion but tends to have more rules regarding procedure.
When is it used ?	– where there is no right answer and where both sides of the argument would benefit from exploration. To enhance formal communication skills in the presentation of an argument.
Examples:	– the use of nuclear power to generate electricity; bring back corporal punishment.

Guidelines:

(a)   Preparation:
– nominate/elect a chair from the students to ensure rules are followed in an impartial manner;

– select a topic which will stimulate debate and allow argument for and against;

– select a main speaker for the motion and one against the motion and give them time to prepare;

– brief the chair.

(b)   Presentation:
– divide group into those in favour of the motion, those against and those uncommitted;

– allow time for research and preparation of arguments;

– arrange debate in steps:

(a) proposer for;
(b) proposer against;
(c) seconder for (to argue against (b));
(d) seconder against (to argue against (a));
(e) open debate;
(f) Vote.

– teacher summary of main points and assessment of communication skills.

Relative merits:
– has a clear structure and an element of competition. All students can participate. Students can take the leading roles. Good for contentious issues.

Summary:
– student centred, structured technique for learning communication skills and extracting key points of a topic.

3.1.5 *Question and Answer*

What it is ? — Posing a series of questions to students in order to promote thinking and understanding.

When is it used ? — It is an informal assessment technique which is used with groups of up to 30 students. It is a way of ascertaining the existing level of learning or entry behaviour in the introduction to a lesson and/or, assessing the learning that has taken place at the end of a lesson (or during it).

Example: — building concept attainment (e.g. a tourist).

Guidelines: — questions need to be carefully considered so that the learners supply their knowledge and do not simply answer yes or no;

— ask simple questions first and then move to more complex ones;

— spread the questions so that all learners respond;

— ask the questions, allow thinking time and then ask students to respond. This may involve setting rules to avoid chorus answers;

— praise a correct response, praise the correct part of a partially correct response and explore the reason for an incorrect response. Always accept the students' answers to ensure future participation.

Relative merits: — students are involved and feel they are contributing to learning;

— misconceptions may be identified at an early stage;

— can build from simple to complex;

— key questions can be pre-planned;

— feed back on quality of learning is gained;

— you need to be able to respond quickly to the students answers.

Summary: — you need to develop this useful skill. Question and answer may last a few minutes or be developed into a longer session. The feed back showing misconceptions is very valuable. Encourage all answers and build upon wrong or partially correct answers.

When discussing lesson planning in Chapter 1 it was suggested that 'key questions' should not only be planned but be stated as part of the teacher activity in the body of the plan. This means that you need to plan the questions related to the level of the objectives. Figure 3.9 gives an indication of questions at the different levels. Each level in the Cognitive Domain has been included but only up to 'valuing' in the Affective Domain. You might want to combine the higher three levels in the cognitive domain into 'invention'. The reason that the higher levels in the affective domain have not been covered is that post-16 education and training tends not to go higher in this domain.

You will see that, not only do the levels of question get harder to answer the higher they go up the domain, but the length of the responses is also likely to increase. Those questions that warrant a one word answer are termed '*closed*' questions: those that require a sentence or more to answer are '*open*' questions.

Domain	Level	Example Question
Cognitive	Knowledge	What city is the capital of England?
	Comprehension	Explain, in your own words, the meaning of pollution.
	Application	Now that you have studied energy, if you leave a refrigerator door open and switched on in a sealed room, will the temperature of the room rise or fall?
	Analysis	Why do you think that Labour party supporters, after World War II, said that the Conservatives were a party of warmongers?
	Synthesis	Now that you have studied static electricity, how could you stop getting a 'shock' when you slide over the plastic seat covers of a car?
	Evaluation	Describe the fallacies in reasoning in the statement "All ducks are birds. All robins are birds. Thus, all ducks are robins".
Affective	Receiving	How interesting was your visit to the factory?
	Responding	How did you feel after reading "Catcher in the Rye"?
	Valuing	What actions, if any, would you take with a friend who wrote a 'Letter to the Editor' of a local newspaper?

Figure 3.9 Questions at Different Levels in Different Domains

It is useful to have both types in a lesson but it is often the case that closed questions will elicit a 'chorus' response as many will know the answer and want to show that they know.

When you use question and answer technique, you will want as many of the class to respond as possible and you will want them to answer both low and high level questions. The type of questions that you ask are not only classified into levels but also whether you *'nominate'* a student to answer or whether the question is *'un-nominated'* (any student in the class can answer). Consider the response pattern to teacher questions shown in Figure 3.10 which gives an overview of a question and answer session with 9 students siting in a semi-circle. From this you can see that the teacher has asked equal numbers of nominated and un-nominated questions. This is generally useful in that, if you want all of the students to respond, you can nominate individuals to get them to think, involve them in the session, and so on. You will also see that the total of teacher initiated interactions is 36 and the total student initiated interactions (them making comments and asking questions) is 16. Thus a third of the interactions are student initiated which is a good proportion: it is generally useful to get students to talk to you as well as you talking to them. Often this is very difficult and you may find in your classes a very small proportion of the interactions are student initiated.

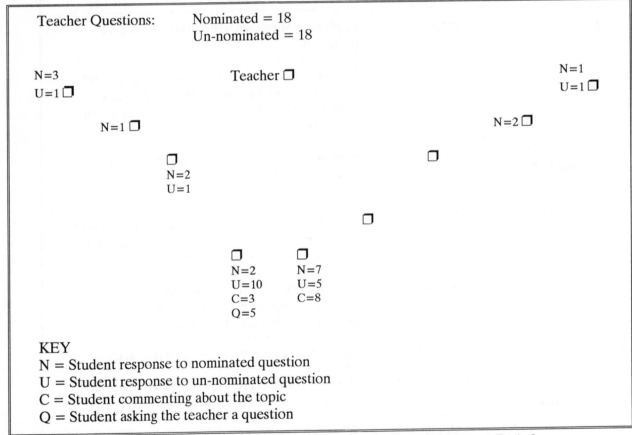

Figure 3.10 **Response Patterns to a Class Question and Answer Period**

However, when you look at the positions of the responses around the class, you will see that a total of 40 of the 52 interactions (77%) were from 2 members (22%) of the class: a very uneven distribution. Also, three members of the class (33%) did not interact at all or only interacted once. Thus 33% of the class were involved in only 2% of the interactions. The questions that need to be answered associated with this type of analysis include:

(a) did it matter that some students did not respond or make any contribution at all?

(b) if it does matter, what might be done to ensure that they participate?

(c) does it matter that 77% of the interactions came from 22% of the group?

(d) if it does matter, what might be done to make them them respond less?

(e) does seating have any influence on the response pattern?

(f) what response pattern would be ideal?

The answer to question (a) depends upon the respective abilities of the students who did not respond. If they are bright students in your subject and they are not introvert, then perhaps it does not matter that they do not answer. They might not like question and answer and learn in spite of the use of this technique. If, on the other hand they are not concentrating and/or do not do very well in your subject, then a series of nominated questions to them will be an advantage. If they are introvert, then nominated questions will have to be handled carefully – you will need to make sure that they are easy questions that they should be able to answer and make sure that you give praise when they respond.

The two who answered so many questions obviously need consideration and action: they have over-dominated the session. They should not be asked nominated questions and a you might have a quiet word with them to ask them to let others participate more. Perhaps the seating has an effect: they are sitting directly opposite the teacher and together. Perhaps dividing them and sitting them at the edge of the vision of the teacher so that not so much eye contact is maintained could be useful.

3.1.6 Video

What it is ?	– a method of bringing realism into the classroom or workshop.
When is it used ?	– can be linked to a range of other teaching strategies as a means of providing variety and realism.
Examples:	– loading nuclear fuel rods; a surgical operation.
Guidelines:	
(a) *Preparation:*	– preview video and identify main points. Pre-select appropriate scenes if entire programme is too long;
	– plan an associated activity for the student to be completed during or after viewing;
	– book necessary equipment (video, tape, room etc.).
(b) *Presentation:*	– introduce the video and the activity and alert students to the key points;

	– after viewing assess the learning;
	– stop for questions or replay any important points.
Relative Merits:	– can bring a well known expert into the classroom;
	– students can see dangerous or one-off situations;
	– a permanent record;
	– can provoke thought – used as a trigger;
	– relatively cheap and very convenient;
	– can be taken home by (some) students;
	– may disrupt class;
	– class handed over to 'another';
	– may be perceived as merely entertainment;
	– can induce sleep.
Summary:	– video used with care can be a stimulating part of a lesson.

There is a danger when using a video to pass the responsibility for the teaching entirely over to the programme: to the voice on the TV and the picture on the screen. Used properly, the video can be an excellent addition to the classroom or workshop teaching of a large group of students.

It is all too easy to select a video, seat the class comfortably in front of the TV, switch on and do nothing more until the programme is finished. If this is the case, not only will you tend not to concentrate upon the programme but your students will do the same. The 'good' use of a video, like so many other teaching strategies, must ensure that the students are *active*.

The major advantages of the video over a film are (i) the video can easily be stopped, rewound and replayed, and (ii) it can be watched in normal light without the need of a darkened room. You need to exploit both of these advantages when using the strategy in order to make the students active.

We have suggested above that you preview the video and highlight the main points: the key features that it exhibits. Either before or after the showing of each main point, you can stop the recorder, emphasise the point, make a note of it on the chalkboard and ask students to note it before going on with the viewing.

In order to take advantage of the normally lit room, you can prepare an incomplete handout for the students which invites them to take notes under the main headings as they are viewing. If you consider that they have insufficient time to make the necessary notes you can again stop the recorder for the activity to take place. Another advantage of such a handout is that your students also have a permanent record of what they have watched.

3.2 Strategies Appropriate to Small Groups

Just as large group strategies are appropriate for certain educational purposes, there are times when you should use strategies that are appropriate to small groups. Students are likely to work in small groups in industry and commerce and, in consequence, we have a moral obligation to use such approaches in our controlled environments.

Industry and commerce are continually telling us of the importance of 'common' skills to be associated with our subject specialism skills and one of these relates to the ability to work 'as an effective group member'. This, generally, means the ability to work in small groups; to be an effective leader as well as an effective follower; to learn to cope with other people's idiosyncrasies; present a logical argument and analyse other's arguments; to co-operate with others and adopt a variety of roles when working co-operatively.

As educators have become dissatisfied with the conventional classroom, its basic assumptions, and its effectiveness, so the strategies associated with small group work have gained momentum. Such strategies include seminar, role play, case study, simulation and the others listed in Figure 3.5. These often employ different aspects of small group discussion where students are able to think things through for themselves without having the direct control of the teacher. Of course, this means that you automatically lose some of your control over what is being said and what is being done. You become more a manager of the situation as opposed to the purveyor of information. You need to set up the situation and take more of a 'back seat' and let the students proceed more at their own pace. This means a very different perspective for you and one that some teachers find, at least initially, very difficult to cope with. You become a more 'humanist' teacher with the concentration upon the need of the student as well as the need of the subject. Students learn from each other.

Because of the different approaches that you have to adopt with a smaller group, the range of objectives that you can achieve is greater. The higher level cognitive and affective domain objectives are more applicable to these methods. It has been argued that in some subjects the major concepts, principles, and methods are so well established that no competent person raises any doubt about them. At the introductory levels in such subjects like science, engineering and mathematics there is much agreement about what is important. In other subjects there is not such a consensus. In the social sciences – in history and economics, political science, psychology, literature, music and art, we do not agree nearly so readily about what is important, good, true, valid or significant. Consequently, in these low consensus subjects, discussion methods may be necessary. Similarly, the discussion method may also be better suited to the changing of attitudes and behaviour. During the discussion, students make public decisions committing themselves to a given course of action.

3.2.1 Seminar

What it is ?	– a student researches a topic, presents the findings to other students and leads the ensuing discussion.
When is it used ?	– widely used with mature students to explore specified topics.
Examples:	– how to deal with problem students; the causes of World War Two.

Guidelines:	– a student should have time to consider relevant readings, view videos, listen to lectures etc. before the seminar. Some questions may be posed in advance. At the seminar, each student should be encouraged to share their views so that the range of issues can be explored.
Relative Merits:	– students involved in the preparation;
	– students know what is to be discussed and that they will have the opportunity to participate;
	– opportunity to ask questions of their peers and teachers;
	– seminars are student led;
	– students may be reluctant to participate at first;
	– need to summarise the main issues at the end of the seminar;
	– can be dull.
Summary:	– a different way for learning and, if the group is small, then opportunities easiest for effective interaction.

The aims of the seminar method include the common skills of 'the ability to find information' and 'the ability to present an argument'. Often discussions take place in class without students having all of the facts and understanding the topic. The advantages of the seminar are that students are involved themselves in finding the information prior to giving a short input, and they then discuss its implications and sustain an argument through the answering of questions on it from their colleagues. Thus, the phases in a seminar are:

(i)   finding information;

(ii)   presenting the information to their colleagues;

(iii) answering questions from colleagues.

The assessment of the work, therefore, can give feedback on the subject matter; the ability to find information; the ability to present the information, and the ability to answer questions from their fellow students.

3.2.2 Workshop

What it is ?	– an opportunity to develop practical skills in a simulated situation and link the theory with practice.
When is it used ?	– in the development of skills.
Examples:	– using a CNC lathe; making a dovetail joint.

Guidelines:

(a) *Preparation:*
- ensure all equipment available and ready;
- consider how to introduce and conclude each session;
- prepare an assessment schedule related to key points;
- prepare worksheet to indicate task schedule and associated assessment points.

(b) *Presentation:*
- often starts with a demonstration;
- manage individuals working at their own pace (question, feed back, rectify faults);
- overtly link theory with the practical aspects;
- monitor safety aspects;
- allow time for a conclusion so that students can see/critically analyse others work/progress.

Relative merits:
- can take place before or after theoretical aspects;
- can be a good basis for problem solving;
- teacher can talk with the learners on a one-to-one basis;
- reinforces learning in a realistic and meaningful way;
- students work at own pace;
- can be seen as tedious or boring;
- expensive in terms of time, equipment and rooms;
- implications for Health and Safety.

Summary:
- a valuable, if not essential part of many courses. Usually enjoyable for the students as it often appears to be real and exciting.

3.2.3 Gaming/Quiz

What it is ?
- games are a learning situation with an element of competition and/or cooperation.

When is it used ?
- can stimulate and involve learners when they interact with other students and/or the game.

Examples:	– team building; effects of an oil spillage.

Guidelines:

(a) Preparation:	– try out and test game prior to use with students;
	– ensure rules are clear and understood by students.
(b) Presentation:	– introduce the game in its learning context;
	– monitor programme and assist only when essential;
	– summarise and consolidate the learning outcomes.

Relative merits:	– can be fun;
	– compete against a machine or situation rather than another student;
	– may have to make your own game;
	– game may not work;
	– immediate feed back;
	– may not be taken seriously.

Summary:	– can be a different type of learning which the students generally enjoy.

The Quiz is a particular form of gaming. Teams or individuals may participate and an element of competition may be introduced. It can be an interesting way of obtaining feed back on the quality of learning and motivating students to revise and study their notes.

3.2.4 Brainstorming

What it is ?	– a problem solving technique used to generate a number of ideas (solutions) in a short time e.g. 5 to 15 minutes.
When is it used ?	– when a problem, real or manufactured, exists, the students are invited to generate possible solutions. Often used in management courses or with problem solving.
Example 1:	– warm-up – uses of a paper clip.
Example 2:	– problem – how to prevent strikes.

Guidelines:	– the students may be 'warmed up' using a trial brainstorm. The students are encouraged to shout out key words – these are all written down without criticism or censure. If the participants dry up, there can be an enforced two minutes silence. Then the brainstorm continues. the key words are then categorised and discussed. Possible solutions are then identified.
Relative merits:	– unusual solutions may be identified;
	– all can participate;
	– needs few resources;
	– seems to be part of the creative process;
	– group needs to learn and obey rules;
	– warm-up sessions may be needed;
	– can be demanding and can only be used for short periods.
Summary:	– a challenging and active learning situation.

3.2.5 Buzz Groups

What it is ?	– a relatively large group of students are divided into smaller groups of about 4 to 6, usually to discuss a problem/situation used for a short time, say 5 minutes. The noise of the several simultaneous discussions give the strategy its name.
When is it used ?	– with large groups where you want the students to interact with each other.
Example:	– merits of an integrated transport system.
Guidelines:	– make sure the groups know what they have to discuss and how long they have. Nominate a leader or tell each group to appoint one. State the manner of feed back e.g. oral from the leader, OHT, flipchart etc.
Relative Merits:	– introduces student activity into what could be perceived as a teacher-centred situation;
	– gives a change of activity and allows the students to express themselves;
	– can be used in a large, formal lecture theatre;

	– gives feed back on the learning;
	– sometimes can be difficult to nominate groups;
	– feed back could take some time (try a maximum of 60 second feed back from each group).
Summary;	– small groups discussing giving a 'buzz' of conversation.

3.2.6 Field Trip

What it is ?	– usually the students are taken out of their normal learning situation to a 'real-life' situation.
When is it used ?	– where realism is essential, or very helpful, in reinforcing the learning.
Examples:	– study of rock formation; a food processing plant.
Guidelines:	
(a) *Preparation:*	– plan links with the theory/learning intention;
	– consider safety and make allowances for delays;
	– prepare handouts and activities;
	– plan for inclement weather;
	– consider insurance and parent/employer permission;
	– brief students before the visit;
	– plan follow up activities.
(b) *Presentation:*	– ensure adequate supervision at all times;
	– 'visit' students, use question and answer.
Relative merits:	– students can see the real situation;
	– realistic and lifelike;
	– motivating;
	– clear links between learning and visit;
	– time consuming for planning and visit;
	– may be costly;

	–	legal/safety problems;
	–	supervision of students on visit.
Summary:	–	can be a very valuable and rewarding experience but may turnout to be a nightmare.

3.2 .7 Role Play

What it is ?	–	students acting a part or a role in events before a situation, during the situation and after the situation.
When is it used ?	–	helping the students to feel the influences and pressures in their role. It is suggested that role play is particularly effective with attitudinal issues.
Examples:	–	conflict in the workplace e.g. receptionist and 'difficult' customer;
	–	conflict within the team in the workplace;
	–	situation where people are disadvantaged due to race, gender, etc.

Guidelines:

(a) Preparation:	–	have role cards for participants.
	–	plan activities for those students not in role, i.e. observers for feed back. nb. players should not see each others' role-play cards.
(b) Presentation:	–	introduce the role play and indicate its function in the learning, i.e. why you are doing it;
	–	monitor the role play and only step in if things go badly wrong, i.e. a student is going to be embarrassed;
	–	debrief the students so that they are no longer 'in role';
	–	ensure that the role play is analysed and related to the intended learning outcome.
Relative merits:	–	a good way to address attitudinal issues;
	–	high degree of student participation;
	–	realistic;
	–	emotions can be felt;

– students can teach their peers about their feelings in their role rather than the teacher telling them;

– usually a safe environment;

– can be threatening – especially for the shy participants;

– needs careful preparation;

– needs careful managing;

– essential to debrief the students;

– can take some time.

Summary: – once written and tested, the role plays can be used many times with different classes. High student involvement with the difficult area of attitudinal change.

3.2 .8 Ice Breaker

What it is ?   – a technique used to get the student to feel part of the group and part of the learning process.

When is it used ?   – often used with the first meeting of a group or when a student or students join an established group.

Example 1:   – ask the group to go into pairs; one person interviews the other and asks their name, their interests etc. (Nothing too personal). The roles are then reversed. The students then introduce each other to the whole group.

Example 2:   – each student writes their first name on the board and tells as much as they know about it e.g. its origin, its meaning, how they feel about their name, famous people with the same name.

Example 3:   – prepare a brief questionnaire which asks, what qualities do you bring to the group? What are you looking forward to? What are your concerns? Display the results and ask the students to look at the responses of the others in the group. n.b. the questionnaires need to be anonymous.

Guidelines: – the balance between helping a group to get to know each other and causing embarrassment is a delicate one. Care needs to be exercised and judgment made so that the student is allowed to develop but is not threatened.

Relative merits: – can help discussion and small group work to achieve maximum effectiveness very quickly;

– students feel part of a group;

– no long silences;

– students pose more questions to the teacher earlier in the course;

– relieve tension;

– can be fun;

– can take a long time;

– may not be perceived as being 'useful';

– some students may hate it.

Summary: – used with care and in a non-threatening way, icebreakers may help establish a group identity in an hour rather than weeks or months.

3.2.9 Simulation

What it is ?   – the simulation of a real or a possible situation.

When is it used ?   – in situations where it is not possible or desirable to undertake learning in the actual conditions.

Example 1:   – computer simulation of the economy.

Example 2:   – flight simulator.

Example 3:   – managers trying to see own skills in prioritising and time management in a stimulated situation.

Guidelines: – the simulation needs to be make as realistic as possible. Supervision of all students is essential at all times in order to avoid reinforcement of errors.

Relative merits: – can be used where the real situation is dangerous, costly, 'difficult' or too time consuming;

– can be repeated until desired level of learning is achieved;

– can be stopped at any stage in order to inject concepts, principles etc.;

– students are active and take responsibility;

– can be a good introduction to the real thing;

	–	can be time consuming to set up;
	–	may be difficult to supervise all students all of the time.
Summary:	–	may be the only way to learn in some situations, with the students being able to stop and ask questions.

3.2.10 Case Study

What it is ?	–	it is an examination of a real or simulated problem which is structured so that learning can take place or be reinforced.
When is it used ?	–	often used on management and business study courses to analyse what went wrong in a given situation and to consider how failure could be avoided. It tends to be used in situations where rules or laws cannot be applied or where there is some ambiguity.
Examples:	–	why a particular company collapsed;
	–	what happened to the British Motor Cycle Industry.
Guidelines:	–	the situation needs to be realistic and as accurate as possible. As much information as possible needs to be given and often superfluous information is given as in real life.
Relative merits:	–	the case study needs to have clear learning intentions;
	–	the aftermath of the study needs to reinforce learning;
	–	can be an individual or group activity;
	–	can be in class or at home;
	–	real, including current, situations can be studied;
	–	needs to be well structured;
	–	a good deal of preparation may be needed.
Summary:	–	takes a good deal of preparation but can bring realism into the learning situation.

3.3 Strategies Appropriate to Individual Work

Just as some strategies are appropriate to large and small groups, there are times when you need to provide opportunities and activities for students to work on their own. What are these? When is a student best left alone with an assignment, a set of printed materials, a set of programmed instruction materials, or a broad mission to be carried out through independent effort and study?

The individualisation of instruction has gained momentum in recent years. Some educators have become dissatisfied with the conventional classroom, its basic assumptions and its effectiveness. The coming of the 'objectives' revolution provided the basis for this to happen and it has gone apace in recent years. Apart from helping achieve educational objectives in general, individual instruction can achieve the objectives of helping students to work and learn independently. It was realised that students must eventually learn on their own and education must assist this process. 'Learning to learn' is now a major objective in its own right with students continuing to learn throughout their lives. This *'humanist'* approach to education, promoted by Dewey (1933) with his 'Project Method', and A.S. Neill (1960) with his 'whole school approach' was formed and has gathered momentum.

There are, of course, cautions in using individual work and there is a difference between 'independent' and 'self directed' study. Independent study is organised by the teacher with suggestions as to what might be completed and, perhaps, when. Self directed study, on the other hand, has its organisation base with the student and, in effect, is even more student centred. It is often the organisation that students find difficult. The 'Keller Plan' (F.S.Keller, 1968) found that students, when left to their own devices for too long a period, would be liable to flounder and the inclusion of teacher centred and group activities when associated with individual work made it much more effective in terms of the amount that was learned.

The 'Personalised System of Instruction' (PSI), which was the outcome of the work by Keller, has the following characteristics:

(i) *Individually paced*: – flexibility in timing can be achieved because students are working to meet specific criteria. The outcomes, then are criterion and not norm referenced.

(ii) *Mastery oriented:* – unless a student demonstrates mastery of a topic they cannot proceed. Testing can be at the request of the students when they feel that they are ready.

(iii) *Tutoring:* – assistance should be available to assist and answer questions which cannot be answered by the individual.

(iv) *Study guides:* – study guides, which contain objectives, offer suggestions for study, point out available resources, describe projects or experiments that could be attempted and provide sample assessment items, are given to the student.

(v) *Supplemented with traditional methods:* – lectures, demonstrations, and so on may be scheduled for stimulation or clarification; they may be used occasionally and attendance can be voluntary.

PSI has many variations but few meet with failure if the basic elements of the system stay intact.

You can use the elements of the Keller Plan in the three methods described below. More and more, the effective classroom teacher is being asked to design their own 'study guides' for use with independent study and the elements of the Plan should be kept in mind during the design process.

3.3.1 Project/Assignment

What it is ?   – the students are usually given an individual topic for an in-depth analysis. They often have to work independently, do research and report either in writing or verbally to a group. The project could involve a group of students working together on different facets of the same problem.

When is it used ?   – often used in advanced courses for training in research techniques but now used in a wide variety of situations including practical work.

Examples: – research the incidence of AIDS in the UK (individual);

      – design and build a wind tunnel (individual);

      – build a house (group project).

Guidelines: – students may need help with the study skills involved, particularly when working on their own. The project has to be realistic in terms of time and cost. Clear learning intentions are needed.

Relative merits: – realistic situation for students;

      – can promote independent learning;

      – student feels in command;

      – tutorial links may be on a one-to-one basis;

      – can be highly motivating;

      – enhances study skills;

      – cross curricular;

      – supervision can take up a good deal of time;

      – some students need a lot of managing;

      – can be costly;

      – resources, library, need to be available.

Summary: – a recognised and realistic alternative to traditional examinations.

3.3.2 Tutorial

What it is ?	– the teacher usually sets the student a task and the tutorial is a means of preparing the student for the task, assisting in the process and then discussing the quality of the learning outcomes. It is essentially a strategy to support and enhance the quality of learning.
When is it used ?	– used in all spheres of learning but may not be called a 'tutorial'.
Examples:	– supporting work on an assignment;
	– checking progress on the course as a whole.
Guidelines:	– it is important to listen to students to see what they know and what they do not know. Positive outcomes should be planned. Tutorial could be on a one to one basis but when students have similar tasks a small group approach can generate valuable discussion and peer support. Students and teacher should prepare for tutorials.
Relative merits:	– individual attention;
	– opportunity to see the quality of learning;
	– valuable support to progress;
	– opportunity to establish a rapport with students and improve communication;
	– confidential aspects can be discussed;
	– individual concerns addressed;
	– costly because of one-to-one relationship;
	– finding a suitable room.
Summary:	– in widespread use and students should find tutorials to be of great value.

3.3.3 Open Learning/Distance Learning

What it is ?	– this is usually where the teacher and student meet infrequently (if at all). It may include videos, broadcast materials, audio tapes, written material, etc.

When is it used ?	– useful for students who cannot attend due to work commitments, or because of distance to travel.
Examples:	– Open University and Open Tech.
Guidelines:	– the materials used must be tried and tested, unambiguous and interesting. Carefully consider the existing materials. If planning your own materials, build in as much activity and feedback as possible.
Relative merits:	– helps students who cannot attend a given location at a given time;
	– student proceeds at own pace;
	– large number of students taught simultaneously;
	– may be seen as a cheap alternative 'to proper teaching';
	– can be expensive to design and produce;
	– teacher feed back could be infrequent;
	– can be difficult to maintain student motivation;
	– feeling of isolation and lack of peer group support.
Summary:	– the only option in some situations but tutorial support is often needed.

4. Evaluation of Teaching Strategies

Improvement in your use of teaching strategies can come from better preparation but this is only a small part of the process. Your effectiveness in the use of the strategies can be achieved through (a) introspection involving you thinking about what you have done after the event, (b) asking a colleague to sit in with you and comment on your approaches, (c) using 'micro-teaching' where you teach a topic to a group of colleagues and they critically analyse what has taken place (this is often video recorded), or (d) asking students what they think of your approaches. Each of these will benefit from some sort of preparation; preparing a questionnaire for the observer(s) to complete; asking specific questions at the end of the lesson; or recording through either sound or video tape, what has taken place. This preparation will provide you with evidence or data upon which you can make judgements and decisions about what changes you might make. This, then, is the process of evaluation.

4.1 Deciding upon what to evaluate

It is all too easy for you to say that you want to improve your teaching and to look at too many things all at once. It is important that you decide the particular aspects that you want to improve and to concentrate upon particular aspects at a time. You might want to improve a particular teaching strategy like question and answer, or an introduction or conclusion to a session. You then need to prepare an instrument to ensure that you collect the information, or data, that you require in order that you can make the appropriate evaluative judgements.

The questions that you might want to find answers to include:

(i)   How can I improve my technique with ... (a specific teaching strategy)?

(ii) How can I improve the interaction of my students?

(iii) What is the effectiveness of my introductions/conclusions to my sessions?

(iv) How well do my students learn?

4.2 Data Collection

One of the easiest methods of collecting data is to audio-record, say, a question and answer part of your lesson, or an introduction to a lesson or a conclusion. The recording will give you specific data upon which to work. For instance, for a question and answer session you can find the following:

(a)   the total number of questions that were asked;

(b)   the number of questions that were open to all the class to answer and the number of questions that nominated a particular student to answer;

(c)   whether you nominated a student to answer either before or after asking the question;

(d)   the number of knowledge and the number of thinking questions;

and so on. The recording provides the evidence for finding out answers to the questions that you have planned. It might be useful to assist with the analysis of the data to make a transcript of either the whole or part of the recording.

Questionnaires to students can also form useful data upon which to make your judgements. The method of questionnaire design is discussed in Chapter 8, but Figure 3.11 gives an example of a questionnaire to be given to students to evaluate your explanations, Figure 3.12 your demonstrations, Figure 3.13 your discussions, and Figure 3.14 your lecturing. The design of each of the questionnaires is slightly different and you should decide which you prefer and which will most likely give you the type of information that you require.

The Explanation guide uses the principle that every explanation should have an introduction and conclusion and that the key aspects of the explanation should be stated and easily identified. It requires the students to answer yes or no (or not observed) and, in consequence is easy, and does not take much time, to complete.

The Explanation Guide

Please mark each aspect below with a 'Yes' or a 'No' or 'Not Observed'.

1. Introduction

    (a) The opening gained and held my attention.

    (b) The opening established rapport.

    (c) The opening told me what was to follow.

    (d) The opening said what was to be expected of me.

2. Key Points

    (a) The key points were clearly expressed.

    (b) The examples amplified the key points.

    (c) The examples added interest to the explanation.

    (d) The timing enabled me to understand the points.

3. The Summary

    (a) The summary brought together the key points

    (b) The conclusions were clearly stated.

Figure 3.11 Explanation Guide for Student Completion

The Teacher's Role in Leading a Discussion

Instructions to students:

Think back to the discussion we have just had and try to recall the role of the teacher in it. Examine each of the following statements and rate each one from 1 to 6 in terms of truthfulness. If you think that the statement is completely true then ring (1). If you think that it is completely untrue then ring (6). Ring numbers in between if you rate the statement as being somewhere between these opposites.

1.	The teacher explained the discussion task clearly.	1 2 3 4 5 6
2.	The teacher asked questions which encouraged group members to talk freely.	1 2 3 4 5 6
3.	The teacher did not interrupt constantly but listened.	1 2 3 4 5 6
4.	The teacher did not try to appear to be superior to the views expressed.	1 2 3 4 5 6
5.	The teacher encouraged the group to describe their own experiences when appropriate.	1 2 3 4 5 6
6.	The teacher attempted to involve each group member.	1 2 3 4 5 6
7.	The teacher did not show irritation with a particular viewpoint.	1 2 3 4 5 6
8.	The teacher did not force own views on the group.	1 2 3 4 5 6
9.	When desired, the teacher gave information/shared experiences.	1 2 3 4 5 6
10.	The teacher allowed unpopular as well as popular views to be expressed.	1 2 3 4 5 6
11.	At the end, the teacher gave members of the group the opportunity to offer their own conclusions	1 2 3 4 5 6

Figure 3.12 Student Rating Schedule for Teacher's Role in Discussion

Rating Scale for Demonstration

Name: Group:

Topic: Date:

Key: T = Transmission
            E = Emphasis
            V = Variation
            M = Meaningfulness

T1	Skilful performance by demonstrator.	Good	1	2	3	4	5	Poor	
T2	All equipment available.	All	1	2	3	4	5	Some	
T3	Equipment visible to all students.	All	1	2	3	4	5	Some	
T4	Clarity of commentary.	Clear	1	2	3	4	5	Poor	
E1	Attention directed at specific points.	Clear	1	2	3	4	5	Confusing	
E2	Well paced step by step procedure	Good	1	2	3	4	5	Too	Fast Slow
E3	Use of Q & A for emphasis	Effective	1	2	3	4	5	Poor	
V1	Variation in student activity	Good	1	2	3	4	5	Too	much little
V2	Variation on in teacher activity	Good	1	2	3	4	5	Too	little much
M1	Integration of demonstration with other subject matter.	Good	1	2	3	4	5	Disjointed	
M2	Involvement of students with other subject matter.	Good	1	2	3	4	5	Too	much little
M3	Best method of teaching the topic.	Suitable	1	2	3	4	5	Not suitable	
M4	Use of Q & A or other method to evaluate the learning	Effective	1	2	3	4	5	Poor	

Figure 3.13 Rating Scale for Demonstration

Feedback from Students

Lecture Rating Schedule

This questionnaire has been designed to inform me of your opinions concerning my presentation. They will be useful to me when giving future presentations. Please indicate your present thoughts by means of a mark on the 5 point scale below. For example, if you found the lecture quite interesting, you will show this as follows:

Interesting	1	②	3	4	5	Boring

Use the reverse side of the sheet for additional written comments.

The Lecturer

Clearly audible	1	2	3	4	5	Inaudible
Lively	1	2	3	4	5	Monotonous
Too fast	1	2	3	4	5	Too slow
Pleasant Manner	1	2	3	4	5	Unpleasant Manner
Well organised	1	2	3	4	5	Muddled
Interprets ideas clearly	1	2	3	4	5	Leaves me confused
Stressed important point	1	2	3	4	5	All points seem the same
Good use of examples	1	2	3	4	5	Examples were confusing
Is up to date with subject	1	2	3	4	5	Not aware of latest developments
Explanations clear	1	2	3	4	5	Incomprehensible explanations
Lectures confidently	1	2	3	4	5	Not confident

Subject Matter

Difficult	1	2	3	4	5	Easy
Too much material	1	2	3	4	5	Nothing much in it
Vocationally useful	1	2	3	4	5	Waste of time
Interesting	1	2	3	4	5	Boring
I will do further study	1	2	3	4	5	I will not pursue it

Use of Audio Visual Material

OHP Transparencies easy to read	1	2	3	4	5	Illegible
Sufficient time to read transparencies	1	2	3	4	5	Insufficient time to read

Activity

Too many different lecturer activities	1	2	3	4	5	Not enough
Too many different student activities	1	2	3	4	5	Not enough

Figure 3.14 Student Lecture Rating Schedule

The design of each of the questionnaires is based on the questions that are required to be answered. The data is provided by the students in answering the range of questions.

Data Analysis

The summation of the data can be achieved by taking a blank questionnaire and, on it, placing slash marks beside each question how the individuals have responded. Summation of the slash marks will give the overall response of the group.

The data from the questionnaires can be analysed by looking at the summation of all of the responses and finding those aspects that are very positive and those that are very negative. These, then, give the good aspects, those that should be kept, and the poor aspects, those that should be changed.

> *Possible evidence to show that you have achieved the competence 'Manage learning situations'*

1. (a) Choose one of your classes and relate the students and their needs to suitable learning activities and justify the choice of teaching strategy used.

    (b) Indicate your role in managing the learning situation.

    (c) Show how you have used a variety of teaching strategies.

2. State the techniques that you have used to ensure that your students have adopted a positive attitude to their learning.

3. Design a questionnaire for your students to answer to evaluate a specific aspect of your teaching. Give the questionnaire to a group of students to collect data, analyse the results by summating their responses and draw conclusions about what are:

    (a) the good aspects that you might accentuate in future;

    (b) the poorer aspects that you might consider changing.

Progress Check

> *If you want to check your understanding of managing learning activities, try the following progress check*

Progress Check 3.2

1. Choose two strategies that are used with large groups and indicate, for each:

    (a) its advantages;

    (b) its limitations;

    (c) the main aspects of its preparation;

    (d) the main aspects of its presentation.

2. Choose two strategies that are used with small groups and indicate, for each:

    (a) its advantages;

    (b) its limitations;

    (c) the main aspects of its preparation;

    (d) the main aspects of its presentation.

3. Choose two strategies that are used with individual study and indicate, for each:

    (a) its advantages;

    (b) its limitations;

    (c) the main aspects of its preparation;

    (d) the main aspects of its presentation.

4. What are the possible methods of evaluating your effectiveness using the lecture method of teaching?

Further Reading and References

Further reading and references relating to the topics in this chapter can be found in the following:

Brown, G   *Micro-teaching: A programme of teaching skills,* Methuen, 1975.

Dewey, J   *How we think: A restatement of the relation of reflective thinking and the education process*, D.C. Heath, New York. 1933

Gage, N.L. and   *Educational Psychology*, Rand McNally, 1975
Berliner, D.C.

Gibbs, G,   *53 Interesting Things to do in your Lectures*, Technical and Educational
Habeshaw, S and   Services, 1984.
Habeshaw, T.

Gibbs, G, and   *253 Ideas for Teaching*, Technical and Educational Services, 1988.
Habeshaw, T and
Habeshaw, T.

Habeshaw,S,   *53 Interesting Things to do in your Seminars and Tutorials,* Technical
Habeshaw, T, and   and Educational Services, 1984.
Gibbs, G.

Jacobsen, D Eggen,   *Methods for Teaching: A skills approach*, Charles ER Merrill
P, et al .   Publishing Co, 1981

Keller, F.S. and   *The Keller Plan Handbook: Essays on a personalised system of*
Sherman, J.G.   *instruction,* 1974

Neill, A.S.   *Summerhill: a radical approach to child rearing*, Hart Publishing, 1960.

Perrott, E   *Effective Teaching: A practical guide to improving your teaching,*
                         Longman, 1982.

Rose, P   *53 Interesting ways to Write Open Learning Material*, Technical and
                         Educational Services, 1992

Rogers, J(ed)   *Adults in Education*, BBC, 1978.

Walkin, L   *Instructional Techniques and Practice,* Stanley Thornes, 1990.

Chapter 4
Learning Aids

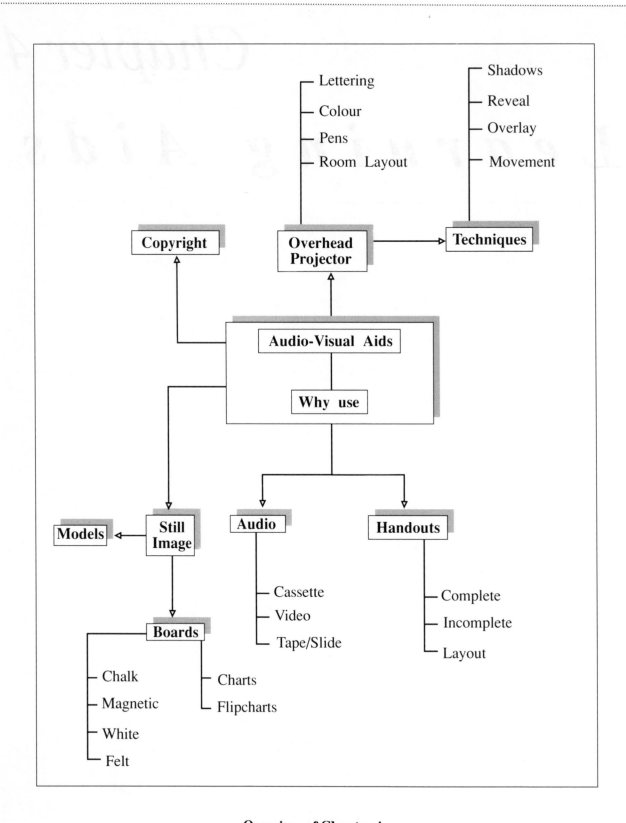

Overview of Chapter 4

Competences Related to this Chapter

The teacher competences and associated performance criteria related to this chapter are:

Major Competence – *'Produce, Use and Evaluate Learning Resources'*

COMPETENCE	*PERFORMANCE CRITERIA*
1. Establish a basis for choosing learning aids.	(a) Classify learning aids. (b) Identify the principles of using learning aids. (c) Use or adapt the environment to optimise the use of learning aids.
2. Use board aids properly.	(a) Establish advantages and limitations of six types of board aids. (b) Design appropriate layouts for use on board aids.
3. Use handouts appropriately.	(a) Classify different types of handout. (b) Establish principles for handout design. (c) Produce and use effective handouts for student use.
4. Use the overhead projector (OHP) appropriately.	(a) Design clear and useful transparencies for the OHP. (b) Use the projector in a way to promote learning.
5. Select, adapt or construct learning resources for a specific programme.	(a) Identify factors which affect choice of visual aids. (b) Consider production and duplication costs, type of audience and content in choice of aids.
6. Evaluate the use of learning resources.	(a) Establish and meet criteria for evaluating the effectiveness of chosen resources. (b) Evaluate learning resources used in relation to established criteria and cost of production and use.

1. What are Learning Aids and Resources?

In Chapter 1, we defined a resource as "a support to teaching strategies which assists learning". We also discussed the use of the different types of board (chalk, white and flipchart), handouts and OHP transparencies. In this Chapter, using a spiral curriculum, we want to return to the topic of aids and resources, to expand upon what we described earlier to include a fuller range of resources and discuss the principles of choice of aids and to evaluate their use.

Learning aids use all of the five senses. They use *hearing* through audio aids (like the cassette recorder), *sight* through visual aids like charts and posters and printed resources like handouts and books, *touch* through resources like specimens and models, and also, to a lesser extent, *taste* and *smell* in, for example, cookery. Also, more than one sense can be combined in a visual aid like a film or a tape-slide presentation which combine both hearing and sight. Thus, anything that you use to augment your teaching or learning strategy, or anything that you get your students to use, can be termed a learning aid or a resource.

There are a great range of resources that are available to you as a teacher. Some are indicated in Figure 4.1. You should consider (a) those that you have used, (b) those that you have not used and (c) those that you would like to use.

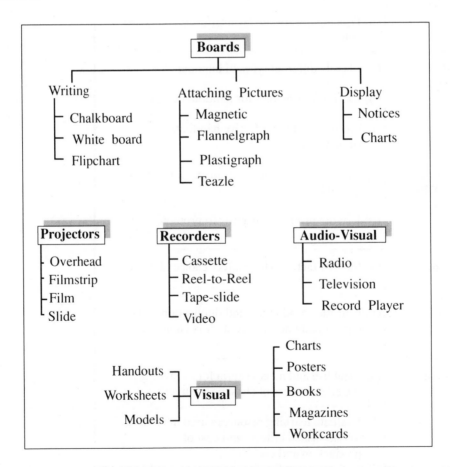

Figure 4.1   Range of Available Resources

1.1 Reasons for Using Learning Aids and Resources

As a new teacher you may say to yourself "Why bother with all of those visual aids? – I can manage without them". Of course it is possible to 'manage' without visual aids but effective use of aids can really enhance your students' learning experience. HMI reports are a rich source of advice, and these reports often link poor learning with the failure to use visual aids and similarly link effective learning to the professional use of well designed visual aids. The link between effective learning tends to be implicit rather than explicit. The inexperienced teacher tends, naturally to dwell on the subject matter – "What happens if I am asked a question on 'x'?" However, there is little doubt that use of more than one sense, for example both sight and sound, enhances understanding and memory. As long as you do not overload your students' sensory input, then the more senses you use the better.

If you consider the traditional methods of teaching, the lecturer standing in front of the class talking, then the main sense the students are using is hearing. Psychologists tell us that only about 12 per cent of what we learn comes in this way. In comparison, they also tell us that 75 per cent of what we learn comes through what we see. Thus, six times more of what we learn is through sight than through listening. This, in itself, has implications for the range of teaching strategies that you use. Do you provide six times the opportunity for learning by sight as you do learning through listening? Do you use visual pictures to accompany what you say? The television news is a good example of the use of pictures to associate with the spoken word. During the news there are invariably either picture stills associated with the news item, or, more often, video recordings of what is being talked about. Rarely do we only see the newscaster alone on the screen. Even when we do, there is often a still picture depicting the story in the background. It would be interesting to see if there were six times as much picture work as there is 'just newscaster' for any particular half hour associated with the six o'clock news programme. Because of the media such as TV, radio, magazines and so on, students are used to the more sophisticated presentation and productions and you, as a teacher, have to compete with this.

You may be tempted not to use some aids because they require a great deal of preparation before the session, they need items to be ordered, specialist rooms to be booked or technicians to be liaised with. All of this may seem to be too much bother. There is also a danger of being obsessed with equipment, or of making the aid more complicated than it needs to be through the use of sophisticated additions. You should aim to use an aid more than once so that the time spent on preparation will be worthwhile.

It is said that all good learning aids start in the mind of the teacher with the idea of putting over the subject matter in the most convenient way that makes the learning easy and interesting for both you and your students. Audio visual aids can be very stimulating to students and provide the often necessary variety to your teaching.

1.2 Speaking Time vs. Thinking Time

How many words per minute do you speak? If you speak very fast you might reach 200 words per minute but the average is much less than that –usually around 150 words per minute. Compare this with the number of words per minute that you can think. Psychologists tell us that the average thinking time is around 800 words per minute. So, there is a *differential* between *speaking time* and *thinking time*.

Consider one of your students listening to you when you are having a good day. You are talking to your students about a topic which has particular interest and relevance to them: they are motivated. They are listening to you talking at 160 words per minute but their minds can think much faster than that. So they are filling the differential between *your* speaking speed and *their* thinking speed by trying to anticipate what you are going to say next, by thinking how they can apply what you are saying in their projects or at work. That is on a good day.

Now consider one that is not so good. You are talking to them, for too long perhaps, about a topic which holds little interest to them and it is approaching lunch time, it is hot and they are hungry and thirsty. They start to listen to you but then say to themselves "What use is this to me? I will never use this topic." So they listen for a minute then their minds wander. "What shall I have for lunch? Shall I go to the canteen or just buy a sandwich at the snack bar?" They tune back in to you and realise that you are still on with the same boring topic. Their minds start to wander again. "What shall I do tonight. Shall I take my girl/boy friend to the cinema? What shall we do after we have been to the cinema?" This is a voyage upon which there is no return. The next thing that they hear is you saying "Thank you very much. I will see you next week" and the other students are putting their books together and leaving.

People *can* do two things at once. They can listen to you *and* they can do something else while they fill the differential between speaking and thinking speeds. The skill in teaching is that you have to fill that differential for your students in a meaningful manner so that they are using the differential to further concentrate upon the topic. This is the place for visual aids. You can provide students with a handout which they can relate to whilst you are talking or, even better, provide them with an incomplete one which they can fill in whilst listening to you. You can get them to take their own notes, draw a diagram during a demonstration or some other activity which will allow some of the differential between the two speeds to be filled.

2. Preparation of Learning Aids

Well designed learning aids should:-

1. *promote perception:*   by adding senses there is greater likelihood that the learner will perceive what is intended;

2. *promote understanding:*   with greater perception there is likely to be greater understanding;

3. *help reinforcement:*   when you use learning aids to supplement your spoken words, as they are invariably, there is more likelihood of repetition and reinforcement. The reinforcement can be both during the teaching (for example with a chalkboard) and after it has taken place (for instance reading from a handout);

4. *aid retention:*   as we said in Chapter 1, an important aspect of memory is repetition (remember learning your telephone number?). So, repetition leads to retention;

5. *motivate and arouse interest:*   as your students use more than one of their senses when you use visual aids, you are more likely to arouse their interest;

6. *provide variety in learning:*   the use of visual aids not only provides repetition, but repetition using a different medium. Hence the provision is more varied;

7. *make effective use of time:*   as students are more motivated and show greater interest, then more effective use will be made of the time they spend learning.

Visual aids should be:

1. simple;

2. to the point (and well related to learning intentions);

3. interesting.

An excellent visual aid is the map of the London Underground

- it is simple

- it makes good use of colour

- it is not accurate (in a geographical sense) but *representative*.

It does take time to make a good visual aid – but it will repay itself – it is relaxing to do – make a hobby of it.

2.1 Room Requirements

Having made and designed appropriate visual aids, it is necessary to show them to their best advantage. You may well have to put up with the accommodation that is allocated to you, but it is possible to make the best of it through the appropriate positioning of tables, chairs, desks and equipment to support your students' learning. All too often teachers tend to accept rooms as they are and do not make the necessary changes because it takes time and effort.

In order to motivate your students and allow them to concentrate upon their subject matter, you need to have a room that is :

- comfortable and quiet as possible;
- the right size for the number of students you have;
- adequately ventilated;
- acoustically good;and
- there should be no direct sunlight.

To apply these principles you should be able to move desks or tables about, have curtains or blinds at the windows, some covering on the floor, and chairs that are comfortable.

Your organisation of the room should depend on the number of students that you have. On the next page Figure 4.2 shows an optimum arrangement for up to 20 students, Figure 4.3 for between 20 and 30 and Figure 4.4 for more than 30

The arrangements shown in Figures 4.2 and 4.3 have the advantage that students have eye contact with each other. Consequently, with a relatively small class size, you can easily use question and answer and whole group discussion and the students will be able to see and hear what others are saying.

The arrangements shown in Figure 4.4 are, in effect, for lectures when the passage of information is from you, the teacher, to the students. The audience is too large for any meaningful interaction to take place and, in consequence, it does not matter that students are not able to see each other.

Each of the room layout diagrams have shown 'formal' arrangements. However, you will realise that many rooms are used as multi-functional accommodation, requiring a formal setting on one occasion and an

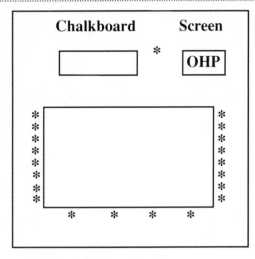

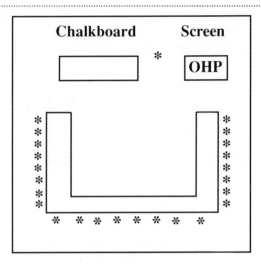

**Figure 4.2 Rectangular
Table for up to 20 Students**

**Figure 4.3 U-Shaped Arrangement
for up to 30 Students**

informal one on another. Usually, desks or tables are capable of being moved and there are great advantages in the less formal arrangements shown in Figures 4.2 and 4.3.

You need to be careful in your siting of both a chalkboard and a screen. Students must be able to see both of these aids clearly and so your position must not obscure their vision of either. This means that you should stand slightly behind the overhead projector, as we show in the diagrams.

This leads us to consider your ability to move about the classroom. It is important, when you move furniture, to consider your ability to move freely about the whole of the room as opposed to just standing at the front. Moving to the back of the class allows you to have a 'student's eye view' of the aids.

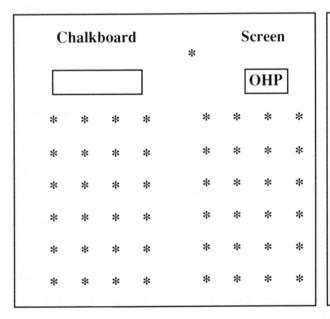

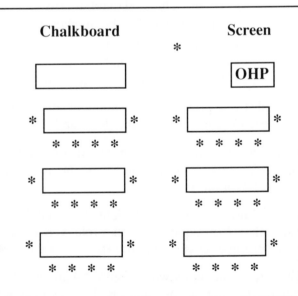

Figure 4.4 Theatre or School-Type Seating for Larger Audiences

> *Possible Evidence to Show You have*
> *Achieved the Competence 'Establish a*
> *Basis for Choosing Learning Aids'*

The type of evidence that you might collect to show that you have achieved the competence involves:

(a) State the learning aids that you:

(i) already use; and

(ii) would like to use

under the following headings:

boards;
projectors;
recorders
visual.

(b) For a lesson plan that you have designed:

(i) decide which aids will assist learning;

(ii) state why you will use them.

State why you have chosen a particular type of test question.

Progress Check

> *If you want to check your understanding of your role in establishing a basis for choosing learning aids, try the following progress check*

Progress Check 4.1

1. State three different types of learning aid under thefollowing headings:

    (a) Boards;
    (b) Projectors;
    (c) Recorders;
    (d) Visual.

2. Give at least SIX important aspects that well designed learning aids should achieve in the teaching and learning environment.

3. How many words per minute are, on average associated with:

    (a) speaking; and
    (b) thinking.

4. Give the advantages and limitations of three different types of room layout, stating, in each case, the size of group for which the layout is most appropriate.

3. Boards

Boards are probably the most popular and most used of all visual aids. The are quick and easy to use and are available in 99% of teaching accommodation. However, they are probably the most *misused* as well. It is all too easy to jot hurried notes on them; complete a quick sketch; or to place student responses to questions on them. To used them well, however, you need to plan carefully and be neat when using them.

There are several types of board in use:

1. Chalkboard

2. Whiteboard

3. Feltboard

4. Magnetic board

5. Flipchart

Boards are in widespread use because of their advantages:

- always available
- easy to alter and amend work;
- versatile - suits any subject;
- colour is able to be used;
- simple;
- cheap;
- students can see the build-up of diagrams;
- easily cleaned;
- no special equipment required;

The disadvantages are few:

- many people have a tendency to 'talk to the board' as they write;
- you cannot see the students as you write;
- your writing needs to be larger than normal;
- if your presentation is unplanned it can be untidy;
- your notes on the board do not provide a permanent record.

You should remember that what you put on the board tends to go into your students notes in the same form. If your writing or drawing is untidy, if you have not drawn parallel lines when they should be parallel, if you have got half incomplete rubbing out, how can you expect your student's work to be neat and accurate

At various times during the lesson, it is useful to go to the back of the room to make sure that your writing and drawings are visible to all of the class, that your writing does not drop towards the right hand side and that you have no spelling mistakes. It is only really from the rear of the class that you can get a true indication of the worth of your chalkboard work.

3.1 Chalkboard

These tend to be either rollerboards or fixed boards. Coloured chalk is very useful but make sure that the colours you use are visible. The main drawback of the chalkboard is that you, and your belongings, tend to be covered in dust – even with dustless chalk. It can be very uncomfortable to those who suffer with a dust allergy.

You can rotate the roller-board around top and bottom rollers. This has the advantage that it increases the amount of space that you have available through the up and down movement that is possible, as well as your being able to push up what you have just written to make it more visible to students. You also do not obscure what you have already written when you put more writing onto the board. A further advantage is that the height of the board can be adjusted to suit your own size. I wonder how many of us have either had to stretch to reach the top of a board or, alternatively, stoop to reach the bottom of it, depending whether we are over six feet in height or under five feet. The advantage of the rollerboard type is that it can be made just the right height for you to be able to write on. This right height is your eye level. If you write at eye level, and walk along the board as you write, your lines should be straight and not drooping towards the end in an arc as you stretch.

However a corresponding fault of this type of board is that, when you rotate it, some of the writing that you have just completed goes over the back of the board and is obscured from the view of the students. You must be careful to aviod 'losing' important material in this way.

For difficult shapes you can use a template made from card or plywood. Such shapes might be, for example, a map of British Isles, a waveform, the human body, or any shape that you constantly draw and it is difficult to achieve quickly and accurately. For some diagrams you can prepare the board using the 'pounce' method. First you draw the diagram (or a pattern of it) on paper and put small holes in the outline. Then before the lesson, you fix the paper pattern to the board and 'pat' the outline with the board duster so that when the pattern is removed it reveals an outline of dots that you can see but the students cannot. At the appropriate time during the lesson you can join up the dots to give the required, accurate outline.

We have already discussed the layout of information on the chalkboard in Chapter 1. It is sufficient here to say that chalkboards are usually either black or green and probably the most effective colour of chalk on this background is *not* white as might be expected, but yellow. However, as we said in Chapter 1, the use of colour for highlighting and drawing distinctions between different aspects is very useful so long as you do not overdo it.

3.2 Whiteboard

Whiteboards are becoming more popular and are tending to replace chalkboards. They are used for exactly the same purpose and the principles of their use are the same. However, they are clean, bright and look modern. They have better visibility than the chalkboard especially when you use colour as they are more like a book with dark print on a white background. Additionally the white background gives the classroom a brighter atmosphere compared to the black of the chalkboard. They have all of the advantages of the chalkboard with very little dust. Beware! you must use a drymarker – that is a non permanent pen. The pens that are used for flipcharts look very similar but if you use one on a whiteboard surface you will not be able to rub it out with a dry duster (in fact you will only be able to remove it with spirit). If you are unsure which type you are about to use, test the marker on a small area and, if you can rub it out easily with your finger, you know that it is a drymarker. You can also use whiteboards as OHP screens but you must be careful of any glare that might be produced from the bright light. Many whiteboards have a steel backing which means they can be used as a magnetic board as well and we will discuss their use later. Writing on whiteboards tends to be more difficult than on chalkboards because there is less surface resistance. It is a little like using a ballpoint pen for the first time when you have been used to a fountain pen. You will find that the pens tend to 'flow' over the surface of the board. 'Poor' writers therefore tend to be even poorer when using a whiteboard. If you have not used one before, have a practise before you use it in front of a class of students.

You can use a whiteboard with an OHP. You can project the OHP slide of, say, the outline of a statistical table, or a diagram of an organisation onto the whiteboard and then use question and answer and write on the whiteboard. This is a very effective technique but, again, be careful of the glare.

3.3 Magnetic board

The great advantage of magnetic boards is that you can use them to depict movement. For instance, consider teaching a group of naval students how to dock three or more navy ships in harbour. What better way than making models of ships and sticking magnets to them, drawing the outline of the coast and harbour on a magnetic board, showing the movement of the ships in formation and the required docking procedures with which should be first, second, and so on and how they might tie-up together? Other examples where you could use movement to some advantage on a magnetic board are the formation and joining of atoms, addition of sinusoidal waveforms, magnetic fields, ploughing a field, indeed, any application where you need to show movement.

You should not just use the magnetic board when you want to show movement. You could cut out pictures from magazines or outlines could be cut from coloured card. Stick magnetic tape to the undersides, for display on the board. For example consider the concept formation of herbs in a horticulture class. You could cut out magazine pictures of basil, dill, parsley, rosemary, thyme, and marjoram and display them randomly with lettuce, tomato, cucumber and turnip. You can then ask your students to come to the front of the class and classify them into herbs and non-herbs.

While many whiteboards can be used as magnetic boards any steel surface will do, for example a filing cabinet, metal cupboard, or the like. You can use magnets to secure posters, diagrams, and so on. However, magnetic tape is available. This is produced in rolls and you cut off the length you require. The self adhesive part goes onto the back of the picture allowing it to be positioned on the board. The pictures and/or words may be moved around easily and repositioned. The whole effect is flexible and realistic.

3.4 Feltboard

The feltboard, using an old blanket and sandpaper stapled or stuck to pictures, is the 'poorman's' magnetic board. It is less fashionable now due to the more widespread use of magnetic boards but used to be used a lot to depict movement. It operates on the same principle as your child's 'Fuzzyfelt' farm animals and consists of two pieces of felt, one of which is background and the other is the shape, which will stick together.

The more modern version uses 'Velcro'. You can use flock paper to cut out the shapes. The flock side adheres to the felt. Again, the shapes and outlines can be moved many times. If no flock paper is available, sandpaper may be stuck or stapled to the display item.

4. Charts

Charts make an attractive display in a teaching base room. You can cover all of the walls with materials which are of interest and are informative to the students. You can make changes regularly depending upon the stage of the course you have reached. As the topic changes, the charts change. Charts form a useful, often colourful display.

Excellent charts are now available, often free of charge, from some manufacturers, for example you can get a cutaway drawing of a gearbox. These are very professionally produced , colourful and use a good grade of paper, often laminated, so that they last and are hard-wearing. However, there are techniques that you can use to make quite a professional job of 'home-made' charts. When you make your own, card is relatively cheap but you may have to use a stencil to help with the lettering. If you cannot draw very well – do not despair. Trace a diagram from a book onto an OHP sheet and project it onto a piece of card. You can then draw around the image that is projected and colour it to give it a professional finish. You can even add lettering using a stencil to give it a more polished look. Alternatively photocopy the picture from the book using a plain-paper copier onto an OHP transparency so that you do not need the tracing part. This has the added advantage that you also have the OHP transparency for class use at the appropriate time. So, you don't have to be a first class artist to produce a very acceptable chart to hang on the walls of your classrooms.

Figure 4.5 shows a different type of chart; notices to be placed at strategic points to indicate the location of the class for the first meeting. You can make these colourful and with interesting shapes so that they catch the eye of the passer-by.

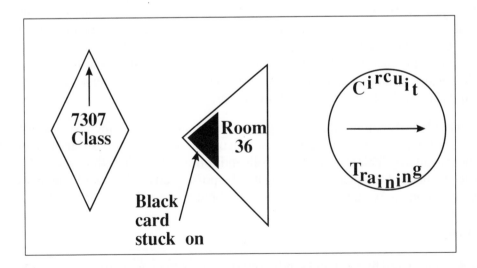

Figure 4.5 - Notice for the First Class Meeting

We have already said that charts should be regularly changed so that they maintain impact . They need therefore to be stored until they are required for the next class. Because of their size they are difficult to store. Ideally they need to be kept flat and out of sunlight. Alternatively, roll them up and place them safely in a cupboard.

4.1 Flipcharts

Flipcharts are essentially large pieces of paper placed on a stand and used instead of a white, or chalk, board. After the initial investment in the easel/stand, the flipchart:

- is low cost as you only need the paper and pens;

- is simple to use, just like writing with pen and paper and, when one piece of paper is full, you just take another sheet;

- is easy to transport from one location to another or across the room to the most appropriate location;

- is unlikely to go wrong (or can it?) as there are no working parts or electricity required;

- can be used with charts, diagrams, and so on or whatever you wish to draw;

- is suitable for use with photos or colour pictures as 'stick-ons';

- allows you to use the reveal technique by sticking pieces of paper over the parts that are not to be seen straight away and then peeling them off as required;

- can be prepared before the lesson so that you can take your time over neatness. Also, in this way they can be reused;

- can be semi-prepared (incomplete) so that you can complete it during the lesson.

The disadvantages are that flipcharts are:

- bulky to transport (depending upon make);

- difficult to store;

- much smaller than a chalkboard which can be difficult to get used to.

It is a very flexible tool and especially useful if teaching away from your usual place – even when no electricity is available– what can go wrong(!)

> *Possible Evidence to Show You have Achieved*
> *the Competence*
> *'Use Board Aids Appropriately'*

The type of evidence that you might collect to show that you have achieved the competence involves:

(a) State six types of board aids indicating, with reasons, which you have used and which you haven't used.

(b) State three advantages and three limitations of using THREE different types of board aids.

(c) With one of your classes, use TWO different types of board aid and, for each:

　(i) describe the layout that you have used;

　(ii) give reasons for your chosen design.

*If you want to check your understanding of your
role in using board aids appropriately,
try the following progress check*

Progress Check 4.2

1. State six different types of board aids.

2. Give at least SIX important aspects that well designed learning aids should achieve in the teaching and learning environment.

3. State three advantages and three limitations of using THREE different types of board aids.

4. Why should charts be:

   (i) displayed in teaching rooms; and

   (ii) changed frequently?

5. Handouts

Teachers vary in their views about handouts from 'essential' to 'the students file them and never read them'.

The copying of notes or diagrams from a chalkboard or OHP transparency is not usually effective use of class contact time. Class contact time is valuable and handouts are one means whereby this time can be saved. However, handouts take time to prepare and are relatively expensive. Consequently, once the decision has been taken to use handouts, you should ensure that they save class contact time.

Also, you should try to make them visually attractive and include some form of activity associated with them (for example incompleteness) so that your students have to use them. They should be 'user friendly' through the use of language and vocabulary that the students can understand. Any new terms should be defined. Sketches and drawings can replace a relatively large number of words. If you give instructions, ensure they are clear and correct – trial test them! Use space and borders to good effect so that the page is not covered with words.

Handouts tend to be used a good deal. They can be used in a variety of ways:

- directly related to lesson content;
- supporting - to introduce the lesson;
- contain relevant (complex) formula;
- as a reading list;
- as a worksheet/jobsheet/operation sheet;
- information sheets - presenting rare or hard to find information.

There are different types of handout but all have one thing in common: they should help the student. *Information handouts* are used to provide students with data and facts. There are three main types:

Notes: these are directly related to the lesson content, for example the main points of a lesson;

Supporting: an introduction to a topic, definitions, complex formulae, graphs, tables and diagrams;

Reading lists: which can be related to the course as a whole or to an individual topic.

A *worksheet* is an incomplete handout which the student is expected to complete during or straight after the lesson. They can be used by individual students which economise of teacher's time allowing time for individual attention. They allow students to work at their own pace, in an independent manner.

Worksheets:

(i)   can save you repeating yourself especially if the students are working at different rates;

(ii)   need to be foolproof or have been tried and tested.

There are several types of worksheet:

(i)   *Job Sheets:* which contain instructions or a specification so that a student can complete a piece of work. An example of a job sheet might be a specification for making a skirt or other article of clothing. Here the instructions are given so that students can complete the article on their own.

An alternative which can be completed by students is shown in the example in Figure 4.6. Completion can be achieved through inserting words in spaces left for the purpose for homework, through exposition as the lesson proceeds or by having an associated OHP transparency on which you can write in the appropriate words in the spaces as you go through each of the steps.

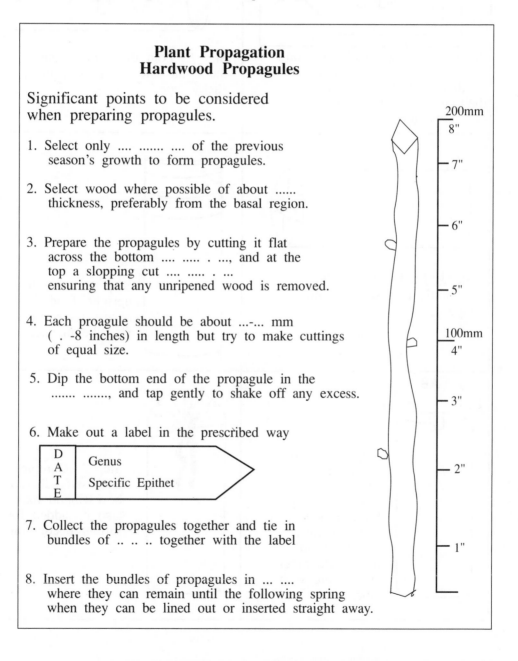

Plant Propagation
Hardwood Propagules

Significant points to be considered when preparing propagules.

1. Select only .... of the previous season's growth to form propagules.

2. Select wood where possible of about ...... thickness, preferably from the basal region.

3. Prepare the propagules by cutting it flat across the bottom ...., and at the top a slopping cut .... ensuring that any unripened wood is removed.

4. Each proagule should be about ...-... mm (. -8 inches) in length but try to make cuttings of equal size.

5. Dip the bottom end of the propagule in the ...., and tap gently to shake off any excess.

6. Make out a label in the prescribed way

| D A T E | Genus |
| Specific Epithet |

7. Collect the propagules together and tie in bundles of .. .. .. together with the label

8. Insert the bundles of propagules in ... . where they can remain until the following spring when they can be lined out or inserted straight away.

200mm
8"
7"
6"
5"
100mm
4"
3"
2"
1"

Figure 4.6 Example Jobsheet - Incomplete Handout

Figure 4.7 Example Operation Sheet Showing Step-by-Step Instructions

(ii) *Operation Sheets*: are used to explain a process or series of operations like how to take blood pressure, how to operate a photocopier, or the 'Decorative Bottle Wrapping' shown in Figure 4.7.

The example shows how each step is highlighted with both pictorial and verbal instructions associated with each of the steps. This seeming repetition ensures that the instructions can be followed where some students (the 'visualisers') will follow the pictures, others (the 'verbalisers') will follow the words, while most will use both the pictures AND the words to ensure understanding. The layout is clear with good use being made of 'white space'. Thus, after a demonstration (or even without one) a students can work on their own to complete the Bottle Wrapping.

(iii) *Assignment Sheets*:usually consisting of a number of questions, problems or tasks to be performed;

(iv) *Experiment Sheets*: frequently used in laboratory work although the 'recipe' approach should be avoided.

Whatever type of handout is used, they should be well designed and checked for errors.

The danger of handouts is that they are distributed and the learner never reads them. To overcome this, the handout should have some learner activity included, for example:

- leave blanks – students have to listen for or find key facts/words etc.;
- give the learner time to read and then ask for a summary;
- or use questions and answers;
- follow with a test.

> *Possible Evidence to Show You have Achieved the*
> *Competence 'Use Handouts aids appropriately'*

The type of evidence that you might collect to show that you have achieved the competence involves:

(a)   Choose THREE different handouts that you have designed and used with your students. For each of them:

    (i)   classify them into either worksheets or information handouts;

    (ii)   describe how each of them was used in your lesson(s); and

    (iii)   explain what students did with them.

(b)   Explain the general design principles that you use when making your handouts.

> *If you want to check your understanding of your role in using handouts appropriately, try the following progress*

Progress Check 4.3

1. Define each of the following:

    (i)   information handout;

    (ii) worksheet.

2. State at least FOUR different types of worksheet.

3. List at least three different types of student activity that might usefully be associated with their completion of a handout.

4. State at least THREE advantages of using handouts with students.

6. The Overhead Projector (OHP)

When to use an OHP

The OHP is in widespread use and has been so for many years. It can be used in a number of ways:

- as a record of discussion through the noting of key points as the lesson proceeds (that is, using it like a chalkboard);

- as a summary at the end of a lesson especially when objectives have been noted in the introduction. At the end these can then become a basis of a question and answer to see how much has been learned;

- to reproduce a chart or map or some other type of prepared material which would take some time to draw in the lesson;

- to build up materials using an overlay technique which is similar to building up a complex drawing as the lesson proceeds except that you can take time and care in its preparation;

- to develop an argument which is similar to the complex drawing above except that it contains key words or phrases;

- can be linked with incomplete handout as suggested in Figure 4.6 to ensure that students read and use the handout when they are completing it;

Merits and Limitations

Its *merits* include;

- it is readily available;
- can be used in daylight conditions;
- it is reliable;
- user can see the learners - observe reaction;
- observe behaviour;
- easy to store transparencies;
- OHT's (OverHead Transparencies) last a long time;
- can make own to suit exact needs; can be colourful;
- can show movement;
- high quality especially when using a photocopier (enlarge/reduce).

The *limitations* include:

- can be noisy due to the fan which operates all of the time to cool the bulb;

- can generate heat/draught from the fan;
- needing a screen or light coloured wall onto which to shine the image. This can be a disadvantage when sun shines onto the image surface. The screen should not be placed in the direct light but a silver screen can be used where the daylight is strong

6.1 Care of an OHP

Care needs to be taken with OHPs:

- do not move them when hot. This can damage the bulb;
- do be careful of the cable so that you, yourself, or your students do not trip over the trailing wire;
- do not 'open' OHP to change the bulb unless the institution allows you (Health & Safety), and, if you do, ensure that it is switched off at the mains and the plug is removed;
- do not handle the bulb directly (use a soft cloth) as the grease from your fingers will cause a 'hot spot' on the glass from the intense heat that is produced;

It is good practice to check the room first in order to make sure that the projector works, to focus the projector, to ensure that the screen is visible from all parts of the room, and to make sure the projector is clean and not covered in chalk dust.

The projector and screen should be positioned to avoid keystoning effect (where the image is wider at the top of the screen than it is at the bottom). This can be achieved by slanting the screen away from the wall at the top (see Figure 4.8). The keystone effect can be eliminated if the light beam projected by the OHP is at right angles to the screen

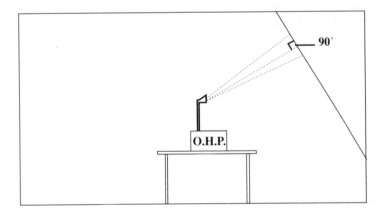

Figure 4.8 Positioning of OHP to Avoid Keystoning

You can use the OHP with the whiteboard as a screen. The OHP gives the outline of, say, a statistical table, a map of the country, and you, or the learners, can write on the whiteboard and build up the image. However, the whiteboard may have a surface which reflects some light which appears as a bright spot - hence limited vision.

6.2 Using the OHP

When using the OHP:

- switch off when the image is not needed in order to reduce any possible distraction due to glare and noise;

- keep out of the way of the image by standing, neither in front or behind the projector, but to one side of it;

- use a pointer on the top of the OHP to indicate key points rather than pointing to the screen. When you point to the screen you obscure part of the image by standing in front of it. Even resting a pencil on the top of the OHP is effective;

- give your students a chance to see the whole image before you start talking. This provides an 'advance organiser' for the students and can assist them in making their own notes;

- keep the caps on the OHP pens so that they do not dry up quickly due to evaporation from the heat of the room and the projector;

- don't mix up your transparencies – have a system. Pick up from left hand side - place on projector, remove and store on right hand side.

- try to involve the learners in your presentation of the transparencies. This might be achieved through question and answer, leaving spaces for either yourself or the students to complete, or just through expecting them to make their own notes;

- link with incomplete handouts as was suggested with Figure 4:6. This helps with the involvement of the students.

6.3 Design Principles

The following design principles are valuable:

- keep it simple;

- not too much information in words;

- not too many drawings;

- not too much detail;

- one topic at most per transparency;

- design on plain paper before making the transparency;

- put the main idea in the middle of the image;

- ensure an adequate space at each edge of the transparency;

- simple words – key words instead of sentences;

- not all upper-case – use both lower and upper case.

The example shown in Figure 4.9 tries to follow the above design principles for a session dealing with 'Design of OHTs'.

From the example, there is a heading (which should always be there even if it is a continuation sheet) at the top, it is simple and the focal point is in the centre. You should remember that the transparency should not transmit *all* of the information, but *only* be a basis for reminding you of the important points of your exposition and as an aid to students structuring their notes.

Skills in Making Transparencies

Making OHTs demands a whole new set of skills. If you are a good artist to begin with, then so much the better - you will already have a clear appreciation of design principles.. But you do not need to be a good artist, there are many ways in which you can 'cheat' to produce a very professional effect.

Lettering may be achieved by:

- using computer or desk top publishing (make original on plain paper and use a photocopier with special OHT original). This produces a good quality but colour is not possible;

- dry letter e.g. *Letraset*. Good quality and available in colour. Letters and diagrams tend to age and crack;

- stencil – should be used with a drawing board. The quality is high but it can be time consuming;

- freehand using pens. Quality depends upon handprinting/handwriting but colour can easily be added;

- Remember that the size of lettering is important and the following can be used as a guide:

  * 5 mm lettering seen from 10 metres max

  * 10 mm lettering seen from 10-15 metres max

  * 15 mm lettering seen from 15-20 metres max

Pens

Pens may be permanent (i.e. spirit based) or non-permanent (i.e. water based). These can be used as follows:

- Alterations may be made when you use spirit-based pens using an alcohol-based fluid or an OHP rubber/eraser;

Design Principles for an OHT

1. *Only one subject per sheet.*
   (Max 6 lines of six words)

2. *Lettering – clear, large, lower case*
   and consistent.

3. *Colour – some but not too much.*
   Choose suitable colour for the
   purpose.

Figure 4.9   Example OHT using Design Principles

- Water-based are easily changed. Unfortunately perspiration on hands removes the image. Ideal to have a permanent structure using spirit based pens and add temporary information using water based pens which may be removed before the OHP is used the next time.

Pens are available in various thicknesses:

- superfine - ideal for detail and lettering;
- fine;
- medium;
- broad – ideal for main headings;

You need to experiment with each and decide on the range which suits you. Store pens in the upright position, caps firmly on, away from heat or sunlight. Special compasses are available if you wish to draw circles e.g. for pie charts. Templates are also available which help with drawing a wide variety of shapes. Highlighters are even available which have been especially designed for use on OHPs.

Colour often improves an OHT. It may be achieved using pens – (tends to be streaked) or with highlighters and colour film.

Colour Film

When colouring large areas with a pen (such as the different segments of a pie chart) it can prove difficult to achieve the same density of colour throughout. Colour film is material which can be cut to shape to colour areas on your transparency and is an alternative to colouring-in large areas with a pen. It comes in a range of colours. At first it appears to be expensive but it does seem to last a long time.

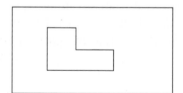 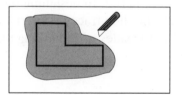 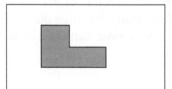

To colour an 'L' shape first draw the shape on an acetate sheet. Then roughly cut out a piece of colour film and stick it over the drawn 'L' shape. Finally, using a craft or stanley knife and a metal ruler, cut to the exact outline. The skill is using just the right pressure – to cut the colour film but not the transparency. Three colours on any transparency is sufficient.

Overlay Technique

Overlays help you to present complex issues. The base OHT is attached to a card frame and the overlaps can then be positioned. Masking tape gives a firm line whereas sellotape ages, bubbles and cracks. A maximum of 5 sheets is advised.

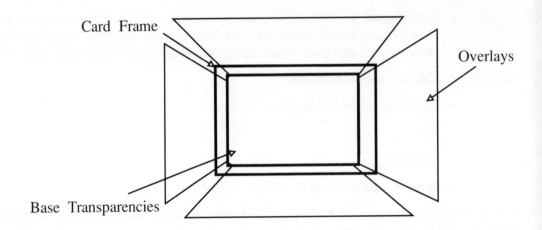

Card Frame

Overlays

Base Transparencies

Overlay are ideal for:

- Bricklaying;
- Circuits (electrical/hydraulic);
- Maths solutions;
- Maps;
- Graphs;
- Chessboards, etc.

The example shown in Figure 4.10 indicates how you might design an overlay. You need to use a number of transparencies (two in the example). The first one (a) has the title and the first part to be shown (Part 1) while the second (b) has the addition of part 2. In designing the overlay it is an advantage if you draw the whole thing first on a piece of paper and then trace first part 1 (a) and then part 2 (b). The two (or as many as you have, can then be hinged at the sides with masking tape to ensure that the parts fall over in place easily.

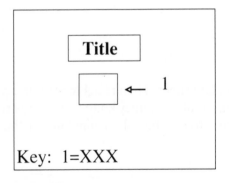

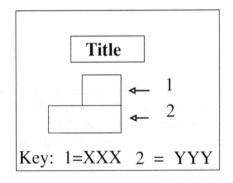

(a) Showing Part 1   **(b) Adding Part 2**

Figure 4.10   Transparency Overlay Technique

Reveal Technique

A reveal technique is where part of the transparency is initially shown, then a little more, and so on until all is revealed. A piece of tracing paper may be used to cover what you wish to reveal. This allows you to see what is covered - but which is not projected. Plain paper may be used under the OHT as an alternative. Strips of card or paper may be used to mask lines or key sections or you may reveal area by area. In the example transparency shown in Figure 4.11, first the main title would be shown by covering up all of the material other than the title with tracing paper. While it is revealed, you would explain the title, its importance to the students (why it was being discussed). The paper can then be pulled down to reveal the first sub-title, then each of the lines one at a time so that each is explained, commented upon and applied to a specific situation. You proceed in this way until all of the transparency has been revealed. The use of the reveal technique ensures that students concentrate on a particular aspect of the transparency at a particular time.

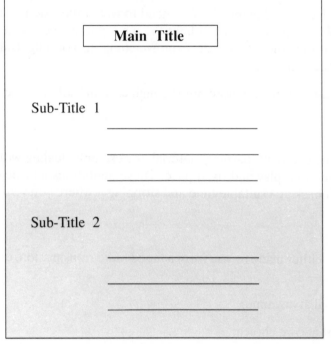

Figure 4.11 Reveal Technique

Transparency Storage

Storing OHTs need not be difficult. Card frames are very useful and special ring binders and boxes may be bought. You can write on the frames any notes you may wish to make.

A4 wallets/Sleeves are relatively cheap and have the advantage of having 'multiholes' so that they can be stored in a ring binder. Do remember to buy glass quality so that the image is projected through the wallet.

Silhouette Effect

The OHP can be used to produce shadows e.g. of a leaf, layout of a room cut in card, moving figures/mechanisms etc. This silhouette effect can be very impressive. Animation can be achieved e.g. clock with pointers. A most effective example is demonstrating magnetic fields using magnets and iron filings. Be certain to have a blank OHT on the projector first so that you can remove the iron filings.

7. Other Techniques

7.1 Video

Videos are being used more and more in teaching. Unfortunately, this powerful medium is often used as a time-filler to keep the learners quiet for an hour. It has taken over from 8 or 16 mm films with the advent of television, having the advantage that it can be shown in daylight conditions. This means that students can take notes (or complete a handout) whilst they are watching.

Videos should be used with care and planning. You need to watch the video yourself prior to showing it to a class. From this initial showing you can highlight the main points, see if you want to show all of it or just parts, and decide what the students will do from watching it. You might also design an associated (incomplete) handout to accompany it.

Interactive video is being used more and more but the high cost and solo use are drawbacks.

7.2 Audio materials

The radio can provide some excellent learning material, for example dealing with politics. The problems are fixed transmission time, no replay and fixed pace. These limitations may be overcome by taping the transmission and playing it back at a suitable time and stopping it where you want to.

7.3 Audio Cassettes

The use of audio cassettes, either made by you from a taped radio transmission, or bought specially for the purpose, allows you to:

- use of material at any time;
- stop and start at own choice;
- replay;
- edit.

It is widely used for foreign language training and special language laboratories are used for the purpose where students have their own headphones and can start and stop the tape themselves. This allows an activity to be built into the process where students can speak the foreign language and hear themselves using a playback facility. In these laboratories, the teacher can 'tune in' to any particular students and monitor their progress.

7.4 Tape Slide Programmes

The use of audio cassettes can be supplemented by 35mm slides so that the showing of the slides can have an accompanying commentary. The two can be synchronized so that a pulse on the tape will automatically change to the next slide.

Tape-Slide can be made by most people. It is relatively cheap.

The pictures may be taken by yourself or they may be bought.

This medium is ideal to recap on a visit to a factory, foreign location or field trip where you have taken slides which can be shown to the class to remind them of specific points.

7.5 Use of IT

Information Technology, particularly the use of computers has greatly enhanced the ability of the individual teacher to produce quality visual aids. The word processor (WP) is much more widely used than ever the typewriter was and you should at least have a working knowledge of it and you should be able to use the keyboard with a certain amount of skill. Most teachers have access to a personal computer (PC) with a word processing package attached. This has resulted in much better production of handouts. The use of Desktop Publishing (DTP), although not as common as word processing, is available in most organisations and an increasing number of teachers are familiar with its use. The use of DTP packages gives an even more enhanced production of handouts than the use of the WP. It also has the added advantage that diagrams and pictures can be added quite easily.

The use of DTP enables different character fonts to be used. Thus, you can design your own OHP transparencies with a font size appropriate for projection onto a classroom screen. The computer print can be directly transferred onto a transparency using the appropriate materials on a plain paper copier.

*Possible Evidence to Show You have Achieved
the Competence
'Use the Overhead Projector appropriately'*

The type of evidence that you might collect to show that you have achieved the competence involves:

(a)   Choose THREE different overhead projector transparencies that you have used with your students. For each of them:

    (i)   state how you made them (e.g. drawn freehand, traced from books, what type of pens you used);

    (ii)   describe how each of them was used in your lesson(s); and

    (iii) explain what students did with them.

(b)   Explain the general design principles that you used when making your transparencies.

(c)   Explain how you set up the room to use the overhead projector.

*If you want to check your understanding of
your role in using the
overhead projector appropriately,
try the following progress check*

Progress Check 4.4

1. List FOUR advantages and TWO limitations of the use of the overhead projector

2. List FOUR different ways in which the overhead projector might be used as a learning aid.

3. List at least FIVE principles of design of overhead projector transparencies.

4. Describe the difference between water and spirit-based overhead projector pens.

5. Explain at least TWO different techniques that you might use for the production of an overhead projector transparency.

6. Describe what is meant by 'reveal' and 'overlay' techniques.

8. Copyright

There is a tremendous amount of printed and recorded material available and some of it is ideal for teaching purposes. The use of photocopiers, video recorders and other relatively recent technical innovations have made it easy and cheap to make copies of these works. However, the need to protect copyright is important if we wish people to keep publishing and making valuable works. Copyright law is a specialist area of law and, before making copies, you need to be clear about your right to do so. If you work for a college or training organisation you should be able to seek guidance from your management colleagues.

Briefly, copyright is a right given to or derived from work and not a right in the novelty of ideas. The types of materials included under copyright include:

- literary works, written and including written tables or compilations;
- music works;
- dramatic works;
- artistic works;
- sound recordings;
- films;
- broadcasts;
- published editions.

An exception to copyright is for 'fair dealing' which in this case means research or private study. You are allowed to make one copy of anything which is protected under copyright so long as it is only for your own research or your own private study. Also, you are allowed to copy part of a document, so long as it is *not a substantial part* of the work. This, however, is not very helpful to us as the definition of a 'substantial part' is open to interpretation. A substantial part could be 'the most vital part' of a book, the main thesis, even though in terms of volume, it is not a large proportion.

However, many colleges and institutions, through their Local Education Authorities, have a CLA (Copyright Licensing Agency) Licence which allows them to copy 'for immediate use in no more than one course of study in any academic year:

- up to one chapter or (if greater) 5% of a book

- up to the number of copies required for the personal use by each member of the class plus the teacher ...'

Clearly this scheme is of major benefit to us but, before using this process, you should ensure that your organisation is a member of the scheme and you should read the conditions very carefully.

9. Selection of Visual Aids

Having described some of the important design characteristics of a range of visual aids, it is necessary for you to select a particular type of aid for a specific purpose.

Unfortunately, like so many aspects of teaching, there are no definitive answers for the selection of a particular aid. The design of aids starts in your own mind. A good aid is one which does a particular job to assist in the learning of a particular topic for a particular group of learners. But all learners are different. So, what works for one group does not necessarily work with another. However, there are some general rules that you can use as a guide.

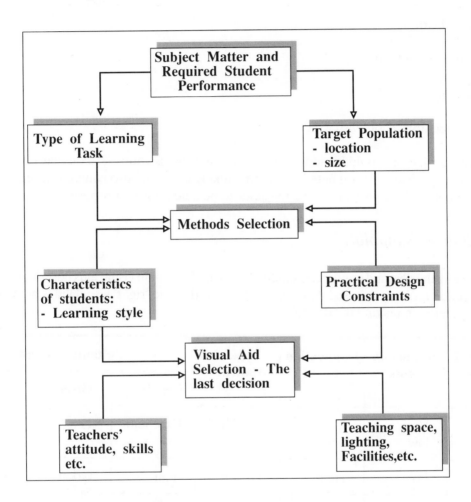

Figure 4.12 Factors Affecting the Choice of Visual Aids

9.1 Factors Affecting Choice of Visual Aids.

Some of the factors affecting the choice of visual aids are shown in Figure 4:13. First, the choice of a particular method will often dictate (or at least limit), the choice of aids. For example, if you decide to use a method involving group discussion and the sharing of experiences, then obviously the use of a one-direction medium such as a film would not be suitable as it limits the opportunity to exchange ideas. Secondly, the type of learning task facing the learner will eventually influence the choice of visual aid because it dictates the choice of teaching method. Thirdly, the special characteristics of some learners will also bear an influence on choice. For example it would be unrealistic to instruct a group of slow readers using handouts. Finally, the practical constraints, both administrative and economic, will limit the choice of methods and aids. It appears reasonable, therefore, to consider:

> teaching methods;

> learners;

> type of learning;

> practical considerations;

> *and then*

> make decisions about visual aids

Perhaps one further factor should be added to the list - and that is yourself. You may either love or hate using the overhead projector. If you hate it, you are unlikely to use it. Also you may have no training in its use and be afraid of it. Thus, you must have the skills to be able to use it properly.

Cost and Content Suitability

Figure 4.13 reviews the cost and content suitability for each of the main visual aids described in this chapter. These two selection tools can be used with some assurance that the 'right' visual aid is being selected if all factors are considered in making the decision.

Type of Aid	Production Costs	Duplication Costs	Type of Audience	Suitable Content		
				Cognitive	Affective	Motor
Handouts	Very low	Very low	Individual	Excellent	Fair	Good
Boards	Low	High	Group	Fair	Good	Poor
OHP	Mod low	Low	Group	Fair	Fair	Fair
Film/ TV/video	High	High	Group or Individual	Good	Poor	Fair
Charts	Low	Low	Group	Fair	Poor	Poor
Work card	Low	Low	Individual	Fair	Poor	Good

Figure 4.13 Suitability Factors of Common Visual Aids

Evidence that you might collect to show that you have achieved the competence
'Select, adapt or construct learning resources for a specific programme'.

(a) Identify and present a number (at least three) lesson plans which use a range of learning resources.

Justify the choice of resources in relation to the objectives of the sessions.

(b) Identify the constraints and problems that might exist in the use of the chosen resources.

(c) State how you have shown an awareness of equal opportunities in the design or use of the resources (for example how you have considered all ranges of ability).

N.B. In collecting this evidence it is suggested that you use at least five different resources and that at least one of these should use information technology in its production.

If you want to check your understanding of your role in selecting, adapting or constructing learning resources for a specific programme try the following progress check

Progress Check 4.5

1.   State how you would choose aids for a specific session.

2.   For a chosen visual aid, indicate the process that you would go through to design it.

10. Evaluation of Aids

As with all of your teaching, it is important that you consider how to evaluate the aids that you use and to feedback your findings into the subsequent use of that aid (as you will surely use it more than once) and other aids.

The checklist shown in Figure 4.14 on the next page will help you in considering the aspects that you might use to evaluate your design and use of aids. It should be completed through answering all of the 18 questions with either a 'YES', 'NO' or 'NOT APPROPRIATE'. In evaluating the aid ALL of your questions should be answered with either a YES or a NOT APPROPRIATE. If you have any answered with a NO, you should reconsider that aspect of the design, use, etc. For each of the questions asked, *tick the appropriate column* to indicate whether each aspect has been considered or not, or if it is not applicable in this instance.

An alternative way to evaluate your aids is to ask students questions about their suitability, whether they assisted the learning, whether they appreciate them, and so on. Students are the ones for whom the aids are designed – they have to suit their needs.

Also you might ask colleagues what they think about your various aids. Indeed, it is useful in a department to have a pool of aids so that you can use each others' and file them in a central place. In this way the time taken in their design and production is shared.

Evaluation of Aids

	YES	NO	N.A

Preview

1. Have you checked in advance:

    (a) that you have not used too many aids?
    (b) that you have not used too few aids?
    (c) that your aids work?

Presentation

2. Can the aid be seen/heard?

3. Is it used for too long/not long enough?

4. Is it clear (does it aid learning)?

Design

5. Will it work (blackout, bulbs, leads)?

6. Is there a logical sequence?

7. Is the time for use about right?

8. Can it be misinterpreted?

9. Is there enough/too much variety?

10. Is there enough/too much colour?

11. Is it well made?

Use

12. Have you invited co-operation of the students?

13. Does it attract attention?

14. Have you decided how it will be introduced?

15. Does it supplement verbal information?

16. Does it hold attention?

17. Is it challenging for the students?

18 Does it consolidate learning?

Figure 4.14 Checklist for the Evaluation of a Learning Aid

Possible Evidence to Show You have Achieved the Competence 'Evaluate the use of visual aids'

The type of evidence that you might collect to show that you have achieved the competence involves:

Design a visual aid for use in one of your classes and then and make, use and evaluate it.

1. State the objectives that it will achieve, where it will be used and how it will assist in the learning process.

2. Use it with a class.

3. Evaluate its effectiveness through completion of the checklist in Figure 4.14.

4. Evaluate its effectiveness through its efficiency (for example time taken to prepare compared with increase in learning effectiveness), suitability for the content and gather learner views.

5. State what amendments are necessary before it is used on another occasion.

If you want to check your understanding of your role in using evaluating your use of visual aids, try the following progress check

Progress Check 4.6

1. Explain at least FOUR factors that effect the choice of visual aids when used with students.

2. Which TWO aids have low production costs?

3. List an aid which is suitable for each of the following:

   (i) group audience;

   (ii) individual student.

Further Reading and References

Further reading and references relating to this chapter can be found in the following:

Audio Visual
Products Division
How to Make Successful Overhead Projector Transparencies,
3M UK plc, 1987.

Brown, G. *Micro-Teaching: A Programme of Teaching Skills,* Methuen, 1975.

Buzan,T. *Use Your Head*, BBC, 1974.

Curzon, L.B. *Teaching in FE*, Cassel, 1980.

Folex Ltd. *Successful Presentations*, Folex, Zurich, 1988.

Kemp, J.E. *Planning andProducing Audiovisual Materials*, Harper and Row, 1980.

Lloyd-Jones, R. *How to Produce Better Work Sheets,* Hutchinson, 1986.

Newble, D. *A Handbook for Medical Teachers,* MTP Press,1987.

Osborne, P et al. Graphics in Training, Vol 8, *Training Technology Programme,* Parthenon Publishing, 1987.

Perrot, E. *Effective Teaching*, Longman, 1982.

Pringle, J. *Chalk Illustration,* Pergamon, 1966.

Rominszowski, A.J. *The Selection and Use of Instructional Media,* Kogan Page, 1988 (2nd Edition).

Thorpe, R. Projected Still Images in Training, Vol 10, *Training Technology Programme*, Parthenon Publishing, 1987.

Walkin, L. *Teaching and Learning in Further Education*, Stanley Thornes, 1990

Waller, Chris *Using your overhead projector and other visual aids*, Fordigraph, 1983.

Chapter 5

Planning and Design for Teaching and Learning

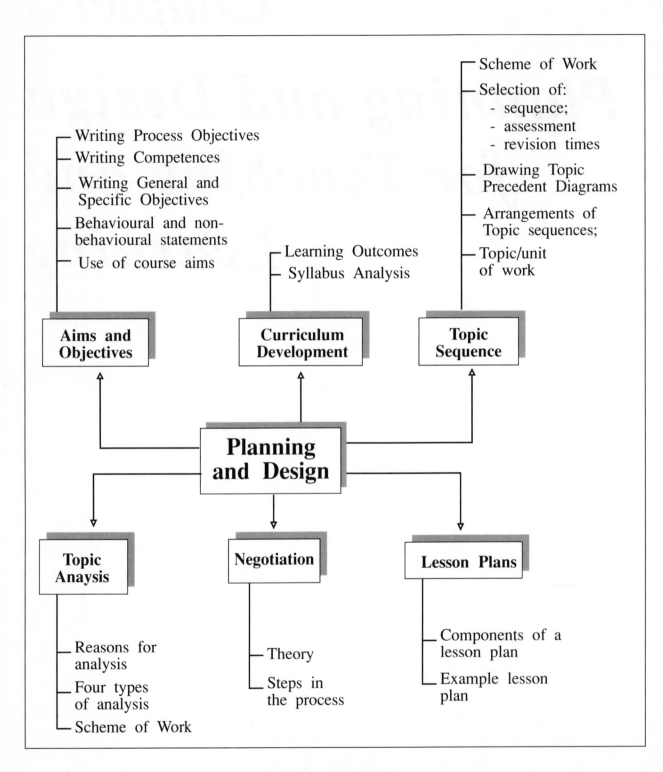

Overview of Chapter 5

Competences Related to this Chapter

The teacher competences and associated performance criteria related to this chapter are:

Overall Competence – *Design Learning Programmes and Schemes of Work*

COMPETENCE	PERFORMANCE CRITERIA
1. **Analyse a syllabus document for deficiencies.**	(a) List possible deficiencies in a syllabus document. (b) Identify measures that may be used to overcome deficiencies.
2. **Identify learning outcomes for specific programmes.**	(a) Specify learning outcomes which include conditions and criteria for success. (b) Relate outcomes to identified needs.
3. **Design learning programmes related to specific needs of learners.**	(a) State learning needs, prior experience and capabilities of the learners. (b) Clearly state outcomes. (c) State relevant factors influencing the programme design (syllabus, etc.). (d) Seek active participation in the design of the programme. (e) Specify learning resources, time and other factors in the design of the programme. (f) Specify content, learning styles and student activity in the design of the programme. (g) State the means of assessment clearly in the programme design.

1. Curriculum Development

1.1 Introduction

Educational institutions are fundamentally about learning. It follows that one of your duties as a teacher and a classroom manager is to review your curriculum at regular intervals. This involves you in reviewing what you teach and what your students learn, how that learning is organised and with what success. Any resulting changes from these reviews can be called development of the curriculum.

Thus, if curriculum development is to take place, it is your job as classroom teacher, with some assistance from your managers to make sure that it does take place. If the curriculum is about learning as we have suggested, then you need to increasingly ask: "What is it that I want my students to learn?" This leads to the following interlocking questions:

(a)   How can I get them to learn it?

(b)   How will I know when they have done so?

Although you are generally presented with some form of syllabus document upon which to base your teaching, the answer to all of these questions falls firmly on your shoulders, not on those of the syllabus designer. In order to find answers to these questions, you must look at the aims and objectives of what is intended to be learned, sequence the objectives into a learning sequence, and choose appropriate teaching, learning and assessment methods. This, then, is what curriculum development involves.

Your 'syllabus' document may be stated in terms of the aims of the subject, a list of objectives, a list of competences with associated assessment criteria, a list of topics, or a mixture of some or all of these. It may also indicate the common themes to be developed and assignments that are to be completed by the students. This document is the official guide to the course of study which is prepared by administrators, supervisors, an examining or validating body or by you yourself.

The following characteristics *can* be identified for a syllabus document:

(a)   aims of the course of study;

(b)   pre-requisites/entry behaviour expected of the students;

(c)   expected outcomes (objectives, competences, etc.);

(d)   number and names of major topics (they may or may not be stated in any logical teaching/learning order);

(e)   time allocated for the coverage of the course (it may be very general such as 60 hours or it may be as detailed as to indicate the time expected for each topic);

(f)   suggested teaching/learning strategies;

(g)   recommended textbooks and references;

(h)   assessment procedures to be used.

However, not all syllabuses have all of these features incorporated into them which means that the curriculum developer – you, the teacher – have to interpret them for the students.

1.2 Possible Measures to Minimise Weaknesses in a Syllabus

By analysing a document, you can identify its weaknesses. If these weaknesses are not rectified they exert negative influences on the teaching and learning process. Indeed, if they are not rectified, it is pointless analysing the syllabus at all.

You might use the following suggestions to minimise the effects of these weaknesses:

No.	Syllabus Deficiency	Possible effect on Teaching/ Learning Process	Measure to minimise the effect
1	Absence of depth of treatment	Previous exam/test papers become the only guide. The usual effect of this is that the teaching becomes based on recall of factual information.	(a) Convey thoughts to syllabus designers. (b) Decide, with colleagues and industry what depth is required.
2	Absence of indication of ability and skills expected of student	As (1) above	As (1) above
3	No indication of teaching strategies to be used	Most teachers revert to the style they have used before and to the needs of the examination/assessment	List all possible teaching strategies and show how much time is to be associated with each during the completion of the syllabus
4	No indication of 'best' resources to be used	As (3) above	List all necessary resources for 'best' coverage of the topics and ensure that they are available when needed

5	Not enough information on testing procedures	The classroom testing may be done on an ad-hoc basis with little thought to remedial and enrichment teaching and to the modification of the teaching	Review with colleagues how best to test and how best to use the results of testing
6	Absence of logical sequence of topics and content	This is likely to lead to a serious discontinuity in the learning process	Individual teachers to plan a logical sequence and make any additions/changes thought necessary
7	Absence of indication of useful links with subjects	Compartmentalisation of teaching in isolation from other related subjects. Can also lead to repetition of topics	All teachers who are involved in teaching the subjects, to share their individual schemes of work and identify links
8	Absence of indication of links with industry	This will likely lead to inadequate and inappropriate learning experiences	Review tasks required of course graduates in industry and build these into the course
9	Absence of abilities skills and attitudes to be developed	This can lead to different teachers developing different abilities, or ignoring some important ones	Write objectives for knowledge, skills and social abilities that are needed in industry
10	Absence of lesson plans	As in (9) above	Individuals to write lesson plans and to share them with colleagues teaching on the same course

> *Possible evidence to show that you have achieved the competence 'Analyse a Syllabus Document for Deficiencies'*

The type of evidence that you might collect to show that you have achieved this competence involves:

For a syllabus that you use for one of the classes that you teach:

(i)   state the characteristics;

(ii)   using the list of characteristics given in section 1.1 of this Chapter, identify those that are missing

(iii) for the characteristics that are missing, explain how the deficiency might be overcome.

Possible Evidence

> *If you want to check your understanding*
> *of syllabus analysis*
> *try the following progress check*

Progress Check 5.1

Explain what measures you would take to minimise the effects of the following:

1. Abilities and skills to be developed in the student which are not stated in the syllabus documents.

2. Lack of information on class and practical tests.

3. Lack of information on teaching strategies to be used.

4. Lack of information on time to be devoted to each of the topics.

2. The Process of Specifying Learning Outcomes

Before we consider the details of course planning and design, it can be helpful for you to consider the totality of the process and the components that are involved in the specification of learning outcomes. The diagram below (Figure 5.1) shows the various components of the curriculum development process: the manner in which a syllabus may be expanded for teaching purposes to show the learning process.

The diagram shows us two main things:

    (a)   that the development process is *sequential* in nature starting with the aims of a course and progressing through increasing detail to the more specific outcomes of the learning process; and

    (b)   that there are *alternative specifications* of learning behaviour that can be written. These are:

        (i)   product objectives which concentrate upon what the student will be able to do as a result of learning;

        (ii)   process objectives or statements which specify the use and application of knowledge and skills that are required for work;

        (iii)   statements of competence which specify the knowledge and skills required in the workplace for a particular occupation and, in consequence, what is required by employers.

The diagram suggests that the objective statements are offered as alternatives. This is sometimes true. It is, however, often the case that there is a need to be eclectic: that is borrowing from each of the sources as the need arises for a single syllabus.

The next sections of the chapter expand upon each of the aspects identified in the diagram and, indeed, show the importance of the increasing specificity: from aims to specific objectives, to common skills and to competences.

3. Course and Subject Aims

Curriculum development of a course or subject (where a course consists of a number of subjects, for example a business studies course consists of subjects such as accounts, law, shorthand and word processing) can be considered at two levels: course and subject.

Course Aims – development at this level is concerned with the whole of what the student is intended to learn. It is sometimes, but not always, carried out by examining or validating bodies.

Subject Aims – sometimes called a module or, as BTEC call it, a Unit. Quite often a subject is apportioned to one member of staff and the development is the responsibility of that member of staff. The subject is broken down into lessons or other learning situations.

Most teachers are required to complete development work at subject and lesson levels. However, most of the external bodies like BTEC, City and Guilds, as well as CNAA and the GCSE Boards are changing and placing more and more responsibility for the development work in the hands of the teacher.

The starting point for this development work lies with the *aims*, or direction of what is to be learned by the student. Again, the aims are at the two levels indicated above. Course aims are fairly general and describe the overall purposes of the course. Davies (1971) describes these as 'ultimate goals' – goals that are to be reached by the student at the end of the course. A course aim is a general statement which gives both shape and direction to the more detailed intentions of the course. Aims are a starting point for curriculum development and are necessary in order to mould the more precise decisions that are to be taken about the curriculum.

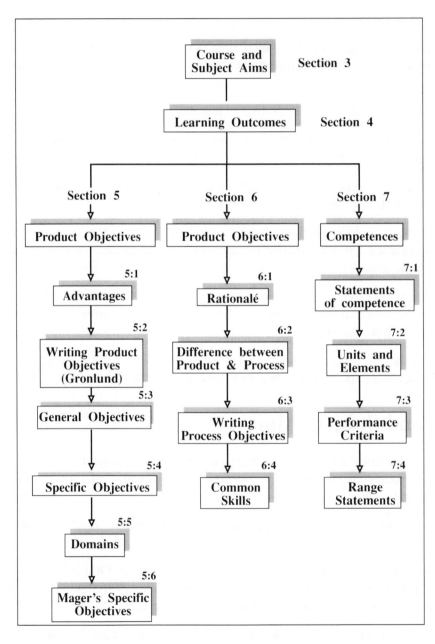

Figure 5.1 Specifying Learning Outcomes

The aims of a Civil Engineering technician course might be to:

- develop accuracy in measurement and methodical scheduling of quantities;

- assist in understanding the factors which affect the cost of buildings;

- develop knowledge of contractual procedures concerned with construction;

- develop the ability to work as an effective member of a team;

- develop the ability to prepare working drawings, sketches, specifications and planning data.

You will see that the aims are all related to the course of civil engineering and are obtained from the specific requirements of the industry. However, the course will consist of a number of subjects (i.e. surveying, mathematics, services, building science, drawing) and each of these subjects will require its own aims. The course aim 'to develop the ability to prepare working drawings and sketches' suggests a drawing subject. This will have its own aims and these might be to:

- develop skill in the use of formal drawings as a means of communicating technical information;

- understand architectural and working drawings containing services in symbol form;

- show skill in the production of simple working drawings of plant rooms and their associated equipment;

- etc.

It is important that you are able to differentiate between aims and the more specific forms of learning outcome – objectives. The usual characteristics of aims are that they:

(i)   are broad ranging covering several subjects or topics;

(ii)   cover more than one domain of learning (that is cognitive, psychomotor and affective);

(iii)   are long term (ultimate goals);

(iv)   are difficult, in themselves, to observe and measure.

To be of most use to you as the teacher as well as the curriculum developer, the aims at this level of specificity should give a direct indication of the ability that the subject will produce (that is cognitive, affective or psychomotor) and the level within the ability (that is knowledge, comprehension, etc.). In this way the subject aims give you direct assistance in gauging the level of teaching that is required.

The list of verbs shown in Figure 5.2 can be useful to you when you are writing your own aims or when you classify them for curriculum development purposes:

Cognitive	Affective	Psychomotor
Identify Develop knowledge Give an understanding Apply Enable Provide a foundation Equip students with	Develop confidence Give an appreciation Enhance motivation Assist flexibility Promote a positive attitude in	Develop skill in Develop competence

Figure 5.2 Useful Verbs for Writing Course or Subject Aims

You can use the checklist shown in Figure 5.2 for either writing your own aims or, alternately, for analysing aims that are presented to you as part of your syllabus.

	YES	NO	NOT REQUIRED

1. Do the aims cover:
   (a) knowledge required?
   (b) skills required?
   (c) attitudes required?
   (d) personal development?			

2. Do the aims identify priorities or are they all inclusive?			
3. Do the aims identify competences to be developed as well as topics or subject areas?			
4. Are the aims of practical use to the teacher or just decorative?			
5. Can the aims be used to write objectives?			
6. Are the number of aims about right to be useful (not too many or too few)?			

Figure 5.3 Checklist For The Evaluation Of Aims

Not all of the aspects identified in the checklist will be required in all specifications of aims. Consequently, when completing the checklist for a specific set of aims, you will tick one of the columns 'yes', 'no' or 'not required'. For a well written set of aims, none of your ticks should appear in the 'no' column. If they do, the aims should either be re-written or modified.

Possible evidence to show that you have achieved the part of the competence 'Identify Outcomes for Specific Programmes' related to Aims.

The type of evidence that you might collect to show that you have achieved this part of the competence involves:

1.   Identify and list the aims of a subject that you currently teach.

2.   Critically analyse the aims using the checklist given in Figure 5.3

3.   For any deficiencies that you find, rewrite the aims stating how such new aims will overcome the deficiency.

Check

Progress

> *If you want to check your understanding
> of the writing of aims try the
> following progress check*

Progress Check 5.2

Consider the aims for the course given below:

Aims for a Vocational Preparation Course

1.   To identify the vocational aspirations, potential abilities and aptitudes of trainees.

2.   To provide the opportunity to develop basic skills in a number of areas and then develop particular knowledge and skills in a specific field.

3.   To give the trainee an appreciation of opportunities in local industry.

4.   To develop confidence, motivation and interview techniques to improve the prospect of gaining employment.

5.   To develop personal qualities relevant to maintaining employment including safety consciousness, mature attitudes, response to discipline, time keeping and tidiness.

(a)   What do you consider have been used as sources to arrive at these aims?

(b)   Classify each of the aims into the domain which each predominantly falls, i.e. cognitive, affective or psychomotor.

(c)   Critically analyse the aims by the completion of the checklist given in Figure 53.

4. Learning Outcomes

4.1 Different Types of Learning Intentions

In the previous section we discussed the aims of a course. This, however, is insufficient to convey to the teacher (or the students) the intended learning. More specific intentions, in other words objectives, will be needed. As we can see from the examples below an objective is a mixture of a student behaviour together with an element of subject content. Consider the following three different categories of objective:

Objective Type	Example
Product Ojective	Define raising agents in a recipe
Process Objective	Prepare a window display
Competence	Demonstrate competence in laying a table for guests

Figure 5.4 Examples of Different Types of Objective Statements

It is important that you can not only recognise each type but can also write them. Therefore when we discuss each type we will give you suggestions for writing and interpreting them. Although we will consider each type of objective individually you should remember that in a syllabus, or for a learning experience, a mix of types might be appropriate.

4.2 Learning Behaviour

As a teacher, your concern is that your students should *learn* aspects which are considered desirable or educationally important. When we use the words 'learn' or 'learning' they can often have many meanings. To be useful to us as teachers we have to agree upon an operational definition of the term.

Suppose the students mentioned below were observed on two different occasions. Say that they were observed for the first time a year ago and then a year later. There will be a difference between the two observations such as:

- Alan can read music

- Susan can solve equations

- Kalo can turn a table leg on a lathe

- Ram can recite a poem

- Jane observes laboratory safety precautions

- Ali can ride a bicycle.

Between the period of the two observations something must have occurred so that these students can now do what they did not or could not do earlier.

What happened during the intervening period is known as learning. Alan has learned to read music, Susan has learned to solve equations, Kalo has learned to turn a table leg on a lathe and so on.

You will see that what the students have learned is very different: each of them involved different behaviours. In educational terminology *behaviour* is used to represent any act that is performed by a person, physical, mental or emotional. We must remember that this use of the term behaviour is different from the one used in everyday language when it is normally used to describe the *good* or *bad* behaviour of a person.

If we agree that the term behaviour is used to denote any activity, it can be said that learners are displaying a behaviour *after* learning that they did not display *before* their learning. In other words, the process of learning has resulted in a *change of behaviour*.

Note: We may not know *how* the change occurred, that is what the process of learning was, we only know what the end *product* of that process is: a change in behaviour.

Therefore, if we can observe a change in behaviour of a person, we may conclude that learning has taken place. In education, learning may be defined as:

a relatively permanent change in behaviour as a result of experience, training or practice.

Our activities as teachers are directed towards bringing desirable changes in the behaviour of our students.

If you want to check your understanding
of the concept of behaviour,
try the following progress check

Progress Check 5.3

You have observed that students in the list below have learned certain things during a particular period. Against each statement write:

Y   If you think that this is a result of instruction from a teacher;

N   if you think it is *not* because of instruction from a teacher;

U   if you are unsure whether it is or it is not a result of instruction.

1.   John has learned to appreciate poetry.   ____

2.   Ram has learned to hate history.   ____

3.   Rahim has learned to swim.   ____

4.   Jane has learned the definition of force.   ____

5. Product Objectives: A Concept

5.1 The Advantages of Product Objectives

Product objectives were the first of the three types of learning behaviour shown in the diagram at the start of this chapter. Earlier in the book we suggested that objectives were useful for:

1.   Communicating intended learning outcomes

2.   Teachers in teaching

3.   Students in learning

4.   Assessing the learning that has taken place

5.   Improving teaching.

We should also have noted that objectives should be written in terms of the intended learning outcomes that are expected after instruction.

The second point to note here is that as objectives are used by so many people (such as students, teachers and examiners), to be effective they must convey the same meaning to everyone who reads them. In other words, they must be unambiguous.

Consider the following statement written as a product objective:

"This lesson is intended to demonstrate the working of a petrol engine to the students".

What is wrong with this? You will notice that it describes the method of instruction but it does *not* specify the intended learning outcome. What does the teacher expect the students to learn? What changes in behaviour will the students display? If the teacher does not know this, how can the learning be verified?

Technically speaking, the objective will be achieved as soon as the teacher completes the demonstration, irrespective of whether the students have learned anything or not.

Now consider the following objective:

"At the end of instruction the student will understand the working of a petrol engine."

Note that in this case the objective is stated in terms of a *learning outcome;* in other words, that at the end of learning, the student will *understand.*

But, does it convey the same meaning to everyone? What does the term 'understand' mean? What will the students have to do to demonstrate that they actually understand? Will they have to describe the petrol engine? Will they have to draw a sketch of the parts? Will they have to identify the working parts? Or will they have to complete all of these?

Although the understanding of the working of the petrol engine may be a desirable learning outcome, the use of the word 'understand' does not communicate clearly the intent of the objective and therefore it is not useful in guiding the teaching and testing. The term has to be further clarified.

There are many verbs similar to the verb 'understand' which are open to many interpretations; for example, such words as 'know', 'appreciate', 'enjoy', 'believe', 'think critically' and many others. The main reasons for the different interpretations are that these verbs attempt to describe what goes on in the mind of the student. Since an observer cannot enter the mind of the student, a teacher does not know when students understand or when they appreciate.

What is required is a description of some observable behaviour which can be accepted as proof or indication of the students' understanding or appreciation. In other words, a product objective should specify what the student should be able to do which can be observed by an outsider. For instance, if it is agreed that a learner can *do* the following, it should be accepted that they understand Newton's Laws:

1.   *States* the laws in own words.

2.   *Gives examples* where each law is applicable.

3.   *Distinguishes* between the situations where each law is applicable.

Note: Each of the words that are in italics describes actions which can be observed and indicate specific behaviours which can be measured (tested) to find out if the objective has been achieved.

When the objective is written using a verb which specifies an *observable behaviour* it is known as a *product objective* (or sometimes called a 'behavioural objective').

Verbs such as 'write', 'state', 'identify', 'classify' or 'draw' describe actions which can be observed and, therefore, can be used when writing product objectives. Verbs like 'know', 'understand', 'appreciate' or 'think' do not describe observable actions; hence they cannot be used in specific product objectives.

Progress Check

If you wish to check your understanding of the concept of behavioural objectives, try the following progress check

Progress Check 5.4

1.   Which of the following correctly describes an instructional objective written using observable behavioural terms?

A.   Communicating the activities of the teacher in behavioural terms.

B.   Containing words to indicate what is expected from the learner at the end of instruction.

C.   Containing words to indicate changes in learner behaviour that can be measured.

D.   Communicating learner behaviour in measurable terms prior to instruction.

2.   Two objectives are stated below. Which of these objectives uses observable behavioural terms to describe the learning outcome?

A.   At the end of instruction the student should be able to appreciate the importance of heat treatment of steel.

B.   At the end of instruction, the student should be able to select an appropriate heat treatment process for steel.

3.   A list of verbs usually used to indicate learning outcomes is given below. Indicate which of these verbs is open to many interpretations and which is open to few interpretations.

(a)	Know	(i)	Distinguish
(b)	Understand	(j)	Compare
(c)	Write	(k)	Differentiate
(d)	Construct	(l)	Enjoy
(e)	Explain	(m)	Believe
(f)	Really understand	(n)	Remember
(g)	Think	(o)	Draw
(h)	Solve	(p)	Design

5.2 Writing Product Objectives - Gronlund's Approach

In the previous section we defined Product Objectives as a statement which uses a verb specifying observable behaviour and we identified the difference between observable and unobservable behaviours. There are situations where the teaching of specific observable behaviours is very useful, particularly for knowledge level objectives.

However, much education is directed to the more complex behaviours of understanding and applying knowledge. Employees need not only to know the principles of their vocation, but they need to understand them so that such principles can be applied to specific situations.

Earlier, we also noted that verbs like 'understand' and 'apply' do not describe an observable behaviour. Hence they cannot be used for writing product objectives in behavioural terms. If we sought to specify all of the learning outcomes, the number of objectives required for a subject/topic would be too great. Too many product objectives may restrict the scope of teaching.

In an attempt to ensure that (a) the totality of the subject matter for teaching purposes is covered and (b) the specific behaviours are suitable for the formulation of assessment, Norman Gronlund (1970) suggests writing product objectives at two levels. These are:

1. *General objectives*, and

2. A sample of *specific objectives* corresponding to and representative of each general objective.

Gronlund further suggests that *teaching* should be directed towards the achievement of the general objectives whereas the specific objectives should form the basis of *assessment*.

An example of the Gronlund approach is shown in Figure 5.5.

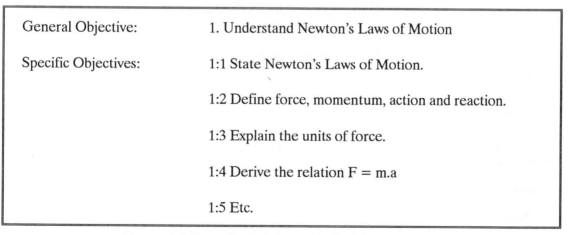

General Objective:	1. Understand Newton's Laws of Motion
Specific Objectives:	1:1 State Newton's Laws of Motion.
	1:2 Define force, momentum, action and reaction.
	1:3 Explain the units of force.
	1:4 Derive the relation F = m.a
	1:5 Etc.

Figure 5.5 Example of Gronlund Specific Objectives

Note that verbs like 'know', 'understand' 'apply' and 'appreciate', which we considered unsuitable for stating behavioural objectives, may now be used for stating general objectives. The general objective describes a general learning outcome which, by itself, is not observable. It is, however, further clarified through a representative sample of specific behaviours which use terms to describe observable behaviour.

> *If you wish to check your understanding of the difference between general and specific objectives try the following progress check.*

Progress Check 5.5

A list of product objectives is given below. Indicate which of them are general objectives and which of them are specific objectives.

1. Understand the working of the heart.

2. Calculate the power required to lift water through a given height by a pump.

3. Apply Pythagoras' Theorem.

4. Appreciate the need for providing incentives to workers giving excess production.

5. Erect a tripod with the help of given tools and equipment, so that the apex is 3 metres above the ground.

6. Measure the length of a wall using a tape to an accuracy of 0.1 mm.

7. Understand the method of setting-up a levelling instrument using a bubble tube.

8. Know the steps in boning a chicken.

5.3 General Objectives: Guidelines

Guideline 1.   Objectives should be stated in terms of student performance.

Consider the following two objectives:

1.   *To teach Faraday's Laws of electro-magnetic induction.*

2.   *Understand Faraday's Laws of electro-magnetic induction.*

The focus of the first of the objectives is on what the *teacher* does whereas the attention of the second one is what the *student* does: in this case what the student understands. Objectives should always be stated in terms of student behaviour rather than in terms of teacher behaviour.

Guideline 2.   Objectives should be stated in terms of the learning outcome and not in terms of the learning process.

Examine the following statement:

"*The student gains knowledge of Bernoulli's theorem*".

The statement emphasizes the gaining of knowledge (the learning process) rather than the type of behaviour that provides evidence that learning has taken place.

Words like 'gains' 'acquires' and 'develops' generally indicate the learning process rather than the desired outcome of the learning experience.

Guideline 3.   Statements of objectives should be an amalgamation of subject matter and the desired behaviour.

Examine the following:

1.   *Armature reaction.*

2.   *Understands armature reaction in a D.C. machine.*

The first statement is merely subject matter and contains no verb or student behaviour. The second tells the general outcome of learning with the addition of the desired student behaviour; it is an amalgamation of the subject matter and the student behaviour.

Guideline 4.   Avoid the use of more than ONE type of learning outcome in each General Objective.

Read the following objectives:

1.   *Uses appropriate experimental procedures in solving problems.*

2.   *Knows the scientific method and applies it effectively.*

The second objective includes both 'knows' and 'applies' as possible learning outcomes. It is better to have a separate statement for each because some students may 'know' the scientific method (that is to be able to state it) but may not be able to 'apply' it effectively.

The checklist shown in Figure 5.6 can be used for either writing your own general objectives or for assessing those written in your syllabus. It indicates the important aspects of the writing of these objectives.

	YES	NO
1. Does the general objective indicate an appropriate outcome for the instructional unit?		
2. Does the general objective include desired outcomes as knowledge, skills, attitudes, etc.?		
3. Is the general objective attainable taking into account the ability of the learners, facilities, time, constraints, etc.?		
4. Is the general objective relevant to the course aims?		
5. Does the general objective begin with a verb?		
6. Is the general objective clear, concise and well defined?		

Figure 5.6 Checklist for Evaluating General Objectives

5.4 Specific Objectives: Guidelines

The following guidelines will assist you in writing specific objectives which will expand upon the general objective and give a representative sample of behaviours to show how the general objectives will be assessed.

1.   State the general objective.

2.   Begin each specific objective with an action verb which communicates the terminal behaviour of the learners.

3.   Write the specific objectives which are relevant to the general objective.

4.   State the objective including condition and criterion components if these reduce any ambiguity.

5.   Do not omit complex objectives (e.g. appreciation) simply because they are difficult to state in behavioural terms. Reference materials may have to be consulted in such cases.

6.   Write a sufficient number of specific objectives for each general objective so as to adequately describe the student behaviours for achieving the general objective.

7.   Write a specific objective to communicate one learning outcome.

8.   Sequence the specific objectives in such a way that the learning outcome of one becomes the pre-requisite for achieving the learning outcome of the next.

A checklist is shown in Figure 5.7 which is similar to the one for General Objectives. It, again, provides the important facets for the writing or checking of this type of objective.

	YES	NO
1. Are the specific objectives relevant to the general objective?		
2. Does the specific objective contain a verb which is an observable behaviour?		
3. Is the specific objective stated in terms of student behaviour as opposed to teacher behaviour?		
4. Does the specific objective communicate only one learning outcome?		
5. Have the specific objectives been arranged in a logical sequence?		
6. When seen as a whole, does the list of specific objectives reflect what is intended by the corresponding general objective?		

Figure 5.7 Checklist for Evaluating Specific Objectives

Writing general and specific objectives must be within one of three domains and at a specific level within that domain. The process relies upon the specification of the *verb* which is specific to both domain and level. The lists shown in Figures 5.8 and 5.9 are adapted from Gronlund (1970) and give an indication of the verbs that you might consider using when writing general and specific objectives. Notice that some of the verbs appear in more than one domain and more than one category in the cognitive domain. The reason for this is that the verbs are only *illustrative* of the domain and level and the specific level depends upon the context within which the verb appears. For instance the verb 'solve' (a specific objective cognitive verb) can be at three levels.

'Solve two times two' is recalled as 'four' and is *knowledge*. 'Solve a problem' by putting numbers into an equation is *comprehension*. 'Solve the height of a building' by devising an equation for the first time is *application*. Thus, the verbs given in the lists are there to help you write objectives: there are many others and the ones shown are only an indication of those that you might use.

Level	Illustrative General Objective	Illustrative Verbs for Specific Objectives
Knowledge	Knows common terms. Knows specific facts. Knows basic concepts. Knows principles states.	Defines, describes, identifies, labels, lists, names, outlines, selects.
Comprehension	Understands facts. Interprets charts and graphs. Translates verbal material to maths formulae. Estimates future consequences from data.	Converts, defends, distinguishes, estimates, explains, extends, generalises, gives new examples, infers, paraphrases, summarises.
Application	Applies concepts and principles to new situations. Applies laws/theories to practical situations. Constructs charts and graphs.	Changes, computes, demonstrates, discovers, manipulates, modifies, predicts, prepares, produces, relates, shows, solves, uses.
Higher than Application (Analysis, synthesis & evaluation).	Recognises unstated assumptions. Integrates learning from different areas into a plan for solving a problem. Judges the logical consistency of written materials.	Breaks down, discriminates, infers, outlines, relates, separates. Categorises, combines, devises, designs, modifies, plans, rewrites, summarises. Appraises, compares, concludes, justifies.

Figure 5.8 Illustrative Verbs for Specific Objectives in the Cognitive Domain

Domain	Illustrative General Objective	Illustrative Verbs for Specific Objectives
Affective	Appreciates the need to show sensitivity to human needs and social problems. Appreciates the need for class discussion. Appreciates safety rules. Appreciates a healthy diet.	Asks, chooses, selects, answers, assists, complies, practices, follows, forms, initiates, influences, shares, studies, works on own volition.
Psychomotor	Shows skill in writing. Shows skill in operating. Shows skill in typing. Shows skill in preparing food. Shows skill in cutting hair.	Assembles, builds, calibrates, changes, cleans, connects, composes, creates, designs, hammers, makes, manipulates, mends, paints, saws, sews, sketches, starts, stirs, weighs.

Figure 5.9 Illustrative Verbs for Specific Objectives in the Affective and Psychomotor Domains

> *If you wish to check your understanding of writing general and specific objectives try the following progress check.*

Progress Check 5.6

1. Write two general objectives for a unit or topic of the course subject you are presently teaching and, for each general objective, write at least three specific objectives which will allow achievement of the general objective.

2. Use the checklists (Figures 5.6 and 5.7) to evaluate the objectives that you have written.

3. State whether the following general objective behaviours are likely to represent Cognitive, Affective or Psychomotor behaviours.

    (i)   understands
    (ii)   appreciates
    (iii)   shows skill in
    (iv)   judges
    (v)   knows

4. State the level in the cognitive domain that the following specific objective behaviours are most likely to represent.

    (i)   list
    (ii)   explain
    (iii)   predict
    (iv)   justify
    (v)   give new examples
    (vi)   name

5.5 Domains of Learning Behaviour

Selecting the Domain

You should note that few objectives are purely cognitive, psychomotor or affective. The major criterion that we use in selecting the domain in which the objective belongs is the *primary behaviour* called for: if it relates primarily to 'knowing' about the subject, it is cognitive; if it relates primarily to 'skill behaviour', it is psychomotor; and if it relates primarily to 'feelings' or 'attitudes', it is affective.

The checklist shown in Figure 5.10 can be used for either writing your own product (general and specific) objectives, or for assessing those written in your syllabus.

	YES	NO
1. Does each objective use an observable verb?		
2. Does each objective contain only one behaviour?		
3. Does each of the objectives in the cognitive domain deal with knowledge and intellectual skills?		
4. Does each of the objectives in the psychomotor domain deal with physical skills?		
5. Does each of the objectives in the affective domain deal with attitudes, feelings or emotions?		

Figure 5.10 Checklist for Evaluating Product Objectives

Progress Check

> *If you wish to check your understanding of domains of objectives try the following progress check.*

Progress Check 5.7

The following is a list of product objectives. Read each and indicate the *domain into which each primarily falls* by placing the letter 'C' if it is cognitive, 'P' if it is psychomotor, or 'A' if it is affective.

1. _____ Stitch given materials.
2. _____ Identify the given samples of legume seeds by name.
3. _____ In the clinical setting, demonstrate concern for apprehensive patients by answering the call lights promptly.
4. _____ Define the editing symbols on a given list.
5. _____ Select the appropriate forms for transferring doctor's orders.
6. _____ Given ten lists of three digit numbers, calculate totals for the lists on any calculators found in the simulated office practice laboratory.
7. _____ Choose the most suitable option among several alternatives in business careers.
8. _____ Specify any missing or incomplete information on the completed short-term loan contracts provided.
9. _____ Compute the missing value on a given list of Ohm's Law problems.
10. _____ Determine the kinds of nutrients to be applied to a given soil to grow a certain crop.
11. _____ Select the proportions of concrete mix required for a given job.
12. _____ When confronted with a hazard, demonstrate concern for safety practices by observing all safety precautions.
13. _____ Given ten shafts with differing diameters, measure the diameter of each with a micrometer.
14. _____ Outline the qualifications for a given job.
15. _____ Change the ribbon of a typewriter.
16. _____ Identify the sequence of operations for constructing a house.
17. _____ Grease all points in a car, as outlined by the manufacturer for routine maintenance.
18. _____ After reviewing a film presentation, analyse the presentation using the outline form provided.

Precision in Classification into Levels within a Domain

In many instances you can classify a given objective as belonging to one level from one point of view and to another level from a different point of view. In such cases, particularly for psychomotor and affective objectives, it may not be advisable for you to classify them as strictly belonging to one level or another: the dividing line between any two successive levels is not sharply defined and either level would be acceptable. For most occasions you will find it acceptable if the following simplification of the levels is used for operational purposes:

1.   The levels in the cognitive domain are classified as:

   (a)   Knowledge

   (b)   Comprehension

   (c)   Application

   (d)   Higher than Application

You should note that level (d) includes the levels of Analysis, Synthesis and Evaluation. This level is sometimes called 'Invention' and this is descriptive in that it is a high level cognitive behaviour which involves the student in doing something new. Very little of many syllabuses will contain a high percentage of this level and some, particularly in the initial years of a course, may not contain any at all.

2.   No sub-division of the Psychomotor and Affective domains need be used.

Instructional Uses of Taxonomic Levels

You will notice that classifying product objectives into the different levels in domains will assist you in your teaching in the following ways:

1.   To *sequence* objectives for teaching so that learning progresses from known to unknown and simple to complex.

2.   To include objectives at all of the required levels within a domain. This ensures that you emphasise the different levels required by the overall aims of the course.

3.   To construct *appropriate test questions* to measure desirable changes in behaviour at the required levels.

Taxonomic Levels in Teaching/Learning Programmes

You may not find it possible or desirable within the time available to develop all cognitive, psychomotor or affective abilities to the highest level in each domain. For example, some motor skills may be developed to a naturalization level (done automatically and with ease), but it would not be possible or even realistic to expect all skills to be developed to this level. Similarly, in the affective domain you will find it likely that most of the objectives may not go farther than the valuing level and it has already been indicated that the Higher than Application level in the cognitive domain is a high level skill with only small amounts in any one year of a course. The tasks which students have to perform determine, to a large extent, the taxonomic levels to which students have to be developed during the educational programme.

If you wish to check your understanding of taxonomic levels try the following progress check.

Progress Check 5.8

Identify the levels of objectives in the list below as Knowledge (K), Comprehension (C), Application (A) or Higher than Application (HA) by placing the appropriate symbol in the blank space adjacent to the item.

(a)		Identify the given samples of legume seeds.
(b)		Define the editing symbols on a given list.
(c)		Select the appropriate forms for transferring doctor's orders.
(d)		Specify any missing or incomplete information on the loan contracts provided.
(e)		Determine the kinds of nutrients to be applied to a given soil to grow a certain crop.
(f)		Select from the tables the proportions of concrete mix required for specified jobs not previously tackled.
(g)		State the qualifications for a given job.
(h)		Design a method you would use to accomplish the given task.
(i)		Identify the objectives on a given list as primarily cognitive, psychomotor or affective.

5.6 *Mager's Approach to Writing Product Objectives*

In the previous sections we described Gronlund's approach to writing general and specific objectives and we identified the taxonomic levels of the three learning domains. Gronlund's approach to writing objectives has much to commend it. However, you will find that the specific objectives, due to their being only a representative sample of behaviours, are often open to interpretation. Robert Mager (1962) suggests a method of overcoming this problem.

Since the intention is to make specific objectives unambiguous so that everyone who reads them get the same meaning, there are two ways in which we can achieve this:

1.   Write all product objectives using terms which describe only the specific observable behaviours as intended learning outcomes; or

2.   Use non-observable terms to describe the intended learning outcomes *but* further clarify such terms by indicating a sample of specific behaviours which can be accepted as representative of the intended general learning outcome.

The first method of writing product objectives is the one favoured by Robert Mager while the second one is the one that we have already described as suggested by Norman Gronlund.

As a teacher you will find both methods of use as you will find some situations in which the Mager type objective is useful and others where the Gronlund approach helps.

Mager suggests that objectives should be written which specify what the student should be able to perform or do to demonstrate mastery of the subject/topic. As many statements as necessary should be written, he suggests, to describe all of the learning outcomes.

He further recommends that to make the objective more specific, it should contain three elements. According to Mager it is, however, not always essential to include all three elements in every objective. The main intention is that the objective should communicate the intended learning outcome as unambiguously as possible. If all of the three elements reduce ambiguity, then they should be included. The three elements are:

1.   *Terminal Behaviour* (behaviour to be demonstrated by the student at the end of instruction).

2.   Important *conditions* under which the terminal behaviour is expected to occur.

3.   *Criteria* of acceptable performance.

Terminal Behaviour

The terminal behaviour describes what the student will do or perform after instruction. It is essential that it should specify observable behaviour like 'repair', 'state', 'write', 'select'. Verbs like 'know', 'understand' and 'appreciate' which are not observable behaviours do not qualify to describe terminal behaviour in Mager's approach.

Conditions

Conditions refer to what the student will be given, for example, with the help of 'handbook', 'tools' and 'references'. It can also specify what the student will be denied, for example 'without the use of a calculator', or, 'from memory'.

Criteria

Criteria refer to the extent or standard of attainment. They may specify speed or efficiency, for example, 'within 40 minutes'. They may make reference to quality or quantity, for example 'to the second place of decimals', or 'eight out of ten correct'.

The following example may assist to clarify for you the three elements:

> Given a 7.5 kW DC motor, that contains a single fault and given a standard kit and references, the student must be able to repair the motor within 45 minutes.

In the above objective:

1. *repair* communicates the desired terminal behaviour.

2. *given a 7.5 kW DC motor, that contains a single fault and given a standard kit and references* indicates the conditions under which the behaviour is expected to occur.

3. *within 45 minutes* tells us the criteria of acceptable performance.

> *If you wish to check your understanding of Mager's approach try the following progress check*

Progress Check 5.9

Complete the table below to identify the three components of the objectives (a) to (e). If you do not find a particular element in the objective, leave the cell blank.

Objective No.	Terminal Behaviour	Conditions under which behaviour occurs	Criteria of acceptable performance
a.			
b.			
c.			
d.			
e.			

(a) Given ten rock specimens, identify all sandstones without the use of any equipment.

(b) The students shall be able to name the parts of an electric motor.

(c) Using the standard code of practice for Steel Design, the students shall design a suitable section for the column (pillar).

(d) Given samples of bricks from four brick-makers, the students shall select those that are first class.

(e) The students shall state the quantity of bricks required for wall construction to an accuracy of 10%.

6. Process Objectives

6.1 Rationale for Process Objectives

In the previous section, we concentrated upon writing product objectives and, in that section, we suggested that general and specific objectives were a useful method to convey their meaning. We further suggested that they were useful for the acquisition of knowledge and skills. However, apart from knowledge and skill, a workforce needs to be adaptable and flexible due to the rapid changes in technology. The knowledge and skills associated with product objectives do not necessarily give us this required flexibility - hence the need for process objectives which concentrate upon the use and application of knowledge and skills and attempt to provide us with the additional competences that are required for work.

It is important that we make courses reflect as accurately as possible the skills and processes encountered in the workplace and to enable our students to perceive a close relationship between their education and their employment. This close relationship can infer a fairly obvious need for work experience and simulation to be associated with our courses. It can also mean that the processes experienced by our students realistically reflect the processes that they experience at work. For example, in the case of assessment, there is often a marked difference between the examination and the form of assessment that they experience at work.

Traditional examination assessment is characterised by:

- a dependence on memory and speed
- a judgment made on a single occasion
- a judgment made by someone remote from the student
- the need for contrived problems to suit designated examination times
- a lack of acknowledgement of transferable skill development
- a likelihood that it is norm referenced.

We can identify two major problems with product objectives:

(a)   there is a likelihood for curriculum developers to (over) concentrate on the low level skills associated with knowledge because these are the easiest product objectives to write and assess;

(b)   teachers tend only to teach to the behaviours stated in the specific objectives and ignore the more all-embracing general objective which precedes them.

Work-based assessment is characterised by:

- a need to investigate, inquire and be reliable
- the fact that assessment is continuous
- judgment being carried out by oneself and peers, providing feedback
- real-life problems

- skill development being continuously demonstrated as circumstances change

- being criterion referenced because a certain level of competence is required.

If our courses are to closely reflect the needs of the workplace then the intentions must specify objectives that are written in terms of these processes or competences that are important at work.

The addition of process objectives to a course specification is an attempt to ensure that students not only acquire knowledge but, also, apply it. Such activities are more likely to lead to learning which is flexible and durable over time as it will allow our students to change to meet the needs of a changing technology. Additionally, the inclusion of such process objectives is likely to lead to increased student motivation when they realise that the competences that are being learned are those that they require at work and that they are not just learning knowledge for its own sake.

Justification for the process mode is given by Cole (1982) where he suggests that promotion of process education 'stems from the realities of a satisfying and productive life in the present world'. He suggests the following eight justifications:

1. The world is changing so fast ... that it is impossible to predict what knowledge individuals will need in the next few years.

2. The state of knowledge is so vast that only a small proportion can be taught to students.

3. The acquisition of processes ensures an individual who can solve problems.

4. Processes are more widely applicable than knowledge and information.

5. Processes are more permanent than other types of learning.

6. Information is easily obtained when needed but processes cannot be 'looked up'.

7. An emphasis on processes is needed to prevent academic isolation and social irrelevancy.

8. Processes are required for learning to occur through formal education.

> *If you wish to check your understanding of the rationale for product objectives, try the following progress check*

Progress Check 5.10.

Give three reasons for the inclusion of process objectives within a course specification.

6.2 Differences between Process and Product Objectives

The key features of the process model are:

(a)   a focus on student activities, and

(b)   the teaching and assessment of transferable skills which are common to a number of subject disciplines.

These key features mean that process-based curricula focus on a clear description and identification of the learning activities that are to be pursued. In order to ensure that transferable skills are learned, they are based on competences that are common to a number of subject disciplines (for example mechanical, electrical and motor vehicle). This does not mean that the competences that are identified are only the simple ones, but that they form the basis of the thinking of, for example, a technical person. Thus, competences like the following would be included:

- communication skills

- problem solving skills

- self appraisal and evaluation

- working as an effective group member.

As you will see, this type of competence is common to all work personnel and are required as life skills. Of course, they need to be aligned to relevant subject content and it is suggested that this is completed in one of the two ways shown in the next section.

The examples given in Figure 5.11 will serve to illustrate the main facets of the model. First, you should notice the difference between product and process types and see that product objectives concentrate upon student terminal behaviours whilst the process type concentrate upon student activities.

PRODUCT OBJECTIVES	PROCESS OBJECTIVES
– State the principle of moments.	– Establish the effect of a force rotating about a point.
– Draw a histogram from specific data.	– Collect, tabulate and summarise statistical data.
– List at least 5 reasons for planning lessons.	– Participate in a discussion on lesson planning.

Figure 5.11 Examples of Product and Process Objectives

In order that you can make a direct comparison the same subject matter has been used with the different types of objective. This is not usually, of course, either possible or advisable.

If you wish to check your understanding of the differences between process and product objectives try the following progress check

Progress Check 5.11

Below are ten objectives. Choose those that are product objectives and those that are process types.

1. _____ State the principal sources of hydrocarbons.

2. _____ Work on tasks where measuring and estimating of materials and time are required.

3. _____ Define the meaning of the term petty cash.

4. _____ Choose from a given list, the tools required to carry out a major service on a motor car.

5. _____ Prepare a window display.

6. _____ Obtain, by a variety of means, information on the characteristics of the range of job opportunities available in the catering industry.

7. _____ Investigate how a business is run by identifying the factors involved in selling, choosing location, borrowing, employing, etc.

8. _____ Convert fractions to decimals and vice-versa.

9. _____ Experience various roles in groups (e.g. leader, recorder, participant, chair).

10. _____ State the ingredients required to make chilli.

6.3 Writing Process Objectives

You will remember from the previous section that process objectives concentrate upon student experiences. You will also remember that curricula will benefit from the inclusion of a mixture of process and product objectives.

You can use the following criteria when writing your own process objectives. You should:

1. Reflect the general learning that the subject/course aims to achieve.

2. Blur the boundaries between topics and often make reference to personal qualities, skills, attitudes and practical knowledge which often go unmentioned in traditional syllabuses.

3. Rely more on the generalised process skills of analysis and problem solving, personal qualities such as resilience and responsibility, the ability to transfer knowledge and skills acquired in one context to other problems and situations.

4. State them in terms of the experiences that students will undergo.

BTEC (1988) suggest two methods of writing process objectives for their courses. Both of these employ what they call, principal objectives; the bases of learning, and these are supported by indicative objectives or indicative content. The two methods are outlined in Figure 5.12 below.

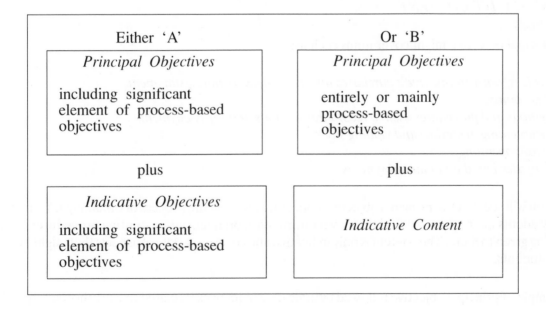

Figure 5.12 Methods of Writing Process Objectives suggested by BTEC

You can see from this that a system of principal objectives is the start of the curriculum specification and that these are like the general objectives discussed earlier. However, it is suggested that they contain a *significant* amount of process-based objectives. Associated with these principal objectives are either *indicative objectives* or *indicative content*. The word 'indicative' is obviously important in that the principal objectives may be achieved in a number of different ways. The subsequent content or objectives is just *ONE* of the ways in which this might take place.

The main difference between the two methods of specification is that 'A' has less process-based objectives than 'B'. If indicative content is given as in 'B', then more of the principal objectives are required to be process-based.

It is evident that both of the systems will include product-type objectives to support the process-based ones. Thus, the process model attempts to combine both process and product elements.

To illustrate the use of principal objectives and indicative objectives and indicative content, the following examples are given.

PRINCIPAL OBJECTIVE

'Obtain information on basic financial accounting procedures used in a variety of offices.'

INDICATIVE CONTENT

The principal objective might cover items such as:

invoices, order forms, credit purchases and sales, delivery notes, statements of accounts.
methods and procedures used to record transactions and verify payments.
documenting, recording and valuing stock.
payroll operating.
computer-based and manual systems.

Here, you will see that the principal objective concentrates upon the process of obtaining information; that is that students are required to find their own information on financial accounting procedures as opposed to it being given to them. The content is only indicative and covers a variety of aspects that might be obtained by the students.

An example of principal objective followed by indicative objectives is related to workshop safety and shown below.

PRINCIPAL OBJECTIVE

'Simulates the appropriate procedures which should be adopted in the event of workshop accidents.'

INDICATIVE OBJECTIVES

The principal objective might cover items such as:

> *giving mouth to mouth resuscitation using dummies,*
> *describing the effects of various types of fire e.g. oil, electrical, chemical,*
> *bandaging various types of physical injury.*

Here the process involves the simulation of procedures in the event of workshop accidents. The indicative objectives are of the process type except for the describing the effects of fire – which is a product type.

You can use the following checklist for writing process objectives or for evaluating those process objectives that are presented to you as part of a syllabus.

	YES	NO
1. Are the principal objectives written in terms of processes (e.g. as a statement of a competence)?		
2. Are the process objectives written to: (i) Reflect the general learning of the course? (ii) Blur boundaries between topics? (iii) Rely on process skills? (iv) State experiences that the learners will undergo?		
3. Do the indicative objectives include a significant element of process-based objectives?		
4. Are the student learning experiences explicitly defined?		

Figure 5.13 Checklist for Evaluating Process Objectives

> *If you wish to check your understanding of*
> *writing process objectives,*
> *try the following progress check.*

Progress Check 5.12

The four criteria for the writing of process objectives are:

(a)   Blur subject boundaries

(b)   Experiences of students explicitly stated

(c)   Reflect aims of the course to give general learning

(d)   Generalised process skills stated.

Choose which of the four criteria is predominant in each of the following statements.

1.   –   Experience, either vicariously or directly, a variety of personal encounters and a range of responses in them.

2.   –   Be able to read and understand written questions and requests (e.g. memos, questionnaires, worksheets).

3.   –   Investigate the outlets for surplus fish and poultry.

4.   –   Recognise the basic personal and technical skills necessary in electronic engineering with particular reference to hygiene, cleanliness and appearance.

5.   –   Identify and assess the nature of specific environmental problems.

6.4 Common (Core) Skills

The term skill denotes thinking (or cognitive) skills as well as the more purely technical or manipulative (psychomotor) abilities. Thus, we see that there are two kinds of skill:

- *vocationally specific*, that is those applying to a particular vocational area;
- *common*, that is those general or transferable skills like the ability to acquire new knowledge or to cope with problems of an unpredictable character which are common to many vocational areas.

We previously suggested that the key features of the process model are the transferable, or common, or core skills and that these are based on competences that are common to a number of subject disciplines. The term 'common skill' is to be used in this book but synonyms for it are often used like 'transferable skills', 'general skills', 'core skills' or 'core competences'. It is, however, important to note the definition:

Definition of Common Skill

A common skill can be defined as:

> *The possession and development of sufficient knowledge, appropriate attitudes and experience for successful performance in life roles. This includes employment and other forms of work; it implies maturity and responsibility in a variety of roles; and it includes experience as an essential element of competence.*

BTEC has defined seven major common skill areas for technology although, they agree, these will be developed in different ways for different courses to take into account the needs of their vocational area. The seven areas are detailed below with each area given examples of how they might be achieved.

self-development skills e.g.:

- manage own roles and responsibilities;
- manage own time in achieving objectives;
- undertake personal and career development;
- transfer skills gained to new and changing situations/contexts.

working with and relating to others e.g.:

- treat others' values, beliefs and opinions with respect;
- relate to and interact effectively with individuals and groups;
- work effectively as a member of a team.

communication e.g.:

- receive and respond to a variety of information;
- present information in a variety of visual forms;
- communicate in writing;
- participate in oral and non-verbal communication.

managing tasks and solving problems e.g.:

- use information sources;

- deal with a combination of routine and non-routine tasks;
- identify and solve routine and non-routine problems.

applying numeracy e.g.:

- apply numerical skills and techniques.

applying technology e.g.:

- use a range of technological equipment and systems.

applying design and creativity e.g.:

- apply a range of skills and techniques to develop a variety of ideas in the creation of new/modified products, services or situations;
- use a range of thought processes.

Thus, when you write process objectives, you might well use a representative sample of the above seven areas of common skills *together with* process objectives from the other skill areas associated with your specific subject area. Apart from BTEC, common (or core) skills are identified for YTS, CPVE and TVEI post-16 year old courses. The common aspects of these are indicated in Figure 5.14.

	YTS	BTEC	CPVE	TVEI	
Knowledge about IT	*	////	////	////	Knowledge and Understanding
Knowledge about industry and commerce	////	////	////	////	
Knowledge about society and the environment	*	*	////	*	
Communication	////	////	////	////	Skills
Numeracy	////	////	////	////	
Using IT	////	////	////	*	
Problem Solving	////	////	////	////	
Practical Skills	////		////	////	
Working Cooperatively	////	////	////	////	Attitudes and personal qualities
Adaptability	*	*	////	*	

KEY: //// = Formal Requirement
             * = Generally needed for success

Figure 5.14 Requirements of Common Skills for Different Courses

Figure 5.14 shows that common skills, when given as part of the curriculum requirements, usually include:

- Communication (oral and written)

- Problem Solving

- Practical Skills

- Personal and Social Qualities, especially:

    - team working

    - adaptability.

They also include:

- IT: an appreciation of its implications and basic skills in its use;

- Industry, Commerce and Society: an understanding of their nature and scope; familiarity with changes in society and the world of work.

An example of a mixture of vocational and common skill process objectives related to mechanical engineering is given in the example below.

1. Selects appropriate tools and cutting fluids for various machine operations including:

    - identification of relevant angles on common cutting tools;

    - identification of drilling faults and reasons.

2. Plan, organise and complete a machine cutting task working in a group of three students. The work to include:

    - negotiating in the group, individual contributions;

    - working as an effective member of the team;

    - presenting a report, including the relevant drawings, any problems encountered and conclusions reached.

You will see that the first of the principal objectives is written in terms of a process and is from the vocational area. The second one, however, involves the common skills of 'communicating' and 'working with others'.

7. Competences

7.1 Statements of Competence

The National Council for Vocational Qualifications (NCVQ) was established following a review of vocational qualifications in 1986. Industry is seen as the 'owner' of National Vocational Qualifications (NVQs) – the qualifications which receive the seal of approval of NCVQ. In practice, industry often means 'employers'.

NCVQ has adopted a competence-based model, an American import, for the specification of its qualifications. An NVQ is based on a 'statement of competence' in a particular vocational area and the task of setting standards in the area of competence is entrusted to an Industry Lead Body.

The NCVQ 'hallmark' signifies:

- a defined level of competence in a nationally recognised system;

- an acceptable national standard for the qualification;

- assessment based on skills, knowledge, understanding and ability in application;

- no unnecessary barriers to access;

- routes for progression.

In effect, the qualification is based upon competences that are required in the workplace and, in consequence, is what is required by employers. In the future it is anticipated that all vocational qualifications will be competence-based and validated by NCVQ through national awarding bodies in order to provide a coherent system of vocational qualifications. It is argued that this is necessary in order to give both employers and students an understanding of qualifications and the relationship between them.

NCVQ state that *'a vocational qualification is a statement of competence relevant to employment'*. It is this statement which specifies the competence to be achieved for the award of a National Vocational Qualification. It is the basis from which assessment procedures, recording and certification are derived. This brings about changes in further education which include:

1.   identification of competences for all vocational areas;

2.   identification of theory related to each competence;

3.   specification of assessment criteria for each competence and each part of the competence;

4.   liaison with industry for:

    (a)   assessment of competence (e.g. in the workplace);

    (b)   provision of prior skills.

5.   greater marketing procedures.

7.2 Units and Elements of Competence

The Manpower Services Commission (MSC 1988) define a competence as *'the ability to perform an activity within an occupation'*. Competence, they say, is a wide concept which embodies the ability to transfer skills and knowledge to new situations within the occupational area and includes aspects which we have already described as 'common' or 'core' skills.

NCVQ require an NVQ to be a statement of competence and intend that learners will be able to qualify for NVQs by accumulating units of competence.

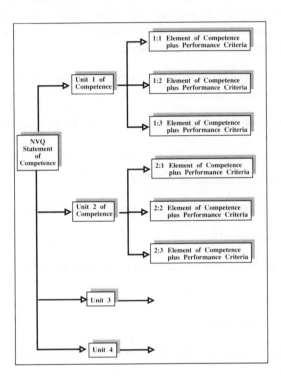

Figure 5.15 Sub-divisions of Statements of Competence

Figure 5.15 shows us that a Unit is made up of a number of elements of competence (with associated Performance Criteria) which together make sense to, and are valued by, employers so that they warrant separate accreditation. Vocational qualifications are usually made up of a number of related Units which together comprise a statement of competence relevant to an occupation. Examples of Unit titles from different occupational areas are:

- Establishing ornamental borders (from Horticulture)
- Designing posters (from Design)
- Handling power-aerated doughs (from Bakery)
- Analysing metals using electrochemical techniques (from Chemical Analysis)
- Filing (from Business Administration).

An element of competence describes what can be done; an action, behaviour or outcome which a person should be able to demonstrate: that is, a product objective. Alternately, an element of competence may describe knowledge or understanding which is essential if the performance is to be sustained or extended to new situations. Each element of competence has associated performance criteria which give us the expected level of performance.

7.3 Performance Criteria and Range Statements

NCVQ require each of the Elements of Competence to have performance criteria associated with them. These criteria give an indication of the required assessment for each of the competences. Range statements (or range variables) are also required for each of the Elements. These give suggestions of the range of situations against which the competence will be assessed.

Thus, the 'Filing' competence from Business Administration (see above), one of the units, has the following units, performance criteria and range statements.

Unit 1:1   File documents and open new files within an established filing system.

Performance Criteria

1:1:1 File all documents without undue delay.

1:1:2 Store all material without damage in a safe and secure manner.

1:1:3 Classify all documents correctly.

1:1:4 Refer all uncertainties in classification to an appropriate authority.

Range Statements

(a)   Paper-based filing systems covering:

   (i)   the storage and retrieval of information using alphabetical and numerical filing and indexing systems;

   (ii)   lateral and vertical filing systems.

(b)   The element requires competence in:

   (i)   pre-sorting documents for filing;

   (ii)   setting-up, sorting and sequencing card indexes and cross reference material for filing;

   (iii)   preparing and introducing new files.

Example Material Incorporating Competence

You will realise that areas that have strong links with industry have made rapid advances with competence-based courses. Catering and Hairdressing have strong links with Training Boards as well as having simulated work areas in colleges. 'Caterbase', the Catering Industry Training Board, have produced a competence-base for the catering industry which has been accepted by City and Guilds as the basis for training with the

Catering and Food Service industry. The links with construction have been made through the Construction Industry Training Board and have pioneered competence-based assessments in colleges in that discipline.

Example 1 – Catering

The catering example below shows the competence required for both 'preparing' and 'end of service' tasks for Food Service. Thus, this is what the trainee waiter must achieve for preparing the restaurant for customers and clearing-up after the customer has left. You will see that the example is in three sections:

(a) the competence statements;

(b) basic knowledge and understanding associated with the competence; and

(c) syllabus items - in effect, an analysis of the requirements of the competence.

Competence in Basic Preparatory and End of Service Tasks

A. In a task at work, in training or in college, the candidate must:

1. Demonstrate a competence in basic preparatory and end of service tasks;

2. Be assessed in accordance with the assessment schedule.

B. As a result of tutored experience in the task described in 'A', the candidate should, in a written examination or in an appropriate assessment, demonstrate a generalised command of the basic preparatory and end of service tasks.

The candidate must be able to:

(i)   define mis-en-place;

(ii)   identify the different areas of preparation;

(iii) state the specialist requirements necessary for items on the menu;

(iv)   select the correct equipment for service;

(v)   identify the correct positioning of equipment on the table.

Syllabus

4:1 Define mis-en-place

(a) preparing items of equipment and other requirements for a food service operation.

4:2 Identify the different areas requiring preparation

(a) table and chairs   (i) cleaning and dusting, (ii) positioning, (iii) lay-up

(b) sideboards   (i) cleaning and dusting, (ii) positioning, lay-up, cloths, equipment, commodities, accompaniments.

(c) etc.

Example 2 – Electrical

The construction (electrical) example given below is concerned with the testing and inspection of an electrical installation after it has been wired. That is testing the wiring of a house circuit that has been wired for lighting, power circuit, cooker circuit, etc.

Here the competence is stated together with the criteria for assessment.

Competence

     12.   The candidate must show competence in Testing and Inspection of Installations.

Performance Criteria

The candidate shall meet the following performance criteria:

     12.1 Visually inspect the installation taking into account the necessary factors.

     12.2 Test the ring circuit continuity using an ohmmeter and state the acceptable readings

     12.3 Test for continuity of protective conductors using an ohmmeter and state acceptable readings.

     12.4 etc.

You will note that the examples show that the components of a competence are not only the 'skilled processes' but also knowledge and required background theory. This is shown diagrammatically in Figure 5.16.

In terms of the writing of competence statements, the *Skill* is usually accompanied by *Performance Criteria* and *Range Statements*.

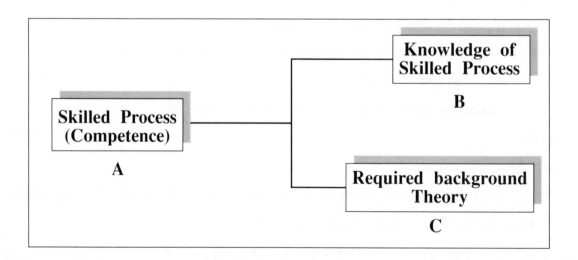

Figure 5.16 Components of a Competence

> *Possible evidence to show that you have achieved the competence 'Identify Learning Outcomes for Specific Programmes'*

The type of evidence that you might collect to show that you have achieved the competence involves:

1. For a subject or topic that you teach, write learning outcomes in the form of:

    (i)   general and specific objectives;

    (ii)   Mager type product objectives;

    (iii) process objectives which include both subject and common skills areas;

2. From the different types of learning outcomes that you have written state which are more likely to be appropriate to meet the needs of

    (i)   your students;

    (ii)   the vocational area that you serve; and

    (iii) your own teaching.

3. Write a critical analysis of each type of learning outcome in (1.) above.

Possible Evidence

> *If you wish to check your understanding of competence, try the following progress check.*

Progress Check 5.13

1.   Define the term 'common' skill and give three examples from your own subject area.

2.   Define the term 'competence'.

3.   State what is meant by an 'Industry Lead Body'.

4.   Explain what competence statements require each of the following:

     (i)   performance criteria;

     (ii) range statements.

8. Scheme of Work (sequence of topics)

8.1 Definition of a Topic

At the start of a course, as the teacher, you are faced with the task of planning a series of learning experiences for your students. This plan is sometimes known as a Scheme of Work. There are many ways of deciding upon the order of topics but, perhaps, difficulties occur in the identification of 'topics'.

There is no fundamental definition of the term 'topic' (in the educational literature) as it is applied to a learning experience . It may be defined as 'part of a subject which has a separate learning entity'. Although this is a vague definition, it may not be possible to be more rigorous than this. A topic may be the subject of one lesson (or session) or it may span two or more lessons: there may be more than one topic in a lesson. Certainly a topic should not be too large as students might have difficulty in following its logic. Also, if too large, there will be insufficient detail to plan a useful sequence, state the intended learning outcomes and assess the topic. Conversely, if the topic is too small, there will be a plethora of topics which makes planning very difficult. Perhaps, as this discussion proceeds, your understanding of 'topics' will be refined.

For an Introduction to Teaching Course (like C & G 7307) the following may be identified as topics:

- Lesson Plans;

- Evaluation;

- Memory;

- Motivation;

- Law and the Teacher;

- Profiling.

These are topics which are readily identified. Topics like 'assessment'' 'psychology' and 'preparation for teaching' are all too large to be usefully considered as topics. Thus, a topic is part of a subject.

8.2 Sequence of Topics

The sequence of topics is often derived from a syllabus or list of issues to be taught. There are, however, several ways in which you can establish your order of teaching. Some of these are:

1. easiest topics first.   in this way you can gain the confidence of students before addressing the more difficult issues;

2. a theme.   some courses can be seen in terms of themes and two or more themes make-up the scheme of work. For example Parliament: theme, elections;

3. logical sequence.   in mathematics there is a need to learn addition and subtraction before multiplication and division so it is logical to have that sequence;

| 4. | begin with the topics that you as the teacher are familiar with. | you may be in a position that you are familiar only with part of the syllabus and teaching what you know allows you time to prepare the other topics. |
| 5. | Historical/Chronological order. | the causes of the First World War are taught before the battles. This is a logical and natural order. However, if you start the teaching with a major battle and its effects, you might create impact and the interest to see the causes. |

A scheme of work may be defined as:

> *a series of planned learning experiences, sequenced to achieve the course aims in the most effective way.*

The scheme of work may include subject content, teaching strategies, student activities, assessment, evaluation and resources.

The decision making process you go through in designing a scheme of work is complex and, may be influenced by such aspects as:

- student entry behaviour
- course aims
- course content
- time available for learning
- teaching strategies to be used
- assessment techniques required
- resources available.

The process is further complicated when 'your' subject is part of a course which must develop common (or core) skills and may have core themes as with BTEC courses. Each subject planning is interdependent on the other subjects. A procedure that can be used is the Topic Precedent Diagram (TPD). This gives you a useful overview from which you can achieve an optimum learning sequence for your students. Usually, there is no right or wrong sequence but, of all the possible permutations, some sequences are better than others.

8.3 Topic Precedent Diagrams

You should try to make the planning process as rational as possible and Topic Precedent Diagrams will help. It is a means of achieving a logical sequence of topics so that both the learning and the teaching are readily understandable to the students. The following series of steps provide the essentials of the process:

| Step 1 | Identify the topics. This is not as easy as it sounds as topics vary in length and importance. |
| Step 2 | Write each topic on an individual card. Place the cards in random order and then number them. This process is one way of changing the order of topics as provided by the syllabus or by your own experience of teaching the topics. |

Step 3   Now introduce the precedence of topics. If the first two cards selected are 'A' and 'B', then:

(i)   must 'A' be taught before 'B'? Yes   (A) → (B)

(ii)   must 'B' be taught before 'A'? Yes   (B) → (C)

(iii) no relationship between 'A' and 'B'   (A)
                                              (B)

Thus, depending upon the precedence decided by the criteria
that you are using, such as historical, logical, simple to complex,
decides how the cards are positioned to give the teaching and
learning sequence.

Step 4   Now pick a third topic card, 'C' and, using the criteria for precedence again, compare it with the topic in the earlier pair that
has the greater precedence. For example in (i) above, compare
'C' with 'A' (the topic with the greater precedence). If 'C' must
precede 'A' then use the following linear sequence:

However, if 'C' does not have to precede 'A', compare it with 'B'.

You might find points of divergence when there is no direct relationship between 'A' and 'B' but 'C' must be taught before 'A'
and 'B'.

Alternately you may find points of convergence when 'A' and 'B'
have no direct relationship but must be taught before 'C'.

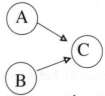

Step 5   Use a table or desk, and arrange the cards to form the TPD of
the subject. This allows you to modify the TPD by moving the
cards. Once you have completed the procedure, the results are
recorded in a diagram as shown in Figure 5.17. Remember, the
topics to the left must be taught before those to the right.

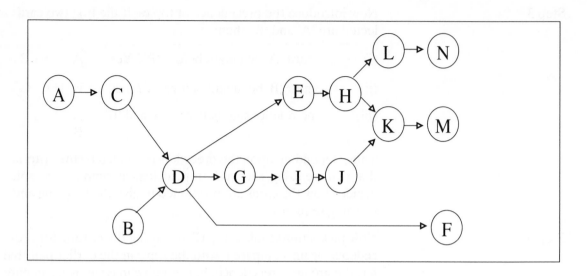

Figure 5.17 Typical Format of a Topic Precedent Diagram

The diagram shows alternative starts (for example you may start with topics 'A' or 'B') and multiple finishes (you can have three optional finishing points, 'N', 'M' or 'F').

You should note that the points of convergence ('D' and 'K') indicate that the entry behaviour to that topic is complex and, you may need careful revision before tackling them.

Note that the points of divergence (that is 'H' and 'D') show the importance of these topics for subsequent learning. As such, you need to ensure that these topics are understood before you progress.

Once you have completed the diagram, the important topics that need assessing should be clear to you. These are the points of convergence and divergence. Also, you may need to revise certain topics before you can make progress. For instance, if the order is:

you may find it of value to revise 'H' before starting to teach 'K'.

Figure 5.18 shows a Topic Precedent Diagram for a course of applied mathematics of approximately 'A' level standard. It may be seen that the topics are linear and show their relative interdependence. Some topics are dependent upon others and themselves serve as an essential for others (for example topic 8 - basic differentiation). Other topics are relatively independent and you could consider teaching them at almost any time (for example topic 23 – complex numbers).

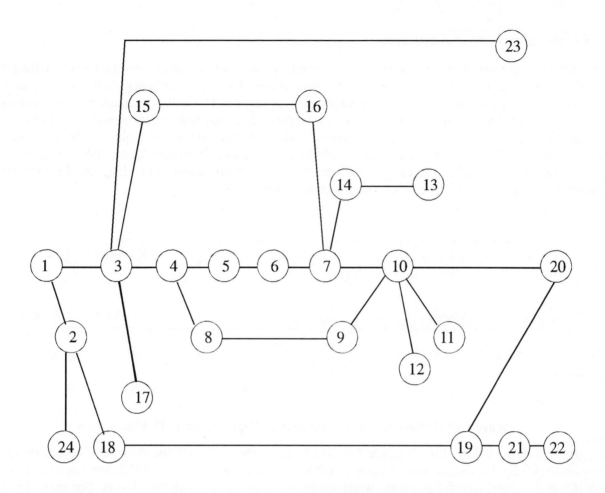

1. Sets
2. Binary OPs
3. Mappings
4. Sequences
5. Limits
6. Basic Differentiation
7. Differentiation Techniques
8. Basic Integration
9. Theorem of Calculus
10. Integration Techniques
11. First Order Diff. Eqn's
12. Application of Integration
13. Taylors' Approximation
14. Optimisation
15. Functions
16. Particle Differentiation
17. Morphisms
18. Vector Spaces
19. Vector Space Trans
20. Second Order Diff Eqn's
21. Matrices
22. Linear Equations
23. Complex Numbers
24. Relations

Figure 5.18 Example Topic Precedent Diagram – Mathematics

8.4 Optimum Linear Sequence

The TPD provides you with a framework for planning and you can determine your order of teaching from the diagram. Note that there are a number of permutations of teaching sequences that you could choose. But you must select the 'best' one to suit your particular situation. This will depend upon a variety of issues such as the availability of resources, personal preference, demands from other subjects and the requirements of the students. The 'best' sequence is often called the 'optimum linear sequence'. Such a sequence for the sample TPD shown in Figure 5.17 might be as we show it in Figure 5.19. Note that the revision (topics shown below the line) and assessment times have also been shown on the diagram which have been chosen from convergence, divergence and finishing points.

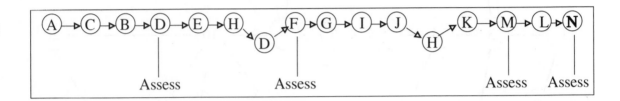

Figure 5.19 Optimum Linear Sequence of Topics from TPD, Figure 5.17

Figure 5.19 shows a TPD for Electrical Principles and it also indicates the designer's Optimum Linear Sequence (OLS). This is only one of many possible permutations. 'A' on the OLS denotes an assessment point and is usually placed after a topic which forms the basis for more advanced work. For example, many topics depend upon the learner understanding Topic 10.

You may also usefully indicate revision points on the OLS. For instance, you might find it beneficial to revise topics '2' and '9' after topic '28' before proceeding to topic '37'.

Mathematical, scientific and historical subjects lend themselves to this type of approach to planning a Scheme of Work. However, can the more creative subjects be considered in this structured manner? This really depends upon the subject matter and the will of the planner to reflect upon the planning process with care.

The world of Fashion is a creative area and Figure 5.21 shows an approach to planning this subject. There are fewer topics in the TPD but the use of the diagram helps stop a 'random' approach which sometimes is a feature of creative subjects. The need to be able to *justify* the sequence of study is an important part of the professional's task.

The use of the Word Processor is a rich area for training. One approach to planning is to divide the subject into practical and theoretical elements (see Figure 5.22). This may have benefits at the planning stage whilst in practice, learning theoretical and practical skills are well integrated.

The teaching of various techniques in Graphics could take place in a number of different sequences. A justification of a well ordered approach is shown in Figure 5.23 which indicates a very structured sequence.

The design of a Topic Precedent Diagram together with the addition of the Optimum Linear Sequence gives you the basis for your Scheme of Work. It allows you to logically plan the sequence of topics and determine the assessment times. In order to complete your Scheme you could add the most appropriate teaching strategies, resources and student activities.

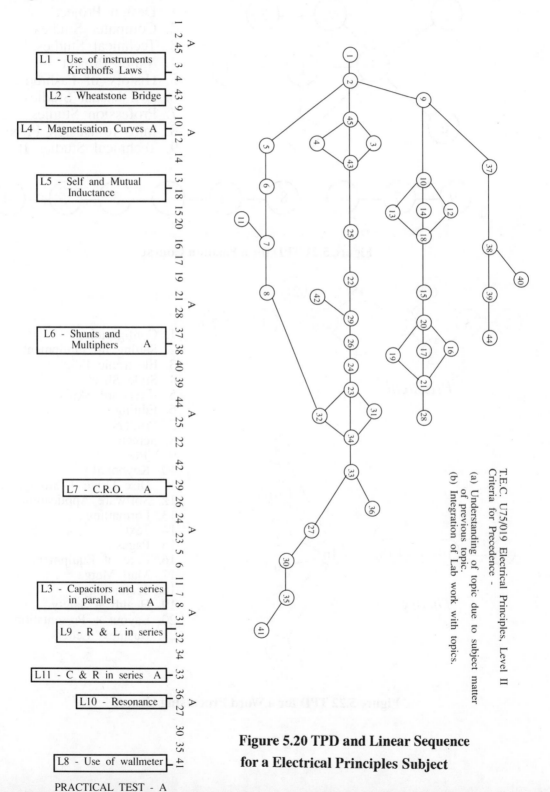

T.E.C. U75/019 Electrical Principles, Level II
Criteria for Precedence -

(a) Understanding of topic due to subject matter of previous topic.
(b) Integration of Lab work with topics.

L1 - Use of instruments Kirchhoffs Laws
L2 - Wheatstone Bridge
L4 - Magnetisation Curves A
L5 - Self and Mutual Inductance
L6 - Shunts and Multiphers   A
L7 - C.R.O.   A
L3 - Capacitors and series in parallel   A
L9 - R & L in series
L11 - C & R in series A
L10 - Resonance
L8 - Use of wallmeter

PRACTICAL TEST - A

Figure 5.20 TPD and Linear Sequence for a Electrical Principles Subject

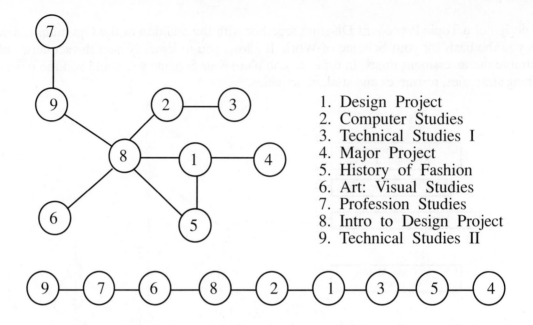

1. Design Project
2. Computer Studies
3. Technical Studies I
4. Major Project
5. History of Fashion
6. Art: Visual Studies
7. Profession Studies
8. Intro to Design Project
9. Technical Studies II

Figure 5.21 TPD for a Fashion Course

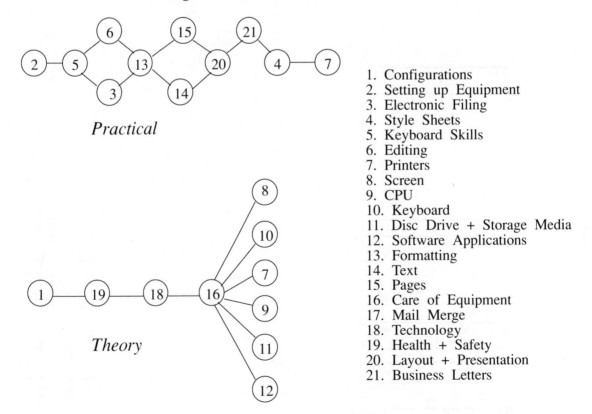

Practical

Theory

1. Configurations
2. Setting up Equipment
3. Electronic Filing
4. Style Sheets
5. Keyboard Skills
6. Editing
7. Printers
8. Screen
9. CPU
10. Keyboard
11. Disc Drive + Storage Media
12. Software Applications
13. Formatting
14. Text
15. Pages
16. Care of Equipment
17. Mail Merge
18. Technology
19. Health + Safety
20. Layout + Presentation
21. Business Letters

Figure 5.22 TPD for a Word Processing Course

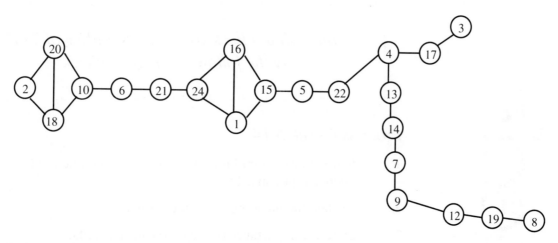

2—20 –18 –16 –6 – 21— 11—16 – 1 –15— 5– 22– 4—17— 3 —13—14–7– 9 –12 - 19– 8

1. Line - Pen + Ink
2. Correct Procedure - Drawing up art work
3. Positive + Negative - Gouache
4. Gouache Consistency - Flat colour
5. Halftone - Pen + Ink - Technical + felt
6. Image Grid - Enlarge/reduce
7. Cut paper - coloured
8. Applying Knowledge to Design Problems
9. Using Markers
10. Use + Care of Equipment: Brushes, Pens, Light box etc.
11. Awareness of Techniques + Media
12. Experimental Approach
13. Gouache - Halftone
14. Coloured Pens - Halftone
15. Halftone - Monotone - Graphite
16. Basic use of Media. Line Graphite
17. Flat Colour - Gouache
18. Correct use of Tracing Paper
19. Choice of Ground
20. Stretching Paper
21. Presentation of Finished Work
22. Understanding of Colour Theory

Figure 5.23 TPD for a Graphic Techniques Course

If you wish to check your understanding of TPD's, try the following progress check

Progress Check 5.14

1.   State at least four different criteria which may be used to sequence topics in a TPD.

2.   Explain the meaning of the term 'topic'.

3.   State the importance of the following in a TPD:

   –   point of divergence;

   –   point of convergence;

   –   finishing point;

   –   optional starting points.

4.   From a TPD, how could you decide:

   –   where best you might assess learning?

   –   where to revise a topic?

9. Topic Analysis

Having used the course aims, identified the main topics and organised the Optimum Linear Sequence for teaching, your next step in the planning process is to consider how you can present each of the topics to the students to make learning as simple and easy as possible. Some teachers go directly from the identification of the topic to the intended learning outcomes, for example by writing objectives or competences. If you wish to adopt a more rigorous approach, then you would include Topic Analysis which assists you to identify the main components of the topic (the sub-topics). Then proceed to order the sub-topics into a learning sequence which you will use in your lesson plan.

There are four main models of Topic Analysis which we will consider and these are ascribed to Davies (1971), Rowntree (1974), Gagné (1975) and Stenhouse (1975). Each model has its own advantages and limitations. Some subjects lend themselves to analysis by one (or more than one) of the models. Equally important is your preference for a model. If the model helps you to plan, then it serves a need. It is a valuable exercise to try each of the models in order to find which is the most helpful to you. You might find that you could use a combination of models for part of the subject (for example cognitive domain) and then use another for a different part (for instance affective domain).

Each model is considered in turn, together with an example.

9.1 Davies' Model of Topic Analysis

Davies suggests that you should ask five questions for each topic:

1. *What do you expect the students to demonstrate in order to show that they have learned the topic?*

This concentrates your mind on the objectives to be achieved through the learning of the topic.

2. *What questions do you expect the students to be able to answer?*

The questions that are to be answered by the students give an indication of the sub-topics that are required from the topic.

3. *What tasks, procedures and techniques should the students perform?*

Your response to this question forces you to concentrate upon the students' activities required in the learning of the sub-topics.

4. *What discrimination must be made?*

Where a comparison is made between what has already been learned and what needs to be learned.

5. *What total change in behaviour do you expect and how will this be observed and measured?*

Your response comes back to the objectives and gets you to add criteria of acceptable performance.

Your responses to these five questions provide you with a framework for Topic Analysis and a series of prompts. It is a useful exercise in identifying sub-topics and objectives but is less helpful in the formulation of a learning sequence (that is the ordering of the sub-topics).

Figure 5.24 shows a Davies-type analysis applied to a Painting and Decorating topic of 'Painting a Door'.

Davies Question	Response
How will learners demonstrate that they have learned the topic?	The students shall show skill in the application of undercoat and gloss paint to a door by brush.
What questions must the learner answer?	The students must answer questions about: need to protect surroundings from paint splash; – application of undercoat; – between coat procedures; – application of gloss paint; – the cleaning of tools, equipment and surroundings after each process.
What tasks, procedures and techniques must the learner perform?	Skill of preparation. Skill of application of paint by brush. Working with others. Ability to work tidily.
What discriminations must be made?	Students should understand the difference between undercoat, gloss and emulsion paint. They should know how to avoid runs, misses, curtains, nibs, etc.
What total change in behaviour is expected?	The learner shall show skill in painting a door to a professional standard in a real or simulated environment.

Figure 5.24. Application of Davies Topic Analysis to Painting a Door

9.2 Rowntree Model of Topic Analysis

Rowntree's model uses a two dimensional perspective to Topic Analysis which allows you to use a chart or diagrammatic approach. The horizontal analysis shows you the 'component behaviours' while the vertical one shows you the 'contributory' or 'enabling behaviours'.

In the example given by Rowntree (Figure 5.25) the cognitive domain is on the left hand side of the diagram with the right hand side concerned with psychomotor abilities.

The horizontal aspects show the various components (that is the type of charts available). The vertical view shows what is needed to achieve the components (for example for a pie chart - draw a circle, divide the circle using a protractor, and so on). Thus, the horizontal analysis provides you with the sub-topics and the vertical provides you with the sequence with an indication, perhaps, of the required entry behaviour. This required entry behaviour is shown in italics at the bottom of each of the lines in the figure.

The Rowntree analysis can also be applied to 'Basic Graphics Techniques' and this is shown in Figure 5.26. Clearly this is a large topic but the analysis yields valuable insights which will enable you to identify the intended learning outcomes (that is the objectives and competences).

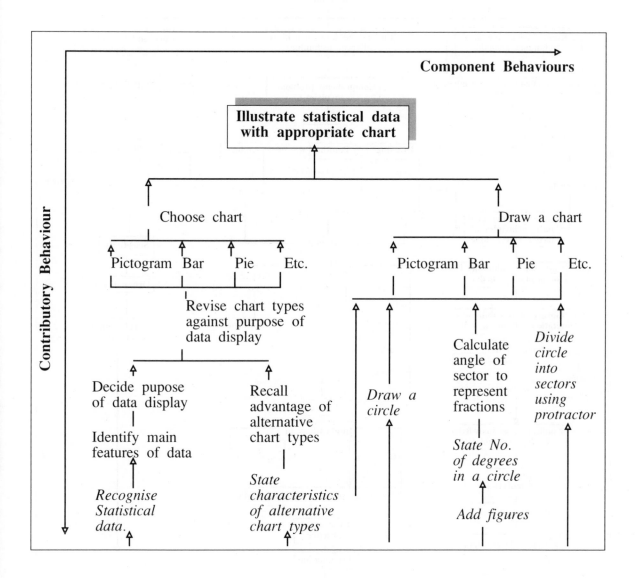

Figure 5.25 Application of Rowntree Topic Analysis to Chart Drawing

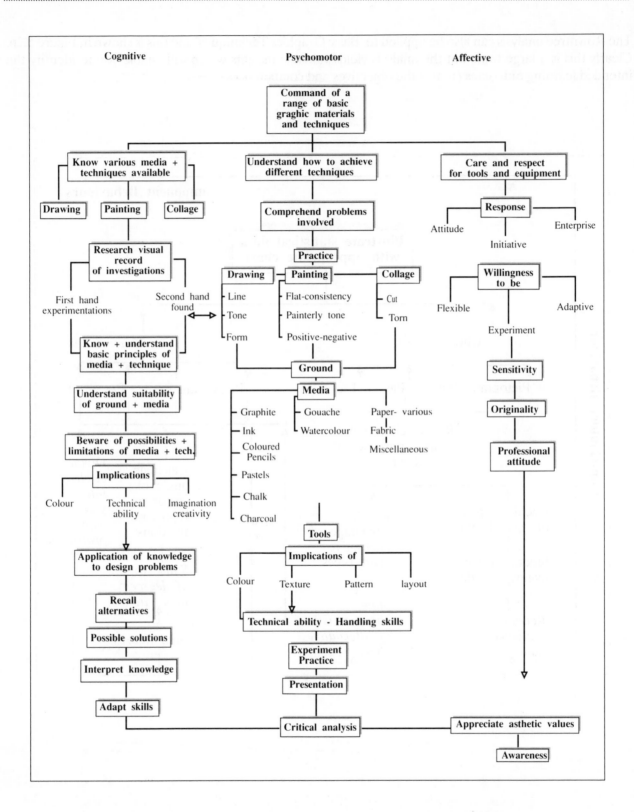

Figure 5.26 Application of Rowntree Topic Analysis to Basic Graphics Course

9.3 Gagné Model of Topic Analysis

The Gagné model is based on a hierarchy of learning; that is the student must learn simple things before learning complex ones. An example of the use of the model is shown below in Figure 5.27 with each of the Gagné stages identified for solving the problem 'How to Select an Appropriate Type of Holiday'.

Gagné Hierarchy	Example
Problem Solving	Selection of an appropriate type of holiday.
↑	
Principles	If you have good weather, food, companionship and accommodation, then you will have a pleasant holiday.
↑	
Concepts	Accommodation, weather, food, holiday.
↑	
Discriminations	Activities for work and pleasure.
↑	
Simple Types of Learning	

Figure 5.27 Application of Gagné Topic Analysis to Selecting a Holiday

In this way, learners start with simple types of learning (stimulus-response) leading to discriminations, through concepts and principles until, finally, they can use all of this learning in the solving of problems; the most difficult type of learning.

The advantage of the Gagné-type of Topic Analysis is that it allows you to sequence the work in terms of the order in which learning naturally takes place. The problem for you is that, in order to use the Gagné model, you must be able to identify the types of learning with accuracy. Indeed, not all teachers subscribe to the Gagné learning types.

9.4 Stenhouse Model of Topic Analysis

The Stenhouse model suggests that some course aims may be difficult to achieve merely by using the teaching topics. It suggests that you can use some aims directly to formulate the sub-topics and that you can use the model to achieve them. In the example given in Figure 5.28, 'To Develop an Enquiring Mind and a Scientific Approach to Problems', learning may be achieved incidentally, but Stenhouse believes the analysis will help you structure teaching to ensure that activities take place which make the achievement of such aims more likely.

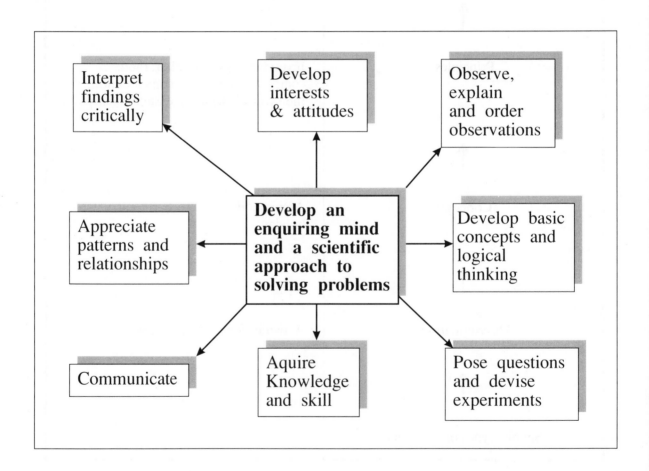

Figure 5.28 Application of Stenhouse Topic Analysis to Problem Solving

You will find that the Stenhouse Model is particularly useful with 'creative' subjects as it allows you to 'map' the various elements of the topic. The example (Figure 5.29) shows the key elements in a first course in 'playing the violin'.

Note that you may use the Stenhouse Model to brainstorm the various elements involved in the topic. You may find it useful, however, to consider each of the three domains of learning (Cognitive, Affective and Psychomotor) in turn during the brainstorming so that you can be sure that you are being comprehensive in your coverage.

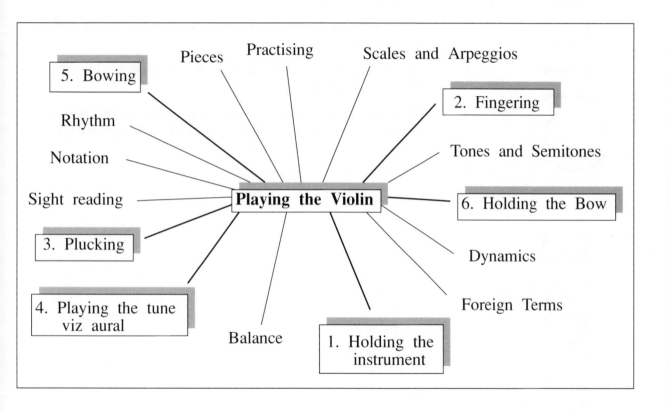

Figure 5.29 Application of Stenhouse Model to Violin Playing

> *If you wish to check your understanding of Topic*
> *Analysis try the following progress check*

Progress Check 5.15

1.   What are the 5 questions that Davies suggests should be answered to analyse a topic?

2.   What, according to Rowntree are meant by 'contributory' and 'component' behaviours?

3.   Explain Gagné hierarchy of learning which he uses as his basis for Topic Analysis.

4.   What, in your opinion, is the most likely type of subject matter that can be applied to the Stenhouse method of Topic Analysis?

10. Lesson Planning

If you observe experienced teachers you may find a wide variation in practice with regard to their approach to lesson plans. Some teachers have very detailed plans while others 'appear' to have little at all in the way of a plan. What is important is that the lesson is always planned with care. What follows is a guide to some ways in which you may plan. You should experiment with planning until you find the method which works best for you.

When you are planning a lesson you will find that a range of factors influence you. Figure 5.30 gives a brief overview of the process you could use. The student, of course, is at the centre of the process.

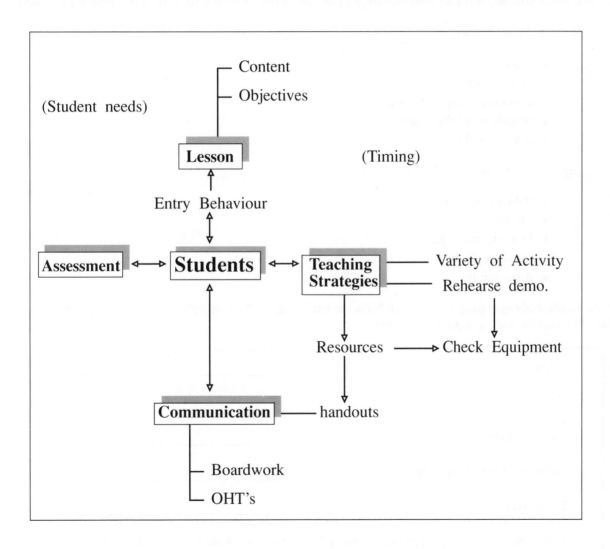

Figure 5.30 Factors which influence the Lesson Planning Process

You need to consider several strands. The starting point of the process is the intended learning outcomes (objectives/competences). Aligned with the statement of learning outcomes is the need to identify the entry behaviour of the students. It could be that learners know (a) too little and you have to start at an 'easier' level or (b) too much so that they do not need instruction. You should plan your communication with the learners and plan and encourage communications between students. You should use a variety of activities to maintain interest which will, in turn, influence your timing and your use of a range of teaching strategies and resources. When you use resources check that the equipment does work and that you know (or remember) how to use it. For example, with demonstrations check before you start that all of the equipment that you require is working. How long will it take to complete the demonstration?

At this stage you may wonder how you might plan all of this. The key features for a lesson plan include:

(i)   Initial information:

- topic
- class details
- expected entry behaviour
- objectives of the session
- time available.

(ii) In the Body of the Plan:

- student activity
- timing
- teaching strategies
- resources/aids
- assessment.

One method of organising these variables is shown in Figure 5.31 with the initial information at the top of the plan and its body in a column format.

Topic :	_____
Class :	_____
Time available :	_____
Expected Entry Behaviour :	_____
Objectives :	_____

Key/Time	Teacher Activity	Student Activity	Resources

Figure 5.31 Possible Layout for a Lesson Plan

It is vital that you consider the lesson in three stages:

(i)   introduction

(ii) development (the main body), and

(iii) conclusion (summary).

We have said of the lecture that the good lecturer 'tells students what is going to be told', 'tells them' and then 'tells them what they have been told'. This, in effect, corresponds to the three stages of a lesson.

In a student-centred lesson, your first phase may be to outline the activity to your students and check what they should know in order to complete it (the entry behaviour). This may be followed by getting the students to attempt the activity. Finally, ensure that the learning has taken place through question and answer or a test or activity that makes the required check or, alternately, review the main points of the lesson (the conclusion).

The following lesson plans explain how you might complete these points in practice. The first example (Figure 5.32) is for a psychomotor skills lesson, the second (Figure 5.33) is to learn attitudes and the final one (Figure 5.34) is to achieve an objective with indicative content.

Topic :	Temperature Measurement
Class :	10 Student Nurses
Time available :	60 minutes
Expected Entry Behaviour :	Knowledge of mercury-in-glass thermometer.
General Objective :	Show skill in the procedure for body temperature measurement.
Specific Objective :	Measure a person's temperature using a thermometer. Accurately record results.

Key/Time	Teacher Activity	Student Activity	Resources
Recap last lesson 5 min	Q. Normal readings of blood pressure?	Answering	OHP transparency
Introduction 5 min	Need to take temperature. Thermometers. Uses of records.	Listening	Thermometer
Development Temperature 30 min	Q. Why take temp? Q. How gain/lose heat? Use a thermometer. Demonstration	Answering	OHP 1
		Watching/Listening Practise on each other	Mediwipes
	Body Temperatures		List on Chalkboard
Conclusion 10 min 5 min	Recap main points Question Objective Test	Answer	Test No 6

Figure 5.32 Lesson Plan for a Psychomotor Skills Lesson

Topic :	Simulation of a meeting.
Class :	15 communication students (Bus Stud).
Time available :	70 minutes.
Expected Entry Behaviour :	Knowledge of procedures of formal meetings.
General Objective :	Appreciate the relative merits of meetings as part of the decision making process.
Specific Objective :	Listen to others. Contributes to decision making process. Supports other members of the class.

Key/Time	Teacher Activity	Student Activity	Resources
Introduction 5 min 5 min	Purpose of simulation. Issue/allocate roles.	Listening Reading	Suitable room. Role cards.
Development 30 min 20 min	Agenda item 1 Agenda item 2 Agenda item 3 Debrief - questions	In role Feedback/ discussion.	Agenda items.
Conclusion 10 min	Summary of key learning issues.	Note taking	OHP transparency.

Figure 5.33 Plan for Lesson to Teach Attitudes

Topic :	Making a video 'Interviewing Consumers' Lesson 1 .
Class :	10 Personnel Officers.
Time available :	3 hours.
Expected Entry Behaviour :	No previous experience.
Objective :	Participate in the making of a video. Observe reactions of the interviewer and interviewee.
Indicative Content :	Use of camera. Team work. Planning work.

Key/Time	Activity
9.00	Meet class - discuss overall task. - distribute duties to students e.g. collect camera, etc.
9.45	Meet at 'scene'.
9.50	Confirm/discuss duties with individuals.
10.10	Coffee
10.30	Questions
10.35	Record interviews .
11.15	Adjourn to room to see tape.
12.00	Lunch (p.m. editing, etc.)

Figure 5.34 Example Lesson Plan Related to Indicative Content

> *If you wish to check your understanding of lesson planning try the following progress check*

Progress Check 5.16

1. List the six main aspects which could be included in the introductory information of a Lesson Plan.

2. Give two useful activities which could be included in the introduction to a lesson.

3. Identify the headings that are useful for the body of a Lesson Plan.

4. What percentage of the total time for the lesson might be given to:

    (i)   the introduction;

    (ii) the summary;

    of a lesson.

11. Negotiation

The approaches to course planning we have discussed so far have been based on a prescribed course content. However, the use of negotiation in learning is becoming more prevalent, particularly with adult learners. Perhaps the thought of having to negotiate the learning programme for each student fills you with horror! One thing it is not: and that is a soft option. Do not negotiate the hard topics out of the learning – this is the hallmark of the bad teacher.

If your students have not negotiated their learning before, they too may be filled with horror. Perhaps your ideal approach is to start with what is non-negotiable, gain their confidence and gradually wean your students into the negotiation process.

11.1 What is Negotiation?

Some people tend to associate negotiation with conflict or with the final stages of conflict, for instance at the end of a war, at the end of a strike or wage bargaining process. This is not a very helpful perspective. The negotiation of learning is about you and the student engaging in a process where you agree on a course of action whereby the student is to achieve the intended learning outcomes whether they be in the form of aims, objectives or competences.

11.2 Why Negotiate?

The needs of students clearly vary enormously and this is particularly true of adult learners. Using a standardised course you cannot hope to meet the range of abilities, expectations and temperaments of all of your students, but can only hope to meet some of their needs for some of the time.

If you negotiate an individual programme with a student, there is a greater likelihood that it will suit the needs of that individual. However, the system is not without its problems and in Figure 5.35 we outline some advantages and limitations. From this it will be seen that, generally speaking, the advantages outweigh the limitations. This is especially true in learning social skills that are concerned with processes. The limitations of negotiation are generally involved in the working of the process and can be overcome if you negotiate skilfully enough.

Advantages of Negotiation	Limitations of Negotiation
– Increased motivation.	– Can be difficult to manage.
– Course seen as 'right for me'.	– Can be bureaucratic.
– Student active in the learning process.	– Learners may not want to take on role.
– Closer Student/teacher relationship.	– Lack of rapport leading to lack of agreement.
– Early identification of learning problems.	– Unrealistic goals may be set.
– Increased opportunities for pastoral counselling.	– Practical considerations (e.g. laboratory availability) may cause difficulties.
– Good for social skills.	
– Highlights (unknown) student skills.	

Figure 5.35 Advantages and Disadvantages of Negotiation

11.3 The Process

The process of negotiation may be seen as a five stage model.

(i)   Preparing for Negotiation

(ii)   the first session(s)

(iii)   the contract

(iv)   monitoring the learning

(v)   the review

(i) Preparing for Negotiation

Before entering into the negotiation process, you should have a very clear idea of what your student is to achieve. The limiting factors, or constraints that you need to establish are, for example, whether the assessment is to be determined by a third party, if the institution has constraints such as 'supervision' at all times, what is the time scale (not only the end dates but, also, regular reviews). Unplanned difficulties arise and you need to build in some contingency for them. The student may be unfamiliar with negotiation and your planning needs to take this into account. Finally, decide where is the best place for the first and subsequent meetings.

(ii) The First Session(s)

Students often find negotiation difficult, if only because they may be adolescents dealing with an adult in a new situation. It is important, therefore, that you quickly establish a rapport. Perhaps a useful way to start is to find out more about the student as a person by asking about their interests and ambitions. Establish the framework and limits or boundaries of the negotiation before the process begins properly. One approach that you could use is to start from details and proceed to agree detail by detail. This involves great expertise and time. You may, however, find it more useful to secure a broad, wide ranging agreement and then explore area by area. Your role is to listen to the student, confirm beliefs and agreements by repeating them, and then to probe a range of issues. You will find that sticking points do occur. It is often useful not to spend too much time on these but to refer to them at a later stage.

(iii) The Contract

At some stage you will need to 'firm-up' or agree the proposals. You can do this in the form of a contract or agreement. This is best in writing and needs to be in a language that the student understands - in fact, get the student to draft the contract. You need to be sure that the intended learning outcomes are valid, the learning can take place within the constraints of the institution, the time-scale is realistic and finally, it is within the ability of the student. Your contract needs to give the student clear guidelines for progress but be flexible enough to overcome unforeseen problems. Regular reviews need to be a feature of the contract. From the contract, your student should be clear about what is the intended learning, what is to be done, how it is to be done, what resources are available, what is the time-scale, how the outcomes are prescribed and, finally, what are the assessment criteria.

(iv) Monitoring the Learning

It is important to have regular reviews. In this way you will set the student a series of deadlines in which to work thereby giving a structure to the process. You can identify progress, or lack of it, so the final outcomes should be no surprise to you. The student should do most of the talking at the reviews. You can achieve this by posing questions such as 'How is the project going'? 'Have you any problems'? or 'What problems have you had'? 'What are you going to do next'? You might find it useful to note some of the outcomes in the contract itself.

(v) The Review

Your final stage is to review what has been done and learned. Your ultimate question is 'Has the student achieved the intended learning outcome?' This may include a discussion of a formal assessment. What is also important is 'What would you do differently?' and 'What have you learned in other (negotiated) learning?'

11.4 Summary

As you can see, the negotiated curriculum places very different demands upon both you and the student. The benefits for the student have been discussed. The benefits for you come when you can see your students working on their own initiative and discussing their work in an adult or even enthusiastic manner. You need to have, or develop, the skills of a negotiator, manage several different learning activities and, very importantly, manage your own time to ensure all students have sufficient support.

> *Possible evidence to show that you have
> achieved the competence
> Design Learning Programmes related
> to specific needs of students'*

The type of evidence that you might collect to show that you have achieved the competence includes:

1. Draw a Topic Precedence Diagram and Optimum Linear sequence for your own subject area. To complete this you will need to:

    (a) define the topics;

    (b) follow the suggested steps to produce the TPD;

    (c) design an OLS from the TPD and, on it, show revision and testing time.

3. Using the OLS as a basis, design a Scheme of Work where, for each topic, you indicate the learning time required, the teaching methods and resources to be used, and the assessment procedures that you will plan.

4. Select a topic from your TPD and apply the most appropriate methods of topic analysis to it. Give reasons for your choice of method.

5. Using the topic analysis that you have completed, plan a lesson using the criteria that have been suggested.

6. Critically analyse the written lesson plan either from the basis of having written it, or after you have used it with a class, from the basis of having used it.

7. Design a pro-forma which could be used as a basis for a contract for your students to negotiate effective learning. Critically analyse the design of the contract.

> *If you wish to check your understanding of negotiation try the following progress check*

Progress Check 5.17

1.   List the 5 stages that might usefully be used in negotiating a learning programme with a student.

2.   Identify at least three aspects that you should prepare before negotiating a learning programme with a student.

3.   Define a learning contract.

4.   Why are regular reviews important when questioning a negotiated learning contract with a student?

5.   List the important questions that you should ask a student in the final review of a negotiated learning contract.

Further Reading and References

Further reading and references relating to the topics in this chapter can be found in the following:

BTEC — *Course and Unit Design*, BTEC, 1988.

Bloom, B S — *Taxonomy of Educational Objectives: Handbook 1:Cognitive Domain*, Longmans, 1964.

Cole, H.P — *Process Education*, Education Technical Publications, 1982.

Davies, I K — *The Management of Learning*, McGraw Hill, 1971.

Fletcher, S — *Competence-based Assessment Techniques*, Kogan Page, 1992.

FEU — *Learning by Doing*, FEU, 1988.

Gagné, R M — *Essentials of Learning for Instruction*, Dryden Press, 1975.

Gronlund, N E — *Stating Behavioural Objectives for Classroom Instruction*, McMillan, 1970.

Krathwoal, et al — *Taxonomy of Educational Objectives: Affective Domain*, David Mckay, 1964.

Mager, R F — *Preparing Instructional Objectives*. Fearon Publishers. 1962.

Newble, D and Cannon, R — *A Handbook for Teachers in Universities and Colleges*. Kogan Page. 1991.

Newby, T — *Validating your Training*, Kogan Page, 1992.

Popham, W J — *Criterion Referenced Measurement*, Prentice Hall, 1978.

Reece, I H (ed) — *Aspects for Curriculum in Technical Education*, Colombo Plan Staff College, 1982.

Romiszowski, A J — *The Selection and Use of Instructional Media*, Kogan Page, 1976.

Rowntree, D — *Educational Technology in Curriculum Development*, Harper Row, 1974.

Simpson E J — *The Classification of Educational Objectives: Psychomotor Domain*, University of Illinois, 1976.

Stenhouse, L — *An Introduction to Curriculum Research and Development*, Heinemann, 1975.

Vargas, J S — *Writing Worthwhile Behavioural Objectives*, Harper Row, 1972.

Chapter 6

Communication and the Teacher

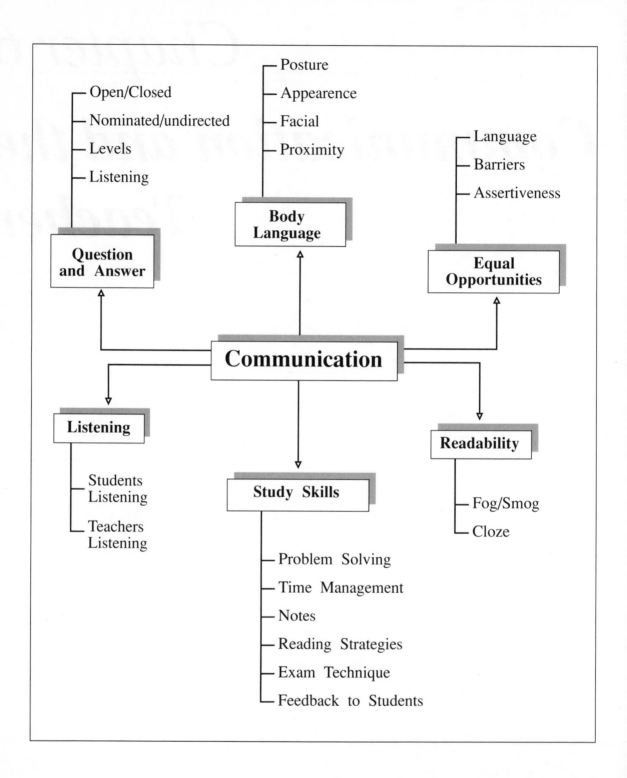

Overview of Chaper 6

Competences Related to this Chapter

The teacher competences and associated performance criteria related to this chapter are:

Overall Competence – Employ effective Communication Techniques.

COMPETENCE	PERFORMANCE CRITERIA
1. **Demonstrate effective communication skills**	(a) Use language appropriate to the ability of the students. (b) Use a variety of stimuli to enhance communication (c) Select appropriate means of communication to suit the learners and the topic. (d) Use question and answer technique effectively.
2. **Assist students to develop their communication skills.**	(a) Identify the communication skills required by students. (b) Monitor progress in skill development. (c) Assist students to develop these skills. (d) Provide opportunities for students to practise these skills.

1. Model of Communication

Comunication is essentially about one person who sends a message which is received by a second person. Some form of channel, or means of communication is needed. This channel could be sound, it could be movement, it could be smell. We have used models elsewhere in this book and Figure 6.1 shows us a basic model of communication

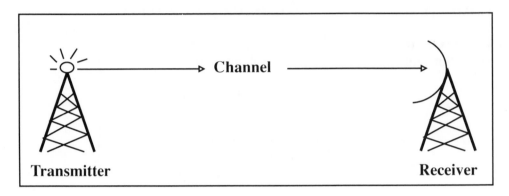

Figure 6.1 Basic Communication Model

The model is satisfactory for most situations for example speech, nonverbal communication, reading; but in practice the situation is more complex.

In practice there are factors which distort the message or signal. This is called 'noise' and is a barrier to good communication. If your classroom has a poor layout, the students may not be able to see or hear you. The lighting may be poor or there may be excessive sunlight. 'Noise' could be from traffic or people outside the room or it could be from the students themselves. Noise could be more difficult to identify like pitching the level of the learning too high or too low for the learners. The vocabulary you use could be too difficult for the learner or too much use of unfamiliar jargon. We have to do our best to minimise noise and make our message clear. Non verbal signals - or even verbal signals, from the students should give us valuable feedback on the quality of communications.

2. Reading Age and Readability

All the students, with whom we come into contact, have attended school until they were at least 16 years old. We make assumptions about that experience and, in particular, we often assume that students have the ability to read the information we present to them. We give the students handouts, we write on the board and we recommend textbooks. But how often do we really consider the difficulty of the reading and the ability of the students to read well? Difficulties in learning may not be caused only by the way in which we teach, or the lack of intelligence of the learner but may be the result of a reading problem. Consequently we should now look at how we can determine the reading age of a students and the readability of written materials.

Reading age is related to the reading age of the average child. So a reading age of 14 is the ability to read at the standard of the average 14 year old. *Readability* on the other hand considers the degree of difficulty with particular reading materials. Consider 14 year old pupils. If they are presented with material requiring a reading age of 16 then there could well be problems. However if the material has a reading age of 12 then there should be no problem. Problems with reading are not confined to students. Many people, for example, experience problems with official forms such as those relating to Social Security and income tax, although progress has been made in making such forms more easily understood. There is a Plain English Society whose main purpose is to reduce the amount of material in circulation which is unnecessarily difficult to read. Official jargon is often called 'Gobbledegook' and this word is used in the title of two of the techniques we will look at.

Remember that calculating readability (or the reading age required to understand a text) is an inexact science. So, two of the techniques used, the FOG index and the SMOG index, and the results they produce should be seen only as guidelines.

2.1 Reading Age

2.1.1 The Fog Index

The Fog index is one of the indices used to calculate the required reading age of written materials. You can use it on your handouts to give an indication of whether you are writing at an appropriate level for your students.

FOG is the *Frequency Of Gobbledegook* and may be calculated as follows:

1. Select a passage of 100 words

2. Count the number of complete sentences

3. Count the words in each of the complete sentences.

4. Find the average sentence length (L) by dividing the number of words in all of the complete sentences by the number of complete sentences (i.e. divide your answer to '3' by your answer to '2').

5. Count the number of words of three or more syllables (N) in the 100 word sample

6. Add L and N, multiply by 0.4 and then add 5 ie $0.4(L+N)+5$

7. This is the reading age

You may wish to select three or four passages of a textbook to find the average reading age.

The following text is designed for use with students who have a reading age of 14. The FOG index has been applied to determine its suitability for such students.

Note that in the following passage there are 100 words between the two stars.

Lamps and Lighting

*Filament lamps are available with a single coil of tungsten wire or with a double coil, or coiled coil, which gives more light. All common filament lamps have an average life span of one thousand hours. This light is best for normal domestic usage since it gives a good balance between the amount of life obtained and the cost of the electricity.

Filament lamps should be bought to suit the voltage of the mains supply. If, for example, your residence is supplied at 240 volts, buy lamps of the same voltage. The common size of domestic filament lamps range from about * 8 watts (for the dimmest of night lights) to 200 watts. Almost all household lighting needs are met by 40, 60, and 100 watt lamps but the greater the wattage, the greater the heat generated and the greater the cost.

Number of complete sentences	= 5	
Average sentence length (L)	=	$\dfrac{\text{No of words in all sentences}}{\text{No of complete sentences}}$
	=	$\dfrac{90}{5}$
	=	18
Number of polysyllabic words (N)	=	11
Reading Age	=	$[(L + N) \times 0.4] + 5$
	=	$[(18 + 11) \times 0.4] + 5$
	=	$[29 \times 0.4] + 5$
	=	$11.6 + 5$
	=	16.6 Years

This means that the material would be unsuitable for students who have a reading age of 14 years. They would have too much difficulty reading the text let alone with its content. You should recognise that the important aspect of Required Reading Age that makes the text difficult to read lies with the number of polysyllabic words and the length of the sentences. So to bring down the required reading age you must reduce the number of long words and the length of the sentences.

Consider the following text about the design of a teaching programme. It is intended to be used as a handout to students who have a reading age of 14 years. Will the students cope with the demands of the language?

(*) *"Basically* a teaching programme is a course prepared as a result of an *intensive analysis* of the learning task. It is *generally* presented to the students one stage at a time. Each stage presents *information* and demands a response from the students. They may be required to answer a question, make a *decision* or practise a *procedure*. The response that students make has two functions. First it ensures that they are *actively* involved in the learning process and practise the tasks that they are to master; *Secondly* it provides a measure of their progress. This measure can be used by the (*) students as knowledge of results or by the course designer to identify and remedy weaknesses in the teaching. "

Again use the FOG index to gauge the suitability of the text for these students. The two stars (*) represent the beginning and end of the 100 words. Within the extract there are:

(i)   six complete sentences within 94 words giving an average sentence length of 94/6 = 18.3 (L);

(ii)   nine words have 3 or more syllables (N) – these are shown in italics.

Thus, for this extract the Required Reading Age is:

Age	=	$[(L + N) \times 0.4] + 5$
	=	$[(18.3 + 9) \times 0.4] + 5$
	=	$[27.3 \times 0.4] + 5$
	=	$11 + 5$
	=	$\underline{16}$

The extract is too difficult for the students and should be simplified. To do this you need to either reduce the length of the sentences or the number of long words or both *without* losing the sense of the original text.

We have rewritten the extract to reduce the number of long words to six, the semicolon has been omitted and an extra sentence has been created. Thus, the extract becomes:

(*) "In essence a teaching programme is a course prepared as a result of a thorough breakdown of the learning task. It is *generally* presented to the students one stage at a time. Each stage presents *information* and demands a response from the students. They may be required to answer a question, make a *decision* or practise a *procedure*. The response that students make has two functions. Firstly it ensures that they are *actively* involved in the learning process and practise the tasks that they are to master. *Secondly* it provides a measure of their progress. This measure can be used (*) by the students as knowledge of results or by the course designer to identify and remedy weaknesses in the teaching. "

Thus

L	=	95/7
	=	13.6
N	=	6
Age	=	$[(L + N) \times 0.4] + 5$
	=	$[(13.6 + 6) \times 0.4] + 5$
	=	$[19.6 \times 0.4] + 5$
	=	$8 + 5$
	=	$\underline{13}$

and the text will now be suitable for the students in terms of its Required Reading Age.

2.1.2 The SMOG Index

SMOG is the *Simple Measure Of Gobbledegook* and may be calculated as follows:

1. Take a sample of 30 sentences
2. Count the number of words with three or more syllables
3. Find the square root of this number
4. Add 8

This gives the reading age of the material. Again, three or four samples should be calculated to gain an average age of, say, a textbook. If your material contains fewer sentences you can try the following which should give very similar results.

1.   Take a sample of 10 sentences

2.   Count the number of words with three or more syllables

3.   Multiply this answer by 3

4.   Find the square root

5.   Add 8

It has been said that calculations of Required Reading Age is an inexact science and, in fact, the SMOG index tends to indicate a required reading age about 2 years above that of the FOG calculation.

If the required reading age of the written materials appears to be too high then you can redesign the handout by reducing the number of words in each sentence and by reducing the number of words with three or more syllables. You cannot do this with books but you can consider recommending other books which the learner may find easier to understand.

2.2 Readability

2.2.1 APU Vocabulary Tests

The Assessment Performance Unit (APU) have produced tests which measure the reading age of learners. These are relatively quick and easy to administer and are considered to be reliable.

The test that they have produced consists of 75 multiple-choice questions asking students to identify the meaning of words. The initial questions start off very easily. For example, which of the following words means the same as the one printed in capital letters?

BEGIN   1. ask   2. start   3. plain   4. over   5. away.

However, later in the test the words become much more difficult. For example, the final question is:

PUSILLANIMOUS   1. loud   2. living   3. timid   4. averse   5. correct

Thus, not only is the test assessing students' ability to understand words but it is also a time test. Once the test has been completed, it is marked and the raw score is placed on a graph to translate it into a reading age of the student.

2:2:2 CLOZE

Another technique that can be used to gauge whether students are able to cope with specific reading materials is the "cloze" technique. This, unlike the APU test, does not give us a specific reading age, but allows us to assess whether a student can cope with a particular part of a book, a specific handout or worksheet.

So far we have considered the required reading age of materials and the reading age of learners. The cloze technique can be used with your own materials to find the required Reading Age. It is based on 'closure' a concept used in Gestalt psychology.

For example when we look at the figure we see a circle because we close the gaps.

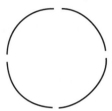

Similarly when we see gaps in prose we consider the meaning of the words before and after the gap and 'complete' the gap. The technique may be used on handouts, books, instructions etc. It matches an individual student with written materials and identifies if they have a concern.

The technique is relatively simple

1.   Take a passage and omit every 'n'th word (say every 5th word)

2.   The learners have to supply the correct word.

Interpretation of the scores is not exact and tends to vary with n, ie nth word which has been omitted. Figure 6.2 may act as a guide,

n = 5	n = 7	Comments
Score 30% +	Score 80% +	Learners should have no problems
Score 30%-50%	Score 65% - 80%	Some guidance needed
Score less than 30%	Score less than 65%	Materials too demanding

Figure 6.2 Interpretation of Cloze Technique to Determine Readability

Despite the problem of interpretation, the Cloze technique has several advantages.

1.   It can be set for any learner at any level because the learner relates to your material

2.   Your own relevant text can be used

3.   It is realistic to the learner (own subject area)

4.   It tests recognizing words, semantics and skimming.

3. Listening Skills

"Some students just don't listen." The adage "in one ear and out the other" describes fairly accurately what happens in some lessons with some students. Students, and teachers, sometimes hear what they want to hear and this invariably results in a breakdown in communication.

Listening, like reading and writing and, indeed, all communication skills, needs practising and can be improved. The skill for the teacher involves motivating students to listen. It involves more than telling them to listen hard and trying to pick out all of the important points. While motivation is necessary and should be encouraged, it is not enough. Students need to know when to "tune in" and what to listen for.

To start with no one listens intently from one minute to the next. Students may look as if they are listening. But, while they may be hearing all of the time, only some of the time are they listening, that is, taking in information, storing, analysing or evaluating the content, and summing up what they hear.

The attentive periods when students listen vary depending upon their tiredness, anxiety, boredom or interest, the stimulation which you provide, and the extraneous noise that makes it difficult for them to concentrate. All people listen for periods ranging from twenty to forty seconds. This is followed by periods of processing of information. Listening involves this continual process of making sense of what is heard. If your talk has your student's attention, then the talk is making sense and students retain more information and are able to recall more details than if they are bored by what you are saying.

Both students and teachers listen: students listen to your explanations and you listen to your students, questions and explanations. Getting students to listen attentively involves using techniques of good talking. These are shown in Fig 6.3.

- Speak clearly and loudly so that all can easily hear;

- Do not read from notes; look at students when speaking and maintain eye contact;

- Be enthusiastic about the topic;

- Use gestures for emphasis and avoid distracting mannerisms;

- Use visual aids to assist the spoken word but be careful that they do not become the main form of communication;

- Encourage questions from the students.

Figure 6.3 Talking Techniques to Assist Student Listening

Each of these assist with student listening and, combined, should ensure that most concentrate. Each of the techniques will be more or less attractive to individual personalities and, as such, will assist the concentration.

Teacher listening skills involve skills that students should be encouraged to use. These are shown in Figure 6.4.

- Organise
- Summarise
- Beware of Distractions

Figure 6.4 Listening Skills for the Teacher

The first of these skills involves *organisation* and can be achieved through asking questions in your mind whilst the student is talking. Such questions are:

(a)   What are the main points that the student is making?

(b)   What supporting facts or reasons are given?

(c)   What advantages are being claimed?

(d)   What disadvantages are mentioned?

The answers to these questions can usually be summarised from the key words that the student uses. Most student answers contain relevant and irrelevant information and you need to sort these out.

Secondly, it is useful, when a student has finished speaking, to *summarise* the main points that have been said. This ensures that the main points have been understood and greatly assists with two-way communication.

Most classrooms are noisy places. So, finally, any *distractions* can be a barrier to effective listening. If the noise is too great, quieten the class, move closer to the students and delay the communication until it can be heard. Sometimes the distraction is due to differences in accent or dialect or the disorganised way of speaking.

4. Questioning

Oral questioning is a very powerful way for you, the teacher, to interact with the students. It involves the studentlearner in the session through thinking and provides you with feedback on the level of learning.

Questioning is a skill which needs to be developed. 'Closed' questions usually only require the student t answer 'yes' or 'no' and as such are not particularly valuable. 'Open' questions cause the student t formulate a response. If you ask students to explain 'Why vaccines work', then they have to state in their own words their own understanding. This gives you feedback especially if you observe the students' body language – are they unsure?

Questions may be asked at various levels. For example in the Cognitive domain you could ask: "What are the main parts of a flower?" (Knowledge). "What does this abrupt change in the graph mean?" (Comprehension). Knowing the properties of Sulphuric acid and the composition of water, predict what would happen if the two were mixed (Application).

Questions may be built up from knowledge to comprehension to application and above. You may pose questions at comprehension level and find no response from the students. In that case you ask questions at knowledge level to ensure that the students have the basis upon which they can answer the question.

Communication is a two-way process where you want to communicate to your students and you want your students to communicate with you. Question and answer is a good way to develop this interactional style of communication.

As a teacher you need a certain amount of confidence in order to develop questioning skills in yourself and in your students. When you pose a question, you have no ideas as to what the student is going to say, despite your hopes! So, it means that you have to have the courage and confidence to deal with any answer no matter how bizarre. When you develop the questioning skills of your students, you are going to experience a wide range of searching questions which places significant demands upon you. You have to be confident in your subject matter and be well prepared even though the best of teachers are sometimes posed questions which they cannot answer. If you do not already use question and answer in your teaching, plan a short questioning session in the near future. You can then gain experience and extend the duration and frequency of the question and answer sessions.

Pate and Bremer (1967) show that most teachers ask closed questions (that is questions that relate to specific facts and mainly to do with recall). What we should be trying to do is to get the students to think aloud. This gives a real insight into students thought processes and assists both you and the peer group. You are also trying to get students to generate ideas and thoughts of their own and to explore the implications.

One of the first stages in questioning is getting the students to talk. This may seem strange when we are often trying to get them to be quiet. Students will engage in social talk very easily but your task is to get them talking about some aspect of your subject. It may be that the talking starts with an aspect not of immediate concern to the current topic.

For example you may be dealing with electrical circuit design and ask questions about the relative merits of using alternative sources of energy. Students talk to you but can also talk to their peers and it is at this stage that you ensure that you have control of the situation and not allow a 'free for all'.

One thing about teachers is that we tend to talk far too much! What we need to do is to let others have a chance to speak. We need to plan our questioning rather than hope a question pops into our minds at the appropriate moment. Before the lesson starts we need to think about what are the *key* questions which we should ask. The *order* in which we ask these questions is also important. Although we prepare these key questions before the lesson, we have to be prepared to change these questions, or use a series of unrehearsed questions, in order to respond to the answers that we receive. In other words we need to plan a questioning *strategy* but be prepared to develop *tactics* on the spot.

In chapter 3, open and closed questions were discussed where closed questions require a one word answer or there is a single correct answer. Open questions, on the other hand, allow the students more scope to state their views, postulate what could happen or put forward an argument. Developing the technique to pose open questions is a skill that teachers should develop. These questions need not just be at the start of a lesson or during the development phase. It may be useful to pose open questions at the end of one lesson which stimulates curiosity about the next lesson.

Another facet of of good questioning technique is to distribute questions around the whole class so that answering is not left to a few students. One technique to achieve this is:

1. Pose the question to the whole class

2. Pause - allowing all students to think of the answer.

3. Nominate/name a student to answer

4. Listen to the answer

5. Reward correct answer with "yes, correct, that's right" etc

6. Incorrect answer should not be ridiculed either by yourself or the remainder of the group of students.

7. Spread the questions around the class so that all can participate.

8. Encourage all to join in – in a regulated matter – by for example by saying – "Jean, can you give an example of what David means?"

However, non-verbal cues can be given by establishing eye contact, raising eyebrows, and so on. If you work around the class in an obvious systematic order, those who have answered tend to relax a little. Use a technique which is not obvious. There is also a tendency for us to act like a torch beam as shown in Fig 6.5.

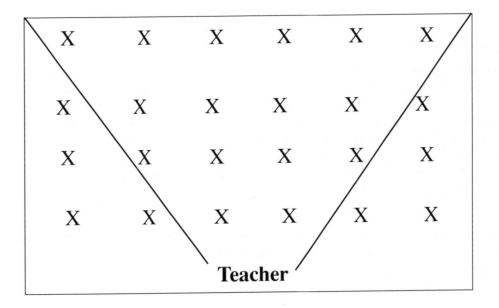

Figure 6.5 'Torch Beam' Arc of Questioning

If we are aware that most of us tend to concentrate our attention for questions on those students who sit in the beam, then we can deliberately pay attention to those we normally omit. There is also a tendency for students to sit in a classroom such that it reflects their interest. Figure 6.6 shows the three zones into which students tend to sit according to their interest and you should try to relate it to one of your classes to see if it is true.

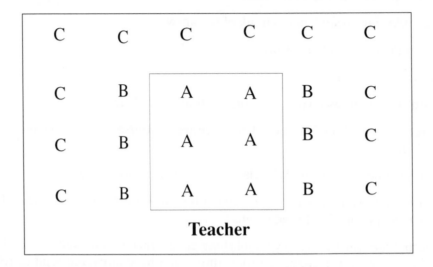

Figure 6.6 Areas of Maximum and Least Interest in a Class

The figure shows that 'A' is the area where student sit who have the most interest and 'C' is where they sit when they have the least interest. The least interested try to hide in the back corner of the room where they may not be seen and they may not have to answer questions.

Having posed our questions, dealing with the answers is another dimension. Student answers are sometimes difficult to hear. Have you ever been to a lecture or a public meeting where someone at the front speaks to the front, and you, sitting at the back, are unable to hear? This can happen in the classroom and you can assist communication by saying "Yes, that's right, Sophie, the paint will blister." Thus, repeating the correct answer so that all of the students are able to hear. Problems occur when students give incorrect answers. Derision from other students must be stopped otherwise some students will fail to answer for fear of ridicule. If you understand why a student has given an incorrect answer, you could reply, "I can understand why you said that Alan, but ...". If you are puzzled by the students answer try "Could you explain that a little more, Peter?" This, then should identify the cause of the misconception.

Sometimes incorrect answers or no answers at all are due to the fact that students do not understand the question because of the vocabulary that has been used. You must take care to explain jargon or words that are familiar to you but may be outside the range of vocabulary used by the students. Remember, you are probably a generation removed from your students and language does change!

One of the problems that we encounter when we first start to use question and answer may be nervousness. We pose the question, no immediate response, so we answer our own question. If we are asking an open question, the students need time to recall facts, think about the relationships and formulate a response. Give the students time and look at their faces for clues about puzzlement, deep thinking or even pain.

Encourage the answerer with nods and other non-verbal encouragement. Praise good answers without becoming sycophantic. In Chapter 3 we looked at the level or order of questions. It may be useful to 'warm-up' the students with questions of the lower order like recall, before going onto the higher order questions.

So far we have concentrated on our role as teachers and posing questions to students. But how about getting students to ask us questions? We could set up a situation where the students have to formulate questions to us for which we can reply either "Yes" or "No" and *only* "yes" or "no". We will not give any other responses at all. This places real pressure on the questioner. An example could be: "My car will not start. Why?"

Student Question	Answer
Is there any petrol in the tank?	Yes
Is the petrol getting through to the carburetor?	Yes
Has the battery given trouble recently?	No

and so on.

The above technique helps the students to develop their communication skills and grow in confidence. However, there is a bonus. Such techniques give you interesting insights into how the students are thinking and, perhaps, the concepts that they have attained and those that they have not.

Teachers at some stage in their careers, must be concerned about questions they cannot answer. The usual advice is to say that you do not know the answer but will find out for the next time. Perhaps someone else in the class may know. However, beware of the class who look for the most obscure question they can find for you each week! If you suspect this, give that question, or another, to the whole group as homework!

5. Body Language

A knowledge of body language is vital to every teacher. You need to be able to 'read' the students' body language and you need to be aware of you own. You cannot disguise your body language – but you may be aware of what sends negative feelings. You may not want to teach this particular group – and this may be communicated to the learners. You can minimise the negative signals and project more positive ones - which often means appearing to be more enthusiastic than you feel.

There are no scientific type rules for body language but there are indications. It is useful to watch a television programme without the sound. Try to guess the moods and relationships. Then try with the sound. Watch people in everyday life, those at work, at home and in social settings.

5.1 Posture

How you stand, sit and move indicate or communicate messages to others. Someone who stands and is constantly moving about is unsettled. Leaning forwards indicates interest, folded arms tends to indicate a defensive stance. A person who moves with confidence is very different from one who feels insecure .

5.2 Appearance

How you dress has an impact on those you meet. There are codes of dress which we know. We dress more formally for an interview than we would for a social event with close friends. A dinner party with friends would indicate less formal dress than for an official dinner. We all tend to wear uniforms. Teenage students tend to wear jeans and tee shirt type clothes. Look at your fellow teachers – you can often see an indication of their subject specialism from their choice of clothes.

5.3 Facial

The face is sometimes called the window on our feelings. When we are happy, we smile. It is difficult to stop doing so! Frowning can indicate difficulty with understanding or disagreement. There are a host of facial expressions and you need to look for the ones that signal the students are in trouble or following well. Asking if they understand almost always gets a "Yes" – not always a reliable indication. Eyes are a key to feelings. Strong eye contact is usually a good sign. Think of someone who wears dark glasses, try to 'read' their feelings. It can be difficult and frustrating.

5.4 Proximity

We all have our own 'personal space'. If we are talking to a stranger and they come too close, we move to increase the space. We feel threatened. However too much space can indicate a barrier. Walk around the classroom, move from the front and show the students that you are not frightened of them.

6. Equal Opportunities

6.1 Language

Most of us become teachers because we enjoy helping others to learn. We must agree that all students must have a fair and equal chance to learn. This essentially is embodied in equality of opportunity. We may be creating barriers to some students merely by the words we use. The following gives some examples.

Male - dominated language

Much of our language has expressions which contain 'man' eg mankind. We can, quite unconsciously, be creating barriers to some of our students. We could use 'humanity' instead of mankind. Some other examples are listed below.

man in the street	average person
master copy	original copy
to man (the reception etc)	to staff (the reception etc)
to master	to learn
manpower	staff, workforce
manmade	synthetic, artificial
spokesman	official representative

Some examples of pronoun problems and how to overcome them are:

The student can complete his own enrolment form	Students can complete their own enrolment form
A student with a physical disability should be able to gain entrance himself	A student with a physical disability should be able to enter without help
A student could get lost finding the college if he did not have a map.	One could get lost without a map.

There are many, many other examples and you can see that you really do need to take care. Perhaps it is worth looking at some of your existing handouts and notes to see if you are guilty.

6.2 Barriers

There are barriers to equality and you need to look carefully at your own practice and that of the organisation for which you work. Mistreatment of one group by another, more powerful group is possible in three main ways,

1.   individual eg verbal or physical abuse

2.   structural eg employment, legal systems

3.   Institutional practice eg unequal provision of service

Values, attitudes and assumptions may be transmitted in three main ways,

1.   Expressed beliefs   – e.g. they are all the same

2.   Cultural forms   – e.g. books, jokes, literature

3.   Systems   – e.g. the curriculum, learning resources

You must not allow any form of discrimination in your classroom or learning situation. Not only is it morally wrong, it is likely to be illegal.

6.3 Assertiveness

6.3.1 Definition

There are quite a number of people who feel the need to go on assertive training courses because they feel that others are exploiting them in some way. It may be that they feel isolated in the team in which they work, for example the only man or woman, the only Asian, and so on. Assertiveness can help you to exercise your rights when you need to. The danger is that you meet some people who have had assertion training who appear to be demanding all of their rights all of the time. It is analogous to attaining the age of 18 and having the right to drink alcohol in a public house so spending all day, every day drinking. That is a sign of immaturity. You need to appreciate the rights of others and use assertiveness in a mature and sensitive manner.

This section deals with some of the techniques which may help you to become more assertive. However, it is necessary that you practice these techniques. The likely situations in which you sometimes need to be assertive is in dealings with colleagues and some students. When we get into situations where there is a difference of opinion we can become aggressive; we can get angry and fight to win our 'rights'. We may get our own way on one occasion but it is likely to be a hollow victory because of the ill feeling it causes. On the other hand, we could act in a submissive way, agreeing with everyone and thinking it is not worth making a fuss or making enemies. We could even lose the respect of others, certainly the students, and even lose self-respect. Between these two cases lies being passive and manipulative. We actually do as we are asked but let it be known, perhaps through non-verbal signs, that we are resentful. None of these three positions are really satisfactory.

Being assertive can help us to improve or retain our self respect and self esteem. This, in turn, should increase respect with the communities of colleagues and students. Assertion is all about being able to express our thoughts, opinions and feelings whilst at the same time allowing others to do the same. Expressing our own values without listening to others is not being assertive, it is being rude! We should not expect to get all our own way all of the time but should be prepared to negotiate to find a common workable understanding and agreement.

The situations in which assertiveness might be necessary include 'refusing', 'poor treatment', 'anger', 'criticism', and 'activity'. Each of these have possible techniques, argues Lindefield (1987), for dealing with them and are discussed separately below.

6.3.1 Refusing

Most of us when asked to do something we do not want to do either say "Yes" and resent or regret doing so, or say "No" and feel guilty. What we should do is think about the request and, if we do not want to do it, say "No". A technique to avoid feeling guilty is to rationalise it to refusing the request and show that you are not refusing the person. Suppose your immediate superior wants you to take on a responsibility which is clearly beyond your role and it is something that you do not want to do, or your students want 'time out' without sufficient reason, you should say "No". They are likely to persist and approach you from all angles saying why it is in your interest to do it. You should not respond to these more devious approaches but you should continue to say "No, I do not want to". This reaction is often called the 'broken record' technique. Other helpful tactics are to ask for time to think about it and clearly important issues should be considered. You might ask for more facts or information before making up your mind. If you decide to say "No", say "No" without thinking up excuses which could be attacked by the requester. Make it clear that it is you saying "No" and not someone else putting pressure on you to say "No". Finally, you have said NO, so do not linger to reassure that person, move on.

6.3.2 Poor Assignments or Poor Treatment

Sometimes students present work to us which we feel is well below their best. When we try to redress the situation, we are presented with responses which are intended to sidetrack us. Consider the following situation:

Teacher:	Sam, I want you to resubmit this assignment. There are several spelling errors and your printer obviously needs a new ribbon. I can barely read the type.
Sam:	I was in a rush and have a lot to do today - other assignments. I am happy with it.
Teacher:	I appreciate your workload but I want the errors removed and a new printout.
Sam:	Could I pencil in the corrections? The content is O.K.
Teacher:	No, Sam. A new printout please. It is important that you present your work well at all times.
Sam:	But the printer was rubbish!
Teacher:	Some of the equipment should be serviced more effectively and I appreciate your frustration but please resubmit.
Sam:	O.K. I'll try my best.

This exchange showed the teacher using the 'broken record' technique, repeating the need to correct errors and for a new printout. The teacher was clear that the high quality of presentation was important and no amount of sidetracking had any effect. The teacher remained calm and did not criticise the student for sloppiness.

6.3.3 Anger

We are very fortunate if we never have to face a person who is angry with us. We tend to feel guilty and wonder why we have caused the situation. But, have we caused the anger? Perhaps it is up to that person to deal with situations without getting angry. Your task is to try to engage the person on a calm and rational basis. Dickson (1982) suggests a step-by-step approach similar to the following:

1. Gain the person's attention by repeating a suitable phrase such as, "Could I say something please?"

2. Establish and maintain eye contact.

3. As eye contact is established, try to make progress with something like, "I can see you are upset, could you explain to me why?"

4. Try to get a 'sitting down' situation as people tend to be less aggressive in this situation.

5. Listen to the person and determine why the anger is there. Move closer if you are at some distance to the person to avoid the need for shouting.

6. Finally, if you reach this stage, you should now be able to move to try to solve the problem.

6.3.4 Criticism

We all like to be appreciated by others and be held in high esteem. However, we are all subject to criticism from time to time; hopefully, not angry criticism. We have to be honest with ourselves about whether the criticism is justified. A way of coping with criticism is to use a technique called "Fogging".

This involves the following options:

1. You can agree with those issues that are true and say things like "Yes, you are right about that. I will get in on time in the future".

2. You can agree with issues which might be true and say something like "Yes, you could be right about that. I'll check it".

3. You can see why certain perceptions are held and say "I can see why you think that".

Negative enquiry can be used with fogging or in place of it and involves asking for more information and/or asking for more criticism. For example, the following might be said:

"Why do my comments upset you so much?"

"I don't understand. What do you expect me to do?"

"Could you explain why I should give you special treatment at the expense of your peers?"

7. Spider Diagrams

At the start of each chapter of this book there is a diagram which gives an overview of what is in each chapter. There are many names for this type of diagram such as 'spider diagram', 'concept map', 'framework' and 'mind map'. Using a diagram drawn by another person can be helpful because you can see the structure very quickly. However, drawing your own diagram really does help you to learn and understand. The diagrams are valuable for revision purposes.

A way to draw your own map or diagram is to place the main theme at the centre. Try to make this as visual and memorable as possible. Each strand may then be developed so that a branching network is developed. You may find it useful to start drawing diagrams from your existing topics but then, when you feel proficient, you could use the diagrams to plan the topic. You can even make an OHT so that the students can share the concept!

Figure 6.7 shows an example of a Spider Diagram for a lesson dealing with the 'Calculation of Area'. This subject was first dealt with in Chapter 1 where a lesson plan was presented for the topic. It is of interest to compare the lesson plan and the Spider Diagram.

At the end of a lesson, as a conclusion, it can be very useful to ask students to draw their own Spider Diagrams of their idea of what has taken place in the lesson. Such an activity not only provides a useful conclusion, but also provides you with an indication of what has been learned and what the students' perceptions are of the content of the lesson.

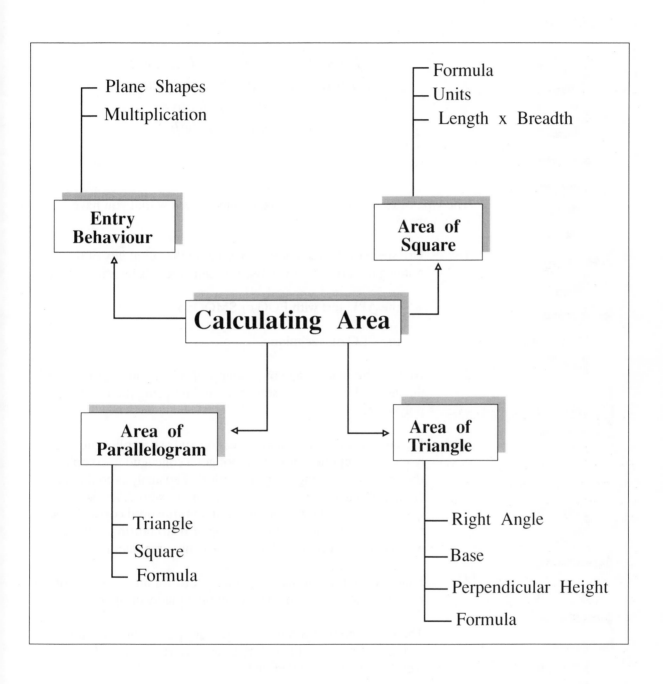

Figure 6.7 Example Spider Diagram for a Lesson 'Calculating Area'

> *Possible Evidence to Show that*
> *you have Achieved the Competence*
> *'Demonstrate Effective*
> *Communication Skills'.*

The type of evidence that you might collect to show that you have achieved the competence involves:

1.   Use some of the techniques to examine the suitability of the reading materials that you use for your students by using either:

   •   the APU test with FOG or SMOG; or

   •   the CLOZE technique.

2.   Reduce the reading age of an inappropriate handout, say, by reducing the length of the sentences and reducing the number of polysyllabic words.

3.   Design a question and answer session and ask a colleague to analyse what happened (if you cannot get a colleague to complete the analysis, try using a tape recorder). The analysis could include how many questions each student answered, levels of questions, time allowed before students answered correctly/incorrectly, questions needing rephrasing or restructuring, difficulty with language, verbal and non-verbal encouragement.

4.   Examine your handouts, assignments, etc. for any signs of words, phrases or activities which may inhibit equality of opportunity.

5.   The next time that you feel that you are getting into a conflict situation, take a breath and try to use assertiveness techniques. Record what you did and said.

6.   Observe a conflict situation between two colleagues, between two students or between a colleague and a student. See what assertion could bring to that situation. Again, record what happened and what thoughts you have on the situation.

If you want to check your understanding of your role in Effective Communication Skills try the following Progress Check

Progress Check 6.1

1. Explain the basic model of communication.

2. State at least one way of ensuring that reading materials are suitable for your students.

3. Explain how you can reduce the reading age of written materials.

4. State at least three ways of helping students to listen.

5. Explain the difference between open and closed questions.

6. Explain the difference between nominated and un-nominated questions.

7. State at least two important categories of body language.

8. Give two examples of how to make language more gender neutral.

9. State two barriers to equality.

10. Draw a spider diagram for a topic that you are about to teach.

8. Study Skills

8.1 Introduction

Teachers teach and students learn! We have seen in chapter 3 how people learn but we can help the learning process by helping the student develop study skills. What are study skills? This is a difficult area but if we can help students take more responsibility for their own active learning processes then these can be included in study skills.

8.2 Problem Solving

Problem solving skills are important in everyday life such as how to travel from A to B, the best way to combine the demands of home life, working life and studying - and enjoy and benefit from each. With active learning we often ask the students to investigate a situation, explore a case study, etc. We often leave the learners to develop their own strategies for this and concentrate on our subject matter. Yet if we were to help with these problem solving strategies then the learning might be so much better. Three problems solving models are presented and these are linked to Business, Science and Technology. You should use only one model depending upon the subject you teach. The models are only models and if experience shows that they could and should be improved to suit your students and their learning, then modify the models.

(i) Business Problem Solving

Problems in the Business Studies area often involve people and their behaviour. For example, why is absenteeism higher in one section than another? A structured approach which involves separating fact from opinion is achieved as shown in figure 6.8.

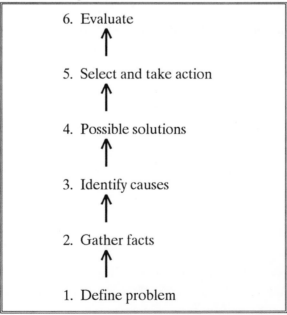

Figure 6.8 Model for Solving Business Problems

The first step is to state what is the problem. This seems to be rather obvious but if four people are working as a team to solve this problem then they may hold four very different perceptions so it is useful to agree the problem (and any limitations). Secondly facts need to be gathered and these need to be kept separate from opinions or conjecture. The third step involves exploring the cause or causes of the problem. There may be several interlinked causes. Some causes may be within your control but some may not be. The fourth step is perhaps the most difficult. You need to get the students to generate at least three possible solutions. The danger, and it is a common trait in most of us, is that we identify a solution – the first idea – and use that. The difficulty is to structure the learning activity so that a number of solutions are generated. When using the problem solving model for the first few times, you may wish to set time limits for each stage and not allow progress until there are a number of possible solutions. The next step is to select the best solution and apply the solution to the cause(s) of the problem. Finally the learners need to check that the problem has been solved by evaluating the solution.

(ii) The Technology Model

Technological Problem solving model is similar but often involves making something. The model is shown in Figure 6.9

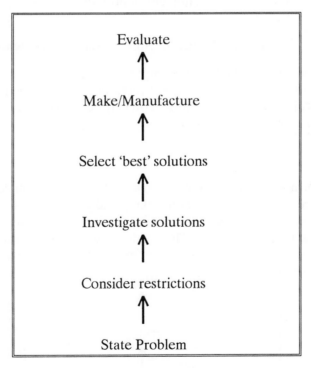

Figure 6.9 Model for Solving Technology Problems

In this case the restrictions could include limitations on space available, costs, material etc. An example could be to make a building without internal supports e.g. aircraft hanger, so that supporting the roof becomes the major design problem.

(iii) The Science Model
Science Model is yet another variation as shown in Figure 6.10

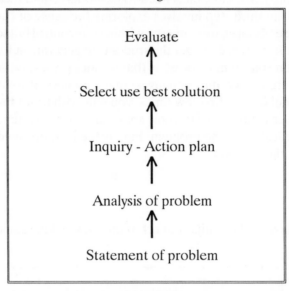

Figure 6.10 Model for Solving Science Problems

In this case the means of inquiry may be the most important stage. For example how does temperature and humidity affect the strength of, say, nylon ropes. A structured approach to problem solving should give the students a framework for their learning activities. You may need to control the first uses of the models by setting timelimits, checking progress, etc.

8.3 Making notes

We often assume that because we can make notes that students can also make their own notes. Just check and see! We need to encourage the skill of note-taking and you can do this by starting with small topics and gradually building up to larger ones. Note making needs to be an active process and you may wish to start with helping with the first few sessions. The students need to know the three stages:-

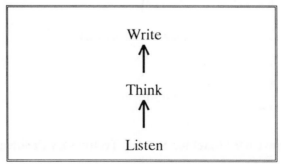

So the students listen to what has been said. They think – "What is the main issue here?" and write short/brief notes re key points. You can help by giving cues by saying "There are four major points which influence ...". "The first is ..."At the first attempt at note taking you could promote examples of what the learners notes should contain.

8.4 Reading Strategies

We have already seen the importance of reading but know we need to help the students to develop good reading strategies. This may seem to be strange. If the students are good readers, what is the problem? The problem is that the students read everything in the book from start to finish when they need, and you want them to be selective, that is read only 3 or 4 important pages. You may also want your learners to be able to skim read a chapter in order to identify and learn one or two key issues.

There are three approaches to reading a book, journal or part of them. These are:

(i) *Skimming* – is where the purpose is to get a general idea of what the writer is saying. The reader looks at the headings, general points etc in order to get a quick overview of the text.

(ii) *Scanning* – is when we are trying to find specific information – for example finding out what brainstorming is and how to use it.

(iii) *Intensive reading* – is where the text is read very carefully and thoroughly. You should only use this technique when you find the specific information you are looking for or when an item of interest is found when skimming.

Can you help your students develop these skills? The answer is for you to design activities which are an integral part of your teaching, which allows the students to develop these skills. If you want to try a more structured approach you could use the SQ3R method (Ref Gibbs). SQ3R stands for

Survey
Question
Read
Recall
Revise

You could set a research exercise, based on this technique, which could involve the use of the library.

Survey – is where you ask the learners to 'skim' the source of information in order to find specific information.

Questioning – includes asking, for example, is this the most appropriate source of information? Is it providing the answers I need? Is it too basic? Is it too advanced and detailed?

Read – is reading with a purpose e.g. scanning, and then intensive reading. Note making may be part of the process.

Recall – after reading is a good check on understanding and helping memory.

Revise – does not mean intensive reading for examination but the periodic revision of the key points.

You may wish to structure an exercise in your own subject area based on this technique. We are being asked to 'teach' more material in a shorter time. This may be one approach which may be helpful.

8.5 Examination Technique

There are still a great many courses which have formal written examinations. We often assume that our learners know all about examinations and how to pass them. Are you sometimes disappointed with the scores of students who you consider to be 'bright'? This could be because of poor examination technique. It may be worthwhile asking the students to form small groups and consider what are their worries about examination, this may generate an agenda for discussion. The following five points may be in this agenda.

(i)   *Research the Examination*

It is always valuable to see what the previous examinations were like. Again, the students should be guided to do this themselves. You could give them a framework as follows:

- Look at the syllabus
- Look at past papers - What questions are likely to be asked?
- Are the questions based on facts and/or application?
- Practice on previous questions

(ii)   *Practice Questions*

It is usually valuable to set the students some questions from previous papers – even under simulated examination conditions – and give the learners feedback which could include the following. Have they:

- read the question carefully?
- answered the question that has been asked and not what they hoped it would be?
- answered all parts of the question and included all relevant facts?
- gives no superfluous information? – this is wasteful.

Essay type questions should have answers which:

- have paragraphs
- introduction
- middle which contains key facts and argues the case, gives examples and generally demonstrates understanding
- conclusion

(iii)   *Before the Examination*

The students need to be well prepared with all of the necessary equipment. It would be unfortunate if they were upset by forgetting some simple piece of equipment. You may get the students to draw up a 'be prepared' checklist which may look like this.

Pens + spare (or refill, bottle of ink)	Instruments e.g. protractor, ruler, set square
Pencils (sharpened) plus sharpener	Eraser
Coloured Pencils	Reference books if allowed
Calculator	e.g. textbooks, dictionary
Watch/Clock	Sweeties!!

(iv) *In the Examination*

Techniques which are common sense to you and I, often need to be explained to learners.

(a) Read through the Paper

- read instructions – any changes to previous papers
- identify the questions you can – and want to answer

(b) Plan the time

- equal marks for each question then spend an equal amount of time on each
- plan your answer (see mind maps)
- leave space at the end of each answer in case you want to add anything
- allow pre-reading time
- allow time at the end for checking through all answers
- allow time for planning answers

(c) Answering the questions

- answer your best question first – but still to the time limit!
- do not do less than the specified number of questions
- write legibly
- check spelling and grammar (when checking answers)

(v) *Multichoice Questions*

Multichoice questions are common because they give good coverage of the syllabus and are easy to mark. Marking can even be automated. Students definitely need practice with this type of examination because the instructions need to be understood. Guidelines could include the following points:

- read the instruction carefully
- do you have to answer all questions?
- is there only one answer?
- how much time is allowed?
- work straight through the paper and return to difficult questions later
- do not spend too long on any one question

8.6 Time Management

If you were to ask your students when they plan to go shopping for a new dress/shirt, to a disco, buy the latest pop CD etc, they can probably give you a specific time because these are important events. If you were to ask which times in the week are set aside for study then you will probably find out that studying is fitted into 'spare' or unplanned time. It is important that time planning includes a positive approach to including studying.

(i)   Planning the year

This indicates examinations and could include deadlines for various assignments and projects. Indication of review and revision times is important.

(ii)   Planning the week

Some times cannot be changed e.g. coming to classes. It is important to stress that the students need to include time for sport, recreation, resting, meeting friends etc but should also include study time. Does the planned study time reflect the importance of the learning programme?

(iii) Planning the studying

Research shows that an hour or so is the optimum time for studying a topic. For each hour the learners should:

- set aside a few minutes to collect books etc
- set goals for the learning time
- work for about 20 minutes
- spend 3/4 minutes reviewing what has been learned
- 5 minutes rest
- 20 minutes working
- 3/4 minutes reviewing
- rest for 5 minutes or so
- next topic or end there.

The above needs a disciplined approach but it is surprising how many learners find it useful.

Feedback to Students

As we have said in Chapter 1, we tend to concentrate on the teaching of subject matter to the exclusion of core skills. But employers often tell us that they want their employees, your students, to be good communicators. The skills of communication pervade all subjects and all forms of education so each of us should help students to develop skills in oral and written communication. The use of question and answer will help students to receive oral information, process it and respond. Developing the students' own questioning skills is also a valuable asset. So, the frequent use of question and answer sessions in our teaching not only helps subject matter development, it aids the development of the students' oral skills. It is important that we encourage and support each student by giving feedback and encouragement. Written communication can be practised through assignments and homework tasks. You should mark this and return it to the students promptly. You should comment on the work rather than a mark of 6 out of 10. Comment about:

- how the work can be improved;
- what elements were missing;
- were some sections too verbose or unclear?

You should also correct any spelling and grammar errors. If you do not do it, no one else will and it is the only way that students will improve their written skills. With report writing, many students have problems writing in the third person, past tense. Re-write some sections for them correctly and get the students to practise this skill.

> *Possible Evidence to Show that You have Achieved the Competence "Assist Learners to Develop their Communication Skills".*

The type of evidence that you might collect to show that you have achieved the competence involves:

1. Put the students into the role of questioner and pose them a problematic situation chosen from your subject area for them to solve. Tell them that you will only answer "Yes" or "No" to their questions to assist them to solve the problem.

    Record the situation and write a comment on how individual students respond.

2. Set tasks or homework in which students have to use a problem solving model. Comment on their use of the model. What aspects are well achieved and what aspects less well achieved?

3. Check student notes on a specific topic and compare with what you expected to see.

If you want to check your understanding of your role in Developing Student Communication skills try the following progress check

Progress Check 6.2

1. Describe the problem solving model that is most applicable to your subject area.

2. Explain a technique that you might use to improve your students' reading skills.

3. Explain what you would include in a one hour session to teach study skills to your students.

4. Explain the aspects that you might teach students about examination technique in terms of:

- practice questions;

- before the examination;

- in the examination.

5. How might you help students with their time management?

6. What aspects might your comments include when you mark your student's work?

Further Reading and Referenes

Reading and references relating to the topics in this chapter can be found in the following:

Brown, G.A.   *Microteaching: A programme of teaching skills*, Methuen, 1975.

Collins, N.   *New Teaching Skills*, Oxford University Press, 1986.

Curzon, L.B.   *Teaching in Further Education: An Outline of Principles and Practice,* Cassell, 1990

Dickson, A.   *A Woman in your own right*, Quartet, 1982.

Kery, T.   *Effective Questioning*, Macmillan Education, 1982

Lindefield, G.   *Assert Yourself*, Self-Help Associates, 1987

Pate, R, and   Guiding Learning through Skillful Questioning, *The Elementary*
Bremer, N   *School Journal,* 69(8),1967

Perrot, E.   *Microteaching in Higher Education*, SRHE, 1977.

Rees, S.   *Assertion Training*, Routledge, 1991.
and Graham, R.S.

Turner, C.   *Developing Interpersonal Skills*, FE Staff College, 1983.

Chapter 7
Assessment of Student Learning

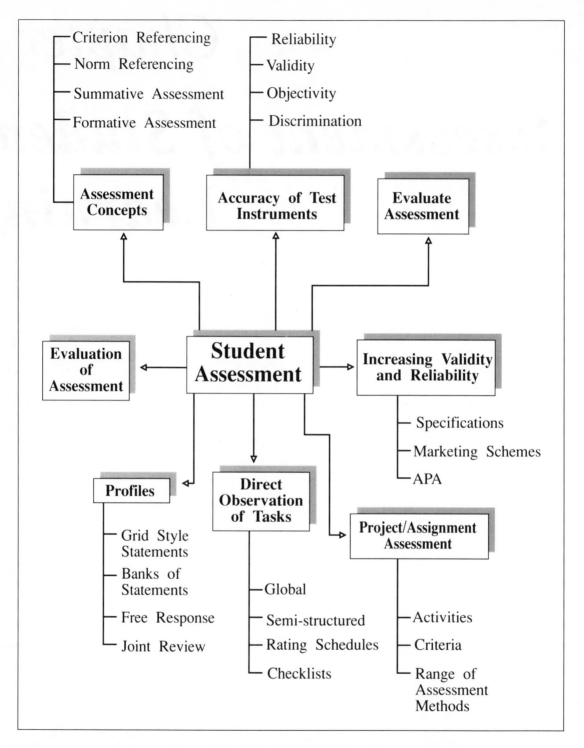

Overview of Chapter 7

NOTE: This chapter should be read in conjunction with, and after, the Assessment section in Chapter 1,Section 4, where the principles and techniques of supply and selection test questions are discussed.

Competences Related to this Chapter

The teacher competences and associated performance criteria related to this chapter are:

Overall Competence – *Employ a variety of effective methods of student assessment.*

Competence	Performance Criteria
1. Assess learners during a lesson or learning period.	(a) Employ suitable short-term informal assessment methods. (b) Rapid feedback is provided for the students. (c) Select assessment methods according to learning process and stated outcomes. (d) Motivate students through feedback. (e) Plan assessment into an overall lesson design.
2. Justify, use and record appropriate forms of measuring learner achievement.	(a) Provide a rationale for the methods and processes of assessment. (b) Clearly relate methods of assessment to appropriate objectives or competences. (c) Provide a rational explanation for any weighting, marking or grading employed.ative and summative methods employed. (d) Employ accreditation of prior achievement (APA) techniques as appropriate. (e) Record students' progress on suitable documentation. (f) Identify procedures for feedback to the students. (g) Review assessment procedure and provide evaluative comment as to its success, suitability and development. (h) Draw clear distinctions between form.
3. Employ appropriate asssessment of student practical work.	(a) Use a range of test instruments for the assessment of practical tasks. (b) Use appropriate formats for the assessment of projects/assignments. (c) Employ effective student profiling formats. (d) Present feedback to students in a positive manner.

1. Introduction

It is important at the start of any study of assessment of student learning that you recognise the distinction between two types of assessment: formative and summative. The distinction between assessment to satisfy the needs of society (which normally take the form of 'summative' assessment) and assessment to help in both teaching and learning (which is most usefully 'formative' assessment).

Thus, summative assessment is that which takes place at the end of a course or topic and is used for certification purposes. It is used to see if a student has learned the material and is capable of going onto further study. Formative assessment, on the other hand, is that which takes place during the course and is useful to tell the student how the learning is proceeding as well as telling the teacher about the success of the teaching. Figure 7.1 shows the different techniques that can be used for the two types of assessment.

Formative Techniques	Summative Techniques
Question and Answer Supply type questions Selection type questions Projects Assignments Essays Practical Tests	End examinations Supply type questions Selection type questions Projects Assignments Essays Practical tests

Figure 7.1 Formative and Summative Assessment Techniques

As you can see many of the techniques are the same but the purpose to which they are put is what distinguishes them. Figure 7.2 indicates the different uses to which the techniques can be put.

Uses of Formative Techniques	Uses of Summative Techniques
Teachers for ensuring that learning has taken place. Teachers for improving methods of instruction. Students to gain an idea of their success in achievement of objectives and learning methods.	Employers for job selection. Curriculum developers for curriculum reviews. Examining/Validating bodies for award of grades and diplomas. Students for selecting courses of higher study.

Figure 7.2 Uses of Formative and Summative Assessment Techniques

2. Formative Assessment

You will realise that, as the teacher, the use of formative techniques are important in that they have a direct effect on the way in which you treat your students as it is your aid to teaching and student learning. You are no longer thinking of putting your learners in rank order, but simply deciding whether or not they have succeeded in learning what it is you intended them to learn. Careful use of formative techniques should not be a hurdle to students like a summative external examination is, but rather a natural part of the learning process.

If you are to carry out these suggestions for formative techniques in the classroom it means that every effort must be made to divorce them from the ideas and thought processes that are present in the mind of students that are associated with the summative examination. Thus, the testing situation and the marking process must be seen, not as a threat, but as part of the teaching and learning process. That is not to say that the process should be slipshod – it needs to be thorough, but that it should be based on the needs of the individual student. The term continuous assessment comes to mind but this is somewhat of a misnomer. Assessment cannot be continuous as you do not have the time to devote to an individual that you would like. Continuous assessment generally means intermittent assessment but the focus is that which is required by the individual student. Not in terms of pass or fail but in terms of whether the quality of the work is good or not so good and what might be done to make improvements. What are the good aspects of the work and what are the not so good aspects?

Perhaps the most undervalued part of the formative assessment process is the potential of students to assess and record their own progress. Yet, in effect, this is what all forms of external teacher, particularly formative, assessment is about. The type of feedback should be such as to assist students to be able to judge the worth of their own work. When self assessment is used it has the added advantage of releasing you to deal with individual problems and giving the feedback in a form which closely parallels the assessment which students continually make of their own learning.

The nature of formative assessment, then, is essentially diagnostic. Black (1989) quotes research carried out by The Scottish Council for Research in Education, where teachers saw diagnostic assessment in terms of three basic modes as shown in Figure 7.3.

Mode	Focus of Assessment	Areas of Concern
I	The Class	The success of the class in learning what was intended.
II	The Individual Leaner	Which learners have not attained the intended learning?
III	The Individual Learner	What is/are the reason(s) for the learner not attaining the intended learning?

Figure 7.3 Assessment as a Contribution to Learning

The answers to the question in Mode III pose other questions such as:

(a)   are the objectives suitable?

(b)   is the teaching strategy suitable?

In this way, both you and your students see assessment as a positive contribution to learning.

So, how do you use formative techniques; what must you do in the classroom to ensure that these ideals are achieved? We have already said in Figure 7.1 that most of the normal techniques, like question and answer and test techniques, can be used. The following three principles can be employed.

(i)   *Use short-term informal assessment.*
This first principle often means the use of question and answer but can also mean the use of test or homework questions which are given informally. What do we mean by informally? It is the way in which the feedback is given. The feedback concentrates upon the ways in which improvements might be made as opposed to giving a mark for the work. This, of course needs much more thorough marking and it can be time consuming. It not only involves assessing aspects which are right and wrong but saying, for the aspects that are wrong, why they are wrong and how they might best be put right.

(ii)   *Provide rapid feedback.*
Research tells us that if feedback is to be of most effect then it should be given immediately or as soon as possible. This is most effective through question and answer or through a tutorial situation. An effective technique, should time allow, is to get students to describe what they have done. In this way their understanding can be gauged and rapid feedback provided.

(iii)   *Ensure feedback gives motivation to the student.*
The third principle relates to the manner in which the feedback is provided. It is often said that students are not really motivated to learn until they revise for an examination. Yet, here, we are making a case for you to use assessment methods which are part of the learning process; where feedback can be given without the formality of an examination or test situation and removes the stress factors as much as possible. In consequence, the motivation must come from the *manner* in which the feedback is given. The adage that 'nothing succeeds like success' is very true in the learning situation and so, the concentration must, at least initially, concentrate upon what has been done well. The aspects that are done less well must be highlighted as opposed to being condemned and suggestions as to how they might be corrected. This principle is expanded upon in Section 10 of this chapter.

These three principles for formative assessment are outlined in Figure 7.4 with the suggestions as to how they might be achieved.

To apply these principles means that the you should plan the use of the techniques as part of your overall lesson plan. It is probably sufficient to plan the assessment times in the overall plan and to ensure that you adhere to the principles giving feedback when this is appropriate. In both Chapters 1 and 5 suggestions were made as to the layout of a lesson plan with columns for teacher and student activities and that the introduction could assess entry behaviour and the conclusion assess learning.

Principle	Methods of Achievement in the Classroom
Use short-term informal assessment	Concentrate upon way in which improvements can be made. Say why things are incorrect. Give comments as opposed to marks.
Provide rapid feedback	Use question and answer as an assessment technique. Use tutorials to supplement assessment. Get students to describe their work.
Ensure that feedback gives motivation to the learner	Comment upon the good aspects first. Ensure that praise is given where due. Don not condemn the incorrect responses.

Figure 7.4 Achievement of Principles of Formative Assessment

Formative Assessment Techniques

The types of technique that you can use for formative assessment have been outlined in Figure 7.1. You can, however, use each of the different types of question in a variety of situations. One of your roles as a teacher is to decide which type of test to use in a particular situation. The main type of questions that are used are the various types of objective questions and essay type questions. The definition, description and construction of these questions have already been described in Chapter 1.

Well constructed *multiple-choice* questions can comprise an effective test. They are suitable for:

- measuring a variety of complex learning outcomes such as vocabulary, explanations, calculations, facts and applications;
- providing diagnostic information to help with the identification of student learning problems;
- ensuring high test reliability.

Alternate-Choice (True/False) questions are not particularly helpful as they are open to guessing. As there are only two alternatives, students have a 50% chance of getting them correct.

Matching Block questions are suitable for matching dates with events, causes with effects, principles with applications and symbols with meanings they represent. They are most suitable when:

- lower level (knowledge) outcomes are to be tested;
- associations between things are to be identified;
- all the responses are plausible alternatives to a premise.

Short answer questions can be useful for testing students' recall of names, dates, terms and generalisations. They can help minimise the students guessing the correct answer. They are most suitable when:

- the learning outcome is recall rather than recognise information;
- simple computational problems are used;

- a selection-type would be too obvious.

Essay questions usually allow greater freedom of response to students than other test questions. They test the students' ability to structure a response; other questions are unable to provide this. Both structured and extended essay type questions are most suitable when:

- the objectives specify writing or recall rather than recognition of information;
- the number of students is small.

Figure 7.5 gives a comparison of factors which are to be considered when selecting test questions. In general, multiple-choice questions give greater coverage of the syllabus and are easy to mark, but, on the other hand they are difficult to write. Essay questions are just the opposite to this, easy to write but difficult to mark and they do not give very great coverage of the syllabus.

Factors to Consider		Selection Type		Supply Type	
		Multiple Choice and Matching	True/False	Short Answer	Essay
Learning Outcomes	1. Number of specific learning outcomes which can be tested at a given time.	Many	Many	Many	Few
	2. Coverage of the syllabus.	Wide	Wide	Wide	Limited
	3. Abilities which can be tested.	All	Knowledge Comprehension	Knowledge Comprehension	High Levels
Influences on student behaviour	1. Suitability for testing writing ability.	Least	Least	Least	Most
	2. Suitability for testing reading ability.	Most	Most	Medium	Least
Teacher Requirements	1. Ease of preparation	Hard	Hard	Medium	Easy
	2. Degree of skill required in preparation	High	High	Medium	Least
	3. Speed of marking	Quick	Quick	Medium	Slow
	4. Degree of skill required in marking	Low	Low	Medium	High
	5. Objectivity in scoring	High	High	Medium	Low

Figure 7.5 Comparison of Different Types of Test Items

> *Possible Evidence to Show that you have achieved the objective*
> *'Assess Learners during a Lesson or Learning Period'*

The type of evidence that you might collect to show that you have achieved the competence involves:

Designing a lesson plan and highlighting the assessment points in the lesson and:

(a) select appropriate assessment techniques showing how these are related to the learning processes and learning intentions;

(b) describe how the feedback is to be (or has been) provided and show its rapidity and motivational intentions;

(c) after using the assessment methods, evaluate their effectiveness.

> *If you want to check your understanding*
> *formative assessment techniques, try the*
> *following progress task*

Progress Check 7.1

1.   Write a definition of:

    (a)   Formative assessment, and

    (b)   Summative assessment

which draws a comparison between the two types.

2.   Give three uses to which formative assessment could be put.

3.   What type of test would you construct for
the following situations?
You should list the types of question you would include
and explain why you would use them.

    (a)   A class of 20 students doing advanced chemistry
need to be quickly tested across a range of topics.
You do not have much time to prepare the test.

    (b)   You have an average ability class in English.
You want to test students' ability to
present an argument.

    (c)   You wish to test the students learning of a topic in
mathematics at the end of term to see if your are
able to go onto subsequent learning.

    (d)   You are taking a cookery theory class for the first time
and wish to assess their entry behaviour.

3. Norm and Criterion Referenced Assessment

Two other important concepts relate to how the assessments are marked. End examinations are traditionally marked so that the normal curve of distribution (that is, a small percentage achieve distinctions and a small percentage fail, but the majority of the students achieve 'average' marks of between 40 and 60%) is achieved. This is termed *norm-referenced* assessment due to its relationship with the curve of normal distribution. This system is often employed in external examinations to ensure that standards are maintained. The argument is used that the level of the examination is difficult to maintain from year to year, whereas the level of students (especially where large numbers take the examination) is more likely to be the same; the population remains more static than the level of the examination.

The forms of assessment associated with norm-referenced assessment are, therefore, the more traditional forms of end examinations which include essays and other forms of 'paper and pencil' tests, and practical tests. These, of course, only assess a representative sample of the syllabus topics as time is limited in the amount that can be tested.

In terms of the marking of norm referenced tests, in order to ensure the normal curve of distribution, scripts are awarded a 'raw' score depending upon the correctness of the student response and they are then 'adjusted' to ensure that the range of scores fit the curve of normal distribution. This, of course, is usually only done by the larger examination/validating bodies. However, you can achieve similar effects by not awarding full marks and also giving a minimum mark (often for effort).

More recently, it has been realised that the concept of *mastery* learning is important where all students need to master a subject prior to moving onto another subject. This has been facilitated by the introduction of specific criteria stated in terms of objectives and competences which state in detailed terms what the student must achieve. Thus, *criterion-referenced* assessment, as this is called, is becoming more widely accepted.

The forms of assessment associated with criterion referenced assessment relate to the 'newer' types of assessment of assignments, projects with profiles to record achievements as well as the more traditional forms of essays and the like. Also, criterion-referenced assessment is associated with continuous (or intermittent) assessment so that many more of the objectives and competences are assessed.

The marking of criterion-referenced assessment relates to the criteria (the objectives/competences). In this case all of the students can achieve full marks if they complete the required standard suggested, or, alternately, they can all fail, if they do not reach the standard.

You, as the teacher, need to decide whether ALL of your students need to master the objectives of a topic before moving onto the next topic or whether only a certain percentage will achieve all of the them. This latter approach leads to the identification of minimum essential objectives (or competences) and developmental objectives. All students will need to learn the minimum essentials with the better students achieving the developmental ones.

In Chapter 1 of this book we described assessment in terms of the basic teaching model as the part of the teaching process after the instructional techniques has taken place and, as such, provided you with information about how well the student has achieved the objectives, whether the entry behaviour had been at the correct level and whether the instructional techniques had been appropriate. We also described several types of assessment technique (supply, selection, practical and observation) and made some suggestions as to when the different techniques might be employed. We now need to look deeper into the assessment techniques, consider schemes of assessment and evaluate the use of the different methods.

4. Accuracy of Test Instruments

A test is a *measuring instrument*; it measures the achievements of the students. The desirable characteristics of a test are similar to those that would be looked for in any instrument. A set of scales is an instrument that is designed for weighing articles. The scales will have a tolerance of, say, plus or minus two grams to which it will be accurate. Thus, if you wish to weigh 200 g with the scales, you can be sure that the actual weight will be accurate to within 198 and 202 g. Similarly, a test needs to be accurate, within limits, to what it is testing. As it consists of a series of items, questions or tasks, the quality of these is determined by their accuracy. Some of the desirable characteristics of the items, questions or tasks that effect their quality are:

- power of discrimination;

- objectivity of scoring;

- validity;

- reliability.

4.1 Power of Discrimination

A test that consists of all easy items cannot bring out the differences in achievement of different students. All will score well in such a test and so it will not be effective in discriminating between good and poor achievers.

When the results are required for the ranking or grading of students, as in norm-referenced assessment, then they should *discriminate* between the good and the poor students. Thus, a good test should have this power of discrimination.

You should, however, bear two points in mind about this:

(i) not on every occasion is it necessary to discriminate between the students;

(ii) how easy or difficult the question is depends upon the group of students. A question, for example, may be difficult for first year students but easy for final year ones.

4.2 Objectivity of Scoring

Depending upon the type of questions that are included in a test, the test will be either objective or subjective.

If different people are asked to independently score an essay question they will probably award different marks. This is because they will place different emphases on various parts of the essay. In other words *subjective* judgment or personal preference will influence the score. Essay questions, therefore, cannot be scored with complete objectivity.

An objective test is one which is scored *objectively*. That is, the same scores will be awarded by different people. The multiple choice type of question has only one correct answer (for example the choice of (e) option as correct) and can be marked by computer. Thus, a test made up of multiple-choice questions is objective in its marking.

4.3 Validity

When temperature is to be measured, the appropriate instrument is the thermometer. A thermometer is used and NOT a metre rule. Thus, a thermometer is a *valid* instrument for the measurement of temperature.

Validity, in terms of assessment, is how well the test measures what it is supposed to measure. A paper and pencil test, therefore, has low validity when assessing a student's ability to carry out a psychomotor skill but can have a high validity in assessing if a learner *knows* how to complete it. You need content validity for your assessments which means how well your test measures a representative sample of the syllabus topics. Thus a valid test is one which assesses a representative sample of the content.

It is evident that a valid assessment must also assess a sample of the abilities that are required in the curriculum. The questions must not only test the knowledge levels but also the comprehension, application and psychomotor skills; a cross section of all of the abilities that are required.

So, a test, having high content validity should:

    (i)   be based on a sample of the objectives in a curriculum; and

    (ii)   have all of the questions relevant to the objectives which have been chosen from the sample.

What has been described above is 'content' validity. However, validity is also affected by the appropriateness of the method of testing (using paper and pencil to test skills). This latter type of validity is termed 'construct' validity. The construct validity of an assessment is the extent to which it is appropriate to the course, subject or vocational area concerned. Assessment of work done in the student's own time, group work, assignment work, oral work or assessment of skills at work might all be relevant to the course. If methods of assessment are chosen purely because they are easy to administer or because they are easy to mark, the construct validity of the assessment may be questioned.

The possible uses of different types of assessment have already been discussed in Chapter 1. Ensuring that a particular type of test is used for a particular application ensures construct validity. Figure 7.6 shows this in a different way.

Objectives	Possible Assessment Methods
Lower level cognitive	Multiple Choice questions Matching Block questions Short answer/completion questions
High level cognitive	Structured/Extended essay Assignment or Project
Psychomotor	Skill test observation Assessment of skills at work Self assessment related to a checklist Assignment or Project
Affective	Tutorial or discussion Peer assessment Observation
Personal effectiveness	Self assessment Discussion or tutorial Peer assessment

Figure 7.6 Possible Assessment Methods to Improve Construct Validity

There are, of course, no right or wrong answers of where you should use a particular test. There are too many variables to give more specific guidelines. What is right for a course might be different for different subjects or for different vocational areas. In consequence, only a range of possible methods can be given for the different types of objective.

4.4 Reliability

The reliability of a test refers to the extent to which it *consistently* measures what is is supposed to measure. A perfectly reliable test will give identical results in all conditions. If a test is reliable then the following things should happen:

(i)   different examiners assessing the same work should award the same scores;

(ii) examiners award the same score to the same script if they score it again on a subsequent occasion;

(iii) students get the same score on the test when it is administered at different times.

The reliability of a test is influenced by the objectivity of the scoring. If examiners are looking for the same aspects there is more likelihood of them awarding the same marks. Hence an effective marking scheme influences the reliability of a test. Also, the length of a test influences its reliability. The effects of chance factors on students' scores can be reduced by increasing the length of the test paper.

The following chart (Figure 7.7) gives an indication of the possible relative merits of different forms of assessment in terms of the four constructs outlined above.

Assessment Form	Power of Discrimination	Objectivity of Scoring	Validity	Reliability
Essay	Medium	Low	Low	Low
Supply-type	Low	Medium	Medium	Medium
Selection-type	Medium	Medium	High	High
Project	High	Low	High	Medium
Assignment	High	Low	High	Medium
Practical test	High	Medium	High	Medium

Figure 7.7 Possible Merits of Different Forms of Assessment

You will see from the chart that some forms of assessment are better in some respects than others. Indeed, the essay type of assessment, the conventional form of assessment, scores quite low in all of the aspects. The selection type, on the other hand, scores quite high on all aspects. So, why do you use essays at all and why do we not all only use selection type questions. The rationale, you will remember from Chapter 1, is that some forms are more applicable to some types of learning than other forms. The multiple choice type of assessment is more applicable to knowledge and understanding whereas essays are applicable to the sorting and presentation of an argument. Thus, if the presentation of an argument is required to be assessed, you have to accept the low validity and reliability that is likely to result. However, there are techniques that can be used to increase validity and reliability and, if it is necessary to use forms of assessment that give these low values, you should use these techniques to improve your marking.

5. Increasing the Validity and Reliability

5.1 Increasing Validity by Designing an Assessment Specification

The success of your test instrument depends, to a large extent, upon your ability to design a high level of content validity and a high level of reliability.

You can increase content validity through the design and use of an *assessment specification*. This is a technique which attempts to ensure that you sample:

(a)   the content of the course/topic; and

(b)   the different abilities to be tested.

It is probably impossible that you will be able to cover *all* of the objectives or competences and all of the content in the time available for testing. Thus, you have to sample both content and abilities. You must ensure that this sampling is representative of both the content and the abilities in order that you increase the validity of the assessment. The *table of specifications* is used to show the relative importance of the various topics and abilities that are to be tested.

The following example specification (Figure 7.8) shows the percentage marks allocated to each topic distributed over the different abilities in the cognitive domain.

Topics	Knowledge	Comprehension	Application	Higher than Application	Total
A	6	6	2	3	17
B	8	6	2	2	18
C	4	6	2	4	16
D	6	4	4	3	17
E	6	8	10	8	32
Total	30	30	20	20	100%

Figure 7.8 Specification to Increase Content Validity

You can see from this table that, for instance, topic 'C' has been allocated 16% of the total marks and topic 'E', the major topic, has been allocated 32%. The first four topics have been allocated almost equal marks with the final topic is allocated almost twice as much. On the other hand, the abilities of knowledge and comprehension are allocated the largest percentage of the marks (30% each). So, more marks are allocated within the assessment for the recall of information and its understanding.

You can design such a table by reflecting the objectives related to each of the topics and the abilities. This can be achieved either:

(a) by completing the totals columns first (say, from a count of the objectives) and then the cells;

or alternately,

(b) by completing each of the cells from the objectives and then the totals to see if this reflects the time allocated to the learning of the topics.

Once the specification has been completed you need to design questions which match both the abilities and topics with marks being awarded on the basis of the numbers within the cells. If you are using multiple choice questions with one mark per question, you will need 17 questions at the different ability levels for topics 'A', 18 for topic 'B' and so on (or a percentage of these). If, on the other hand, you are using supply-type questions (say, structured essay-type) the number of marks need to be awarded as stated in the cells.

You will see that designing questions and awarding marks in this way ensures that a representative sample of the content is assessed and marks awarded accordingly which will ensure a high value of content validity. The test is assessing what is is supposed to be assessing as given in the aims and/or objectives.

5.2 Increasing Validity by the Design of a Marking Scheme

The value of *reliability* can be increased through using a *marking scheme* to mark all of the scripts. A marking scheme is particularly important for those assessment forms which have low reliability like essays.

An essay marking scheme, where the overall mark might be 40 marks, can be sub-divided as shown in Figure 9.

Aspect	Marks	Aspects
Style	15	Effectiveness of presentation in terms of sentence structure, and vocabulary range.
Accuracy	10	Spelling, grammar, sentence construction and use of tenses.
Content	15	How original and how relevant to the title.

Figure 7.9 Essay Marking Scheme to Increase Reliability

If you use a marking scheme such as this, whilst it does not ensure that all of the essays will be marked in exactly the same way, it goes some way ensuring that the basis of marking will be the same. You know that you are looking for the same things in each of the essays and, in consequence, you have increased the reliability of the marking.

A similar type of marking scheme can be used for a practical task where the abilities to be tested in each of the stages of the process are identified and marks awarded accordingly. An example for 'Flower Arranging' is shown in Figure 7.10 where the task is:

"You are asked to decorate a table for a formal dinner party in June. All flowers and foliage must be available from the garden. Fruit and accessories may be included if desired.
Table size 4ft 6in x 2ft 6in. Suitable covering to be used.
Prepare a list of all plant materials used giving common and botanical names where possible.
Describe briefly the china , glass, and cutlery that will be used."

This marking scheme could be applied to almost any task in flower arranging (or, for that matter, other similar subjects) particularly for the horizontal and vertical axes. Any differences could be catered for in the individual cells. A further advantage of keeping to the same marking scheme throughout the course, is that students get used to it and know upon the aspects upon which to concentrate.

Assessment Stages	A Technical Skills	B Method of Work	C Use of Resources	D Application of Knowledge	E Creative Ability	Marks Available
1. Choice of design (style)			Related to materials (5)	Suitable for occasion (5)	Concept (theme) (5)	15
2. Selection of plant material.	Knowledge of plants (plant identif). (4)	Sorting and packing (3)	Est. of amount req'd (5)	Appropriate design qualities (4)	Unusual colour, texture, etc. (4)	20
3. Selection of other components		Faultless appearance (2)	Ingenuity (3)	Harmony and Compatible (3)	Harmony and Compatible (2)	10
4. Mechanics	Neat, firm and well hidden (3)			Suitable for type of plant material & style of design. (2)		5
5. Execution of design	Manual dexterity (5)	Tidy and methodical work (4)	Materials used well (6)	Application of design principles (10)		25
6. Presentation	Condition of plant material (3)	Staging and display (6)	Value for money (6)	Degree of craft skill (overall standard attained) (6)	Originality & Distinction (4)	25
Marks % available Awarded	15	15	25	30	15	100

Figure 7.10 Marking Scheme for a Practical Task

5.3 *Weighting, Marking and Grading*

Reliability can also be influenced through, instead of awarding the same marks for each question, awarding more marks for the more difficult questions and less for the easier questions.

The problem with the weighting of questions is how do you decide what is a difficult question and what is an easy one. There are two ways in which you can do this:

(i) those questions that take longer to complete can be considered to be more difficult and be awarded more marks.

(ii) those questions that require higher level abilities to be used (like application as opposed to knowledge) can be given higher marks. This is relatively easy with multiple choice questions as knowledge questions can be awarded 1 mark, comprehension level questions 2 marks and application level questions 3, and so on. With other types of question it is not so easy as, say, an essay question requires a number of different abilities together.

Whatever weighting factors are used it is always advisable to tell students specifically what marks you intend to award for what questions or what parts of questions. When you do this, students know where to place their time and energies to obtain maximum marks.

Marks are notoriously unreliable as related to the assessment of student work. Even with a marking scheme it is very difficult to say with any conviction that a particular piece of work is worth, say, 56%. Depending upon the success of the marking scheme and the skill of the marker, there is probably a tolerance of plus or minus, at least, 5% on this mark. One way of overcoming this is to award grades instead of marks (as is often done with essays which are even more unreliable than the marking of science or technology questions). On a graded mark scale the predetermined points are the pass and distinction or pass and merit points. For example a graded mark scale might have a pass mark of 40% and a distinction mark of 70%, or a pass mark of 50% and a merit mark of 65%. During result determination the examiner or teacher decides what raw marks are to correspond to these marks. In order to make marking more reliable, you can decide upon your own categories of the relationship between raw scores and grades. For example you might use:

Grade A - 75% and above
Grade B - 61% to 74%
Grade C - 45% to 60%
Grade D - 31% to 44%
Grade E - 30% and below

with D and E as fail, C as pass, B as merit and A as distinction. Also, for true criterion referenced assessment, this scale can be related to only Pass and Fail to indicate whether the objectives have been achieved or not.

5.4 Assessing Group Work

It has been suggested to you in various places in this book that group work has various advantages; indeed, certain objectives can only be achieved through the presentation of group tasks. In group work students work as teams in small groups. Each group does work and produces either an artefact or report or both. The work is then marked.

The size of the group depends upon the task and what is to be produced. However, you should remember that small groups are probably better than large ones due to the ability of the weaker members being able to 'hide' in larger groups. Some teachers do not like groups larger than three students and, even then, consider this quite large as one will often do less than the other two.

This type of work can give rise to problems in assessment both between groups and within them. Problems between groups relate to the level and range of marks. First, group work tends to be marked higher than individual work: groups can achieve more than individuals and individual weaknesses tend to be covered up by other's strengths. Secondly, group marks tend to vary less than individual marks. If groups are randomly formed the average ability will be similar and individual differences will be less. Problems within groups arise due to the differences in individual contributions. It is common for some members to contribute more than others and, those who contribute less may deserve a lower mark than those who contribute more.

To overcome some of these problems you can use mechanisms which will allocate different members of a group different marks which reflect their relative contributions to the work. Gibbs et al (1986) suggest that this can be achieved through (a) shared group grade, or (b) peer assessment.

The shared group mark means that students themselves, who have a much greater idea about individual contributions, are invited to distribute a teacher's group mark amongst themselves. For instance if a group of four students were awarded 60% for a piece of work, they would be given $4 \times 60 = 240$ marks to distribute amongst themselves. Gibbs suggests that this distribution might be achieved by three different methods:

(i)   groups agree at the start of the work that all marks will be equally shared. This tends to motivate members into sharing the work equally.

(ii) groups can agree the basis upon which marks can be divided. This might include creativity, some value of workload, leadership, communication, and so on.

(iii) groups can decide at the outset of the work who will do what part of the work. For instance one might do the research, another the practical work, a third the writing up and so on. This gives all members a specific task and, if this relates to the criteria for assessment can also lead to equitable distribution of the marks.

Another method is to allow, with the use of a rating sheet, each group member to rate every other member of the group in terms of several key aspects of their contribution to the group's work. Such criteria might be as shown in Figure 7.11. These, of course, are only suggestions and might be very different depending upon the task. The average rating for each individual is then deducted from the group mark and allocated to that individual as their mark. Thus, a student who made a major contribution in every respect would have an average rating of zero and receive the group grade. Another student who contributed little in all aspects would receive the group grade minus 20 marks.

	Major	Some	Little
Leadership and direction	0	–1	–2
Organisation and management	0	–1	–2
Ideas and suggestions	0	–1	–2
Data collection	0	–2	–4
Data analysis	0	–2	–4
Report writing	0	–3	–6

Figure 7.11 Peer Assessment Sheet for Group Work Abilities

6. The Accreditation of Prior Achievement

6.1 Assessment of Competences

With the introduction and proliferation of National Vocational Qualifications (NVQs) major changes are occurring in the assessment systems of education and training of adults. Fundamental to these changes is the competence-based approach and the ways in which we assess and accredit the levels of attainment achieved by adults.

Assessment is the key which provides the impetus for a competence approach. Assessment can be diagnostic, by means of which development needs may be identified; formative, in its potential to provide feedback about progress and standards; and summative, making possible valid and reliable judgments about competence.

The basis of Accrediation of Prior Achievement (APA) relates to the generation of evidence by students to show that they can achieve the competences. This evidence can be collected by:

- your students themselves;
- other course members or colleagues;
- the student's line manager at work;
- tutors;
- mentors at the place of work .

Successful completion of a unit of competence will be on the basis of assessment. The requirements are illustrated in the pyramid below:

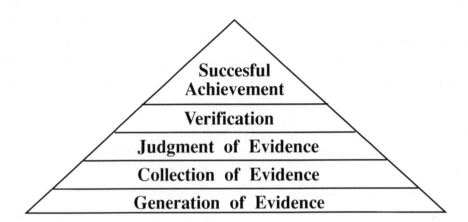

This shows that, at the base of the pyramid and the basis of achievement lies the generation of evidence. Students can generate evidence either on a course, or at work or through exercises which are linked to criteria of assessment associated with units of competence. Once the evidence has been generated it needs to be collected into an acceptable form so that it can be assessed. The collected evidence is then judged as 'reaching the necessary criteria' and then verified by an external assessor.

In order to be awarded an NVQ students need to achieve a number of units of competence which make up the overall competence related to a vocational job. The following principles should be followed for the award:

  (a) all of the competences must be achieved;

  (b) the evidence should relate clearly to the competences;

  (c) the evidence should cover the range of contexts for the competences;

  (d) the evidence should allow distinction between those who meet the criteria and who do not;

  (e) the assessment must be open to verification by external examiners.

6.2 Generation of Evidence

There are four major sources of evidence that you can be collected to show that students have achieved a competence. Sometimes, especially when a spiral curriculum has been designed, it is likely that a mixture of sources will be used. The four sources are:

(a) Historical Evidence: this is evidence resulting from activities that have been under-taken in the past either at work or elsewhere. The evidence may already exist (e.g. curriculum materials) or it may need to be generated (e.g. written reports of projects in which you have been involved).

(b) Performance at Work: this is evidence generated the student at work. Again, the evidence may already exist or alternatively it may be generated as part of the assessment requirements

(c) Performance on Assignments: this relates to the assignments and projects completed as part of course work. This type of evidence gives you greater freedom and students can demonstrate more fully their capabilities. However, there is more chance that the evidence will not relate directly to the competence.

(d) Questioning: this relates to the questioning of you, the teacher, during tutorial sessions. It may be combined with other sources of evidence.

The evidence that is collected to assure a validator that students are competent in a unit can usually be built up into a portfolio of work. The type of evidence of learning that can be included in a portfolio that can be considered for APL (Accreditation of Prior Learning) and APEL (Accreditation of Prior Experiential Learning) includes:

direct evidence (students own work) such as:

projects/assignments from previous courses
tutor assessments of projects/assignments
artefacts - models, videos, photos, etc.
documents used in professional practice
evidence from written tests

indirect evidence (information from others) such as:

reports of professional practice
endorsed statements from an employer
curriculum vitae
certificates and awards
references

This book is partially based on a competence model where, at the start of each chapter you have been given a list of competences to which that chapter refers. Alongside each competence are a series of performance criteria to indicate how the competence can be achieved. Within each chapter are a series of suggestions as to what you might do to collect evidence to show that you can achieve the competence. This evidence, once generated and collected, can be placed into a portfolio and used for APA purposes on courses that you might enter. This will save you having to generate the evidence twice: once at work and secondly by sitting through a course and completing assignments.

Possible Evidence

> *Possible evidence to show that you have achieved the competence 'Provide a rationale for the methods and processes of assessment'*

The type of evidence that you might collect to show that you have achieved the competence include:

(a)   For a particular test that you have used state how you have ensured that it is:

    (i)   valid;

    (ii)   reliable.

(b)   State the reasons for the choice of the type of questions that have been used saying why they are appropriate for the objectives, students, topic, etc.

(c)   For a particular course that you are teaching, write a competence statement and associated performance criteria that would show you that students have achieved the competence. Finally, decide and state the type of evidence that you would accept, that is related to the performance criteria, as proof of competence.

> *If you want to check your understanding of validity and reliability, try the following progress task*

Progress Check 7.2

1. Which of the following correctly defines content validity of a test?

    The extent to which:

    A. The test measures the learning outcome related to instructional objectives.

    B. The process of sampling for test construction.

    C. Different examiners will award the same marks for a question.

    D. An item differentiates between good and poor students.

2. Categorise the following factors into those which predominantly influence validity and those which predominantly influence reliability.

    A. Sampling of objectives.

    B. Marking to a marking scheme.

    C. Relevance of test items to objectives.

3. Describe three different methods you might use in your classroom to assess group work.

4. List three types of

    (i) direct evidence

    (ii) indirect evidence

    that your students might collect to demonstrate their competence.

7. Assessment of Student Practical Work

The usual techniques for the assessment of practical work involves direct observation where you watch the completion of the task and assess the process (how the work is done) and the product (what has been done).

7.1 Problems

Direct observation of practical work may be used to identify learning needs of students in relation to personality, attitudes, behaviours and skills. You can use direct observation in either a formative or a summative manner and, in consequence, it may be used over a relatively long period or in the assessment of a specific task. Observation as a formal means of assessment over a long period, however, is subject to two problems. First, your students may feel threatened and second, your prejudices as the observer can affect the validity and reliability of the assessment. When identifying learning needs, therefore, it is best that you use short, focused periods of observation of a sample of tasks as you are likely to find this more effective than a loose, unstructured general observation system. But, however used, the reports on observations need to be undertaken sensitively which require interpretation and feedback skills on your part.

7.2 Direct Observation Assessment Instruments

There are four common methods of direct observation.

(a) *Global Impression*
which is essentially a technique where you 'look and describe what you see'. The method has no structure and, as such, lacks reliability. However, it is a useful first step in the development of the more sophisticated approaches.

(b) *Semi-structured*
which consists of a number of open questions which you determine in advance and are relevant to the task. You write answers to the questions for each student either during or after observation.

(c) *Rating Schedules*
where you rate a performance on a, say, five point scale as to your impression of each component of the task as carried out by the student.

(d) *Checklists*
where you mark whether the student did or did not carry out specific features of the task.

These four methods range from the global and impressionistic to the relatively specific and analytical. Each has its own strengths and weaknesses. Global methods allow you to take account of individual differences and spot unsuspected learning needs but they are also susceptible to personal idiosyncrasies. By contrast, semi structured observations do provide you with a framework which go some way to checking your idiosyncrasies. Rating schedules concentrate your attention on the major aspects to be assessed but you may differ in your ability to interpret the 5-point scale compared with your colleagues. One assessor's 'very good' may be another assessor's 'mediocre'. Detailed checklists provide a very reliable method of diagnosing strengths and weaknesses but the may exclude some important unforeseen and rarely occurring characteristics. Of the four techniques, the checklist is probably the best for identifying student needs and provides you with some useful feedback for the improvement of your performance as a teacher. Once you have devised a checklist you can use it to develop rating schedules and to provide you with a framework for semi-structured observation.

Examples of the four approaches are shown below so that you can see the relative merits of the different approaches. An example of a global approach is shown below in Figure 7.12.

Please write comments on the student's

ability to use decorate a table for a dinner party.

Ring the grade you feel is appropriate: A B C D E

Figure 7.12 Global Observation

This approach is ambiguous as the instructions do not specify the items that are to be commented upon. Also, the notion of 'ability' is included so you are asked to predict as well as to comment upon present achievement. No criteria are given so it is difficult to compare a group of students. Finally, the meaning of A B C D E is not specified.

The *semi structured* approach (Figure 7.13) provides you with some guidelines in the form of questions. It can be used for observing the student but there is a temptation to answer the questions with a YES/NO. Additional instructions and questions would be required if you intend to estimate the student's achievement.

1.   Did the student choose an appropriate style?

2.   Were appropriate plant materials selected?

3.   Were other components appropriately selected?

4.   Were the mechanics of the design well applied?

5.   Was the execution of the design completed well?

6.   Was the presentation appropriate?

Figure 7.13 Semi-structured Observation Schedule

The *rating schedule* approach, shown in Figure 7.14, concentrates on the five broad dimensions of table decoration which are important. The rating scales are labelled but observers would have to be trained to ensure that they use the scales in the same way. It is, implicitly, a norm-referenced scale.

Please rate the student on the following:

1.	Choice of Style.	6 5 4 3 2 1
2.	Selection of appropriate plant materials.	6 5 4 3 2 1
3.	Selection of other components.	6 5 4 3 2 1
4.	Application of the mechanics of design.	6 5 4 3 2 1
5.	Execution of design.	6 5 4 3 2 1

6 = very good, 5 = good, 4 = quite good, 3 = just satisfactory, 2 = unsatisfactory, 1 = very poor

Figure 7.14 Rating Schedule Observation Schedule

The *checklist* (Figure 7.14) approach sets out the criteria clearly. Even if you do not agree with the criteria you do at least know what they are. The checklist, when given to learners, give them a useful guide on how to cope with the decorating of a table for a dinner party. The terms appropriate and application clearly still require some personal judgment by you as assessor, but different assessors are more likely to agree when using such a checklist than they are when using a rating schedule. The checklist is, therefore, likely to yield reliable assessments and they may also be valid. It is essentially a criterion-referenced instrument.

CRITERIA	YES	NO	NOT OBSERVED
The student related to available materials.			
The design was appropriate for the occasion			
Choice of theme was appropriate.			
lants were identified correctly			
Plants were sorted and packed correctly			
Correct estimate of quantities was made.			
Appropriate design qualities was made			
Unusual combinations of colour and texture			

Figure 7.15 Checklist Observation Schedule

Thus, from the four types, the checklist is the most complex but is more likely to provide accurate results in terms of validity and reliability. It does, however, take more time and expertise to design and you need to observe a student closely in order to complete all of the aspects. In the class situation this latter point might cause difficulties. It is evident that the checklist is at one end of a spectrum with a high degree of structure with its closed, specific and systematic approach but there is less inference involved in interpretation of the instrument. The global approach is at the other end of the spectrum with low structure through its open, general and unsystematic approach with the resultant high inference level required in order for you as assessor to interpret it which results in different interpretations. The rating schedule and semi-structured approaches lie between these two ends of the spectrum as shown in Figure 7.16.

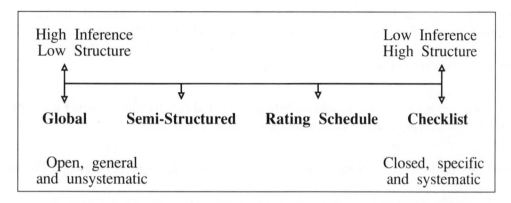

Figure 7.16 Relationship between Different Observation Techniques

7.3 *Preparation of a Series of Practical Tests*

You should follow logical steps in the preparation of a series of practical steps for your students. Such logical steps might be as shown in the following steps:

The *first* step is to prepare, from the syllabus, the objectives that require assessment by means of practical work. This will, in effect, be the minimum essential objectives from the syllabus.

The *second* step is to decide upon the number of tests that will assess the objectives and the type of test exercise that will be required for each of them. For this you will use:

(a)   the number of objectives noted in the list prepared from the syllabus;

(b)   the importance of each of these objectives;

(c)   the ways in which the objectives can be grouped together as relating to similar exercises;

(d)   the time which each of the tests can be expected to take, and the maximum time reasonably available from the course.

The *third* step is to prepare each test exercise. This is sub-divided into four parts:

(i)   Design a test exercise to ensure that students demonstrate attainment of the objectives which have been grouped together.

(ii)   Decide how the test will be marked by designing an assessment scheme which will comprise a list of criteria to show whether the student's performance is satisfactory. This might be a rating schedule, a checklist or a semi-structured format. Probably the most appropriate of these is a checklist which requires either a tick or a cross to show the student achievement or non-achievement of the criteria. The criteria should refer to both the final product *and* the method of work. It might also refer to the speed of work if this is important.

When the criteria are prepared it should be remembered that they will be given to the students as part of their brief and will be presented in the order in which the student will work so that it becomes (a) a guide for the student and (b) easier to mark.

(iii) Decide how the result will be determined. Assessment criteria can be classified as either essential or desirable. Essential criteria are those which, when they are not met, can lead to the complete failure of the exercise, or, alternately, lead to unsafe practices. The remaining criteria can be classified as desirable.

The requirement for a pass should include all essential criteria plus however many of the desirable criteria as is judged reasonable for a student to achieve.

(iv) Draft the test in three sections using clear, simple and unambiguous language. The three sections are:

(a) Preparation which includes:

> where the test will be held;
> details of any necessary preparation;
> a list of materials, tools and equipment required.

(b) Student instructions which include:

> what is to be done;
> what materials, tools and equipment may be used;
> a brief description of how the test will be assessed, including any time limits.

(c) Design the marking scheme which comprises marking criteria listed in the order that it will be most convenient to be checked

The example shown in Figure 7.17, for a task of wiring a three pin plug, demonstrates how such a test sheet might appear.

PREPARATION

The test should be held in normal working conditions. Students should be able to use tools and plugs normally available. They should be instructed to provide their 'usual' tools.

Student Instructions

This test is to assess whether you have reached a basic standard in wiring a 3-pin electrical plug. Using your own tools, a standard 3-pin plug and 13 amp wire, within ten minutes, wire the plug so that it is mechanically and electrically sound.

You should:

(a)   collect the appropriate equipment

(b)   strip the outer sheath and core insulation to the appropriate lengths

(c)   secure the outer sheath correctly

(d)   connect the cables to the correct terminals

(e)   reassemble the plug correctly

(f)   use the appropriate tools correctly

(g)   check your work

Marking

Each point to be marked with a tick if satisfactory and a cross if it is not satisfactory. To obtain a pass, all the square boxes and 50% of the circles must be ticked.

Cable stripper used appropriately.	○
Cable cores bared to terminals but not away from them.	○
Connected cable to correct terminals.	❑
Cables connected securely to terminals.	❑
Outer sheath clamped securely.	❑
Fuse fitted correctly.	❑
Body of plug reassembled securely.	❑
Used correct screwdrivers for different screws.	○
Worked tidily and neatly.	○

Figure 7.17 Example Marking Scheme for a Practical Test

> *Possible evidence to show that you have*
> *achieved the competence*
> *'Use a range of instruments*
> *for the assessment of practical work'*

Design a test for the assessment of a practical skill for your students and describe:

1.   How the objectives are meaningful.

2.   How the test demonstrates achievement of the objectives.

3.   How the preparation includes (a) where the test is to be held, (b) details of student preparation, and (c) a list of materials, equipment and tools required.

4.   How the student instructions include (a) what is to be done, (b) what materials, tools and equipment may be used, and (c) how the test will be assessed.

5.   Show how the marking scheme is valid and reliable including identification of essential criteria, time scale, listed order of tasks, pass requirements, safety requirements, and so on.

> *If you want to check your understanding
> of the assessment of practical tasks,
> try the following progress task*

Progress Check 7.3

1. Describe the differences between the following test instruments:

   (a) semi-structured;

   (b) rating schedule; and

   (c) checklist.

2. Identify the three important aspects that should be included in the *preparation* of a practical assessment.

3. Describe why it is important to:

   (a) design a marking scheme in the order of the completion of tasks;

   (b) give a copy of a marking scheme to students.

4. What are the aspects that define 'essential' criteria of a practical task?

8. Assessment of Assignments and Projects

You may encounter some confusion in the difference between projects and assignments. When used in the context of teaching methods the two are often ill defined despite being widely used and are sometimes inter-changed. The two are very similar and it is the time that is taken to complete them that often differentiates the two: an assignment generally taking a shorter time to complete than a project.

However, the major difference between the two lies in design. In a project the student decides the parameters of the work within overall guidelines whereas in an assignment the teacher decides on the parameters. Thus, a project is more open and is liable to more differences in the way in which it is tackled whereas the assignment has more structure which is likely to lead to similarities in the approaches taken by the students. In many ways a project may be considered as the extreme to which you may go in arranging student-centred learning approaches. Whereas an assignment is more teacher centred.

Both assignments and projects have the advantage that they provide the opportunity for the assessment of a great range of skills within all of the domains and at all levels within the domains. Also, BTEC have pioneered the use of what they term 'integrative' assignments where they also give the opportunity for assessment across the subject matter boundaries. They argue that this is the way that learning takes place at work; not within subjects but across them. The problem is the basis. This has given rise to 'work-based' assignments which also give the opportunity for the assessment of common (transferable) skills, which are problem based.

In this chapter we are going to concentrate only upon the methodology of assessing assignments. The reason for this is that (a) assignments are more commonly used than projects, but (b) the principles and techniques described are applicable to both teaching strategies.

An example of a Work Based Assignment given by BTEC relating to National Awards in Leisure Studies is given below. The general guideline to the student is:

> *'You are to investigate security arrangements in a chosen leisure organisation'.*

This, however, is only a general guideline that is given to the student. Remembering that an assignment has been defined as being:

(i)   structured by the teacher; and

(ii)   giving opportunity for assessment across subject matter boundaries,

both student activities and the objectives from the different subjects need to be identified. These are shown diagrammatically in Figure 7.18 The student activities are shown as a step-by-step guide for the students to follow and, it is from these that the objectives are identified from the different subject areas. The objectives become the basis for the assessment.

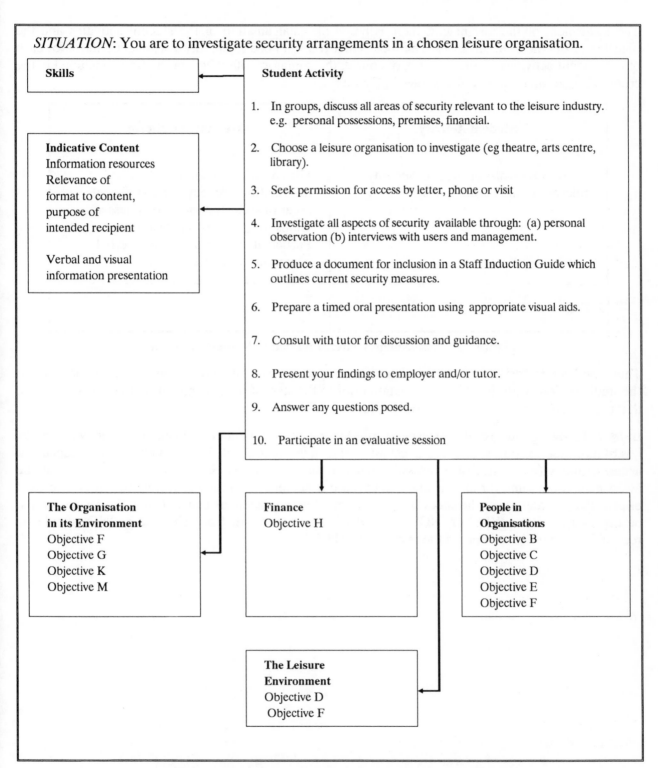

Figure 7.18 Example Layout for an Integrated Assignment

The assessment of the assignment, then, is based on amalgamation of the student activities and the objectives from the different styles. This means that you will need to identify assessment criteria for each of the student activities. There are also, of course, the common skills which must also be included in the criteria. These can be achieved as shown in Figure 7.19.

Student Activity	Assessment Criteria
1. In groups discuss all areas of security relevant to the leisure industry.	Uses a variety of sources of information. At least three different areas of security should be discussed. Helps the group reach decisions. Participate in verbal and non-verbal communication effectively.
2. Etc.	

Figure 7.19 Assessment Criteria related to Student Activities

Thus, you need to design assessment criteria for each of the student activities and these can be given to the students along with the other information prior to the start of the assignment. In this way you ensure that the students know what you are looking for.

Instead of showing you all of the assessment criteria for each of the student activities in the above example, it is of more use to you to indicate a checklist as shown in Figure 7.20. This is subdivided into aspects to achieve validity (ensuring that it assesses what it is supposed to assess), reliability (ensuring that the assessment is the same for all the students that are observed) and utility (ensuring that it can be used effectively). In order to use the checklist for an acceptable assignment assessment all of the aspects should be checked as either 'YES' or 'NOT NEEDED'. Any aspects that are checked as 'NO' should be reconsidered in order to improve the assessment schedule.

			YES	NO	NOT NEEDED
1.	**Validity of Assignment Assessment**				
1:1	Are the objectives of the assignment stated?		1	2	3
1:2	Do the objectives cover:				
	(i)	all the necessary domains?	1	2	3
	(ii)	all the necessary subjects?	1	2	3
	(iii)	all the necessary core skills?	1	2	3
1:3	Are the necessary student activities produced?		1	2	3
2.	**Reliability**				
2:1	Do students receive:				
	(i)	written information of the assessment scheme?	1	2	3
	(ii)	details of how gradings are arrived at?	1	2	3
	(iii)	a timetable of key assessment events?	1	2	3
3.	**Utility**				
3:1	Is there any duplication of sampling of student performance?		1	2	3
3:2	Is there an effective balance between process and product assessment?		1	2	3
3:3	Is informal observation of student performance possible to achieve?		1	2	3

Figure 7.20 Checklist for Assignment Assessment

You might use a wide range of assessment methods for assessing performance in assignments. The following examples illustrate some of the range that you might use:

- *teacher observation* of group activity, team tasks and, sometimes, individual activity;

- *student diaries* of work experience which includes reflections on learning and student's strengths and weaknesses;

- *portfolios/work files* which may include students' working papers as well as completed assignment work and tutor comments;

- *self-assessment statements* on skills development at regular stages during the assignment

- *peer assessment* which may take the forms, for example:

  - agreeing with a team member a statement of their contribution to the task;

  - commenting in a group review on the work of different aspects;

  - making a written comment, against set criteria, of the work of different teams.;

- *assignment products* which may be reports, designs, or artefacts;

- *process reviews* in which the students and tutor review the ways in which the assignment was approached.

> *Possible evidence to show that you have achieved*
> *the competence*
> *'Use appropriate format for*
> *the assessment of projects/assignments'*

For an assignment that you have designed for your students, explain the following for the criteria of assessment that you have included as part of the preparation.

(a) Why are you assessing the assignment?

(b) What are the subject objectives and core skills that are included?

(c) What is the rationale for the criteria?

(d) How does the assessment assist student self-assessment?

> *If you want to check your understanding of the assessment of projects/assignments, try the following progress check*

Progress Check 7.4

1. What three ways can you improve the validity of an assessment scheme for an assignment or project?

2. Explain how giving students:

    (i)   written information of an assessment scheme, and

    (ii)   details of how gradings are arrived at might assist the reliability of an assessment scheme for a project or assignment.

3. Why are a mixture of process and product objectives important to be included in the design of a project or assignment?

9. Student Profile Formats

You will realise from Chapter 1 that a profile is a way of reporting student achievements; it is not an assessment technique in itself. Profiles can be used for both formative and summative processes. Consider the way in which you make reports about the work that your students complete in a year and how these are used by you, your teacher colleagues and employers. Traditional methods of reporting student progress is through an examination and a brief comment about these results, the work completed in class and, perhaps, the attitude of the student. It can be argued that traditional methods :

- are very crude, global and mask individual differences;

- are subject-based reports which tend to hide the overall student abilities;

- offer little incentive to many students;

- offer little worthwhile information to students;

- give no real assistance to students with self-assessment;

- give teachers very little to go on when they are asked to give an account of their work;

- are very impersonal giving students very little opportunity to discuss them.

The intentions of a profile system of reporting is to overcome these problem areas. Summative intentions provide new bases for action by selectors (employers and teachers). Formative intentions provide new bases for action by students.

Consider the aims of a typical vocational course given below in Figure 7.21.

Aims

      To identify personal opportunities and prepare for progression.
      Further explore selected occupational and non-occupational roles.
      To become an effective member of a team.
      Assist an ability for organisation and leadership.
      Develop confidence in working independently.
      Equip students to communicate effectively with a range of people in a variety of situations.

Objectives

      apply enterprise skills.
      recognise the need for a career plan.
      work co-operatively in a team.
      assist colleagues to plan tasks.
      assess results of own work without assistance.
      present a logical and effective argument and analyse others arguments.

Figure 7.21 Typical Aims/Objectives of a Vocational Course

These mainly fall within the affective domain and, it is suggested, are not assessed and reported upon by traditional methods of assessment and reporting. Indeed, generally traditional methods of assessment neglect the affective domain to a large extent. Profiles attempt to pass information onto students, employers and other teachers on all aspects of learning.

Below, four different types of profile are described. When looking at each of them you should consider:

- the method that appears to be particularly helpful to you in your teaching situation;
- methods that might hinder you in your teaching situation;
- methods that might assist you to overcome problems that you might have presently in reporting on student learning.

The first example (Figure 7.22) is a *grid style hierarchical statement* which show the specific abilities that the students must exhibit and, alongside each, a three-point scale of individual progress in the abilities. A space is also provided where examples of how individual students have exhibited the abilities (what task they were involved in when they were observed, what they did, and so on). Additionally there is a space between each statement where either the teacher or the student can sign and indicate a date to confirm that, at that time, the learner had achieved that level.

	Abilities	**Examples of Abilities**	**Progress in Abilities**		
C O M M U N I C A T I O N	*Talking/ Listening*		Can make sensible replies.	Can follow and give explanations	Can present a logical argument.
	Reading		Can read words and phrases.	Can follow written instructions.	Can judge materials to support an argument
	Writing		Can write words and phrases.	Can write instructions.	Can write a critical analysis.
	Use of diagrams.		Recognises everyday sign/symbols	Uses basic graphs/codes/ charts	Can make graphs to support conclusions

Figure 7.22 Grid-Style Hierarchical Profile

Only abilities in communication are shown in the example. However, practical, numerical, social and decision making skills can be added to cover all of the skills in a course of study.

It will be seen that the statements alongside each ability are graded starting from the simple and going to the complex. In the example given a three-point scale is used. This results in quite large jumps between each level. If a five-point scale were used the jumps between each would be smaller.

A completed example for a 'Practical' skill is given in Figure 7.23 to indicate how the spaces might be used. The ability has been assessed on two occasions with different tasks and shows the progression between the two dates.

Abilities	Examples of Abilities	Progress in Abilities		
Safety	1. Changed wheels & oil filter on a car	Can explain the need for rules	Can spot safety hazards	Can suggest safety improvement
		Sig. Date(1)	Sig. Date(2)	
	2. Changed points on a distributor			

Figure 7.23 Completed Grid Style Hierarchical Profile

The advantages of the grid style profile are:

- specific examples for the abilities can be identified;
- reliability is improved through the nominating of the three points on the scale;
- progress can easily be shown;
- can be completed by the teacher, the student, or through a mixture of both;
- can be used as either a formative or summative document;
- contains a lot of information for employers;
- has both tick box and statement information.

However, there are also the following limitations:

- can be restricting as there is no space for abilities other than those listed;
- can take employers a long time to read if they have a lot of them and are used as summative documents;

- teachers might think that all of the abilities need completing;

- can be time consuming to complete;

- there is no specific space for students to write their own comments.

The second example profile format consists of a *Bank of Statements* which the student should achieve. These, basically, are a set of objectives which are available for both the teacher and the student. The intention is that they are used as the basis for negotiation between teacher and student to decide how and when individual students will achieve the statements. The teacher will also use them as a basis for assessment and reporting.

Banks of Statements can be written for any area of the curriculum. However, they are mainly associated with affective domain areas covering the core skills such as 'personal development', 'career development', 'manual dexterity', 'evaluation of performance', and so on. Figure 7.24 shows an example bank of statements from the core area of 'personal and career development'. These are just a representative sample of the type of statement from this core area. Additionally, there would be objectives under other core areas of:

- Industrial, Social and Environmental Studies;
- Communication;
- Social Skills;
- Numeracy;
- Science and Technology;
- Information Technology;
- Creative Development;
- Problem Solving;

or whatever are the demands of the particular curriculum.

It will be seen that these are, as the name implies, just a bank of statements. The use of these in profiling is open to interpretation but, often, they are used as a checklist for teachers and individual learners to check individual abilities.

FACTOR	Ref. No.	CORE COMPETENCE STATEMENT
Personal Development	01.1	Can identify own strengths and weaknesses.
	01.2	Can recognise opportunities to develop interests and abilities.
	01.3	Can make the most of opportunities to develop interests and abilities.
	01.4	Can show initiative in developing own interests and abilities.
Career Development	02.1	Can recognise the need for a personal career plan.
	02.2	Can identify factors influencing local job opportunities.
	02.3	Can make a realistic assessment of own career potential.
	02.4	Can produce a realistic career plan.

Figure 7.24 Bank of Statements related to Personal/Career Development

Again, this system has its advantages and limitations. These might include:

Advantages:

- gives a clear picture of what is intended in the curriculum;
- gives an excellent basis for negotiation with students;
- validity is assisted with the pre-specification of the statements;
- all students know what is required from the curriculum;
- can be used either formatively or summatively;
- contains a lot of information.

Limitations:

- there are a lot of statements;
- it can be difficult to keep track of all of the statements with what students do;
- students might not understand what is meant by the statements when tasks are negotiated;
- some form of overview sheet is needed for individual student records;
- it is likely to be time consuming to assess;
- can be constraining as only the nominated objectives are likely to be reported. There is no indication of need for open comments.

The third type of profile is one which allows for *free response*. This type of format is in the form of a booklet with headings under which both the teacher and the student make comments (see Figure 7.25). It can be completed at any time during the learning process and will form the basis of a summative report.

The advantages of this type of profile include:

- the compilation can be specifically geared to the needs of the individual student and the activities that they have completed;
- having a space for student completion ensures their involvement in the process;
- there are few restrictions for the teacher and the student;
- is used as a formative document but is a basis for a summative report.

On the other hand it also has limitations. These include:

- the openness might lead to bland comments being made about individual students;
- validity might be low due to the open nature of the profile;
- can be time-consuming to complete;
- relies on the writing ability of the tutor and the student;
- reliability might be low.

Page 1 Name of Institution

Student Name: ....

Date: ....

Course: ....

To teacher: this form will provide the basis of the profile to be compiled on the above student during training.
Please complete and return to office by:

....

To student: Your course tutor will complete this form and will discuss any recorded comments with you. Please talk freely with your tutor. If there are any comments you wish to make please do so in the space provided on the back page.

Date	Student Experience

Please comment on the following:
Communication Skills

Practical & Numerical Skills

Page 3

Attitude to Training

Planning & Problem Solving

Manual Dexterity

Computer Literacy

Areas of Aptitude/Improvement
Give details of areas of aptitude and those needing improvement.

Page 4

General Comments
Tutor Please comment on general matters (attendance, self confidence, etc.)

Student Please use this space for any comments about training

Tutor Signature: ....

Student Signature: ....

Date: ....

Figure 7.25 Example of Free Response Profile

The final type of profile is the *Joint Review* between the teacher and the student. This is basically a formative document (see Figure 7.26 for a typical example). It review what a learner has completed over a period of time (say over a month) and sets targets for the following period.

Joint Review

1. What are the main tasks/work completed in the last 4 weeks?

> These reviews are intended to be completed at least once per month.
>
> Review sessions must not be disciplinary sessions.
>
> What is written is intended to come out of a process of feedback to the learner.
>
> The account is agreed between tutor and learner.
>
> The original is on two A4 sheets giving more room than is shown here

2. What has the student done particularly well?

3. After discussion, we have agreed that progress is made in:

4. The next month will be spent on:

Student signature: Date:

Tutor signature :   Date:

Figure 7.26 Example Joint Review Profile Format

The main difference between a Joint Review and the previous formats is the emphasis on the consultation between the tutor and the student. The principle here is that, if student see the need for change, then they are more likely to accommodate that change. Also, it places the emphasis upon self-evaluation by the student. This is a skill that must be learned and the format can be a useful teaching tool for that purpose.

The *Joint Review*, then, has the following advantages:

- the completion can be specifically geared to the needs of individual student and to the activities that they have completed;
- the involvement of the student assists the self-evaluation process and is more likely to be meaningful to them;
- setting targets can be useful for improvements;
- it is used as a formative document but also provides useful evidence for a summative report.

The format also has the following limitations:

- the openness might lead to bland comments being made about individual students;
- validity might be low due to its open nature;
- can be time consuming to complete, especially as it involves discussions with individual students
- discussions must take place in private; a quiet room must be provided for this to take place;
- relies upon the writing ability of the tutor;
- may be used for disciplinary purposes;
- can be difficult to get the involvement of the more recalcitrant students.

We have already described profiling as a *process*; it takes place in a formative framework. In order for you to achieve this, the following principles should be followed:

1.   Profiling requires one-to-one tutor-student reviews on a regular basis.

    The Joint Review format suggests at least once a month. This is time consuming but, it is suggested, is well worth the time that is devoted to it. A further problem is that this tutorial time must be completed in private and the remainder of the class might be unsupervised at this time.

2.   Profiling involves *negotiation* with individual learners.

    The negotiation with individual students, no matter which of the formats is used, is to ensure that students are involved in the process; involved in their own assessments, involved in making judgments about themselves and involved in their own target setting.

3.   Profiling is a teaching strategy which allows student to:

    - reflect on success and failure;
    - take responsibility for their own learning and development.

When considered as a teaching strategy, profiling is looked at in a different light. You should not consider it as an assessment strategy and your students should not look at it as a session for discipline. It is an opportunity to discuss both strengths and weaknesses.

4.   Profiles should record *positive* statements of achievement with respect to:

- abilities or skills/competences demonstrated
- personal qualities exhibited
- tasks or activities experienced

You should note that the intention of a profile is that they report what a student can do as opposed to what they cannot do. You can see that, in all of the examples, the statements are written positively. In addition they should report what abilities, competences, personal qualities, tasks and activities which the student has been successful in.

Four different formats of profile have been identified and the advantages and limitations of each have been stated. The main points relating to these are contrasted in Figure 7.27.

Profile Format	Main Characteristics	Main Advantages	Main Limitations
Grid style Hierarchical Statements	Space for list of activities and nominated scale for indication of progress in abilities.	1. Has tick box and statement information. 2. Progress can be easily shown.	1. Might be restricting for some students. 2. No specific space for student comment.
Bank of Statements	List of objectives as basis of the curriculum.	1. Clear basis for negotiation. 2. Valid and reliable.	1. Lots of statements. 2. Can be confusing and limiting.
Free Response	A list of headings with spaces for mainly the tutor	1. Easy to link what student has achieved.	1. Relies on the tutor writing ability
Joint Review	Similar to Free Response but more open in terms of headings.	1. Easy to link to what the student has achieved. 2. Space for setting of targets.	1. Is very open. 2. Might be hard to get the student involved.

Figure 7.27 Contrasting Different Formats of Profile

Possible Evidence

Possible evidence to show that you have achieved
the competence
'Employ Appropriate Student Profiling Formats'

1.   For a profile format that you have used, give its advantages
      and limitations and state how it achieves appropriate objec-
      tives of your curriculum.

2.   In using your chosen profile format, describe the process that
      you have used and identify the important principles that you
      followed.

If you want to check your understanding of profiling formats try the following progress check

Progress Check 7.5

1.   List FOUR advantages of profile formats that traditional methods of reporting student progress fail to achieve.

2.   Define each of the following profile formats:

   (a)   Grid-style hierarchical statements

   (b)   Bank of Statements

   (c)   Free Response

   (d)   Joint Review

   and give two advantages and one limitation of each type.

3.   Describe THREE principles of the profiling process that are important to make it successful with your students.

10. Motivate Students Through Feedback

You will know that the main aspect of formative assessment is the feedback that is given to students. If the assessment is to provide information that is going to lead to improvement in performance, then it must have a motivational effect. This motivation can be to lead students to greater effort, to make them sustain their efforts for future topics, or to tell them what they have done well or where they have done not so well. Feedback can be given as a mark or grade, or comments, or a mixture of the two. You will also know that if a mark is given then this is what is first looked at and, perhaps, the only thing that is looked at. The comments take time to write, maybe one more difficult to write and should be of much greater benefit to the student in terms of future improvements. Comments can also be very discouraging to the student: often there seems little evidence that students have taken account of what has been said or even understood it.

There is no doubt that immediate feedback is the most beneficial while the work is still fresh in the minds of the student. This, however, is only possible with

(a)   objective-type questions which can be marked quickly immediately after the have been completed; or

(b)   through direct observation when comments can be given either verbally or in writing and the student can question what is said.

In most cases, however, you will not be able to give immediate feedback as you will require time to complete the assessment. Indeed, it is often completed quietly at home or in your office when the students are not present. In order to maintain the benefit of immediacy, you should ensure that the assessment is completed as soon as possible after the work has been done by the student.

There are ways of attempting to ensure that students pay more attention to your feedback. This can be done by relating the assessment and comments to the criteria of assessment which you have previously given to your students. Thus, if they have understood the criteria and put their effort into achieving each of the different aspects, they should more readily understand the feedback. This has the additional benefit, so long as you always formulate your feedback in this way, of ensuring that students pay attention to the criteria.

Alternatively you can ask students themselves what kind of feedback they want. If it is what they have asked for, they will be motivated to take it more seriously. They are in the best position to know what their difficulties are and to judge what kind of feedback is helpful.

You can obtain students' requests for feedback either from individuals or from the group as a whole. If you want requests from individuals you can ask them when they do a piece of assessed work to add a note at the end specifying what kind of feedback they would like. They will probably need some encouragement initially and an explanation of why it is important to them. You might also give some examples of the kind of requests that they might make. Such examples might include 'comment on style as well as content', 'highlight any inconsistencies', 'if I have gone wrong, please point out where this is and show me the correct way', or 'have I answered the question in the easiest manner? If not, how could I have answered it more easily?' The type of feedback, of course, depends upon the type of question. An essay would require feedback on style and grammar as well as content, where as a science or mathematical question would require answers in the most direct manner and with accuracy.

Individual students often require different kinds of feedback and what suits one might be irrelevant to another. If you want a request from a whole group, you can set up a pyramid exercise to enable students to clarify and pool their ideas. This pooling of ideas can often be very useful in the initial stages of requesting this type of information from students. Pyramid exercises operate in stages: first students work on their own, then in pairs, then in fours and, finally, as a whole group.

If you ask students what kind of feedback they want, not only are they more likely to receive it but they are getting practice in self-assessment. It is also more motivating if they identify their own strengths and weaknesses.

Figure 7.28 (adapted from Gibbs, et al, 1986) gives a checklist for giving feedback to students.

---

1.   Keep the time short between the student writing and the feedback. Where possible make it instantaneous.

2.   Substantiate a grade/mark with comments both in the text for specific aspects and with a summary at the end.

3.   Balance negative comments with positive ones and ensure that negative ones are constructive.

4.   Follow-up written comments with oral feedback and aim for a dialogue.

5.   Make the criteria clear to students when setting the work and give them written criteria where possible.

6.   Make further suggestions (e.g. for further reading or for further developing ideas).

7.   Give periodic oral feedback on rough drafts.

Figure 7.28 Guidelines For Giving Feedback

If you are able to follow these guidelines you should ensure that students are motivated by the feedback that you give them. It can be beneficial rather than developing your own checklist (or using ours) to get members of a course team to devise their own; the items on such a checklist arising out of discussions about assessment within the team. Alternately, you can devise your own checklist in consultation with your students.

11. Assessment in Overall Lesson Design

The timing of assessment throughout a course has already been discussed in Chapter 5 (section 8.4) when discussing the design of an Optimum Linear Sequence where it was suggested that assessment points could usefully be included at the end of a teaching sequence of topics. It has also been discussed for an individual lesson, in Chapter 1 (section 1.3) when talking about the three phases of a lesson suggesting that assessment could usefully be completed in the introduction to assess entry behaviour and in the conclusion to assess terminal behaviour related to the objectives of the lesson. Both of these are important aspects but assessment should be an on-going activity throughout both the lessons and the course. You will not only assess through written work but through question and answer of both individuals and the class. The Basic Teaching Model gives the basis for this activity and the complete model can be completed several times during a lesson. This, you will remember, goes from a statement of objectives, to entry behaviour, teaching strategies, to assessment with feedback loops from assessment to each of the previous components. The suggestion was that the assessment could take place during the entry behaviour phase (to assess the extent to which the entry behaviour has been gained), and the assessment phase (to see the amount of learning that has taken place). Different types of cognitive lessons are shown in Figure. 7.29 with different types of assessment taking place during the lesson. Three different sequences (A, B and C) are shown, but you must remember that these are only three from a whole number of different possibilities. The assessment can be by either a formal test or through informal question and answer. The test can be either supply or selection types and can be completed either individually or in groups. Whichever sequence is used, you must plan the assessment in your lesson planning so that it becomes a learning activity as well as an assessment opportunity.

	Introduction		Development				Conclusion	
A	State Lesson Aim	Entry level test	Concept No 1	Concept No 2	Review of Concepts	Test	Homework & next lesson topic	
B	Review test last lesson	State lesson aim	Introduce concepts by Q & A		Concepts 1 and 2	Application of concepts through Q and A	Test of concepts and next lesson topic	
C	Q & A last lesson	State lesson aim	Entry level test	Concepts1 and 2		Review of concepts through Q and A	Test	Next lesson topic

Figure 7.29 Assessment in a Cognitive Lesson

12. Revising Assessment Procedures

In section 5 of this chapter we have already discussed methods of increasing validity (through a table of specifications to ensure that a representative sample of topics and abilities are assessed) and reliability (through a marking scheme to ensure all scripts are marked in the same manner). The use of these techniques should not stop you from putting anything right that has been found wrong in the scheme. Indeed, you should still look for things that might be wrong. An appraisal of the table of specifications and the marking schemes can be useful in providing you with information on the aspects of the assessment which have worked the best. This, in turn, can improve your own techniques with assessment. You also need to consider the questions that you are using. You can use statistical analyses to show you whether the questions are too hard or too easy for the students and whether they discriminate appropriately between the more and the less able students. If they are too difficult, is it the wording of the questions that is misleading or is it the subject matter that has not been learned or was your teaching poor? Do the better students get the questions right and the poorer ones get them wrong?

It is suggested that you periodically check all of these aspects. This can be done with other teachers, examiners (if an external examination is used), students and employers. The checking may lead to recommendations for the change of syllabus content and course objectives as well as in the assessment itself. An evaluation might consider the following points which have been adapted from Ward, C. (1980):

(a)   Does the assessment appear to be valid? Is it assessing all of the required topics and abilities in the right proportions?

(b)   Does it appear to be meeting the needs of employers or prospective employers?

(c)   Do the students see the assessment as valid and reliable? If not, why not?

(d)   Is the standard of assessment appropriate to the aims of the course? i.e. does the table of specification relate to the course aims?

(e)   Are most of the students succeeding in the assessment? If not does the fault lie in the selection of the students, in the teaching, in the student's motivation, or in some other factor?

(f)   Are the results of most of the students consistent with your expectations? If not, why not?

(g)   Were most students able to complete the work in the time available?

(h)   Was the assessment of appropriate difficulty judged by the average mark obtained?

(i)   Does the assessment differentiate between students of different levels of ability? This may be indicated by the numbers of students with high, low and middle range marks.

(j)   Are all of the questions in the assessment appropriate, clear and technically correct?

The answers to all, or some, of these points can assist in giving you an overall view of how your assessment is working. The main point, however, is that you should periodically try to identify any problems that might occur in your assessment procedures. From any problems that you have identified you should also try to find reasons why they are occurring and, once the reasons are identified, rectify the faults.

Check

Progress

> ### Possible evidence to show that you have achieved the competence 'Justify appropriate forms of measuring learner achievement'

1. Describe the process that you have gone through in designing a scheme of assessment at both course and lesson levels. You should draw the distinction between formative and summative procedures.

2. For particular assessment tests, describe how you have ensured:

    (a) Validity, and

    (b) reliability

3. Evaluate the assessment test by answering some of the questions:

    • Is the assessment appropriate to the aims of the course?

    • Are most students successful? If not, why not?

    • Were the average marks as expected? If not, why not?

    • Was the range of marks as expected? If not, why not?

    • Were the questions clear?

    By answering the questions above, what changes would you make in the future if you were repeating the assessment to these students?

If you want to check your understanding of evaluation of forms of measuring learner achievement, try the following progress check

Progress Check 7.6

1. Explain why it is important to give student feedback:

   (a) as quickly as possible, and

   (b) in a positive manner.

2. What ways can you ensure that criteria of assessment are understood by your students?

3. Suggest THREE techniques that could usefully be employed to evaluate your assessment techniques.

Further Reading and References

Further reading relating to the topics in this chapter can be found in the following:

Black, H. et al   *The Quality of Assessment*, Scottish Council for Research in Education, 1989

City and Guilds   *Constructing Practical Tests,* 1979

Gibbs, G. et al   *53 Interesting Ways to Assess Your Students*, Technical & Educational Services Ltd, 1986

Law, W   *Uses and Abuses of Profiling,* Harper, 1984.

LLoyd-Jones, R and Bray, E.   *Assessment - From Principle to Action*, MacMillan Educational Ltd, 1986.

Ward, C   *Designing a Scheme of Assessment*, S Thornes, 1980.

Chapter 8
Evaluation of Self and Teaching

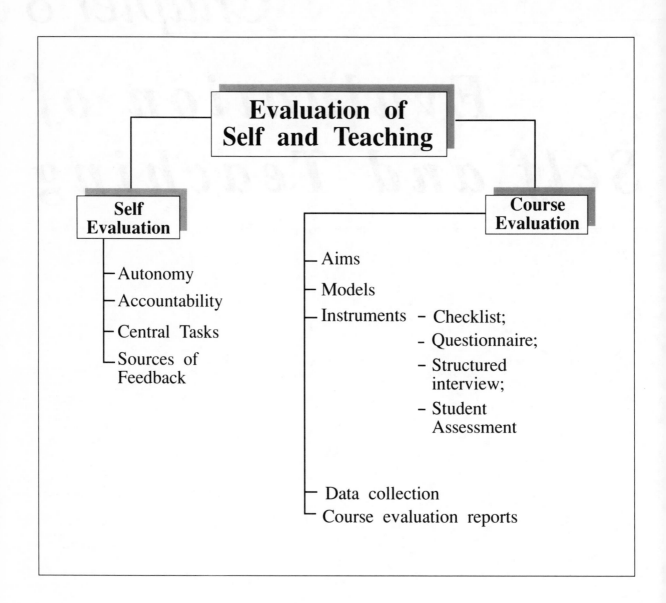

Overview of Chapter 8

Competences Related to this Chapter

The competences and associated performance criteria related to this chapter are:

Overall Competence – *Employ effective evaluation techniques*

Competence	Performance Criteria
1. **Engage in evaluation of own and other's teaching**	(a) Identify central teaching tasks and other professional duties. (b) Devise strategies for monitoring and evaluating the effectiveness of teaching roles. (c) Develop appropriate feedback mechanisms. (d) Use feedback from students, peers and colleagues to aid self-evaluation.
2. **Engage in the evaluation of your courses.**	(a) Consider methods of course evaluation. (b) Assess useful aspects to be evaluated. (c) Identify the components of an evaluation report. (d) Make suggestions for course improvements based on data from the evaluation.

1. Introduction

Evaluation has already been described as the provision of the feedback loop of the Basic Teaching Model (Figure 8.1). Box D, assessment, consists of tests and observations that we use to determine how well the student has achieved the objectives. If this assessment tells us that the students, or even some of them, have fallen short of their learning, then one or more of the previous components of the model may need adjustment. This adjustment involves the making of judgements and these judgements involve the evaluation of both ourselves and the courses that we operate.

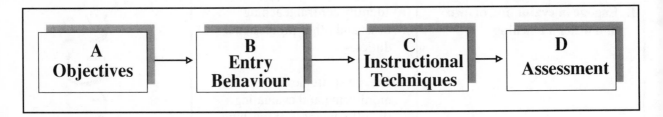

Figure 8.1 Complete Basic Teaching Model

Thus evaluation, in its simplest form, is finding out as much as you can about the quality of teaching and learning and how to improve the various aspects which influence this quality.

2. Autonomy and Accountability

Evaluation, especially course evaluation, is relatively new but is likely to develop further and, perhaps, become a requirement in most areas of education and training. It has emerged, and will probably continue to develop, because of the increasing acceptance of two related concepts: professional autonomy and accountability.

The idea of autonomy is that professionals should be free to determine how they practice but, in return for this privilege, they should be rigorous in maintaining and developing their standards of practice. Accordingly, examining and validating bodies increasingly allow you, the teacher in post-16 education, to determine what you teach, to whom, and how you teach it. Your external syllabuses and externally set examinations are being replaced by college devised and assessed courses which are approved by central bodies. However, in return, these central bodies are increasingly requiring you to monitor, review and evaluate your courses and to report on them periodically. Such reports contain a critical analysis of the operation of the course together with proposals for improvements.

The public served by professionals increasingly expect those professionals to be accountable to them or their representatives. No longer can doctors, lawyers, engineers, architects, and so on, expect to escape scrutiny and criticism by lay people by claiming special expertise, mystique and status. In education, the move to accountability has been promoted by public concern over the relevance and standards of education in schools and colleges.

In consequence, apart from these external pressures, for your own piece of mind, you need to acquire knowledge and skills that are required to evaluate your own performance and your courses. Some headings have already been suggested in Chapter 1 (Figure 1.7 and Figure 1.18) that might be used for a self-evaluation diary and that your own students might be used to provide data on the effectiveness of your teaching.

3. Central Teaching and other Professional Tasks

In consequence of increasing autonomy and accountability, we need to consider what are the main tasks for which we, as teachers of post-16 education and training, are responsible. Once these have been identified, they can be the focus for a self-audit to see how we are operating and what areas we need to improve.

There has been a move recently to base many of the teaching tasks on a competence model. These moves have been spearheaded by two national bodies: the Training and Development Lead Body (TDLB) and the Management Charter Initiative (MCI). These, however, as yet, are far from being accepted generally by the teacher training profession. Not least of the problems is that there is no overt collaboration between the two. Yet teaching involves aspects of both; the teaching aspect as put forward by TDLB and the management (of the classroom) as put forward by MCI. Thus, in terms of competences that are required by the teacher, we need to consider (a) those aspects required to teach our subjects and (b) aspects of management of both the classroom and the curriculum. Thus, these tasks can be sub-divided into (i) teaching and (ii) other professional duties.

3.1 Teaching Tasks

Teaching tasks can be sub-divided into six main elements that reflect the job of the teacher in operating with students. These elements, broadly speaking, have been at the base of the thinking of TDLB and have various competences associated with them. The first of the elements relates to the preparation that you complete for your teaching. The associated competences are given in Chapter 1 and are:

    (i)   Preparation

- identification of student needs;
- analysis of a subject/topic into a logical sequence;
- indication of expected student learning;
- selection of appropriate teaching/learning methods;
- writing systematic lesson plans;
- selecting and prepararing learning resources.

The second element relates to how this preparation is put into practice when teaching students: the application of the preparation. Aspects related to this element therefore include:

(ii) Presentation

- the implementation of selected teaching/learning methods;
- provision of appropriate:
  - introduction;
  - development; and
  - conclusion to a session;
- flexible response to classroom situations;
- using learning resources effectively.

The third element relates to the manner in which you as the teacher are able to relate to your students. This operates on the premise that the better the relationship between you and your students, the more likelihood there is of optimising learning. Aspects relating to this element include:

(iii) Trainee/Student Relationships

- securing student participation in lessons;
- promotion of a classroom climate that facilitates learning.

An element that could be considered as going across all of the other elements is communication: the basis of all teaching. However, it is considered so important that it is thought worthwhile separating and making an element on its own. Aspects relating to communication include:

(iv) Communication

- using appropriate language registers;
- employment of effective skills in verbal and non-verbal communication.

The next element is the final one in the basic teaching model, assessment of student learning. It is from here that you are able to identify any problems that might have occurred with the operation of the previous elements. Thus the aspect to be considered is:

(v) Assessment of Learning

- making an assessment of the extent to which the students achieved the stated intentions.

The final element relates to your knowledge of the subject that you are teaching. It is thus:

(vi) Subject Matter

- demonstration of mastery of the subject matter.

These aspects, then, provide you with the basis on which you can evaluate your own, or someone else's, teaching ability, or, on the other hand, the basis on which someone else might evaluate your teaching ability. They can be used in total to give an overall impression or they might be used one at a time to provide feedback on specific elements.

If you are inviting someone else to evaluate your teaching performance you might use a pro-forma like the one indicated in Figure 8.2.

PRACTICAL TEACHING OBSERVATION PRO-FORMA

Date: Class:

Time: Subject/Topic:

Place:

Competences to be displayed and assessed with associated comments:

Competences *(completed by you)*	Comments *(completed by observer)*

Additional comments by the observer:

(i) Preparation:

(ii) Presentation:

(iii) Trainee/Student Relationships:

(iv) Communication:

(v) Assessment of Learning:

(vi) Subject Matter:

Figure 8.2 Sample Pro-Forma to Assist Feedback from Observation

From the lesson plan it will be possible for you to identify the range of competences that will be used and upon which feedback can be given. If you identify these prior to the observation and write them onto the pro-forma, you will obtain the specific feedback that you desire. These might be, for instance:

(a)   use teaching strategies that are appropriate to the group;

(b)   organisation of the environment in a way that assists learning;

(c)   use appropriate language;

(d)   analyse strengths and weaknesses of the students.

It may be that you want to practise and gain feedback on a specific skill, like your ability to use the question and answer technique effectively. In this case you might design and use a schedule only related to this specific aspect (see Figure 8.3).

An advantage of such a schedule is that you think about the main aspects of the competence related to question and answer both in the planning and the presentation stages. That is, you plan your question and answer technique to try to ensure that you cover the aspects that you have highlighted.

QUESTION AND ANSWER TECHNIQUE		
	Circle as appropriate	
1. Questions were clearly understood by students.	YES	NO
2. Pauses were used after asking most of the questions.	YES	NO
3. Some of the questions were asked of specific students.	YES	NO
4. The questions were distributed amongst the whole group.	YES	NO
5. Prompting techniques were effectively used to assist students in answering.	YES	NO
6. Some of the questions were at the higher levels of thinking.	YES	NO
Comments:		

Figure 8.3 Example Schedule about a Specific Aspect of Teaching

This can, then, be used either by yourself or by an observer. If it is to be used by yourself, it can be useful to (a) write your impressions of what happened immediately after the teaching episode and (b) to arrange to either audio or video tape and, at your leisure, watch/listen to the tape and remark your schedule in the light of what you hear/see.

This type of self-evaluation allows you to compare your initial reactions with that which is available when you have specific data (in this case a tape) available to you.

3.2 Other Professional Tasks

Teaching is not only related to what you do in the classroom or in preparation for it, it also involves many other aspects that go to make up the 'extended professional'. Tansley (1989) suggests the following list of tasks when discussing the role of the course team:

- Managerial and Administrative Tasks — timetabling/ accommodation, resource allocation

- Liaison with outside bodies — arranging work experience, liaison with schools and employers

- Liaison within the organisation — reporting to line management, liaison with other departments

- Student responsibilities — student guidance and tutoring/assessment/discipline

- Course responsibilities — curriculum development, course evaluation and profiling

- Examination administration — clerical administration, examination administration, liaison with exam bodies.

This list gives some idea of the complexity of other tasks that the teacher is expected to complete. Although they are directly related to a course leader, many such people tend to delegate these duties to different members of the course team. Indeed, there are distinct advantages in this delegation taking place so that it gives all of the course team members an overview of the whole of the course, its changes and developments. The line management and the course team are the best places for you to gain feedback about how you are doing with such tasks. Alternately, you can make your own checklist of tasks and rate yourself on each of them.

3.3 Sources of Feedback on Teaching

There are several sources for obtaining feedback on your teaching performance which can give assistance with your evaluation. These include your students, peers, and your line manager or tutor. However, all of these people should give you feedback in such a manner as to assist with your own self evaluation. They can provide information (data and impressions) which it is difficult for you to gather when you are involved in the teaching yourself. The only true evaluation, however, is self-evaluation. You can find a multitude of excuses why someone else's evaluation is incorrect but, when you find it out for yourself, there is less scope for such excuses. In consequence, the principles of providing feedback should be:

(a) to apply and have assessed competences identified by you;

(b) for the observer to provide constructive feedback about the identified competences and about aspects of practice;

(c)   for the observer to collect data about practice for detailed subsequent analysis;

(d)   for you to try out new methods and approaches to the development of student learning and obtain feedback on them as opposed to obtaining feedback on aspects in which you know that you are proficient;

(e)   to assist you to evaluate your own teaching.

If these, are the principles, it is important to look at the pros and cons of the different sources of feedback so that you can try to accentuate the positive aspects and minimise the negative ones.

Students are the people who have to suffer our teaching quirks and styles. They are omnipresent and, in consequence, you are not able to 'put on a show' for them. If you do something that is not usually done, they will be aware of it and are able to comment upon it from the standpoint of comparison with what they are used to. Thus, they have distinct advantages over the casual observer.

On the other hand students, especially adolescent ones, might not have the skill to be able to express themselves and tell you their feelings. Also, as you have the upper hand especially as you assess their work and say whether they are to pass or fail their course, they are likely to give you answers that they think you expect. They might well be fearful of being honest, especially if this involves critical comment in that they think that it might have a bearing on their chances of success. Even if they complete a questionnaire anonymously you are going to know their handwriting so you are likely to be able to trace who has said what.

When you ask *colleagues* and *peers* to give you feedback, they are likely to be busy people and will have to find the time to complete the observation. Thus, any instrument that is given to them will have to be easy to complete and will have to be completed during the period of observation. Also they may make unfair comparisons between your practice and their own.

The main advantage of *tutors* is that they will have gained skill in observation and can provide effective feedback to you. However, they only see you on a limited number of occasions and might have some difficulty in 'tuning-in' to both your needs and requirements.

Possible Evidence to Show You have Achieved the Competence 'Engage in Evaluation of Own and Other's Teaching'

The type of evidence that you might collect to show that you have achieved the competence involves:

1.   Devising a pro-forma (or use the ones given in this chapter) to evaluate your teaching in general or a specific aspect of it.

2.   Completing the teaching to collect data about the episode and summarising the data.

3.   Use the data summary to evaluate or have your teaching evaluated.

Progress Check

> *If you want to check your understanding of your ability to evaluate your teaching, try the following progress check.*

Progress Check 8.1

1. Identify at least two aspects of teaching under each of the six main elements of (i) preparation, (ii) presentation, (iii) student relationships, (iv) communication, (v) assessment of learning, and (vi) subject matter.

2. State at least three different strategies for monitoring and evaluating the effectiveness of teaching roles.

3. State an effective way of developing appropriate feedback mechanisms.

4. Explain the main differences between obtaining feedback from:

    - students;

    - peers;

    - colleagues; and

    - tutors/line managers

    to give feedback on your teaching performance.

4. Course Evaluation

4.1 Aims of Course Evaluation

In order to take part in course evaluation in any realistic and motivated manner, you have to recognise the benefits that will accrue to you personally and to your teaching, your course and your students. This leads you to having to consider what are your aims of course evaluation; what are likely to accrue from them. Once the aims have been formulated, and only then, are you able to formulate an effective scheme to evaluate your course.

One of the problems of formulating a course evaluation scheme is the number of aims that might be achieved. Some of the aims are:

- the appropriateness and achievement of the aims and objectives of your course/subject;

- the structure of your course, its progression, balance and coherence;

- the relevance and currency of the course syllabus;

- the quality and effectiveness of your teaching approach used on the course;

- the abilities and skills of the graduates;

- the student input profile and its match to the initial stages of the course/subject;

- your assessment methods and techniques in relation to the objectives and their effectiveness in revealing student achievement;

- the staff who teach on the course, their development and cohesion;

- the provision and deployment of resources.

As you can see, the aims are very comprehensive and to achieve them all would involve a very stringent evaluation. You need to be selective in deciding what you want to achieve in order to make a manageable task for your evaluation. You might only achieve one or two of the above aims in any one evaluation; you might make a three year development plan in order to achieve them all but only tackle some of them each academic year. You might decide, initially, on more general headings like:

- finding information to improve educational processes and programmes;

- identifying problem areas;

- evolving new approaches; and/or

- improving your ability to plan and effect the necessary changes.

Thus, you as an individual teacher, or with colleagues, might want to find the relevance of your course or subject to industry and students, find out if your teaching approaches are acceptable or if others would be better for your students, and so on. Once you have identified what are your aims, you might want to plan and effect the necessary changes. However, all of these should be reflected in your aims of the evaluation.

Figure 8.4 gives a typical list of aims for the evaluation of a subject.

Aims of the Evaluation of a Subject

1. To consider whether the objectives are consistent with the needs of industry and other subjects in the course.

2. To examine the entry behaviour of the students and to link this with subject objectives.

3. To investigate the appropriateness of the teaching and learning approaches to (a) the curriculum documents, and (b) the students' needs.

4. To find the trends in percentage of passes and 'drop-outs' over the past five years.

Figure 8.4 Typical Aims of Evaluation

Aims 1 and 2 are linked to the appropriateness of the objectives of the subject which will be found in the curriculum documents. However, their appropriateness to: (i) the industry that the course serves; and (ii) to the students indicate that either questionnaires will have to be designed or interviews carried out. Similar methods may be used with respect to aim 3 where it is necessary to find the how appropriate the teaching approaches are to the students. The trends in pass rates and drop-outs will be obtained from course records.

A checklist for writing the aims of course evaluation are given in Figure 8.5.

Are the aims that you have written for the evaluation of your course or subject:	YES	NO
1. of practical use?		
2. able to be used in the design of evaluative instruments?		
3. able to be achieved through the process of evaluation?		
4. within your scope to achieve?		
5. sufficiently comprehensive to cover all of the aspects that you want to achieve?		

Figure 8.5 Checklist for Writing Aims of Course Evaluation

One of the problems that you will find in deciding the aims of evaluation lies in its scope. The aims have to be wide enough to cover all of the aspects that you want to achieve, but, on the other hand, they need only to be enough to be manageable. In other words, you need not too many aims and not too few. They need to be written to be helpful to you in terms of the things that need to be identified and also to assist in the evaluative instruments that you might design.

4.2 Model of Course Evaluation

In order to achieve comprehensiveness in terms of the design of the aims, you need to consider the types of question that you might ask. Several models of evaluation have been suggested but probably the most useful in terms of post-16 education and training is the one suggested by Stufflebeam (1971). He suggests that we should think of evaluation in terms of four main headings:

Context	This is the setting of the course or subject and relates to the aims of the curriculum;
Input	The input elements relate to the students, the staff and the resources that are used;
Process	This relates to the appropriateness of what happens on the course - how the input elements are used to achieve the aims and objectives;
Product	This relates to the outcomes - the students who have gone through the course and what they have learned.

Stufflebeam calls this the CIPP (the first letter of each of the elements) model and suggests that a comprehensive evaluation should answer questions relating to each of the elements. However, this might comprise quite an onerous task especially for an individual teacher, but even for a course team. You might want to consider a long term evaluation and only write aims for one of the elements for one set of students. Thus, the complete evaluation might take two or more years to complete.

The type of questions that you might want to find answers to under *each* of Stufflebeam's elements could be:

Context

1. Are the aims of the curriculum consistent with the needs of industry/society/the individual student?

2. Does the curriculum foster purposeful co-operation and interaction with the world of work?

3. Are the aims broad enough to ensure further education and mobility of the students?

4. Are the aims up-dated regularly?

Input

1.   Do the students possess the entry behaviour assumed when designing the curriculum?

2.   Do the teachers have the competences required for implementation of the curriculum?

3.   Are the resources for teaching and learning explicit or implicit in the curriculum documents, available to the teacher and to the students?

Process

1.   Do the teachers make use of the curriculum documents and, if so, for what purposes?

2.   Do the teachers understand the curriculum documents?

3.   Is there a system of feedback from students and teachers on the problems faced in the achievement of the aims and objectives?

4.   Are the teaching strategies (classroom, laboratory and workshop) in line with those proposed in the curriculum?

5.   What is the extent of the use of instructional resource material?

6.   Is the student assessment system valid, reliable and practicable?

Product

1.   What are the trends in percentage of passes and drop outs?

2.   Do the students get absorbed into industry? Is there a time lag? Do they get appropriate employment?

3.   What are the opinions of students and ex-students regarding the relevance of the course/subject/topics?

4.   What are the staff development needs that have arisen and to what extent have they been met?

5.   What are the views of employers on the curriculum?

This is not an exhaustive list of questions, but it gives an indication of the areas that a curriculum evaluation might want to address.

Each of the aims of evaluation, then, can have questions associated with them. Figure 8.6 shows how questions might be associated with the aims of the evaluation suggested in Figure 8.4.

Aim	Possible Questions
1. To consider if the objectives are consistent with the needs of employers	Do the objectives cover cognitive, psycho-motor and affective domains? Are any additions or deletions necessary? Do the objectives reflect industrial needs? How many employers take graduate students? What questions can be asked of employers to determine if the objectives are relevant?
2. To examine the entry behaviour of students.	Is an entry behaviour test available - if not, can one be designed? What is the best time to give an entry behaviour test? Does the entry behaviour for one subject need to reflect other subjects?
3. To investigate the teaching and learning methods.	What teaching strategies are suggested or implied in the curriculum documents? What teaching strategies are used and what strategies *could be* used? What questions should be asked of students and should these be through interview and/or questionnaire?
4. To find the trends in passes and drop-outs.	Who keeps records over the past five years? How can reasons for drop-outs be found - how can student addresses be found?

Figure 8.6 Questions Related to Aims of Evaluation

These, of course, are only a sample of the questions that might be asked. Each of the aims has a whole host of questions that might usefully be associated with them to find specific aspects of the operation of a course or subject. The skill in evaluation is to ensure that the questions are relevant to what is required to be found and useful to the improvement of a course or subject.

4.3 Instruments for Obtaining Information

If the evaluation is to serve the aims that you have listed, it must be a continuous process rather than an intermittent or once only event. It must consist of constant observation, measurement and reporting of how the course/subject is being implemented so that appropriate corrective measures at the most convenient stage of curriculum development might be taken.

The methods of obtaining information can be:

- questionnaires;
- checklists;
- student performance; and/or.
- structured interview schedule.

These might be used on the following sources of information:

- teachers;
- students   – present
             – drop-outs
             – graduates
             – employed;
- industry;
- support staff;
- organisational set-up;
- text and reference books;
- teaching/learning resources
             – availability
             – use.

4.3.1 Checklists

A checklist can be a useful aide memoir to ensure that you have covered all of the aspects in an evaluation that you need to cover. It can also be used as a basis for the design of a questionnaire.

The example shown below (Figure 8.7) is a checklist of tasks that a course leader might wish to complete in order to consider the staff development of the course team. All that is required in order to complete the checklist is a tick to say that each of the aspects has been considered.

	YES	NO
1. All of the staff teaching on the course understand their roles and responsibilities.		
2. Course team members have received specific training in working as a team.		
3. Structured curriculum-led staff development has been offered to all of the course team.		
4. The expertise of staff in developing other course team members has been used.		
5. The following course tasks have been delegated as far as possible: • – administration;		
• – assessment design;		
• – use of new teaching methods.		
6. Part-time and support staff have been included in all staff development programmes for course teams.		

Figure 8.7 Example Checklist for Course Team Staff Development

Checklists must contain terms which the respondent understands and which more briefly and succinctly express views than would be the case with answers from open-ended questions. They are inevitably crude devices, but careful pilot work and design can make them less so. They are at their best when they are designed and used to be related to specific aims.

4.3.2 Questionnaires

An example questionnaire to be given to students about text and reference books is given in Figure 8.8 The aim of this evaluation is:

'To examine how students use the suggested reading list of books for the course.'

The questions associated with this are:

1.   How useful to students is the list of references given for the course?

2.   Why have students found additional reading useful?

3.   What use has been made of additional reading?

4.   How easy is it for students to locate the required reading?

Student Questionnaire - Use Of Reading List

1.   How useful have you found the reading list given at the start of the course? Circle the number that best represents your feelings.

Of little use   1   2   3   4   5   6   Very Useful

2.   What have you used the readings for? Tick the appropriate boxes.

Doing homework	
Completing assignments	
As a back-up to lectures	
Preparation for examinations	
For topics you were absent	
Others (please state)	

3.   Which of the texts have you found MOST useful:

(a)
(b)

4.   Why have you found them useful?

5.   Which of the texts have you found LEAST useful?

(a)
(b)

6.   Why have you found them least useful?

7.   Where have you obtained the required books? Tick as appropriate.

	YES
Institution Library	
Home Library	
Bought	
Borrowed from friend	
Other (please state)	

Figure 8.8 Example Questionnaire for Students

You will see from the example that there is a mixture of open questions (those that require a written response) and closed questions (those that only require a tick). The closed questions are both easier to answer and easier to analyse and from which to collect the data. Thus, a mixture of both qualitative and quantitative data will be collected.

Whatever the design, it should be easy to answer and not take too long. A lengthy questionnaire will not get the attention paid to it that it should get and will be difficult to analyse. As a general guide, the questionnaire should *not* take longer than 5 minutes to answer. The questions need to be directly related to the aims of what you want to find out and its design should be easy to follow and appealing to the eye. Plenty of white space is useful and each question should be clearly separated from the others. It could be helpful for example for questions 3 and 5 to indicate the titles of the specific texts that have been given as, say, required reading so that you are not relying upon the student memory to answer the questions. If this was the case you could combine these two questions with tick boxes for the most and least useful.

4.3.3 Structured Interview Schedules

An interview Schedule is structured and prepared as a basis of a one-to-one interview with your target audience.

In a structured interview schedule you are unlikely to be able to cover as many aspects as you can in a questionnaire but it has the advantage that you can cover the items in greater depth: subsequent questions being dependent upon the response of the previous one. Also, you have much greater control over the responses in that you can ask the questions to ensure that they are understood and ensure that *all* of your questions are answered.

Although you are going to have a face-to-face discussion with whoever you are going to interview, it is still important that you prepare a schedule upon which to base your questions. In such a schedule you should structure your questions from the general to the specific. You can ask questions about:

(a) knowledge and skills;

(b) common and study skills;

(c) work related skills.

Usually, you will want to find out opinions of individuals about various aspects of the course that you operate. The schedule shown in Figure 8.9 is for an employer to find out their opinion of a course of study upon which they send students.

It will be realised from the example schedule that the actual aims and objectives of the course, the knowledge and skills that are applicable can be inserted into the design itself.

In completion of the schedule, spaces are left for you to insert notes on the responses that the employer makes. You make these notes as the discussion proceeds.

Your design should ensure the following:

- the questions must be directly related to the aims of what you want to find;
- there are a limited number of questions;

Name: Position:
Company:

No of Employees: Course Title:

Q1. Outline of course aims and objectives. Is this how you perceive the course?

Q2.   If this is not what you thought, what differences would you wish to see?

Q3. Do you agree with the course content?

Q4. The course provides training in the following skills and knowledge. Does this reflect your requirements?

Q5. Stress will be laid on the following skills. Do you agree with this?

Q6. Where should the greater emphasis be laid?

Q7. How satisfied have you been with the student(s) who have attended the course?

Q8. How do you see your future needs?

Q9. What should be added or subtracted from the course?

Figure 8.9 Example Structured Interview Schedule for Employers

- adequately prepare both the schedule and any other information that is required.
- structure the schedule from the general to the specific.

4.3.4 Student Assessment

Information about how well the course is going, can be obtained from the results of student assessments. If, for instance, a large proportion of the students fail the end examination, then this is important information and questions will need to be asked as to why this has happened.

This does not only have to be at the end of the course. If students do badly (or well) on your formative tests, then this is also useful information about the success of that part of the course which is being assessed.

4.4 Data Collection from Questionnaires

Data collection can either be qualitative, that is when it is related to opinion, or quantitative when it is related to a numerical scale. For comparative purposes it is easier to deal with and draw conclusions from quantitative data that qualitative. It is necessary, therefore, for us to look at transferring qualitative into quantitative data.

Figure 8.10 shows a small part of a questionnaire given to students to evaluate their opinion of the effectiveness of a short, in-service course for teachers. The part shown refers to the overall organisation of the course.

In your opinion was the overall organisation of the course:					
	QUALITY				
	Poor	Fair	Good	Very Good	Excellent
1. Well prepared					
2. Properly sequenced					
3. Intelligently time-tabled (e.g. to give variety)					
4. Etc.					

Figure 8.10 Part of Student Questionnaire

It may be assumed that the questionnaire is given to a class of 25 students. In order to collate the data, each of the responses from the individual students can be transferred to a blank questionnaire. When this is done the completed blank questionnaire might look as shown in Figure 8.11. In each of the appropriate spaces a slash (/) mark indicates where a particular student student has responded. The slash marks are then summated within each of the cells.

In your opinion was the overall organisation of the course:					
	QUALITY				
	Poor	Fair	Good	Very Good	Excellent
1. Well prepared			///// //// (9)	///// ///// (10)	///// / (6)
2. Properly sequenced		/// (3)	///// (5)	///// ///// // (12)	///// (5)
3. Intelligently time-tabled (e.g. to give variety)	//// (4)	///// / (6)	///// ///// (10)	///// (5)	
4. Etc.					

Figure 8.11 Data Collection on a Blank Questionnaire

The next task involves changing the qualitative scale into a quantitative one (that is assigning numbers to each of the points on the scale). This can be done as follows:

Poor	= 1
Fair	= 2
Good	= 3
Very Good	= 4
Excellent	= 5

Another part of the questionnaire asked questions about the 'group tasks' involved in the course and students were requested to indicate their opinion of the tasks by either agreeing or disagreeing with a number of statements. A five-point scale of SD = Strongly Disagree, D = Disagree,; N = Neutral; A = Agree, and SA = Strongly Agree was used. This type of scale, known as a Likert Scale, is shown in Figure 8.12.

Similarly, the qualitative responses can be given a numerical value by assigning numbers to each of the five values of opinion.

	Opinion				
	SD	D	N	A	SA
1 The group work useful in gaining insights into problems.					
2. The variety of group work helped to maintain interest.					
3. The group work needed more resource materials.					
4. Etc.					

Figure 8.12 Example Questionnaire using a Likert Scale

Once the scale has been decided for each of the questions, the responses to them can be converted to the numerical scale and then correlated. So, for question 1 in Figure 8.11, the number of responses in each cell has to be multiplied with the number assigned to that point on the scale. As nine (9) students considered the preparation to be 'good' and 'good' = 3, a total for this cell would be 3 x 9 = 27. This can be completed for all of the cells as shown in Figure 8.13.

In your opinion was the overall organisation of the course:						
	QUALITY					
	Poor	Fair	Good	Very Good	Excellent	Mean
	1	2	3	4	5	
1. Well prepared			9 x 3 = 27	10 x 4 = 40	6 x 5 = 30	97/25 = 3.9
2. Properly sequenced		3 x 2 = 6	5 x 3 = 15	12 x 4 = 48	5 x 5 = 25	94/25 = 3.7
3. Intelligently time-tabled (e.g. to give variety)	4 x 1 = 4	6 x 2 = 12	10 x 3 = 30	5 x 4 = 20		66/25 = 2.6
4. Etc.						

Figure 8.13 Calculation of a Mean (Average) Response

For comparative purposes the mean (average) response can be calculated for each of the questions. This can be achieved by adding the totals for each of the cells and dividing this by the number of students responding (25 in this case). So, for Question 1 the mean response is (27 + 40 + 30) = 97 / 25 = 3.9.

In consequence, the mean response for each of the questions will allow specific comparisons between the questions to be made. It can be seen that there is 1.1 difference between questions 2 and 3, but only 0.2 difference between questions 1 and 2 and that question 1 receives the 'best' result and question 3 the worst.

4.5 Writing a Course Evaluation Report

A necessary part of any evaluation that you have completed is the preparation of a report to convey the results and conclusions to interested parties. There are many different ways in which your report may be written but generally there are commonalities in the different formats. Reports usually contain four main divisions: an introduction, the methodology used, presentation and analysis of data and conclusions and recommendations. This format reflects the stages of the evaluation process. The headings shown in Figure 8.14 expand upon each of the main divisions and may help you to write your report. This list of items is fairly comprehensive and is not meant to be a rigid guideline of every step you must take.

1.   Introduction

    (a)   Reasons for the evaluation

    (b)   Aims to be achieved

    (c)   Key questions to be answered

    (d)   Any limitations

2.   Methodology

    (a)   Sources of data

    (b)   Data gathering instruments

    (c)   Procedures employed

3.   Presentation and Analysis of Data

    (a)   Presentation of findings

    (b)   Tables and Figures (usually incorporated into the findings)

4.   Conclusions and Recommendations

    (a)   Summary

    (b)   Conclusions

Figure 8.14 Format of a Report

Before deciding upon the final format it is necessary to ask yourself what is essential to be included in order to provide an easily understood report, and how do you provide evidence that the recommendations are solidly based? An outline is effective if it helps to identify and order the sub-divisions of the report's major sections. Obviously the outline must precede the actual writing of the report since it is expected to serve as a guide for the writing that lies ahead. An effective outline is a check for coverage and an assurance for sequence and logical presentation of ideas and items.

4.5.1 Conclusions and Recommendations

These two aspects of the report are very important: they are why all of the work has been completed. Often, the two are confused but, in fact they are very different. The *conclusion* represents your judgment based on the evaluation data. There are two types of conclusion: (i) pre-determined decision situations and (ii) exploratory conclusions. In pre-determined decision situations a conclusion would be based on a synthesis of information about the particular decision. You have to draw your conclusion in the light of, say, political and social forces both inside and outside the education or training establishment. It is no good drawing conclusions that you know could not work due for instance for the need for resources. The second type of conclusion is more exploratory in nature. Exploratory evaluation is initiated to explore general concerns or feelings about the adequacy of a course. That is, if a course leader believes that a course has its shortcomings, but has not collected data on which to base the opinion, an evaluation study may be carried out to identify areas or components of the course which need changes.

Recommendations must be based on the conclusions. It can be useful to organise the recommendations around areas upon which you have placed special importance. For example the recommendations may be organised under content area, instructional methods, personnel, course management, or support services. Good organisation will assist the reader to have a clearer appreciation of the importance of your recommendations.

Conciseness in the recommendations section is a desirable characteristic. A lengthy section may produce boredom and lead to the rejection of even the good recommendations that are presented.

You should remember that the recommendations are a basis for action, and will be translated into policy by the decision makers. Therefore, you need to consider that decision makers have their own barriers to overcome. The recommendations, to assist this, may be presented in rank order. Recommendations that are socially, economically or politically unacceptable need to be adapted accordingly. They should be examined to find out whether a partial implementation does not result in an action being taken which may be unfavourable to the aim of what is being attempted.

Possible Evidence to Show You have Achieved the Competence
'Engage in Evaluation of Your Courses'.

The type of evidence that you might collect to show that you have achieved the competence involves:

1.   Devising a set of aims for a course evaluation and, for each of the aims, writing a set of questions to show how the aims might be achieved.

2.   Devising an instrument to collect data in order to answer the questions in (1) above.

3.   Using the instrument and analysing the data that is collected.

4.   Writing a short report on the basis of the data analysis.

> *If you want to check your understanding of your ability to evaluate your courses, try the following progress check.*

Progress Check 8.2

1. List at least two aspects of your course that might be evaluated under each of the headings of:

   (a) Context;

   (b) Input;

   (c) Process;

   (d) Product.

2. Describe the advantages and limitations of the following instruments:

   questionnaire;

   checklist;

   student performance.

3. List at least five different sources of information that might be used to evaluate one of your courses.

4. Describe how to change qualitative to quantitative data.

5. List, in order, the aspects of a course evaluation report.

Further Reading and References

Further reading and references relating to the topics in this chapter can be found in the following:

Bell, J et al	*Conducting Small Scale Investigations in Educational Management,* Harper, 1984.
DES	*Managing Colleges Efficiently*, Department of Education and Science, 1987.
FESC	*Responsive College Project*, Further Education Staff College, 1988.
FEU	*A Fragmented View? Professional Accountability and Maintenance of Standards in Vocational Curricula*, Further Education Unit, 1985.
FEU	*Supporting Quality in Y.T.S.*, Further Education Unit, 1989.
Gibbs, G and Haigh, M	*Alternative Models of Course Evaluation*. SCEDSIP Occasional paper 13. 1983.
NIACE,	*Replan. Further Education and Employment Training: A Quality Response*, Replan, 1989.
Stufflebeam, D	*Educational Evaluation and Decision Making*, Peacock Publishers Inc. 1971
Tansley, D	*Course teams: The Way Forward* in FE, NFER Nelson 1989

Chapter 9
Evidence of Competence in Teaching

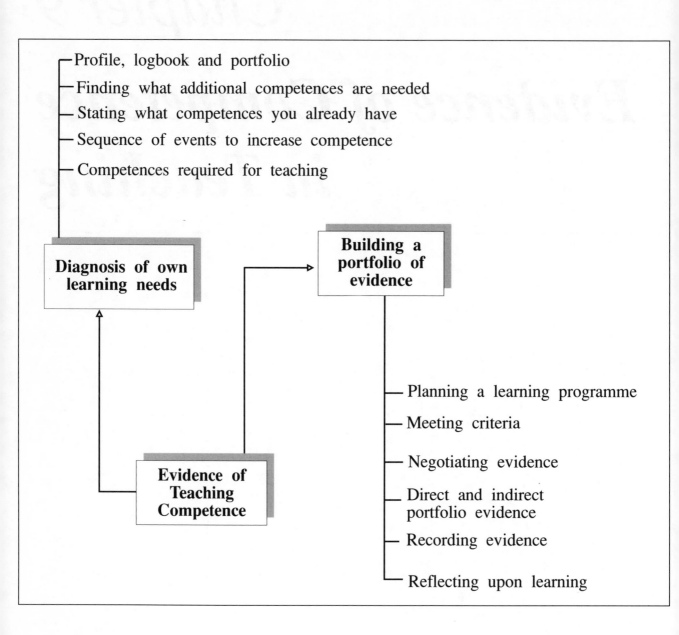

- Profile, logbook and portfolio
- Finding what additional competences are needed
- Stating what competences you already have
- Sequence of events to increase competence
- Competences required for teaching

Diagnosis of own learning needs

Building a portfolio of evidence

Evidence of Teaching Competence

- Planning a learning programme
- Meeting criteria
- Negotiating evidence
- Direct and indirect portfolio evidence
- Recording evidence
- Reflecting upon learning

Overview of Chapter 9

Competences Related to this Chapter.

The competences and associated performance criteria related to this chapter are:

Overall Competence – *Establish an effective system of gathering evidence of teaching competence*

Competence	Performance Criteria
1. Diagnose own learning needs to improve your teaching competence.	(a) Identify present competences. (b) Collect evidence of present competences. (c) Identify competences that require improving. (d) Design a plan to achieve the competences that require improvement.
2. Build a portfolio of evidence of competence in teaching.	(a) Negotiate appropriate evidence of achievement. (b) Collect direct and indirect evidence in building a portfolio. (c) Have evidence validated if necessary.

1. Introduction

Many 'modern' syllabuses are being written in terms of the competences that are to be achieved and the assessment associated with them relates to assessment in the workplace. That is, the assessment is directly related to an individual's ability to perform specific competences at work. This places completely different demands upon the assessment process. The emphasis upon end examinations is becoming less and less and even the ability of an individual in projects and assignments is decreasing.

So, not only are the demands of the curriculum designers changing, but also the demands of the curriculum developers (which, we have already emphasised earlier in this book, is you, the classroom teacher) are changing. The emphasis of the teaching relates the ability of students to perform the specific tasks that are required of them at work and, associated with this, for the student to have the necessary knowledge and understanding to complete these competences. Indeed, each of the Chapters in this book has emphasised the competences that are likely to be related to the knowledge and understanding of the concepts contained within the text. Also, the activities contained in each of the Chapters has tried to indicate how you might obtain evidence to show that you are competent in particular teaching skills. Thus, the skills of assessment in modern syllabuses relate your ability to be able to assess competence in the workplace or similar simulated environment. This means, in your case, the assessment of your skill whilst you are teaching students.

This assessment of your teaching used to be referred to as 'Practical Teaching Assessment', carried out by tutors in Colleges of Education in conventional teacher training courses. This, along with many other courses, is in the process of change so that your practical teaching observation might be 'assessed' by someone in your own institution who will 'accredit your competence'.

As we described in Chapter 7 when discussing the assessment of competences, this requires a sequence of events from the generation of evidence, through collection of that evidence, to a judgement of whether it suggests competent performance or not, to, finally, its verification and successful achievement of competence. What we must do in this Chapter is to look at how that applies to ourselves and to the teaching process so that we might successfully prove that we are competent teachers.

2. Competences Related to Teaching and Learning

At the beginning of each Chapter in this book there has been an indication of the competences that relate to that Chapter. These, we consider, are not the only competences that you will be expected to perform, but are the *key* competences that are required for you to perform effectively in your first years of teaching. Many teacher training courses (for example the Regional Advisory Council Stage 1, the City and Guilds 7307, and some Certificate in Education courses) and Industry Lead Bodies (for example the Training and Development Lead Body and Management Charter Initiative) identify slightly different competences although they have a similar base.

The competences identified as key to the role of the teacher of post-16 education and training are indicated in Figure 9.1.

	Chapter	Competences
1	*Basic teaching.*	1. Adopt a teaching role. 2. Plan and organise learning. 3. Manage learning. 4. Assess learning and evaluate teaching.
2	*Student learning.*	1. Identify the characteristics of the three learning taxonomies. 2. Demonstrate effective design of learning sessions through the identification of variables which effect learning. 3. Use the components of a range of theories of learning. 4. Identify variables which influence student motivation.
3	*Techniques of teaching.*	1. Deliver a programme of learning sessions. 2. Manage learning activities.
4	*Learning aids.*	1. Establish a basis for choosing learning aids. 2. Use board aids appropriately. 3. Use handouts appropriately. 4. Use the overhead projector appropriately. 5. Select, adapt or construct learning resources for a specific programme. 6. Evaluate the use of learning resources.
5	*Planning and design for teaching and learning.*	1. Identify learning outcomes for specific programmes. 2. Design learning programmes related to the specific needs of learners. 3. Develop procedures to assess learning and evaluate teaching.
6	*Communication and the teacher*	1. Demonstrate effective teacher communication skills. 2. Assist students to develop their communication skills.
7	*Assessment of student learning.*	1. Assess students during a lesson or learning period. 2. Justify, use and record appropriate forms of measuring student achievement. 3. Employ appropriate assessment of student practical work.
8	*Evaluation of self and teaching.*	1. Engage in evaluation of own and other's teaching. 2. Engage in evaluation of your courses.

Figure 9.1 Key Competences of the Role of the Teacher

Each of the competences that is listed has its own assessment criteria associated with it. In order to become competent you should ensure that you can achieve *all* of the assessment criteria. There can be no averaging, saying that you are excellent with one of the criteria so you will not bother with another of them. All criteria are equally important to the achievement of the competence.

2. Learning Competences

Every teacher learns to be increasingly competent throughout their teaching careers. The teacher in training, however, needs to be more systematic about this process than does the more experienced teacher. The process described below has the following sequence associated with it:

    (i)   diagnose your learning needs;

    (ii)   plan a learning programme;

    (iii) negotiate the further learning needed to provide evidence to show competence;

    (iv) build a portfolio of evidence of competence;

    (v)   record evidence in a logbook or diary;

    (vi) reflect on the learning activities.

There are many variations to this sequence but it seems to us that this is logical and covers the important aspects of the process. Such a process revolves around the *generation of evidence* to show competence in a particular aspect of the teaching role.

To assist with the learning process and to show that you have achieved evidence to prove that you are competent, it is suggested that you might use a Profile and a Logbook to record the above activities. The *profile* provides an accredited record of your learning activities. It can consist of:

    (i)   a record of the evidence that you negotiate with your accreditor;

    (ii)   your record of learning activities; and

    (iii) reflections on those learning activities.

The *logbook* is a document for recording progress as you tackle the different aspects of competence. It is similar to a diary, and, indeed may be replaced by a diary consisting of A4 pages, and runs parallel with the development of the profile of evidence. It assists you in reflecting on the learning process underlying that development.

It is becoming increasingly important when attending courses and going for job interviews that, as you learn, apart from the profile and logbook, you also keep a *portfolio* of work that you have completed as part of the learning process. This, like an artist's portfolio, gives examples of the different parts of work that you have completed whilst you are learning.

So, there are three important documents that are associated with the development of competence and each of them are interlinked. All of them are your responsibility to keep up to date and ensure that they are well written. You can, if you wish, ask your line manager, tutor, or a colleague to assess what you have done, comment upon it and sign that they have seen it.

The starting point,then, for the achievement of competence lies with the generation of evidence to show that you are competent and this evidence must be related to the assessment criteria.

3. Generation of Evidence

It is suggested below that the generation of evidence requires a sequential structure to ensure that it will be useful, show that you are competent and that you will not repeat what you already have done. In effect, you will need to plan and organise your learning programme. Each of the stages in the process is described below with suggested proformas which may be useful for the process.

3.1 Diagnosis of learning needs

You need to start with a diagnosis of your learning needs. For example, for each of the competences you should find answers to:

- What competence, if any, do I start with?
- What evidence do I have of existing practice?
- What competence do I need or want to achieve?
- What action do I need to take?
- How will I know when competence has been achieved?

Thus, suppose that you want to achieve competence in "employ appropriate assessment of student practical work". In order to diagnose your learning needs it will be necessary for you to think about your requirements about assessment of practical work. If you are attending a course you will be given assistance through the assessment criteria for that area of work. Thus, it might be as shown in Figure 9.2.

Competence	Assessment Criteria
Employ appropriate assessment of student practical work.	(a) Use a range of test instruments for the assessment of practical tasks. (b) Use appropriate formats for the assessment of projects/assignments. (c) Employ effective student profiling formats. (d) Present feedback to students in a positive manner.

Figure 9.2 Assistance with Diagnosis of Learning Needs

You can now link the five questions above with the content areas contained within the assessment criteria. So you ask yourself:

What competence have I with:

- a range of test instruments?

- using appropriate formats?

- employing profiling techniques?

- presenting feed back in a positive manner?

What evidence do I have with:

- a range of test instruments?

- using appropriate formats?

- employing profiling techniques?

- presenting feed back in a positive manner?

What competence do I need to achieve with:

- etc.

Figure 9.3 gives an example of what your diagnosis of needs might look like in response to the questions above.

Diagnosis of Need

I already use what I consider to be valid and reliable test instruments for workshop practical tasks. The evidence that I have for this includes test schedules and associated marking schemes for 1st year work.

I need to consider which type of marking scheme is best for the subject, me and my students. I need to increase my competence in the assessment of project work for the end of year project for 1st year students. I need at least one and possibly three project briefs with associated marking schemes covering both content and common skills.

I have no experience with profiles but could see that they could be useful when associated with the practical work and projects.

Figure 9.3 Example of a Completed Diagnosis of Needs

Such a completed diagnosis needs to be completed for each of the competences that you want to achieve. In this manner you start to identify:

(i)   the competences that you already have together with the evidence that you can assemble to prove that you have the competence; and

(ii)   those competences that you need to achieve to make you better at your job.

Possible Evidence to Show that you have achieved the Competence 'Diagnose Own Learning Needs'.

The type of evidence that you might collect to show that you have achieved the competence involves:

1. Make a list of the competences required by a teacher in your subject area. For each of these competences indicate those that you already have and those in which you need to become more proficient.

    For the competences that you already have indicate the evidence that you can produce to prove your competence.

2. For the competences in which you need to become more proficient, design a plan to show how they will be achieved.

Progress Check

If you want to check your understanding of your role in diagnosing own learning needs try the following progress check .

Progress Check 9.1

1 For each of the following areas of teaching, identify at least two roles in which you should be competent:

(a) Student Learning

(b) Techniques of teaching

(c) Learning aids

(d) Planning for teaching

(e) Communication

(f) Assessment of student learning

(g) Self evaluation

(h) Evaluation of teaching.

2. Place the following into a logical sequence of activities that could be used to increase your competence in teaching.

(i) Record evidence in a logbook or diary

(ii) Plan a learning programme

(iii) Diagnose your learning needs

(iv) Negotiate the further learning needed to provide evidence to show competence

(v) Reflect on learning activities

(vi) Build a portfolio of evidence of competence.

3. Differentiate between the following:

- profile
- logbook
- portfolio.

3.2 Plan a Learning Programme

The next stage in the process involves the planning of a learning programme for yourself to rehearse the competence. From the diagnosis of need you have to sequence your activities to cover all of the aspects that you have identified. Look at each aspect and decide which to cover first, next, and so on. Your aim should be to finish with a full and balanced set of evidence which fully represents your professional ability.

Figure 9.4 gives an indication of what a completed Plan might look like for the diagnosis completed in Figure 9.3.

Plan of Learning Programme

1. Investigate different formats for the assessment of practical work and identify one that will be most appropriate for 1st year students. This to include:

   - whether to give marks, grades or pass/fail;

   - whether the marking will be on-going or terminal;

   - what will be given to the students (brief, assessment scheme, task sheets, and so on)

2. By looking through the syllabus and scheme of work, identify optional (possibly 5) practical tests.

3. Use one of these practical areas, to identify the skills (both subject and common) that students will need to complete the test. These skills to be limited to those that can be assessed.

4. Prepare a possible scheme of work that students can follow in the completion of a project area. This to identify the tasks that they will need to complete to a basis of time.

5. For each of the tasks identify the assessment criteria that will form the basis of the assessment scheme for marking the project.

6. Investigate profile formats to include:

   - where these are best used;

   - teacher and student tasks associated with their completion;

   - aspects to be included in their design;

   - what is available and what I need to design.

Figure 9.4 Completed Example – Plan of Learning Programme

The completed plan indicates not only what is required to be learned, but gives an indication of the order in which this might be completed. The criteria for making these decisions is likely to revolve around what you are doing at work and the type of possibilities that you see in the achievement of the competence with your students.

The argument here is that, when you plan your own programme, it is more likely to be relevant to your needs and be able to be applied, and be related to, your teaching. This, then, is more likely to give you motivation for your learning.

3.3 Understand, Agree and Meet the Criteria

After planning the learning programme, you need to concentrate upon how the assessment criteria will be met when you negotiate, collect and present evidence of your competence.

In meeting these criteria, it means that your work:

1. *'Establishes and maintains quality'*

    In all your work you need to ensure that its quality is the best that might be achieved.
    This is of prime importance in meeting the criteria.

2. *'Diagnoses students' learning needs and problems'*

    Your work needs to be based on the needs of your students.
    If the work is to maintain quality it must relate to the needs of a particular group of students.

3. *'Is based on an understanding of the learning process'*

    Not only do you need to gain the various competences based on doing your job better in the classroom, but the competences need to take account of a clear understanding of the learning processes.
    This might well mean wide reading of educational psychology which can often underpin classroom practices.

4. *'Demonstrates an awareness of the alternatives that can be used in achieving the criteria'*

    Often, in solving a problem, we use the first solution that comes to us.
    It is important that you consider the alternatives that are available to you and choose the most appropriate of these.
    The appropriateness might be in terms of what is available, what will best suit your students, what will best suit your situation, and so on.

5. *'Explores the use of IT'*

    The use of IT is a common skill upon which you must, as a teachers, concentrate.
    Such skills might be for us as teachers to use or for your students to use, or, indeed, a mixture of both of these.

6. *'Contains its own evaluation'*

    In meeting criteria you must ensure that you can evaluate what you are proposing and doing. This self evaluation must become a way of life.

7.   *'Demonstrates your research skills'*

> The achievement of all of the above indicate that you must be able to research what you are doing.
> Such research might involve reading, asking tutors and colleagues, asking students, trying things out and evaluating them, and so on.

All of these will not be achieved with every piece of work, every piece of evidence that you produce and for every competence. However, you should aim to achieve all of them by the end of a period of study. They are all equally important to the practising teacher. How you are to meet the criteria can usefully be recorded in a Logbook or Diary.

3.4 Negotiation of Evidence

The negotiation of appropriate evidence is a key stage in the overall process. Having decided on the competences to be achieved and having undertaken an initial diagnosis, the question is – what further learning and development is needed? What form will it take? What evidence will emerge that learning has occurred and that competence has been gained?

You may decide that no further work is needed to meet a given assessment criteria – you may feel competent enough and you can assemble evidence to prove it from work that you have already completed. If you do feel competent, gather your existing evidence in a document such as a portfolio of your work. You do, however, need to be fully prepared to justify your decision and to show that you have checked out all of the possibilities.

Sharing ideas and practices with colleagues and other teachers on a teacher training course can sometimes enable you to discover applications and practices that you have never thought about yourself. It is sometimes hard to know what you need to know until you know what is available. It is therefore important that you are 'open' about what you have done and be willing to show it to others and discuss its advantages and limitations. This sharing is an important learning tool.

An example profile form that you might use to negotiate your evidence to prove that you are competent is shown in Figure 9.5. Such a pro-forma, when associated with a teacher training course, would need to be completed either in association with the course tutor, or, when not on such a course, with your line manager. Whichever situation, when it is completed it provides the basis for a discussion of what you propose to seek to achieve.

Competence Area: _____	**Negotiation of Evidence of Competence**		
Competence: _____ _____ _____ _____	Establishment: _____		
Aspects of Competence	*Proposed Evidence*	*Location of Evidence*	*Date*
1.			
2.			
3.			
4.			

Figure 9.5 Possible Pro-forma for the Negotiation of Evidence of Competence

The completion of the pro-forma becomes a simple matter when you have competently and accurately completed a diagnosis of need as suggested in Figure 9.3. Such a diagnosis might clearly indicate the type of evidence that is proposed (for example the project briefs and assessment criteria). However, you might have indicated that you can already meet some of the criteria and the type of evidence that you have to show this can be indicated on the pro-forma.

We have provided a completed pro-forma in Figure 9.6 for the assessment of practical work competence which we suggested previously (assessment of student practical work).

Competence Area: Assessment	**Negotiation of Evidence of Competence**		
Competence: Employ appropriate assessment of student practical work.	*Establishment:* XYZ Adult Training Centre		
Aspects of Competence	*Proposed Evidence*	*Location of Evidence*	*Date*
1. Use a range of test instruments for practical assessment	5 practical tests. Marking Schemes.	Year 1	October
2. Use appropriate formats for the assessment of projects.	Year 1 projects. Marking Schemes	Year 1 work.	
3. Employ student profiling formats.	Essay on formats Report on discussion	ABC college	December
4. Present feedback to students in a positive manner.	Results of questionnaire to students practical assessment	Year 1 work.	July

Figure 9.6 Example Completed Pro-forma for the Negotiation of Evidence

The negotiation process can suggest alternative types of evidence that you might collect as well as assisting you with the things that are available.

It is important that you have the evidence agreed before you start work. The evidence builds into a Portfolio which you should maintain and develop as you are achieving competences.

3.5 Building a Portfolio of Evidence

Probably the most important aspect of this new type of learning involves the building of a portfolio of evidence to demonstrate that you have learned a particular competence. Such a portfolio consists of all types of work that you have been involved with and shows the depth of skill that you have applied to the competence. Such a portfolio shows not only your assessor the work with which you have been involved, but is also available for future reference to be used as accreditation of prior learning for your future learning. It will ensure that you do *not* have to go through learning the same competence again.

So, what do you include as evidence in your portfolio? There is both direct evidence, that is the results of work that you yourself have completed; and indirect evidence completed by others as a result of your work, such as testimonials and certificates.

You can include many kinds of *direct* evidence in your portfolio like:

- teaching plans: schemes of work, lesson plans;

- visual aids: handouts, transparencies, slides, charts;

- evaluation materials: tests, projects, assignments, questionnaires, interview schedules, and the data from these;

- course work: papers from working parties, proposals for new courses, reports of meetings, conferences and visits;

- summaries: of books, articles, radio and TV programmes;

- analysis of classroom, workshop and other activities;

- artefacts: photographs, models, video recordings, audio tapes.

The types of *indirect* evidence that you might include are:

- reports on your practice (such as practical teaching reports);

- certificates and awards;

- references and evidence of work done on short courses;

Following the Kolb model discussed in Chapter 1 where we emphasised the importance of reflecting on learning, in addition to all of this material, the portfolio can also be a useful place to file *your thoughts* (or reflections) on:

- learning activities that you have undertaken;

- your development of competence;

- practical teaching visits;

- projects and assignments that you have completed.

Whichever of the above types of evidence that you keep in your portfolio, when it is part of a course, it should be in line with the evidence agreed in advance and must meet the criteria for that particular competence. The portfolio will also help you to decide whether, in your opinion, you are competent or not and, again if it is part of a course, whether you are ready to claim competence. In other words, it will be the means to support a claim for competence to yourself or to others.

The Process of Recording Evidence

A 'Logbook' or 'Diary' can be used to record progress as you tackle the different competences. You can keep a Logbook in parallel with the development of your Portfolio and it enables you to *reflect* on the learning process underlying that development. The process might follow the sequence of:

(i)   start with your diagnosis of learning needs and continue with what has been agreed (Figure 9.3) and then record what is agreed in your learning plan (Figure 9.4); that is, the proposed evidence and the criteria by which it is to be judged that has been negotiated with a tutor (Figure 9.5);

(ii)   make a note in your logbook/diary when you are actually engaged in the learning process. For example, record when you try a new method of teaching, use a particular visual aid, plan a lesson in a different way, try out a particular method of assessment, go to a meeting and try a new skill. A completed example is shown in Figure 9.7

Date	Competence: Assessment of Student Practical Work
Oct 6th	*Practical Test 1* *Designed a marking scheme by completing a breakdown of the complete job and, for each sub-task, allocated marks (as appropriate) to (i) technical skills, (ii) method of work, (iii) use of tools, (iv) application of knowledge, and (v) creativity.*
Oct 10th	*Used marking scheme with Year 1. It was perhaps too thorough in that it took a long time to complete. I only completed three students.*
Oct 21st	*Practical Test 2* *Designed a marking scheme using a rating schedule. The scale designed using sub-tasks like Test 1.* *Designed questionnaire to give to students to see which type of marking scheme they (a) find most helpful and (b) prefer.*
Oct 31st	*Used Marking scheme and distributed questionnaire. The analysis of the results showed ...etc.*

Figure 9.7 Completed Logbook Entry to Show Record of Evidence

This shows the date on which aspects were completed for student practical work and it follows on from the entry in the Negotiated Evidence by expanding on the entry 'Design 5 Practical Tests with Associated Marking Schemes'. The intention being to try different types of marking scheme and to try to find out which is preferable.

(iii)   the next stage is to record how things went – to *reflect*. This can indicate what success you had, how you as the teacher felt about it (was it worth the amount of time and effort that was invested in it?), what results or feedback you obtained, what you need to do next, and so on. It is a record of your thoughts and actions. It does, of course, not only have to be your thoughts but the reflection can often be most useful when you talk to someone else (a colleague, your students, and so on) about it and share and talk through the problems and difficulties. A completed example of such a reflection is shown in Figure 9.8.

Reflection of Learning Activity

Assessment of Practical Work

Test 1:   *The marking scheme took a long time to prepare (about 4 hours).*
                 It was decided to give a copy of the marking scheme to the students (which I had not done before) and they did not really know what to do with it. Perhaps I should get them to mark their own tasks which might make them concentrate more on each of the aspects.
                 It was difficult to use the marking scheme for method of work as it was difficult to watch the 15 students at the same time and felt that I missed some aspects. This was similar for Use of Tools.
                 Students only tended to look at their overall mark when I gave them their results and not the marks for the individual sub-tasks.
                 The reliability of the results was judged to be higher than my previous assessments as it is more closely related to the course aims.
                 The next scheme (rating scale) I will not add the marks for individual students.

Figure 9.8 Completed Example – Reflection of Learning Activity

This shows *what* was done, with what *success* it was thought to be achieved and what would be done *next* in the light of the experience of the activity.

4. Competence Learning

We described the cyclical approach to learning suggested by Kolb (1984) in Chapter 1 and we show it again in Figure 9.9.

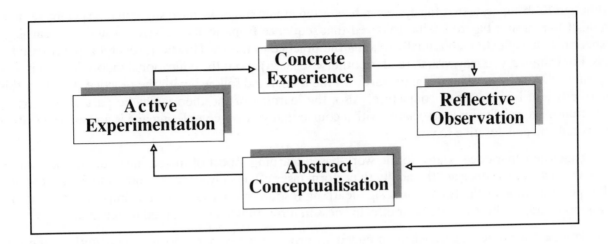

Figure 9.9 Kolb's Four Stage Model of Learning

We suggested that the importance of this model of learning was that included:

(i)   being able to start the cycle at any stage;

(ii)   the importance of reflection as well as experience to optimise the learning;

(iii) once the cycle is started, the sequence should be followed.

This cycle is equally appropriate for your own learning associated with your development of teaching competences. Each of the stages are, in effect, what has been described above in this Chapter. It involves the applications indicated in Figure 9.10.

Active Experimentation	Completing a needs analysis to decide what competences you already have and what are needed
Concrete Experience	Including work-based learning where you design, implement and evaluate aspects of your work in order to gain competence. This, includes the gaining and recording of evidence for your portfolio
Reflective Observation	The final part of your profile design involves reflecting upon what has been completed.
Abstract Conceptualisation	Placing what has been learned with all your previous learning and, perhaps, relating it to educational theory.

Figure 9.10 Relating the Kolb Model to Gaining Competence

Although Kolb suggests that the cycle can be started at any stage, we have suggested a specific sequence in this Chapter and Figure 9.9 has followed that sequence from needs analysis, through the learning by experience, to reflection and, finally relating the practice to theory. However, several aspects arise from this. For instance, you may wish to read (or otherwise learn) about the educational theory first. This would be the traditional way of learning: to start with the theory and follow it with the practice. Whether this is more efficient is a matter of conjecture. Also, the learning of the theory may be part of the concrete experience, especially if it is associated with a course that you are completing and is a result of what your peers tell you and describe to you.

The concrete experience relates to the work-based learning aspect of increasing your competence. We have defined competence as "the ability to perform tasks effectively at work" and, as such, must relate to all aspects of your work. Thus, you design learning resources for your students, implement them in the classroom and, finally, evaluate their effectiveness in terms of what you wanted to achieve.

The competence-based approach is intended to produce a teacher who is skilled *both* in the major occupational roles *and* able to operate as a 'reflective practitioner'. The principle of reflecting upon experience is an essential aspect of professional development. In consequence, it has been suggested that reflection is an important aspect of a profiling system. It is, however, not easy. Once you have evaluated your work you think that you have finished and, indeed, evaluation involves some aspect of reflection. However, you need to reflect upon all apsects of your work; not just in terms of whether it has achieved its aims, but in also terms of how it was learned, whether the best learning techniques were used, whether you might have used different techniques, and so on.

Finally, you need to place what has been learned into your own personal 'concept map'; to align the new learning with what has already been learned. You need to be able to continually enlarge your concept of teaching and learning. Once you think that you know all there is to know, it may be time to give up teaching. We can all continue to learn different aspects all of our lives and, in consequence, continually improve our competence.

Possible Evidence to Show that you have achieved the Competence 'Build a Portfolio of Evidence of Competence in Teaching'.

The type of evidence that you might collect to show that you have achieved the competence involves:

1. Choose a piece of work that you have recently completed for one of your classes (e.g. a lesson plan, a test, a visual aid) and show how that piece of work achieves AT LEAST FOUR of the following:

    *   establishes and maintains quality;

    *   diagnoses student learning needs and problems;

    *   is based on an understanding of the learning processes;

    *   demonstrates an awareness of the alternatives that might have been used;

    *   explores the use of IT;

    *   contains its own evaluation;

    *   demonstrates your research skills.

2. For the piece of work identified in 1. above, indicate whether the evidence is direct or indirect.

3. For a competence that you have decided needs improving, decide upon a plan of action to improve and keep a logbook of all of the aspects that indicate that you are learning to improve the competence. The log should indicate the date and the activities that you have completed.

> *If you want to check your understanding of your role in building a portfolio of evidence of competence in teaching try the following progress check.*

Progress Check 9.2

1.   Assume that you are attending a teacher training course and state at least three types of people with whom you might negotiate appropriate evidence of achievement of competence.

2.   Explain the difference between 'direct' and 'indirect' evidence of competence.

3.   List at least ten aspects of your work that might be included in a portfolio of evidence of competence in teaching.

4.   Explain what is meant by 'validation' of evidence and state at least three people who might carry out this process.

Further Reading and References

Further reading relating to the topics in this Chapter can be found in the following:

Garry, A et al   *Learning from Experience*. FEU/PICKUP. 1986.

Gibbs, G   *Learning by Doing: A guide to teaching and learning methods*, FEU, 1988.

Hall, J   *Crediting Competence - a Portfolio Development Technique for Managers*, in Training and Development, Vol 10 No 6, June 1992.

Kolb, D A   *Experiential Learning - Experience as the Source of Learning and Development*, Prentice Hall, 1984.

Rae, L   *How to Measure Training Effectiveness*, Gower Publishing Company, 2nd Edition 1991.

Chapter 10

The Role of the Teacher in Context

Overview of Chapter 10

Note: The outer circle indicates the *context* within which the roles of the teacher take place

Competences Related to this Chapter

The teacher competences and associated performance criteria related to this chapter are:

Overall Competence – *Recognise your role as a teacher in the overall adult education provision.*

Competence	Performance Criteria
1. **Understand the nature of Adult Education provision.**	(a) Comment upon own courses in the context of Adult Education. (b) Identify source of students and their routes for progression.
2. **Engage in systematic self-evaluation of your role.**	(a) Comment upon teacher's own role in the workplace. (b) Identify functions and relationships between agencies involved in post compulsory education and training.

1. Introduction

Teaching adults is a very demanding job but, when we do it well it can be most rewarding and satisfying. We tend to think of ourselves in isolation. What classes do I have? What am I teaching? What room am I in? How long have I got? What will the students be like? But we are not alone. Even as an adult evening class teacher of non-vocational subjects, we are part of a vast network of people; all like us, teaching students like them!

However, post-16 education and training is a complex arena. We can only hope in this book to outline some of the main aspects to give you a flavour of what it is all about. We must, however, consider our own role as part of this overall network. The figure at the start of this Chapter gives an indication of the complexity of the situation where the inner circle indicates the direct role of the teacher and the outer circle indicating the context in which we operate. If your particular aspect of the context is not included it is up to you to insert it and find out to whom you relate both directly and indirectly. The longer that you work in the system the more you get to know about it but remember that it is not a constant scene. Just as you think that you know about it, it changes and you have to keep up to date.

2. The Administrative Maze

Most people understand some of the education system. For example, everyone knows about Primary schools, Comprehensive schools and Universities. Once we depart from these, the system becomes increasingly complex. The problem is that there are boundaries but these tend to become blurred as time passes.

The 1944 Education Act defined 'Further Education' as that taking place for those who have left school. This later became refined as the term 'Higher Education' was used to denote undergraduate and equivalent levels of work. There are a wide range of courses so it is no wonder that the public are confused. It may be of value to consider the providing institutions as a way of seeing the whole scene.

Tertiary Colleges tend to cater mainly for the 16-19 age range. They often serve a wide area, containing several comprehensive schools, and provide a wide range of 'A' level subjects as well as a wealth of vocational courses such as BTEC National Certificates and City and Guilds Craft studies. Most of the work is known as 'NAFE – Non Advanced Further Education'.

Colleges of Further Education were often known as 'Technical Colleges' but are now usually known simply as Colleges. Again these cater for the 16+ age range but tend to be larger then Tertiary Colleges and have a higher proportion of older students studying higher level courses such as BTEC Higher National Certificates and C & G Advanced Craft Certificates which may be on a full time or part time basis. These higher level courses fall into the category of 'AFE – Advanced Further Education' (and these may be identical to some Higher Education courses - are you confused yet?)

The range of subject matter is formidable. From hairdressing to chiropody, from nursery nursing to mortuary technician – and usually everything in between. From highly specialized technical subjects to hobbies for general interest and Spanish for your holidays. Colleges have been criticized by some for not being responsive to the needs of industry! There can be few institutions which have seen so many changes and have responded so well and so quickly.

Many Polytechnics evolved from 'Technical Colleges' and offer a range of Higher Education Certificates but much of their work is with undergraduates. Many degrees are related to the needs of Business, Industry and Commerce. Most Polytechnical degrees are validated by CNAA (The Council for National Academic Awards) although in 1992 the Government announced that Polytechnics may call themselves Universities and award their own degrees.

Universities tend to have mainly degree courses, again covering a wide range of subjects. Universities usually undertake more research than many Polytechnics and offer more higher degree opportunities which often involve the students in research. These higher degrees, such as Masters and Doctorates, usually require a good first degree as an entry requirement.

3. College Management

The management of colleges has undergone considerable change in recent years. Traditionally colleges were divided into relatively independent units called 'departments', each being under the control of a head of department with their own teaching and non-teaching staff, students, budget and accommodation. Their rationale was that each was a curriculum area such as engineering or business studies. The departments were then often sub-divided into curricular based sections; for example, into mechanical, electrical and automobile sections in an engineering department.

The Principal's role includes co-ordinating the work of the departments. The Vice Principal usually took control of one or more of the cross-college functions like finance or accommodation.

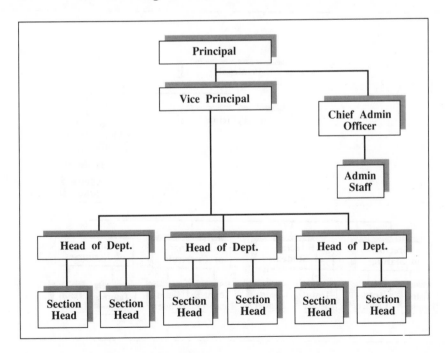

Figure 10.1 Line Management - Departmental

Figure 10.1 shows the line management, not the functional relationships of a typical college. Teaching staff are responsible to the section head for the manner in which they carry out the tasks allocated to them.

Developments in FE have required responses from colleges which have not always fitted easily within the departmental structure. These developments involve :

(a)   extra staff being appointed for specific cross-college roles such as staff development;

(b)   specific cross-college functions added to the roles of the heads of department like resources, staffing, finance;

(c)   flexible cross-college teaching teams intended to make use of greater flexibility of staff so that lecturers could be members of both course teams working entirely within a department and of college teams working across departments;

(d)   cross college units like the library, student services unit and a computer unit.

Such developments have led to some colleges having different organisational structures.

In a non-departmental structure each member of the senior management team usually has a single functional area across the college for which they are responsible. This is shown schematically in Figure 10.2. This figure again shows line management not functional relationships. The line responsibilities of lecturers here is through the leader of their team to the director of staffing. Were the functional relationships to be shown by dotted lines, they would run from each of the teams to each of the directors. In any one teaching team the course leader can delegate responsibility for course management, for curriculum design, for control of resources, and so on. The lecturers taking on these responsibilities would then relate to the appropriate director.

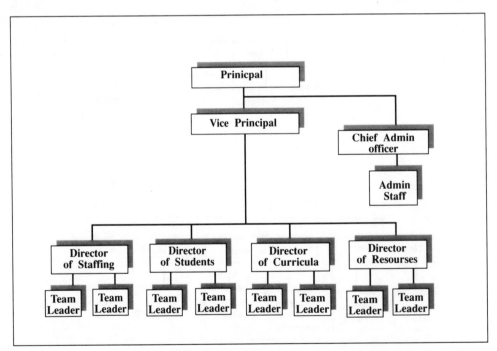

Fig 10.2 Line Management - Non-Departmental

The important aspect for you is to identify the structure in your organisation and to know to whom you need to relate. Such relationships will depend upon your role as well as the organisation of your institution.

4. Post–16 Education and Training Provision

The choice for young people at the age of 16 is particularly diverse. Such choices might be in terms of the kind institution that is to be attended. The range covers sixth forms in schools, sixth form colleges, colleges of further education, tertiary colleges, private providers, and so on. Here, there is considerable overlap in provision. However, the diagram below (Figure 10.3) is divided on the basis of whether or not the 16 year old stays at school, goes to college, or is employed or unemployed.

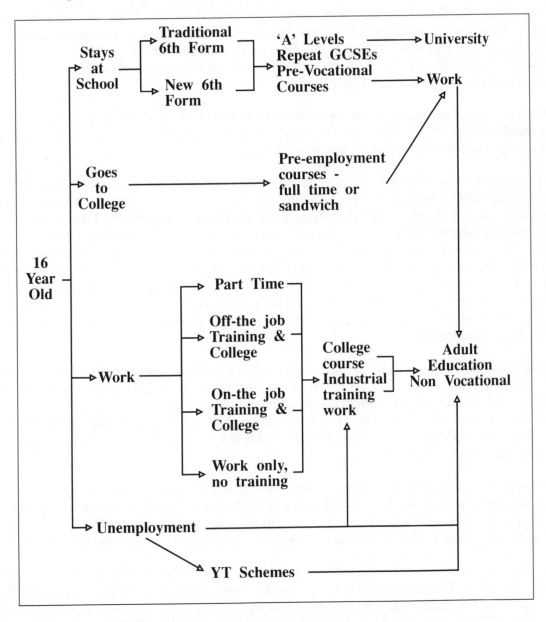

Figure 10.3 Major Education & Training Routes for the 16 year old

One choice for the 16 year old is to stay on at school. This option is often taken because they know of no other. Those who have been successful at General Certificate in Secondary Education (GCSE) can continue into the Sixth Form to complete 'A' Levels as preparation for a University course. A smaller percentage continue into the 'New' Sixth Form to either resit GCSE or take a pre-vocational course like Certificate in Pre-Vocational Education (CPVE) or a BTEC First Award. These give a general training in a range of vocational areas from which 17 year olds can make a more informed choice relating to the vocation they might wish to follow.

An alternative to the Sixth Form and for those who generally know what vocational area they might like to follow is to go directly to college. Here, the 16 year old would follow a pre-employment course. For instance, they might follow a two year Nursery Nurse qualification examined by the National Nursery Examinations Board (NNEB), or a course in Pre-Residential Care assessed by the Central Council for Education and Training in Social Work.

These courses have practical experience built into them, with the student often spending 60% of time in college and 40% on practical placement. There are general and specialist studies in college, often with high importance given to self-development and common skills.

Similar to these two courses are those offered through the Business and Technology Education Council (BTEC). These are in various subjects including Business and Engineering and are sponsored either through individuals or through employers. They are at three different levels: the First Award is general in nature covering basic employment and personal skills; the National Diploma level is more specific to a vocational area but still covers employment and common skills and is for 16 year olds who have three or more GCSEs at grade 'C' and above; the Higher Diploma level is for 18 year olds who have the National award or one or more 'A' levels and the appropriate GCSEs. These are sequential in nature with progression from the First to the Higher Diploma level. The First Award gives more career choice but the National and Higher Diplomas are more for those who have made some decision to persue a career in a specific area of employment.

The third option is for the 16 year olds who have made a specific career choice and are in training for a particular trade or profession. BTEC offer National Certificate and Higher Certificate programmes for this group where students study programmes part-time in college (usually one day per week) with appropriate on or off-the-job training in industry and commerce. City and Guilds (C&G) offer a similar range of courses as BTEC at Technician level and C&G also offer courses at Craft and Operative levels on a similar part-time or evening basis.

Increasingly, there are other providers for this third group of 16 year olds who are in employment. Historically, the growth of Mechanics Institutes as providers of technical education was rapid during the first half of the nineteenth century and they eventually formed themselves into a Union of Institutes which was linked to the Royal Society for the Encouragement of Arts, Manufacture and Commerce (RSA).

In 1855, the Society announced its first public examinations which were eventually run on a regional basis for practical reasons. This, then, is the root of the present system with the RSA and the Regional Examining Bodies all conducting examinations for further education. The first technological examinations for the RSA were held in 1873 and a number of City companies contributed prizes. In 1878 these companies announced their scheme for the foundation of the City and Guilds of London Institute to run courses and examinations in technical subjects.

This section of the RSA's work was handed over to them. RSA has maintained its influence in the non-technical field offering examinations in business studies, especially in secretarial and related office skills.

During the 1960s, 70s and early 80s there was a proliferation of both courses and providers in post-16 education and training. Various government initiatives have come and gone in an attempt to achieve cohesion between the DES (Department of Education and Science – the government department with responsibility for all sectors of education – primary, secondary, further and higher – now called the Department for Education – DFE) and the DoE (Department of Employment – the government department with responsibility, among other things, for training for employment).

You should realise that there is often a fine dividing line between the concepts of education and training and we do not intend to open that debate here. Suffice to say that DFE now has responsibility for education which takes place in an educational institution, as might training, and DoE for training which takes place in the factory or other place of work, or in a training centre run by a company, a private provider or an ITB (Industrial Training Board).

Possible Evidence to Show that you have achieved the Competence 'Understand the Nature of Adult Education Provision'.

The type of evidence that you might collect to show that you have achieved the competence involves:

1.   Commenting upon the type of institution you work in (e.g. tertiary college, Adult Education Centre, private provider) and make a list of the courses that operate in your section of the institution.

2.   Designing a chart of the line management of your institution. Where possible indicate the names of the post-holders whom you have identified.

3.   For a class of students that you teach, identifying and listing where the students have come from (e.g. their educational and work backgrounds).

4.   For the students identified in 3. above, drawing a diagram to show the likely education and training routes that are possible once they have completed your course.

> *If you want to check your understanding of your role in understanding the nature of adult education provision try the following progress check.*

Progress Check 10.1

1. Define the following:

   (a) Tertiary College

   (b) College of Further Education

   (c) University

2. Describe the differences between 'departmental line management' and 'non-departmental line management'.

3. Describe the differences between the 'traditional' and the 'new' sixth forms in schools.

4. What are the three options for training for a 16-year old who is in work?

5. What are the differences between vocational and non-vocational adult education?

6. The Wider Context

6.1 National Vocational Qualifications (NVQs)

In 1986 the National Council of Vocational Qualifications (NCVQ) was established by the government. Its major task was to reform and rationalise the system of vocational qualifications. A priority for the NCVQ was to define the characteristics of a National Vocational Qualification and it subsequently identified criteria for the accreditation of qualifications from the awarding bodies. In the same year the Training Agency (later to be replaced by the Training, Enterprise and Education Directorate (TEED) of the Department of Employment) was given the task of establishing employer groups, known as Industry Lead Bodies (ILBs) to undertake the setting of standards.

By 1990 some 150 ILBs had been established to oversee the development of standards and to promote their adoption by the awarding bodies. The National Vocational Qualifications (NVQs) are awarded by over 300 awarding bodies including examining and validating bodies, professional bodies and industry training organisations. The NCVQ was charged with establishing a framework of NVQs. This framework was originally based on the four levels shown in Figure 10.4, incorporating qualifications up to Higher National Diploma and Certificate level. Subsequently, approval was given to extend beyond level IV.

NVQs attest specific competences required for effective performance at work and they highlight the need for systematic work experience, workshop practice and activities which, if they are completed in further education, closely match the requirements at work. As the qualifications have a competence-base, assessment has moved to the preparation of portfolios by students to show how and why they can be verified as competent at various work activities. The move, then, is away from formal, traditional courses to ones that are related to, and assessed, in the work place or in a simulated work environment.

Level I: competence in the performance of work activities which are in the main routine and predictable or provide a broad foundation, primarily as a basis for progression.

Level II: competence in a broader and more demanding range of work activities involving greater individual responsibility and autonomy than at level I.

Level III: competence in skilled areas that involve performance of a broad range of work activities including many that are complex and non-routine. In some areas supervisory competence may be a requirement at this level.

Level IV: competence in the performance of complex, technical, specialised and professional work activities including design, planning and problem solving with a significant degree of personal accountability. In many areas competence in supervision or management will be a requirement at this level.

Figure 10.4 Definition of NVQ Levels.

In order to gain similarity between academic (that is school) examinations and vocational ones, NVQ introduced a system of 'General National Vocational Qualifications' (GNVQs). These are intended to give a viable alternative to GCE and GCSE qualifications for school pupils and provide them with a vocational bias to their work. The existing qualification system (GCE AS/A Level, GCSE, NVQs, Business and Technology Education Council, City and Guilds of London Institute, RSA Examinations Board, Council for National Academic Awards, Open University,etc.) are, according to FEU (1992) 'closed systems'. In order to link the existing systems to NVQ levels they suggest the comparisons shown in Figure 10.5.

	Genaral NVQ	**NVQ Level**	**Occupationally Specific NVQ**
	Vocationally-related Post Graduate Qualifications	5	Professional Qualification Middle Management
Degree	Vocationally-related Degrees. Higher National Diploma	4	Higher Technician Junior Management
A/AS Level	Vocationally related National Diploma. Advanced Craft Preparation.	3	Technician, Advanced Craft Supervisor. Advanced Craft Certificate
GCSE	Broad-based Craft Foundation.	2	Skilled Craftsman – Basic Craft Certificate.
Nat. Curric	Pre-Vocational Certificate	1	Semi-Skilled Worker

Figure 10.5 The Relationship of National Vocational Qualifications

Thus, the levels in NVQ relate to specific qualifications and such qualifications are intended as preparation for work roles from Semi Skilled worker at Level I to Middle Management at Levels IV and V.

The fourth group of 16 year olds identified in Figure 10.3 are the unemployed. They may, of course, stay at school or join one of the full-time college courses. Alternately, courses for the unemployed have appeared in colleges from the late 1980s as a result of the dramatic rise in unemployment among the young which has risen three times faster than among the adult working population. These courses are part of a package of measures designed to reduce the level of this unemployment. Industrial Training Boards (ITBs) and the DoE funded measures to encourage extra apprenticeships as early as 1971. When the Manpower Services Commission (MSC) was established, the Training Services Agency (TSA) prepared the report *"Vocational Preparation for Young People"* (1975), which describes some of the then limited facilities for training unemployed people and largely excuses itself for limiting training opportunities by describing the lack of motivation among the young. It does, however, give attention to the need for general vocational preparation for the large numbers of employed young people who received no training and suggests that more unemployed young people could be accommodated on these 'gateway' courses, on 'short industrial courses' for skills improvement, and on 'Wider Opportunities' courses for the least well motivated. After 1978, when the MSC was reorganised, new schemes were developed known as the Youth Opportunities Programme and, later, the Youth Training Scheme (YTS). Overall the provision of these courses showed regional variations and the college aspects formed only a small part of the total programme which included work experience, training workshops, community service, employment induction courses and short training courses. This led to an increase in the importance of Vocational Education and Training (VET) today for the majority of firms.

The advent of YTS helped change managerial attitudes by revealing that training can be used as an effective and alternative skill supply source to open market recruitment. The Training Agency sees VET and Human Resource Development (HRD) as important activities that all firms should, at some level, be involved in. Thus, industry and commerce is becoming more involved in their own education and training.

6.2 Further Education Providers

The Adult Education service, usually part of the Local Education provision, offers courses in the Community rather than in a College. Typical meeting places are the Village Hall or Community Centre. This must not be seen as a second class service but as complementary to mainstream education and actually helps people into Colleges, Polytechnics and Universities.

Some Colleges are very specialized. Colleges of Agriculture and Horticulture provide specific training with Certificates offered by BTEC and City and Guilds. Their role is changing as the emphasis moves from farming for example crops and livestock towards a horticultural focus such as sports field management, garden centre staff and landscaping. These Colleges often have their own farm and are situated in beautiful grounds.

Colleges of Art and Design have a long history but have developed as they have met the demands of industry and individuals. Many remain specialist colleges but some of the smaller ones have merged with a nearby college.

There are still a good number of other providers and these include the WEA (Workers Educational Association), industrial training centres, the Prison and Youth Custody Service, Adult Numeracy and Literacy centres and so on.

6.3 Local Education Authorities (LEAs)

Until the 1988 Education Reform Act, Polytechnics were under the control of Local Education Authorities. The LEAs will continue to control College budgets until 1993 when the Education Act will give control of the College budget to the individual College management team. The LEAs' role is to support Colleges with strategic planning. Their role is decreasing with regard to College and Schools particularly as more schools obtain their delegated budget. LEAs have served the provision of education well over a great many years and the reduction of the powers of LEAs is seen by some as an attempt by Central Government to reduce the influence of Local Government.

The Education Reform Act 1988 introduced Local Management for both colleges and schools. Many management responsibilities have since been delegated from LEAs to individual institutions.

The Further and Higher Education Act 1992 allows colleges to take on full control of their own affairs. It transfers the responsibility for funding and planning the sector from LEAs to new Further Education Funding Councils (FEFCs) for England and Wales. The Secretaries of State may take Orders to incorporate most colleges of further education and sixth form colleges, and to designate other institutions as eligible for funding by the FEFCs. It is intended that the date of transfer for all colleges concerned (Vesting Day) will be 1st April 1993. The Act is based on the proposals in the Government's White Paper *"Education and Training for the 21st Century"*, published in May 1991.

6.4 Implications of the 1992 Act

Most colleges which will join the new sector currently operate under Schemes of Local Management, as agents of the LEA. So at present:

- the LEA is ultimately responsible for the financial management of the college, and can withdraw delegation from the Governors if it believes they are mismanaging its funds;

- the LEA is the formal employer of college staff (except in voluntary aided colleges), though many of its powers are normally delegated to governors. The terms and conditions of employment are established by national negotiations, supplemented by some local arrangements;

- the LEA owns college premises (except the voluntary aided colleges), and colleges occupy them under a 'landlord and tenant' arrangement. The LEA is responsible for major structural works and repairs, and cleaning and catering services are generally provided by the LEA's contractors.

From 1st April 1993, colleges will be independent bodies. So, from that date, colleges will:

- be responsible for managing their own finances, for exercising proper control over the funds they receive, and for preparing full audited accounting reports, like those prepared by polytechnics and grant-maintained schools;

- employ their staff directly, with no role for the LEA. The arrangements for national negotiations will change, though it is not yet clear how, and there may be more local agreements;

- own their own premises and be responsible for all aspects of premises maintenance.

Ultimately management responsibility will thus transfer from the LEA to the new governing body of the colleges. Even if the former LEA is used as an agent for some tasks, the final responsibility for seeing that those tasks are performed properly will rest with individual governing bodies and not with the LEA.

Historically, the gulf between the academic and commercial worlds has been bridged in varying degrees by the governing body of further education colleges. College governors have been selected for their business knowledge (industrial, commercial, financial, and so on) for the benefit of the college. The Governing Body, whilst fulfilling a useful function in terms of counselling and guidance, has obviously appeared in any organisational chart, on a dotted line basis, as the straight reporting line between colleges to the LEA.

The LEA function involved a funding responsibility and the provider of a wide range of support and resource facilities. In 1993 these responsibilities will disappear with the Governors assuming a more operational and strategic role with the support and resource function being absorbed by the college itself.

In order to survive, colleges will have to adopt commercial and business strategies which will encompass writing both 'Development' and 'Business' Plans as well as 'Marketing' Plans. All of these will need to address competitive advantages locally, nationally and internationally. In this scene, the role of the governing body will need to become more dynamic and resourceful. In order to provide these plans the new organisations will need to gain experience in intelligence gathering, market research, publicity, advertising, pricing and selling. All of these functions are relatively new to Further Education. Instead of waiting for customers to come 'knocking at our doors', we will have to go out and find them and provide them with what they need. Much of the success of the business will depend upon the excellence achieved in the provision. The quality and delivery of the 'product' (that is the courses) will be of fundamental importance to the survival of the college.

The Governing Body will have to bridge the gap between the academic and commercial worlds in order to ensure that the college not only survives in the years ahead, but moves forward. It will be the responsibility of every teacher to increase his or her role to encompass aspects that will assist governors, such as the marketing function and the ensuring of a quality product.

6.5 Training and Enterprise Councils (TECs)

Some of the responsibilities of managing funds has been transferred from LEAs to TECs, and, in particular funding for non-advanced further education (NAFE) work. TECs do not reflect local political feeling as the LEAs do but reflect the interest of local employers who have a majority interest in the direction of TEC policies. TECs are still being established and it is too early to say what effect these changes will make.

6.6 Nurse Education

Nurse education has been undergoing revolutionary change in the last few years. The old system of State Enrolled and Registered Nurses is being replaced by nurses being educated under the Project 2000 scheme.

Under Project 2000, a student nurse has to study for 3 years in a College of Nursing, 18 months on a common Foundation Programme followed by another 18 months in one of the following areas: adult; child; mentally ill; or mentally handicapped.

The service contribution of the students is only 20% of their time which is a significant reduction.

The aims of Project 2000 are to produce a:

1.   system of education geared to meet future health needs;

2.   group of professionals who will be willing to be adaptable to change;

3.   better relationship between the education and the service sides of the profession;

4.   simpler overall pattern of preparation whilst maintaining and improving standards;

5.   greater degree of professional unity and constructive participation in health policy making.

Perceived advantages include students having more time to study rather than being 'extra hands', more equivalence to other students, a higher qualification (that is Registered General Nurse (RGN) plus Diploma) and an increase in professional status.

However, critics indicate that the disadvantages may be that students lack practical experience, the training may be academic for students expecting practical training, and there could be fewer jobs for registered nurses due to the growth in the number of support workers.

Like so many issues in education, it will take time for the outcomes to be judged fairly and true evaluation is some years away.

The United Kingdom Central Council for Nursing, Midwifery and Health Visiting (UKCC) produced a report in 1990 called the *Post Registration Education and Practice Project*, commonly called PREPP. The reasons for this report included the need to keep qualified nurses up to date in a rapidly changing profession and to enhance the public image of nursing so as to attract people into the profession and to assist adult returners (that is those who are trained as nurses but have not practised for some time due to the attractiveness of other posts or family life). The demographic situation was such that young people were not being attracted in sufficient numbers into the profession and more mature people were entering or re-entering nursing. There are guidelines for training those who have had a significant break from nursing. These are currently being established or are being implemented in their first few cohorts.

The report addressed the issue of those who are newly qualified, including those who are experienced in another area of nursing. It proposed the provision of support by an experienced practitioner known as a 'preceptor'. It also proposed that all nurses, midwives and health visitors should demonstrate that they are maintaining and developing their professional knowledge and competences through the keeping of a *Personal Professional Profile*. The profile is to contain a record of formal continuing education, an analysis of educational needs and a development plan to meet these needs. Each nurse must be registered every three years and, during that time, must have undertaken five days of study.

All of this showed a great concern for in-service training which many professionals would envy. It also explains that a great many nurses need to have some form of teacher training and undertake courses such as ENB998, the City and Guilds 7307, the Certificate in Education and B.Ed.

7. The Role of the Teacher

Did you at one time think teachers only taught and marked? Perhaps they did at one time but not now! The Figure at the start of this Chapter shows some of the main roles of a teacher in an FE College. Some of these duties will be undertaken as part of a team, with you becoming involved in a learning process as well as being a teacher. The duties appear to be off putting but they really are rewarding. You should become involved in these if you want to get the most out of your teaching.

When we first start teaching, we are usually concerned with knowing the subject matter, hoping we will be able to answer any questions and praying that the students will behave. No one expects you to have all skills at once but your colleagues will expect you to develop them and take a share of the responsibilities in due course.

As we grow in confidence we begin to realise that knowing our subject matter and keeping control are important but only part of the overall process of being a 'leader of learning'. Leadership is a key skill which you must have or develop. You have, somehow, to generate an atmosphere which facilitates learning: formal enough for structured learning to take place but sufficiently informal for active learning to develop. Your personality and manner with the students will be key aspects.

7.1 Health & Safety

The Health and Safety at Work Act 1974 applies to everyone on a college site and probably applies in whatever establishment you teach. The Act is detailed but you must be familiar with all safety policies and practices, conform to these practices and set a good example to students.

You must ensure that all students know about safety arrangements and this is particularly important at the start of the course. Students need to know the fire exits, location of first aid boxes, location and use of fire extinguishers and what to do in the event of an emergency. Remember, you are in charge of the students, if you have any doubts about safety, particularly with experiments or in the workshop you must stop any questionable activities, ensure a safe situation and seek advice at the first opportunity.

Workshops and laboratories are potentially hazardous and you are advised to seek detailed guidance on their operation from your employer – who also has a duty to help you carry out your duties in a safe manner.

7.2 Counselling and Guidance

These two words are often used together and even interchanged. Although definitions vary the following may be useful.

Counselling is where your students are helped with problems which, although they may be personal, affect their learning. If the problems are limited, you perform the role of facilitator by helping your student explore the problem and possible solutions in a safe non threatening, non hierarchical manner. It is important that it is the student, and not you, who decides the course of action. It is very tempting to make the decision for the student - resist! The student has to recognise the problem, explore the options and resolve the situation. You may well encounter students with stressful personal problems which you feel are outside your own limitations. Do not be frightened to refer the student, in a kind fashion, to a trained, skilled counsellor. All colleges have the benefit of a counselling service. If you are in an organisation which does not have such a service, ask a more experienced and senior colleague for guidance.

Guidance is a term often used when advising on choice of vocation. You will probably be involved in giving information, without judgement. You may even offer advice based upon knowledge and experience.

7.3 Managing in the Classroom

We started this section by sharing the hope that the students will behave themselves. They generally do if you have planned appropriate learning experiences, provided learning resources, helped with whole group and individual learning and maintained order. It is always better to start in a disciplined way so the students recognise that you are in control. Discipline can then be eased as you and the group get to know each other. A gentle hum or buzz of learning is better than either total silence or uproar. One thing you cannot do is start with a relaxed regime and then try to introduce discipline. There is no single answer when an individual causes trouble. You should have noted in Chapter 1 that students need to be motivated by a range of challenging activities.

Should a small group or an individual cause trouble you need to regain their involvement. The rest of the class will expect you to do this. You need to remain (or appear to remain) calm and in control. A sense of humour is helpful. Avoid confrontation and public threats. You may need to ask problem students to leave the class for a few minutes while you talk to them in private. However if sanctions are needed then you must apply them.

7.4 Curriculum Development

You have probably heard the term 'Curriculum Development' and wonder exactly what it means. You know that the curriculum is what you teach your students, but what about its development? In its simplest form it is changing and responding to factors so that the best possible learning can take place. Remember from Chapter 1 that we defined the curriculum as anything and everything which influences the quality of learning. So you are already involved with curriculum development the first time that you walk into a class of students as their teacher. However, you should now have realised that, in education, things cannot be as simple as that. Much theory has evolved around the curriculum and its development.

Theory and philosophising about issues is fine and an interesting discipline, but as teachers we need the theory to help us in real, practical situations: it needs to be applied theory. A useful model of the curriculum has been developed by the Further Education Unit (FEU). In a simplified form it is a four stage model (see Figure 10.5). In the real world, you could start at any of the four stages, depending upon circumstances or even dealing with two or more stages simultaneously.

When planning a course, the first stage is to identify the learning needs of the students. Many issues may influence the debate including employers and the needs of other courses. Planning the course may be influenced by the nature of the students, appropriate teaching strategies, resources, and the need to allow for Accrediting Prior Learning (APL). The delivery is the implementation phase of the course where the planning is put into practice. Even the most careful planning cannot foresee every eventuality so there is a need to evaluate the quality of each aspect of the course. Our expectations of student ability may have been incorrect, the teaching strategies may have been too demanding or inappropriate, the assessment was too formal or traditional, and so on. Student views of the course are essential. This leads us back to the identification of needs and a review of the needs in the light of the evaluation. So around the cycle we go again.

Each of the four stages is a study in its own right and there are many texts devoted to, for example, evaluation. It may be of interest to note that the Curriculum Development Model used with the National Curriculum is a three stage model with the 'Identification of Needs' and 'Evaluation' being combined. The danger of combining the two issues is that one may become dominant and the other neglected. Why does the difference occur? It may be because that, in schools, the main concern is with the Planning and the Delivery of the courses with the Needs and Evaluation being undertaken by those other than teachers. In Further and Adult Education we are usually involved in all of the four aspects. It is rewarding to be able to respond to the enquiry "Can you provide a course for ...?" and, at a later stage, be able to say that we were able to meet that request. More and more often we are requested to provide a bespoke or tailor made course rather than a course devised by others. Post-16 education and training depends upon the quality of our responses to these demands.

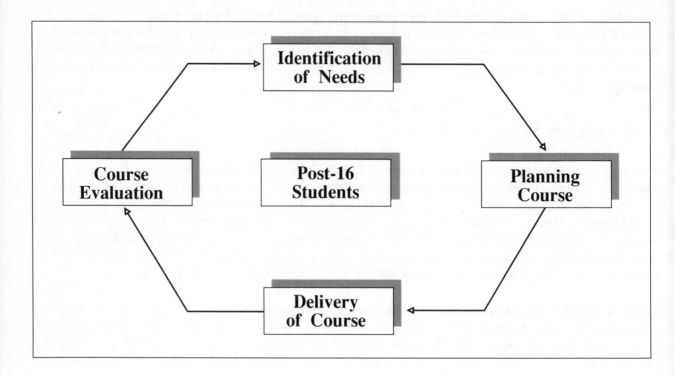

Figure 10.6 Curriculum Development Model

Possible Evidence to Show that you have achieved the Competence 'Engage in Systematic Self-Evaluation of your Role'.

The type of evidence that you might collect to show that you have achieved the competence involves:

1. Identify at least FIVE major aspects of your role in the workplace and comment upon your ability within each of these roles.

2. State, if possible, the role that NVQ is at present playing in your work or is likely to play in the future.

3. Show how you are involved with at least three stages of the curriculum development process.

Check

Progress

> *If you want to check your understanding of your role in engaging in systematic self evaluation of your role try the following progress check*

Progress Check 10.2

1.   What is the role of Local Education Authorities under the 1988 Education Reform Act?

2.   State THREE implications of the 1992 Education Act.

3.   What are "Training and Enterprise Councils"?

4.   What are the aims of Project 2000 in Nurse Education?

5.   Define:

     (a) counselling; and

     (b) guidance

     as applied to post-16 education and training.

6.   What are the FOUR stages in the curriculum development process as identified by FEU?

Further Reading and References

Further reading and references relating to the topics in this chapter can be found in the following:

FEU   *A Basis for Credit? Developing a post-16 crdeit accumulation and transfer framework.* FEU. 1992.

Employment   *Guide to the National Vocational Qualifications*, Employment
Department   Department, 1991.

Open University   *Delivering NVQs: a guide for staff development*, Open University, 1989.

Hall, V.   *Maintained Further Education in the United Kingdom*, Staff College, 1990

Glossary of Terms

Affective Domain	Involves feelings, emotions, attitudes and values.
Angragogy	The science of adult learning (usually related to a student-centred approach).
Assessment	Measurement of how effectively the students have learned; usually measured against stated learning outcomes.
Assignment	Students are presented with a topic/subject or problem for an in-depth analysis.
Behaviourism	The prediction of human behaviour or learning through actions or tasks and based on responses to stimuli.
Brainstorming	Teaching strategy where students generate a large number of ideas in a short time.
Case Study	The examination of a real or simulated situation or problem.
Chalkboard	Either roller or fixed boards with a surface which will take chalk.
Checklist	A list of aspects (for example to assess) which can be 'checked-off' when they are completed.
Cognitive Domain	Involves mental processes.
Cognitivists	School of human learning with the focus on students and how they gain and organise their knowledge.
Common Skill	General or transferable skills (sometimes called core skills).
Competence	The ability to perform actions/procedures effectively in the workplace.
Concept	Mental pictures of relationships and qualities of objects or ideas.
Constructivism	School of human learning which believes in the need to identify current learning prior to constructing new meaning.
Contiguity	The almost simultaneous occurance of stimulus and response in psychomotor skill learning.
Convergent	Search for a single correct answer or solution.
Copyright	The legal exclusive right that authors have to print, publish and sell their own work.
Criterion	Set standard, usually to be attained during assessment.
Curriculum	Programmes for learning and those factors which influence the quality of learning.

Debate	Teaching strategy where students put points for and against an argument or motion.
Deductive	Moving from generalisations to the particular.
Demonstration	Teaching strategy usually associated with showing students a practical skill which they will them practice.
Discussion	Teaching strategy where it is planned that students will talk to each other about a topic and report back on their findings.
Divergent	Process or search for a solution to a problem which has more than one answer.
Domain	A category of learning.
Entry Behaviour	What the student knows about the topic at the start of instruction.
Essay	Student response to a question where they have structure their response themselves.
Evaluation	Means of measuring the effectiveness of a learning situation (which *may* include student assessment).
Extrinsic	Coming from outside oneself. For example, extrinsic motivation is that provided by the teacher.
Feedback	The passing of information to the student of their ability to perform a task.
Feltboard	Board covered in felt which can be used to stick pictures, shapes or words.
Flipchart	Large pieces of paper fixed to a stand to be used in the same way as a chalkboard.
Formative	Type of assessment to help with teaching and learning. On-going assessment throughout the learning process.
Gestaltists	Study of human learning where understanding is based upon insight.
Humanist	Person who believes that learning should be based upon worth, self esteem and dignity of the individual.
Handout	Pieces of paper containing information to be given to students.
Inductive	Going from particular examples to a generalisation.
Intrinsic	Coming from within oneself.
Jobsheet	Handout containing instructions or a specification so that students can complete a piece of work.
Keller Plan	A personalised system of instruction which is individually paced and based on mastery learning principles.
Kinaesethetic	The perception of muscular effort.

Lecture	Teaching strategy where the passage of information is from the teacher to the student.
Lesson Plan	A guide to what the teacher plans for the students to do in order to achieve the intended learning outcomes.
Magneticboard	Board with a steel backing upon which magnets or magnetic-backed pictures can be placed and moved around.
Mastery Learning	Where a student must learn one topic (objective) before proceeding to another.
Matching Block	Type of question where students have to match aspects in one column with those given in another.
Memory	The ability to recall information.
Model	Theoretical relationships between aspects.
Module	Discrete units of identified learning materials.
Motivation	An inclination to become involved in the learning process.
Multiple-choice	Type of question where a student chooses from a number of options.
Norm	Related to the normal distribution of the population.
Norm Referenced Assessment	Relating performance with that of a typical student population.
Objective	May be behavioural (product) or expressive (process) but is concerned with what students must be able to do.
Open Learning	Sometimes called distance learning where the teacher and the student meet infrequently. The learning material is usually written.
Overhead Projector	Machine used to project images (words and projector diagrams) to students.
Pedagogy	The science of teaching (usually related to a teacher dominated approach).
Peer	Of equal rank or status (e.g. a colleague or fellow student).
Principle	A statement of the relationship between two or more concepts.
Problem Solving	A high level cognitive activity using two or more principles.
Profile	A means of recording achievement.
Project	A method of problem solving which involves the student in research, finding a solution and reporting either in writing or verbally.
Psychomotor	Involves physical movement and co-ordination.
Question and Answer	Teaching strategy where the teacher asks a question and a student responds.

Rating Schedule	Rating students according to a fixed scale.
Reliability	The ability of a test to consistently measure what it is supposed to measure.
Role Play	Teaching strategy where students act out a part or role.
Scheme of Work	The sequence in which topics are to be taught.
Seminar	Teaching strategy where a student researches a topic, presents the findings to other students and leads an ensuing discussion.
Simulation	An event or situation that is set up to be as similar to the real thing as possible.
Summative	Type of assessment used at the end of a period of instruction and used for certification purposes.
Transparency	Acetate sheet upon which words or diagrams are drawn to project to students.
Tutorial	One to one learning situation where teacher can give individual and in-depth questioning to a student.
Understanding	Doing something with recalled information (e.g. interpreting, translating or summarising).
Whiteboard	Similar to chalkboard but using water-based pens on a white plastic surface.
Worksheet	Incomplete handout given to students for their completion.
Workshop	Teaching strategy where students are given the opportunity to practice and develop practical skills in a real or simulated environment.
Validity	How well a test measures what it is supposed to measure.